THE NATIONAL ARMY MUSEUM BOOK OF

THE ZULU WAR

Ian Knight is internationally regarded as a leading authority on the history of the nineteenth-century Zulu kingdom and the 1879 Anglo-Zulu war. He studied Afro-Caribbean Studies at the University of Kent and has written thirty books and monographs on the subject, including the widely acclaimed *Brave Men's Blood*, *The Anatomy of the Zulu Army* and a biography of the Prince Imperial. He has contributed to exhibition catalogues for both the National Army Museum and Victoria and Albert Museum. In 2000 he was project historian on the first exploratory archaeological survey of the Isandlwana battlefield. He has also acted as a consultant for a number of television documentaries on the Anglo-Zulu War, including programmes in the prestigious *Secrets of the Dead* and *Timewatch* series in the UK and for the History Channel in the USA. He is vice-president of the Anglo-Zulu War Historical Society and was made honorary research associate of the Natal Museum of Pietermaritzburg, South Africa, in recognition of his work in the area. He is married with two children.

THE NATIONAL ARMY MUSEUM BOOK OF

THE ZULU WAR

Ian Knight

PAN BOOKS

in association with

The National Army Museum

First published 2003 by Sidgwick & Jackson

This edition published 2004 by Pan Books
an imprint of Pan Macmillan Ltd
Pan Macmillan, 20 New Wharf Road, London N1 9RR
Basingstoke and Oxford
Associated companies throughout the world
www.panmacmillan.com

ISBN 0 330 48629 2

A CIP catalogue record for this book is available from
the British Library.

Typeset by SetSystems Ltd, Saffron Walden, Essex
Printed and bound in Great Britain by
Mackays of Chatham plc, Chatham, Kent

All Pan Macmillan titles are available from
www.panmacmillan.com
or from Bookpost by telephoning 01624 677237

Foreword

Ian Knight is one of the world's leading authorities on the Anglo-Zulu War of 1879, knowing intimately the documentary and illustrative sources in both the United Kingdom and South Africa, as well as having a detailed knowledge of the battlefields, including archaeological research at Isandlwana. This profound knowledge is brought to bear on the collections of the National Army Museum, thereby shedding new light on well-known, major engagements of the War, and also explaining interesting aspects of the campaign mentioned in the documents, but not obvious to anyone who has not researched the period in such depth.

The genesis of this book lies in the important National Army Museum publication of 1999 entitled '*ashes and blood*': *The British Army in South Africa, 1795–1914* (edited by Peter Boyden, Alan Guy and Marion Harding), which provided access to the splendid collections of the Museum relating to the history of the British army in South Africa. It was clear that the Museum's archives collection was sufficiently significant to merit publication for the benefit of all, and *The National Army Museum Book of the Boer War* appeared in 1999 to be followed by this further volume so ably written by Ian Knight.

The National Army Museum's collections are very rich in Zulu War material, including the papers of Lieutenant General Lord Chelmsford, GOC Cape of Good Hope during the 1879 war, and important correspondence from other key figures in the campaign, particularly Lieutenant Colonel Redvers Buller and Colonel (Henry) Evelyn Wood. Other Museum archives used extensively include the letters of Major Philip Robert Anstruther, 94th Regiment of Foot, the diary of Captain Edward Essex, 75th (Stirlingshire) Regiment of Foot, and the diary of Lieutenant Julius Backhouse and the letters of Colonel Charles Pearson, both of the 3rd (East Kent, The Buffs) Regiment of Foot.

As Ian Knight remarks in his preface, interest in the Anglo-Zulu War has increased immeasurably compared to its contemporary significance.

Much of this general interest may be attributed to the success of *The Washing of the Spears* by Donald R. Morris, first published in 1965 and reissued with additions in 1989, as well as of the film *Zulu* (1964) and its prequel *Zulu Dawn* (1979). A plethora of publications and documentary films feeding this popular interest has followed over the last thirty years or so. Ian Knight's scholarly weight guides a new generation fascinated by the Anglo-Zulu War of 1879.

Within the National Army Museum, Dr Alastair Massie, Head of the Department of Archives, Photographs, Film and Sound, has been especially concerned with this publication since Marion Harding's retirement, and Debbie Morley, Head of the Design Department, Ian Jones, Head of the Photographic Department and Lesley Smurthwaite, Department of Uniforms, Badges and Medals, have all contributed. Apart from the debt of gratitude to Ian Knight for his exemplary work on the Museum's archives collection, personal thanks are due to William Armstrong and Ingrid Connell of Pan Macmillan for their continued support of another important volume in a series that is becoming well established.

Ian G. Robertson
Director, National Army Museum
22 October 2002

Acknowledgements

My thanks to William Armstrong and Ingrid Connell at Macmillan for their patience, and to Marion Harding at the Reading Room of the National Army Museum for her help in identifying and copying documents. Several debts are of a more long-standing nature; Commandant 'SB' Bourquin, a genuine and unparalleled authority on the history and culture of KwaZulu/Natal, first opened a road to the battlefields for me more than twenty years ago. Ian Castle and Keith Reeves have not only travelled those roads with me but have shared research and debated conclusions over much the same period. Nor could my travels in South Africa have been undertaken without the help of Gillian Scott-Berning, formerly Curator of the Local History Museum in Durban, and Graham Smythe of Rorke's Drift. More thanks are due, too, to Professor John Laband of the University of Natal, Dr Adrian Greaves of the Anglo-Zulu War Historical Society, Major Paul Naish, Ron Sheeley and Ian Woodason, for sharing their ideas and advice. As ever, however, my deepest appreciation goes to my wife Carolyn and my son Alex, who live with the Anglo-Zulu War as much as I do, though perhaps less by choice.

Contents

List of Illustrations xi

List of Maps xv

Chronology of the Anglo-Zulu War xvii

Preface xxi

One 'Half measures do not answer . . .' 1

Two 'They shot us down in numbers . . .' 43

Three 'They died in one place . . .' 76

Four 'They did great execution . . .' 124

Five 'It was a ghastly sight . . .' 176

Six 'They got it today . . .' 214

Epilogue 'Very glad to have finished . . .' 260

Index of Contributors 281

Index 285

List of Illustrations

Section One

1. An historic photograph taken at King Cetshwayo's 'coronation' on 1 September 1873. [79584]
2. A posed studio photograph purporting to show a young Zulu warrior. [23499]
3. Marriage was an important rite of passage within Zulu society, signified in men by the wearing of a head ring known as *isicoco*. [50348]
4. James Lloyd's photograph of John Wesley Shepstone reading Frere's ultimatum to King Cetshwayo's envoys at the Lower Thukela Drift on 11 December 1878. [23479]
5. A naval contingent from HMS *Active*, lined up to overawe the Zulu envoys at the presentation of the ultimatum. [96438]
6. Lieutenant-General Lord Chelmsford, the senior British commander in Zululand in 1879. [96437]
7. King Cetshwayo kaMpande, photographed in Cape Town during his exile. [96434]
8. Colonel Henry Evelyn Wood VC. [6567]
9. General Sir Garnet Wolseley, who was sent to southern Africa to supersede Lord Chelmsford. [96439]
10. A detachment of the 2nd Battalion, 1st Regiment Natal Native Contingent, photographed at Fort Bengough. [23829]
11. An unidentified battalion of the Natal Native Contingent, drawn up with their white officers seated in front. [87307]
12. Officers of HMS *Active*, photographed at the Lower Thukela before the start of the invasion. Midshipman Lewis Coker – lying left – commanded the Gatling at the battle of Nyezane. [30605]
13. Invasion: a company of the 99th Regiment attached to Pearson's column crosses into Zululand by pont at the Lower Thukela Drift on 12 January 1879. [12883]

14. Pearson's first camp in Zululand, photographed from the Natal bank of the Thukela on 14 January 1879. [45890]
15. The Mzinyathi river at Rorke's Drift, where the Centre Column crossed into Zululand on 11 January. [24252]
16. A pencil sketch by Lieutenant William Fairlie of Isandlwana hill, 'from the Zulu side'. [96486]
17. The Isandlwana battlefield, photographed during the burial expeditions of June 1879. [65731A].
18. Isandlwana, June 1879. One of the burial detail, a trooper of the King's Dragoon Guards. [6572]
19. The grave of Lieutenants Melvill and Coghill of the 1/24th. [96443]

Section Two

20. Prince Dabulamanzi kaMpande, photographed c.1882. [18770].
21. A group of Royal Engineers, photographed in the field at the end of the campaign, including Major John Chard VC. [23823]
22. The mission station at Rorke's Drift, photographed six months after the battle. [18806]
23. Rorke's Drift. [6575]
24. Men of the 2/24th build a memorial at Rorke's Drift some months after the battle. [18793]
25. Fort Pine, not far from Rorke's Drift. [87308]
26. Lieutenant Fairlie's sketch of Colonel Richard Glyn of the 1/24th – the commander of the Centre Column. [96484]
27. Colonel Redvers Buller VC, Wood's energetic cavalry commander. [96485]
28. Lieutenant Fairlie's sketch of Louis Napoleon, the Prince Imperial of France. [96482]
29. Major-General Sir Frederick Marshall, who commanded the Cavalry Brigade during the later stages of the war. [96483]
30. The ruins of the mission station at Eshowe, photographed in late 1879. [18791]
31. Officers of the 91st Regiment, the only Highland battalion to serve in the campaign. [96432]
32. An Imperial battalion in Zululand – the 91st Highlanders formed up by companies, pipers to the fore. [23761]

33. An impressive trophy of Zulu weapons, taken by the 91st Highlanders. [96431]
34. The romance and reality of Victorian colonial warfare: a carefully posed study of a 'dead' Zulu warrior. [23497]
35. Zulu skeletons lying on the ground covered by the Zulu right wing at the battle of Gingindlovu. [28318]
36. Irregulars from Raaf's Transvaal Rangers and auxiliaries from Fairlie's Swazi Police march out from Rowlands' column to attack a Zulu outpost at Talaku mountain on 15 February. [71578]
37. Captain Rowland Bettington and a member of his troop of the Natal Horse. [96489]

Section Three

38. Prince Hamu kaNzibe – a member of the Royal House – who surrendered at the beginning of March. [96441]
39. Lieutenant Fairlie sketched Hamu's arrival at Captain MacLeod's camp on the Swazi border on 4 March. [71581]
40. Tommy, the grey horse the Prince Imperial was riding on 1 June. [96440]
41. The donga on the Tshotshosi river where the Prince Imperial was killed; the cairn of stones marks the spot where the body was found. [96444]
42. The Prince's body carried on a gun carriage through the camp at Thelezeni on 2 June. [23831]
43. A Naval Brigade camp above Fort Tenedos on the Lower Thukela. [96435]
44. An unidentified unit of the Natal Native Contingent – probably the reorganized 4th or 5th Battalion. [23495]
45. Lieutenant Fairlie's sketch of auxiliaries of Shepstone's Horse – veterans of Isandlwana – skirmishing on the slopes of eZungeni hill on 5 June. [96491]
46. British artillery shelling Zulu royal homesteads in the emaKhosini valley, 26 June 1879. [96488]
47. British troops and African auxiliaries photographed at Chelmsford's camp on the White Mfolozi in the first days of July. [23832]
48. Major J. F. Owen of 10 Battery, 7th Brigade, Royal Artillery with one of the two Gatling guns he commanded at the battle of Ulundi. [23824]

49. The opening stage of the battle of Ulundi on 4 July; British auxiliaries of Shepstone's Horse goad the Zulu attacking the square. [86832]

50. Lieutenant Fairlie's dramatic sketch end of the battle of Ulundi. [86833]

51. The view from the British camp on the White Mfolozi, looking towards the battlefield of Ulundi, with oNdini burning to the right. [12885]

52. King Cetshwayo on board the steamer *Natal* en route to captivity in Cape Town in September 1879. [23826]

53. The ceremony at Mthonjaneni when King Cetshwayo was restored to Zululand, 29 January 1883. [23505]

54. A contemporary photograph of the Euphorbia Hill cemetery, near Fort Pearson on the Lower Thukela. [562]

Maps

The First Invasion of Zululand, January 1879 5

The Eshowe Campaign, January to April 1879 49

Battle of Isandlwana, 22 January 1879 97

Battle of Rorke's Drift, 22–23 January 1879 119

The Second Invasion of Zululand, March to July 1879 225

Chronology of the Anglo-Zulu War

December 1878

11   British ultimatum delivered to Zulu representatives at Lower Thukela Drift.

January 1879

6   No. 4 Column (Wood) crosses river Ncome into territory claimed by the Zulu.

11   Ultimatum expires; war begins.

11   No. 3 Column (Glyn) crosses into Zululand at Rorke's Drift.

12   No. 3 Column attacks followers of Chief Sihayo kaXongo in the Batshe valley.

17   Main Zulu army leaves oNdini (Ulundi) for the front.

18   No. 1 Column (Pearson) begins advance on Eshowe.

20   No. 4 Column establishes base at Fort Thinta.

22   Attack on No. 1 Column at Nyezane river.

22   Main Zulu army attacks camp of Centre Column at Isandlwana.

22/23   Zulu attack on British border depot at Rorke's Drift.

22/24   No. 4 Column skirmishes with Zulu forces in the vicinity of the Zungwini and Hlobane mountains.

23   No. 1 Column occupies Eshowe mission.

27   First news of Isandlwana reaches No. 1 Column.

28   No. 1 Column decides to hold Eshowe.

31   No. 4 Column moves to a more secure base on Khambula hill.

February

11   Chelmsford's despatch regarding Isandlwana reaches London.

11   Communications between Eshowe and British bases on the Lower Thukela cut.

March

3   First communications by signal established between Lower Thukela and Eshowe.

11   First reinforcements authorized by the British Government arrive in South Africa.

12   Successful attack by Prince Mbilini's followers on convoy of 80th Regiment at Ntombe river.

24   Zulu army leave oNdini for the northern front.

28   Unsuccessful attack by mounted men from No. 4 Column on Hlobane mountain.

29   Main Zulu army attacks No. 4 Column at Khambula, and is heavily defeated.

29   Eshowe Relief Column under Lord Chelmsford begins march from Thukela.

April

1   Prince Louis Napoleon arrives in Natal to join Lord Chelmsford's staff.

2   Chelmsford's Eshowe Relief Column defeats Zulu concentrations on the coast at Gingindlovu.

3   Eshowe relieved.

5   Prince Mbilini mortally wounded in a skirmish near Luneburg.

11   Last of British reinforcements arrive in Natal.

13   Chelmsford reorganizes his forces into 1st Division, 2nd Division and Flying Column.

May

20   British raid across the central Thukela (Twentyman).

21   British Cavalry Brigade visits Isandlwana to bury some of the dead and carry away serviceable equipment.

31   2nd Division crosses into Zululand.

June

1   Prince Imperial killed.

16   Chelmsford receives news that he is to be superseded by Sir Garnet Wolseley.

17   2nd Division and Flying Column link for the final stage of the advance on oNdini.

20   1st Division advances from bases previously established in south-eastern Zululand.

20   First attempts to bury bodies of the 24th Regiment at Isandlwana.

25   Zulu raid across the central Thukela.

26   Troops from the Flying Column destroy Zulu royal homesteads in the emaKhosini valley, the original Zulu heartland.

27   Combined 2nd Division and Flying Column arrive at Mthonjaneni heights, above the White Mfolozi river.

28   Sir Garnet Wolseley arrives in Durban.

July

1   2nd Division and Flying Column establish camp on the White Mfolozi river, opposite oNdini.

3   Mounted men from the Flying Column skirmish with Zulus on the Ulundi plain.

4   Battle of Ulundi (oNdini); final defeat of the Zulu army.

4/5   Surrenders of Zulu chiefs in coastal districts.

8   Chelmsford resigns his command.

15   Chelmsford hands over his command to Wolseley.

19   Wolseley, en route to oNdini, outlines terms of surrender to Zulu chiefs in coastal districts.

August

14   Wolseley accepts surrenders of royalist chiefs including Mnyamana and Ntshingwayo at oNdini.

28   Capture of King Cetshwayo by British Dragoons in the Ngome forest.

September

4   King Cetshwayo taken aboard ship at Port Durnford, destined for exile in Cape Town.

8   Last skirmishes of the war near Luneburg.

Preface

The Anglo-Zulu War of 1879 remains one of the most discussed and analysed of all the colonial wars of the Victorian era. In many respects, in the years since the last shots were fired, it has achieved a prominence out of all proportion to its strategic significance at the time. Certainly, contemporary British analysts were of the opinion that the 2nd Afghan War, which began in 1878 and spluttered on until 1880, was more significant in both military and political terms, while judged by numbers alone, the commitment of troops was far less in Zululand than in the great campaigns of the 1890s in the Sudan and South Africa.

Yet in other respects the Anglo-Zulu campaign remains crucially important, not only in the broader context of the spread of the British Empire, but within the specific framework of southern Africa. The battle of Isandlwana – the worst defeat endured by the British Army in a campaign against an indigenous foe, exceeding in body count even the disaster at Maiwand in 1880 – offered a sharp reminder of the perils of taking military superiority for granted, while the long-term political consequences of the death of the Prince Imperial of France can only be guessed at. Moreover, the determined stand by the Zulu people, in the face of aggressive European interventionism, has come to symbolize the unequal struggle of African peoples in southern Africa across 200 years of white encroachment and dispossession. The defeat of the Zulu paved the way for the greater conflicts to come, between white groups struggling for land and mineral resources, and ushered in a period of oppression and exploitation which has only recently come to an end.

This book is based on material in the collections of the National Army Museum in London, and in particular the superb archive of material relating to the British Commander-in-Chief, Lieutenant-General Lord Chelmsford. As such, it reflects the preoccupations of those in the British forces, at the highest level, in planning, executing and later apologizing for aspects of the campaign. While this gives a remarkable insight into British political and strategic imperatives, the semi-official nature of much of Chelmsford's correspondence does not always offer a personal perspective. Some good collections of letters and diaries from officers of middle and lower ranks exist, and have been extensively quoted here – among them the papers of Major Philip Anstruther, Lieutenant Julius Backhouse and Lieutenant Nevill Coghill. There are, too, a few delightful accounts from ordinary soldiers: Bandsman Tuck's descriptions of false alarms, and the exhaustion of forced marches in the Zululand countryside, are richly evocative.

Nevertheless, the limitations are obvious. There are very few accounts in the collection from Zulu sources, and those that do exist were usually elicited from spies or prisoners, and reflect the preoccupations of their British interrogators. Where possible, I have tried to add in some impression of the events inside Zululand, which were often at odds with the British perception of them, but the book remains very much a picture of the war as it seemed to the British Army prosecuting it.

There are other more curious omissions in the source material. There is very little material on the famous action at Rorke's Drift, and this reflects the fact that to the Army in Zululand at the time the battle was merely one part of a complex and damaging series of events, all of which took place on the same day. The battle was viewed primarily as an example of the courage and doggedness of ordinary British soldiers at their best – arguably the elements which have led to the battle's extraordinary popularity in recent times – and the interest in the battle displayed by the popular press at home came as a surprise to many serving soldiers. The representation of other events, including crucial engagements like the battle of Khambula, is similarly patchy. After careful deliberation, I have made some attempt to rectify this by occasionally including extracts from published sources – either official or private – in the Museum's collections, where they seemed to me particularly revealing, and to provide material not available in the unpublished collections.

The spelling of Zulu words also required some consideration. In 1879 siZulu, the Zulu language, did not exist in a standardized written form, and as a result British observers spelled Zulu words phonetically, often displaying a rich and varied imagination. Thus King Cetshwayo's name was often rendered as Cetywayo, Cetewayo or Ketchwayo; Thukela as Tugela; and Isandlwana as Isandula, Isandlana or even Isandlahana. The old mission station at Eshowe was often rendered in the form preferred by the Norwegian missionaries – Ekowe – while Cetshwayo's principal residence, known variously to the Zulus as oNdini or Ulundi (from the common root *undi*, meaning a high place), was generally referred to by the British as the latter. To complicate matters further, the homestead itself is now generally known as oNdini, while by convention the battle which took place there on 4 July 1879 is known as Ulundi. More curiously, even the names of British officers were sometimes misspelt in contemporary despatches; Colonel Glyn of the 1/24th, for example, referred to his own adjutant, Lieutenant Melvill, as 'Melville'. In a passing nod at consistency, I have followed current usage in my own text, but, to retain something of the period atmosphere, I have left the original spellings in quoted passages. After much agonizing, I have also retained in contemporary texts some words or phrases which would now be considered offensive; the meaning of such phrases (particularly *kaffir*, which was in common usage amongst the Army in 1879, relating either to a person of southern African origin or, more specifically, to a member of the amaXhosa people), was sometimes more ambiguous then than now, and should be taken as an insight into the different racial and cultural assumptions of the nineteenth century.

2002

Chapter One

'Half measures do not answer . . .'

At dawn on 21 May 1879 a column of British troops set out from the border post of Rorke's Drift, in the southern African colony of Natal, to visit the battlefield of Isandlwana, which lay just a few miles away across the Mzinyathi river, in independent Zulu territory. Almost exactly three months before, Isandlwana had been the scene of one of the most dramatic reverses to mar the progress of the Victorian empire; a defeat so shocking and incomprehensible that it had catapulted an obscure colonial campaign to the forefront of public awareness in Britain, and thrust the Zulu people into a searching media spotlight from which they have never really escaped.

Indeed, so catastrophic was the disaster, that in the intervening months the British had lacked both the resources and the will to return to the site. Not only had the threat of a Zulu counter-attack seemed very real, but they had shied away from the spectacle of the dead, who still lay rotting upon the ground. Only a shift in British fortunes elsewhere in the war, combined with the arrival of reinforcements from home and a decidedly pragmatic need to recover military equipment abandoned on the field, had made a return possible.

The force which set out from Rorke's Drift that morning was a strong one, and consisted largely of two regiments of regular cavalry – the 1st (King's) Dragoon Guards and the 17th Lancers – fresh out from England. For the men of both regiments, this expedition was their first venture on to Zulu soil, and it would prove a deeply disturbing experience. There were rumours of Zulu concentrations in the Mzinyathi valley, and the expedition's commander, Major-General Sir Frederick Marshall, had taken no chances. Before dawn, he had pushed a screen of African auxiliaries across the river, followed by a vanguard of mounted men who swept wide of the track, destroying any abandoned Zulu settlements they came across.

The main column crossed at first light. The heavy summer rains

which had plagued the campaign had left the Zululand countryside
greener than was usual for the time of year. The scarlet tunics of the
Dragoons, and the deep blue of the Lancers, with their red and white
pennons fluttering gaily on their lances, provided a striking splash of
colour against the long grass and brown, rocky hillsides. As Marshall's
men advanced, smoke began to rise from the hills to their left, from
Zulu huts torched by the vanguard. It had taken ten days to march down
this same route in January; now, unencumbered by heavy transport
wagons, Marshall made the journey in a matter of hours. At about
8.30 a.m. the cavalry crested a rise, then descended on to the open slope
at the foot of Isandlwana hill, where the British camp had stood four
months before.

What they saw there haunted many of them for the rest of their lives.
The grass had grown up on the old battlefield, at first glance obscuring
the obvious traces of battle. Only the wagons, rising up like islands
where they had once stood in rows behind the tent lines, were obvious
at first. Over 1,300 British troops and their African allies had been killed
at Isandlwana, but there was none of the bloody horror of a fresh
battlefield, and the smell which had characterized the site for months
had largely dissipated. Instead, an air of profound and apocalyptic
stillness hung over the field, a cloying atmosphere of stale death, of
decay and desolation. Many of the bodies had been broken up by the
elements and by scavengers, but in truth there were too many to be so
easily disposed of, and hundreds more lay untouched. Most were
skeletons, held together by the remains of their uniforms, but here and
there the desiccated skin and hair still clung to the skulls, imparting a
macabre parody of life to the features. The story of the battle could be
read in the way the bodies lay, clumped together in some places where
there had been a determined stand, or scattered individually or in twos
and threes where the British line had broken. Among those fascinated by
the evidence of stale slaughter was Captain Stanley Clark of the 17th
Lancers, who wrote to his sister from Rorke's Drift the following evening:

> The sight at Ishandlawana was really very awful and terribly
> interesting. The waggons were the first thing you caught sight of,
> upset and torn about everywhere. The skeletons laid everywhere in a
> wonderful state of preservation, men lay as they were left and the
> natives have not been to touch them. All the Zulu dead are carried

away – ours all there. They were in their clothes – few of which seem to have been taken – trousers, gaiters, boots on – coat, shirt, braces – with their water bottles by their side, the straps round them – but in nearly every case the clothes torn open in front and most horrible atrocities committed on the bodies ... so the corpses – or rather skeletons almost – presented a horrible sight and with great assegai holes in them. Everything was just as left – the horse lines, with the picket pegs and horses laid assegaied in their harness. All the tents are taken but not the ropes – these tents are marked out in many cases with men killed in the tents and all the things strewn about and trampled in by the struggle. I picked up a pamphlet and cheque-book in one – which I'll send you. The mess waggon hastily rifled, tins of milk, sardines and things strewn about. In fact, except for the state of the corpses you might have thought it happened yesterday instead of 4 months ago. We found Col. Durnford's body – his servant instantly recognized it – he had a diamond ring on his finger and a knife in his pocket with his name on. We buried him. I tried everywhere to see if I could see poor Younghusband's body – but of course could not recognize which it was or I could have buried him. You might tell Evelyn that I made every enquiry and found a man – Major Tongue, 2/24th – who saw his body after the battle. He lay near the road, or track which runs thro' the centre of the plain – his clothes on, & the body not mutilated. We fired the kraals around and drove in what little cattle we could catch, harnessed all the waggons that were worth anything – nearly 40 of them – and brought them in here.

In many respects, that image of the terrible field at Isandlwana would prove the defining one of the Anglo-Zulu War, as potent in its way as the flickering silent newsreel footage of men going over the top at the Somme, or of the killing fields of Bosnia in more recent times. It was a register of the shock and horror experienced by the British Empire on finding itself defeated by a people it had painfully underestimated, and it would become a symbol too of the robust resistance mounted by the Zulu people against colonial intervention. More than that, it remains a perfect icon for the violence and brutality which characterized both British progress in southern Africa and the history of the Zulu kingdom. Isandlwana was at once the high point of Zulu warrior tradition and the harbinger of inexorable defeat. Nor would that violence end with the closing shots of the Anglo-Zulu War, for the repercussions of the conflict encapsulated at Isandlwana have continued to echo down the years, framing deep and bitter divisions within South African society to this day.

*

In retrospect, it is difficult to see the British invasion of Zululand in 1879 as anything other than an unjust war of aggression. It did not seem so to the British officials prosecuting it at the time, of course; for them the Zulu kingdom was an anachronism, a symbol of an alien and incomprehensible way of life which must inevitably give way in the face of European-driven concepts of progress. Indeed, with the exception of a few heroic voices crying out alone in the wilderness, British intervention in Zululand was applauded at the time by humanitarian and missionary lobbies in both southern Africa and Europe. For most white observers, the war was fought to overthrow barbarism, to encourage the spread of Christian civilization, European capitalist ideals and the work ethic. Only after the Zulu people were defeated, their young men killed in thousands, their King captured, their royal centres razed and their political and military institutions overthrown, was it possible to reinvent them, with just a hint of nostalgic regret, as 'noble savages'. And therein lies the tragedy of a nation.

The area now known as Zululand lies east of the Kahlamba mountains – known to the first white travellers as the Drakensberg, or 'dragon mountains' – which rise like a jagged spine around the eastern rim of modern South Africa. The country drops in a series of rugged terraces from the cool inland heights to the stifling lowlands which border the Indian Ocean. Rain-bearing winds, blowing off the sea, have scarred the hills with scores of major river systems. The fragile earth which clings to the rocky bones of the land gives rise to a wide variety of sweet and sour grasses which made it in the past both a haven for wildlife and ideal country for pastoral societies dependent on cattle. The origins of human settlement in the area are lost in the mists of time; hundreds of spectacular cave paintings in the mountains and foothills testify that it was home for thousands of years to the Stone Age people who survived into modern times as the San Bushmen. Modern archaeology has discovered the remains of recognizably African peoples which date back to at least AD 800, and by the sixteenth century the accounts of sailors,

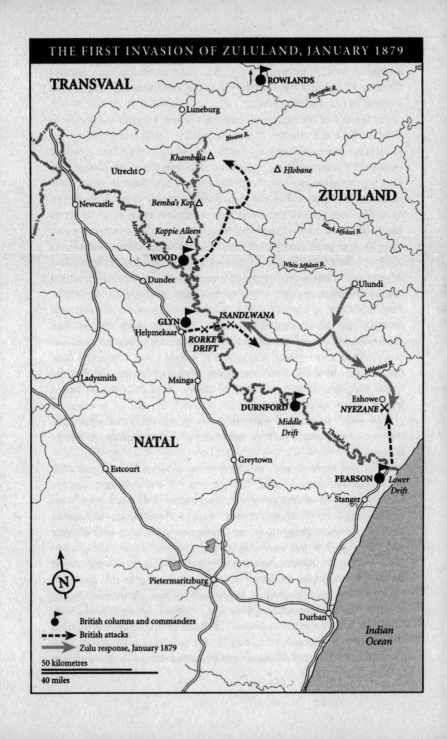

THE FIRST INVASION OF ZULULAND, JANUARY 1879

TRANSVAAL

ROWLANDS

○ Luneburg

Phongolo R.

Bivane R.

Khambula △

Utrecht ○

△ *Hlobane*

Ncome R.

ZULULAND

Bemba's Kop △

○ Newcastle

Black Mfolozi R.

Mzinyathi R.

Koppie Alleen △

WOOD ●

White Mfolozi R.

○ Dundee

○ Ulundi

GLYN ●

ISANDLWANA

Helpmekaar

RORKE'S DRIFT

○ Ladysmith

○ Msinga

Mhlatuze R.

DURNFORD

Eshowe ○

NYEZANE ✕

Middle Drift

NATAL

Thukela R.

○ Estcourt

○ Greytown

PEARSON ●

Lower Drift

Stanger ○

○ Pietermaritzburg

N

● British columns and commanders

- - - ► British attacks

──► Zulu response, January 1879

50 kilometres

40 miles

○ Durban

Indian Ocean

washed up from ships brought to grief on the treacherous coast, describe
the lives of a people who shared much the same language and culture
as the Zulus of modern times.

By the end of the eighteenth century, the area between the Phongolo
river in the north and the Mzimkhulu in the south was populated by
an African group who spoke broadly the same language and followed
broadly the same customs. Organized into hereditary chiefdoms, they
were a polygamous society, in which a man might have as many wives
as he could support. For the most part, ordinary commoners might
have only one or two, but wives were a manifestation of social status
and wealth, and men of importance and rank might have many more.
They lived in small family settlements known as *imizi*, each one a circle
of dome-shaped thatch huts, home to a married man, his wives and
dependants. They were a pastoral people, and much of their social
interaction, religious practice and material culture revolved around cattle.
The only form of storable wealth, cattle were central to the marriage
contract, and the sacrifice of a beast was crucial to every religious rite.
Moreover, while meat was only eaten on important occasions, milk was
a staple food, and a carcass was turned to a wide range of practical uses;
the hide was used for shields or cloaks, the horns for utensils, and the
brush from the tail as a personal ornament. Zululand, with its varied
terrain, good water-supply, absence of tsetse fly, and wide range of
grasses which matured at different times of the year, was ideal cattle
country – a fact which, perhaps more than any other, explains its bloody
history.

Whatever tensions may have riven these societies before about 1750
are lost in the mists of time, but the close of the eighteenth century
brought a period of demographic crisis. Prolonged drought, population
increase, and an economic tension brought about by an increase in
trading activity centring upon the Portuguese enclave at Mozambique
may all have had an unsettling effect, with the result that conflict
between the chiefdoms accelerated. Oral tradition, viewing events
through the rosy glow of nostalgia, suggests that prior to this time such
conflicts were rare, limited in nature and seldom destructive, but as
pressure on the combatants increased, violence became increasingly
brutal as it took on the early characteristics of a struggle for survival.
The result was a profound change in the nature of both the political
and military structures of African groups in the region – a change which

took place on the very eve of the wider and more dangerous challenge posed by white intervention.

The first major clashes took place on the upper reaches of the Mfolozi river complex. Two groups had already emerged to face each other across this line, the Ndwandwe of Chief Zwide kaLanga to the north-west, and the Mthethwa of Chief Dingiswayo kaJobe to the south-east. Both groups were militarily strong and had assumed the role of overlord over weaker neighbours who had gravitated towards them for protection. The exact causes of the dispute between these groups remains obscure, but by about 1800 low-intensity clashes were endemic on the frontier between them.

Into this already unsettled landscape was born a man who was neither an Mthethwa nor an Ndwandwe, but who was destined to overturn the fortunes of both. Arguably one of the most important individuals in southern African history, he is also one of the most ambiguous, shrouded in myth in his own culture, and alternately demonized or lionized in the wider world beyond: Shaka, the Zulu.

At the time Shaka kaSenzangakhona was born – about 1787 – the Zulu were a small group living along the valley of the Mkhumbane stream, on the southern banks of the White Mfolozi. The ancestors of their chiefs had been buried for generations here, in an area still known as *emakhosini*, 'the place of the kings'. Overshadowed by more powerful neighbours, Shaka's father, Chief Senzangakhona, had already given his people's allegiance to the Mthethwa before Shaka was born. Indeed, when a family rift drove Shaka and his mother away from Senzangakhona's royal homestead in search of a protector, it was among the Mthethwa that they came to rest. Here Shaka grew to manhood and learned his craft as a young warrior. Aggressive and ambitious, he soon distinguished himself in Dingiswayo's army, and his prowess is recalled in his praise-poem – the long eulogy by which he was exalted in his lifetime and remembered after his death – by the phrases;

> *Usishaka kasishayeki kanjengamanzi,*
> *Ilembe' eleq'amany'amalembe ngokukhalipha ...*
> *Unomashovushovu kaSenzangakhona,*
> *UGaqa libomvu nasekuphatheni ...*
>
> He who beats but is not beaten, unlike water,
> Axe that surpasses other axes in its sharpness ...

> The voracious one of Senzangakhona,
> Spear that is red even on the handle.

When Senzangakhona died about 1816, Dingiswayo moved to secure his influence over the Zulu. With Dingiswayo's support, Shaka overturned the legitimate successor and installed himself as the Zulu chief. It was a turning point in his own career and in the history of his people. Within two years, by an astute mixture of political manoeuvring, ruthless military action and luck, Shaka had surpassed Dingiswayo, absorbed the Mthethwa into his own confederacy, and defeated and driven out Zwide. Over the following decade, Shaka's influence expanded to encompass most of the groups lying between the Black Mfolozi river in the north and the Thukela in the south, and the emergent state took the collective name Zulu, in the tradition of the ruling elite.

In retrospect, Shaka's rule seems disproportionately short for the impact it had. He was King for scarcely a dozen years – he was assassinated in a palace coup in 1828 – but during that time he created a sophisticated centralized state which went far beyond anything achieved by his mentor, Dingiswayo. The apparatus of the monarchy, centred upon the person of the King himself, shaped and controlled all important religious, political and economic elements within the lives of the subject chiefdoms. Arguably the most important mechanism of state control was the *amabutho* system. The *amabutho* were guilds in which young men of the same age were banded together to undergo the ceremonies which initiated them into manhood. These guilds were required to give a period of service to their chiefs, but Shaka prohibited the regional chiefs from enrolling *amabutho*, and instead summoned youths from across his kingdom to serve him directly. The *amabutho* became in effect a national state-labour gang, which could be employed to fight the King's wars, build his royal homesteads, police his subjects and take part in national hunts or the great religious ceremonies. Although they lived for the most part at their family homes, the men might be assembled at any time on Shaka's bidding, and were subject to such a call-up until they were given permission to marry, a rite of passage which effectively placed them beyond the King's immediate control. To house them when they were assembled, the King established large royal homesteads known as *amakhanda* – literally 'heads' – which served as a focus of royal authority around the kingdom.

Shaka's success as a warrior ensured that his country grew rich in captured cattle, and his army was feared down the length of the eastern seaboard. Yet in his success, as so often in Zulu history, lay the seeds of disaster. The stories of the wealth and power of the Zulu, suitably exaggerated, spread far beyond Shaka's borders to the south and came at last to the ears of British traders on the eastern Cape frontier.

Europeans had established themselves in southern Africa centuries before, of course. In 1652 Jan van Riebeeck had established a toe-hold for Dutch commerce, in the form of the Dutch East India Company, on the extreme southern tip of the continent, easily displacing the indigenous Khoi-san people. The Dutch had little interest in Africa, but the Cape gave them strategic control of the long sea-route round the continent to the immensely profitable Indies, and allowed Dutch ships the huge advantage over rival empires of an opportunity to revictual and water. Gradually, the Cape colony had expanded inland, and produced a hardy breed of frontier settlers, initially Dutch in origin, but mixed with French and German political and religious refugees, who thought of themselves as a new people – the Boers – and were characterized by a tough self-reliance and an isolated and conservative mind-set. With the violent swings of political fortune in Europe which followed the outbreak of the French Revolution, however, the Dutch authorities found themselves displaced at the Cape. The British took over the colony briefly in 1795, left, then returned again in force to seize the place in 1806. Like the Dutch, their interests lay primarily in global strategy, but in the 150 years since Van Reibeeck's arrival, the situation at the Cape had altered drastically.

The inexorable movement of the Boers inland, following the belt of good grazing land that characterized the hills along the eastern coast, had brought them at last into conflict with robust African societies beyond. At least two wars had taken place in what became known as the Eastern Cape Frontier before the British arrived in 1806, and there were to be many more. The British reluctantly found themselves cast in the role of Imperial policemen, a position which earned them little thanks from the Boers, who resented British authority and complained that it failed to give them the uncritical support they demanded. In time, this resentment would lead to a mass exodus from the Cape by the Boers and pave the way for a further century of conflict and dispossession.

It was against this background, in the early 1820s, that the first news of the rise of Shaka Zulu reached the Cape Frontier. The British Empire at that point was awash with ambitious and adventurous young officers, recently made unemployed by the outbreak of peace in Europe, and keen to take their principles of trade and profit into the more exotic corners of the earth. In 1824, a syndicate of Cape merchants devised a scheme to establish a trading presence among the Zulu, and they employed an ex-naval officer, Lieutenant Francis George Farewell, to lead it. A little was known of the coastal geography of the eastern coast – the Portuguese explorer, Vasco de Gama, had first logged its presence to the outside world on Christmas Day 1497, and named it Terra Natalis, in honour of Christ's birth – and Farewell hoped to make landfall at a spot known variously as the Rio da Natal, or Bay of Natal. The bay was a large natural harbour, the best on the east coast, but it was almost enclosed by two jutting spits of land, and a submerged sandbar all but sealed off the narrow entrance. The bar had been sufficient to deter generations of seamen from attempting an entrance, but in July 1824 Farewell's advance party slipped across it without incident. In later years, made wise by bitter hindsight, the Zulu King Cetshwayo kaMpande would remark pointedly on the progress of the British Empire in South Africa. 'First', he observed, 'comes the trader. Then the missionary. Then the red soldier.'

With the arrival of Farewell's party, the first step in the inexorable conflict between the British and the Zulu kingdom had been taken.

King Shaka welcomed the traders. They brought him exotic trade goods and proved a valuable tool in his perpetual political struggle to keep his new state intact. On occasion, the traders did not scruple to add their firepower to Shaka's armies. In return, the King established them as a client chiefdom at the bay, and they ruled as his local representatives. For the first few years it was a gloriously anarchic lifestyle, a long way beyond the reach of any European authority, as the traders hunted for ivory and buffalo hides, took wives after local custom, accumulated retainers from among those dispossessed by Shaka's wars, and grew rich in cattle. They used their influence with the Zulu King to intimidate their African neighbours, schemed and quarrelled among themselves, and, when it suited them, conspired to blacken their host's name for posterity. Keen to obscure their own dubious behaviour, they passed down to history the image of Shaka as a ruthless and capricious despot, a heartless monster who assassinated most of his own family and slaughtered thousands of his own people to satisfy his personal craving for power. In that image of innate and unstable savagery their successors would find a justification for confronting the Zulu kingdom scarcely half a century later.

All subsequent British claims on the eastern seaboard were to depend on that trading outpost of Farewell's. During his last years, King Shaka had established royal settlements closer to the bay, but he was murdered in 1828, and his successor, King Dingane kaSenzangakhona, moved the centres of royal power back to the Zulu heartland on the White Mfolozi, leaving the influence of the traders ascendant in the area south of the Thukela river. Among the whites, this area was increasingly spoken of as a separate political entity – Natal – distinct from the Zulu kingdom itself, and in 1838 a new wave of settlers pushed this schism to its logical conclusion.

In the wake of the Sixth Cape Frontier War (1834–5), many Boer groups on the Cape Frontier had become disillusioned with British authority, and from early 1836 hundreds of Boer families began to migrate from British territory. They simply crossed out of the colonial boundaries and pressed into the interior, looking for new lands to call their own. Their progress was marked by bitter conflicts with African groups living along the way, and in late 1837 the first Boer groups crossed into Natal from the interior. Unlike the British traders at the bay, the Boers were pastoralists, and in direct competition with the Zulu for grazing land. A bitter and brutal war broke out almost immediately, in which the British settlers, pressed by the logic of their own racially defined history, sided with the Boers. At first the war went heavily against the whites, with the Zulu launching attacks against the Boer settlements in the Kahlamba foothills and laying waste to the trading post at the bay. By late 1838, however, the Boers had regrouped and won a significant victory against the Zulu at the battle of Ncome (Blood River).

Yet the Blood River victory was by no means as decisive as has sometimes been claimed. Both sides had fought each other to a standstill, and while the Boers were able to establish themselves in Natal without interference from the Zulu, King Dingane had merely moved his royal capital a few miles further north, beyond the reach of the Boers. It was not until 1840 that a dispute within the Zulu Royal House allowed Dingane's brother, Prince Mpande, to overthrow him with Boer support.

Although the Boers believed Mpande was their puppet, he was in fact an astute political survivor who strove to rebuild the unity and autonomy of his kingdom and to free himself from the constraints of white influence.

The establishment of a Boer republic in Natal alarmed the Colonial Office in London, however. Hitherto, the British had shown no particular official interest in Farewell's schemes and had several times refused his requests to assume control of the enclave. Nevertheless, they had persistently regarded the Boers as errant subjects whose activities needed to be policed, and the Boer presence in Natal was disconcerting in two respects. Not only did it threaten to destabilize still further the already chaotic political situation in southern Africa, but it awakened the possibility of contact with rival European empires through the bay. In 1842 the British acted to isolate the Boers from that contact. Using a dubious grant by King Shaka of land to Farewell, British troops were marched up overland from the Cape Frontier to occupy the trading settlement. The Boers objected of course, and a fierce fight broke out among the sand dunes and mangrove swamps of what is now the city of Durban. The British garrison, under a Waterloo veteran, Major Thomas Smith, dug in and was besieged until reinforcements were rushed up by sea from the Cape. Smith was relieved, the Boers dispersed, and in 1843 Natal was officially annexed to the British Crown. Many Boers were so disgusted that they refused to remain under British control, saying they would rather walk back barefoot over the Kahlamba mountains.

The establishment of British authority changed the character of Natal. King Mpande, delighted to be free of his obligation to the Boers, accepted the situation, and an accord defined the line of the Mzinyathi (Water of Buffaloes) and Thukela rivers as the boundary between the two states. A few republican Boers who did not wish to leave the area entirely prevailed upon the King to allow them to live north of the Mzinyathi, where a tongue of land, belonging nominally to Natal, ran along the mountain foothills. For the most part, however, Natal assumed a British character as immigrants slowly trickled in to claim the best farming land. Port Natal lost its anarchic air, the mixed-race descendants of the first white settlers were brushed under the carpet, and a bustling colonial port known as Durban grew in its place. Ironically, the British chose the village established by the Boer Trekkers – Pietermaritzburg – which lay fifty miles inland as the seat of their colonial authority.

For the African population of Natal, the coming of the British was a mixed blessing. Those groups who had remained in their traditional lands since the days of Shaka had done so largely by accepting Zulu authority. For some of them, British rule apparently offered the chance to stand clear of the Zulu shadow and take back the mantle of a more autonomous lifestyle. For others, who had been displaced by the Zulu, or who had simply fled to avoid direct confrontation, the British offered a protective umbrella under which to return to their former lands. Yet all of Natal's African population soon found that British protection was achieved at a price. Although they continued to live their lives under their hereditary chiefs and in the manner of their traditional customs, their lives little changed on the surface, they were now subject to the supreme authority of the colonial powers. They found themselves living on appointed reserves – known as locations – which were often cramped and impoverished, while the best land was offered to white settlers. Those who were permitted to stay on white farms did so only as labour tenants, though their forebears might have lived there for generations. Gradually, as Natal's administrative infrastructure expanded, the African people found themselves subjected to a variety of taxes, which were intended not only to generate income for the administration, but to force them to abandon their subsistence agriculture and seek paid employment from the whites.

For the most part, the relationship between colonial Natal and the Zulu kingdom remained good for nearly thirty years. Although many white settlers in Natal, acutely conscious of their own vulnerability in the midst of a much larger and potentially hostile African population, were deeply suspicious of their powerful and robust northern neighbour, both King Mpande and the Natal administration were at pains to avoid direct conflict, even when political tensions within the kingdom threatened to spill over into Natal. Nevertheless, goodwill was not in itself sufficient to deflate a growing sense of frustration on both sides, which had much to do with the way the fortunes of the two states were inextricably interrelated.

Mpande, by far the most underrated and misunderstood of the early Zulu kings, successfully rebuilt his nation's fortunes in the aftermath of the disastrous Trekker War of 1838–40, and in the face of growing European economic penetration. In part, however, his success was bought at the price of permanent political insecurity, as he skilfully played one internal interest off against another. In 1856, Mpande's refusal to nominate a successor from among his growing number of sons resulted in a disastrous civil war between two rival candidates, the Princes Mbuyazi and Cetshwayo. Mbuyazi, realizing that he had failed to gain support in the kingdom as a whole, appealed instead for Natal's support. To the consternation of the colonial border police, Mbuyazi and several thousand of his followers tried to cross the Thukela into the colony, and were prevented only by the flooded state of the river. At the beginning of December Cetshwayo's army caught them there, and one of the bloodiest battles in Zulu history was fought out in the undulating grasslands directly opposite the Natal bank. Under the eyes of horrified white officials and traders, Cetshwayo's army utterly destroyed Mbuyazi's faction, overrunning his warriors and slaughtering non-combatants right up to the river bank.

The Zulu succession crisis of 1856 was a sharp reminder that, despite the very different administrations of Natal and Zululand, their fortunes could not easily be disentangled. Since 1824 Natal had always served as a sanctuary for Zulu refugees, and the nominal presence of the border could not by itself contain them. In the years following the civil war, hundreds of Zulu who refused to accept Cetshwayo as heir crossed into Natal, including several of Mpande's sons. The African populations of Natal and Zululand were locked in a political tug-of-war which pre-dated white authority, and which the whites were unlikely to contain. Conversely, the growing penetration of Zululand by representatives of white commercial concerns – hunters and traders – not only served to undermine traditional forms of government within the kingdom, but at the same time linked the two economies ominously together. Much of the balance of trade was in Natal's favour, with thousands of head of cattle extracted from Zululand in exchange for blankets, beads and trinkets, and Zulu trade remained a mainspring of the Natal economy into the 1870s.

The ambiguities of this interdependence were highlighted when King Mpande died in 1872. Cetshwayo had been largely successful in his attempt to eliminate internal opposition to his succession, but he remained wary of his own powerful regional chiefs who had enjoyed a considerable degree of autonomy in his father's time. In an effort to bolster his position, he invited Natal to send representatives to the ceremonies which marked his installation. Without securing permission from London, Natal's Secretary for Native Affairs, Theophilus Shepstone, accepted the invitation. The son of an Eastern Cape missionary, Shepstone was a complex, secretive man who spoke Zulu fluently and was convinced that he understood 'the African mind'. A believer in Britain's manifest destiny in Africa, Shepstone's approach to local politics was machiavellian. By travelling to Zululand with a small escort in August 1873, he initiated a game of tangled political manoeuvre which led ultimately to direct confrontation.

Throughout the expedition, Shepstone's intention was to legitimize Natal's right to intervene in Zulu politics. Many traditionalist Zulu regarded his presence as an irrelevance, and indeed Cetshwayo had already been installed as king by Zulu custom several days before Shepstone's party arrived. For Cetshwayo, it was enough that he appeared to have secured Natal's support to his birthright, a fact which inevitably intimidated internal opposition. Yet Shepstone insisted on staging a farcical coronation ceremony, crowning Cetshwayo with a tinsel crown made for the purpose by a military tailor. Moreover, Shepstone issued a proclamation at the ceremony which Cetshwayo assumed to be a reinforcement of his authority, but which Shepstone later claimed outlined the conditions upon which British support rested. Either way, the time would come when King Cetshwayo would regret ever allowing the British a foot in the Zulu door.

King Cetshwayo was a more direct man than his father, and more confident of his inheritance. Mpande had inherited a country weakened by conflict with the Boers and divided by civil war. He had slowly and patiently restored the power and prestige of the royal administration, but he had never managed to secure the degree of central authority which Shaka had enjoyed. Many of the regional chiefs had sold their allegiance in return for a degree of local autonomy, and royal institutions, such as the *amabutho*, no longer commanded universal support. Cetshwayo, however, was determined to continue his father's work, and in particular insisted that all young Zulu men should join the regiments. This provoked some opposition within the kingdom, especially regarding the King's prerogative to grant permission for the *amabutho* to marry. When, in 1876, the King ordered the iNdlondlo regiment to take brides from a much younger female guild, the iNgcugce, some of the girls, who had lovers in a younger regiment, refused. The King ordered several girls to be executed as an example, and the remainder promptly complied.

The result, however, was not only a simmering feud between the regiments, but a howl of protest from an unexpected quarter.

The first European missionaries had established stations inside Zululand from the 1830s. On the whole, they had not proved very successful, largely because the Zulu were content with their own spiritual beliefs, and evangelical Christianity tended to bring with it a good deal of colonial baggage. Missionary attacks on polygamy, on the power of the spirit diviners – whom traditional Zulus regarded as their first line of defence against supernatural evil – and their support for colonial economic systems like wage-labour and trade were regarded with suspicion by the population as a whole. Mpande had seen some political advantage to their presence, however, within the framework of his own internal struggles. He held them up as representatives of the white world, whose power he could evoke to intimidate his own dissidents. As a result, by the 1870s, a number of mission societies maintained establishments which Mpande had carefully placed in those parts of the country which were already most exposed to white penetration. Cetshwayo, however, was more sceptical, and regarded them openly as agents of Imperial intervention. While he never prevented his subjects from attending mission services, he made it clear that any Zulu converting to Christianity placed himself outside royal protection.

To some extent, of course, Cetshwayo was right; by the 1870s, many mission societies had become disillusioned with their experiences inside Zululand, and had come to blame the King for their conspicuous lack of success. Believing that the only way to open Zululand to wholesale evangelism was to destroy the political institutions upon which Zulu independence and self-confidence rested, they began to agitate for some form of outside intervention. Initially, this took the form of an appeal to the authorities in Natal to use their influence, legitimized at the 'coronation' of 1873, to put pressure on Cetshwayo to accept greater Christian activity. When this produced no obvious results, some societies began a propaganda war, damning Cetshwayo as a bloodthirsty despot, just as his uncle, King Shaka, had once been damned. The 'Marriage of the iNgcugce' incident caused genuine alarm in the Zululand mission community and provided fresh ammunition in the war.

Such a view inevitably found a sympathetic ear in parts of a colony of which a latent fear of Zulu authority had been a characteristic since inception. Nevertheless, although complex factors had created a growing sense of unease in the political relationship between Natal and Zululand since Cetshwayo's accession, the catalyst for direct confrontation was provided by an outside element. By the middle of the 1870s, Imperialism was on the march in southern Africa.

For nearly three-quarters of a century, the British Government had pursued an Imperial role in the region only reluctantly. Global strategy – the possession of the Cape – remained its primary objective, and it had been drawn into the interior only grudgingly, acknowledging the policing duty which devolved upon itself in the wake of settler-driven expansion. For decades southern Africa had been the scene of seemingly interminable conflicts between the British administration, the Boers and indigenous Africans, and every mile the frontiers had advanced had been paid for by a reluctant Exchequer and with the blood of the long-suffering redcoat.

In 1868, however, all that had changed with the discovery of diamonds in the independent territory of Griqualand West. An adroit redrawing of the Imperial boundaries narrowly beat the Boers to these potential riches, and with the growth of a mining boom-town – Kimberley – it seemed that southern Africa might at last offer the British a return on their investment. The prospect of economic development merely highlighted the need for a wider regional infrastructure which was impossible while the area was politically fragmented. To move labour freely to and from the interior, to develop lines of communication and trade which connected southern Africa as a whole to the wider Empire, would require a broader political vision than was current in the introverted and mutually antagonistic British colonies, Boer republics and independent African states.

The solution, advocated by Lord Carnarvon at the Colonial Office in London, was a scheme called Confederation. Based on a precedent which had worked with apparent success in Canada, the underlying principle of Confederation was that the various states of southern Africa should be loosely brought together under British control in order to facilitate a consistent approach to the political economy. Such a plan begged a number of interesting political and military questions, since in the case of the Boers at least, a rejection of British authority had been the very reason why the republics had been established in the first place. Nevertheless, while Carnarvon accepted that the threat of military force was implicit in the scheme, he hoped that recalcitrant groups would soon be won round by the obvious benefits of living under British protection.

The first step on the road to Confederation took place in 1877, when, after a highly selective survey of white public opinion there, the British marched to Pretoria and annexed the Transvaal Republic. From the outside, this was arguably a justifiable reaction to the Republic's chronic instability. Largely bankrupt – self-reliant and suspicious of any form of government, the Boers were perennially reluctant to pay their taxes – the Republic had found itself embroiled in a number of protracted struggles with its African neighbours which it seemed unable to resolve without access to any form of regular army. In particular, a campaign waged against the Pedi confederacy on the north-eastern borders in 1876 had proved farcical, exposing the government to ridicule and alienating its African allies, to whom it had left much of the fighting.

The British, of course, claimed to be able to protect the Transvaal Boers against such enemies, and they counted on the fact that this obvious benefit would inevitably undermine any lingering republican resentment. Ironically, however, the annexation of the Transvaal merely served to intensify the underlying conflict between British and African interests in the area, bringing conflict a step nearer. Imperial theorists on the spot seemed to have missed a fact which is obvious in hindsight; that once the British had confronted and overcome the threat posed by the Transvaal's independent neighbours, the Boers would have no need of the British at all.

With the acquisition of the Transvaal, the British had inherited a long-standing boundary dispute with the Zulu kingdom on the Transvaal's south-eastern border. The origins of this dispute dated to the 1840s, when most of the Boer Trekkers had abandoned Natal. A few, unwilling to give up the lands for which they had fought so hard, had settled in the most northerly part of the colony, where a triangle of land jutted out along the Kahlamba foothills. This area lay north of the Mzinyathi river, the nominal border between Natal and Zululand, and the precise boundary had never been delineated. The area was thinly populated by Zulu groups giving their allegiance to King Mpande, but the King allowed a few Boers to graze their herds in the area. Over the next thirty years, the Boers had edged further and further into Zulu territory – like a toad, as one Zulu described it, hopping and hopping, until it comes unnoticed to the hearthstone of the kingdom. They had even established a village, Utrecht, which formed the basis of an administrative district of the Transvaal. King Mpande had sometimes protested, but had lacked the resolve to take up the issue; Cetshwayo, however, refused to allow the Boers to steal Zululand from under his nose. Several times he had threatened to use force to evict the Boers, but on each occasion had allowed himself to be calmed by British intervention.

For the most part, indeed, the British had supported the Zulu claims prior to 1877, largely because it suited them to play off two potential rivals against one another. Following the annexation, however, the burghers of Utrecht suddenly became British citizens, and the British position changed. Cetshwayo had initially welcomed the extension of British influence, trusting that it would lead to a satisfactory resolution of the border crisis; to his bitter disappointment, he now found that the British appeared to be backing the Boer claims.

This shift had much to do with the character of the British Administrator in the Transvaal, Theophilus Shepstone. Shepstone had given up his post as Secretary for Native Affairs in Natal to take an active role in the implementation of the Confederation scheme. An ardent Imperialist, he also shared a uniquely Natal vision which saw the colony as the gateway to British Africa. Shepstone saw no contradiction in supporting the Boer claims in the disputed territory, where once he had opposed them; in both cases his underlying motive had been the spread of Imperial control. The dispute with Cetshwayo afforded him an opportunity to draw upon his support at the time of the coronation expedition in an attempt to extend his influence within the kingdom. Not only that – he began to look forward to a time when Britain would control Zululand completely, and when the under-utilized disputed territory might prove highly valuable as a theatre for relocating and controlling the broken African population.

For the Zulu, this sudden volte-face was an ominous one, and King Cetshwayo reacted firmly. He continued to repudiate all Boer claims on the borders, and sent representatives to build royal homesteads in the region as a statement of his authority. In particular, the tussle centred upon the small settlement of Luneburg, near the Phongolo river, to the north-east of Utrecht. The settlement had grown up around a German Lutheran mission permitted by Mpande in the 1860s, but the Zulu kings continued to regard Luneburg as built on their land. Although the

German community was peacable and hard-working, the Phongolo region was a long way from any centres of administration, and the African groups there lived largely beyond the reach of the Zulu, Natal and Transvaal, or even of the Swazis, whose borders lay close by to the north. Cetshwayo was determined to assert his right to the region, and a small royal outpost was built within a few miles of the village itself.

To Shepstone, this defiance conjured up the spectre of the myth of Zulu truculence which lay at the heart of colonial perceptions of Zulu culture. He began to refer openly to Cetshwayo's administration in terms which hearkened back to the early settlers' accounts of King Shaka, and which begged an ominous question. In a despatch dated 5 January 1878, Shepstone spelt out his growing conviction that the Zulu kingdom was a threat to the Confederation scheme:

The Zulu constitution is essentially military, every man is a soldier, in whose eyes manual labour, except for military purposes or in furtherance of military schemes, is degrading, he has been taught from his very childhood that the sole object of his life is fighting and war, and this faith is as strong in the Zulu soldier now, and it is as strongly inculcated as it was 50 years ago, when it was necessary to the building up and existence of his nation.

... The Zulu tribe originally insignificant was raised to become the greatest native power in Africa, south of the Zambesi River, by the ability and military talent of Chaka, one of its Chiefs. The genius, instinct and traditions of the people are all military; the nation, which is less than 70 years old, had become a compact military engine before the years of its existence had numbered 20, and its very life depended, at that time of its history, upon the perfection of its aggressive and defensive powers.

... Before Natal became a British colony there was plenty of work to which the ever accumulating forces of this engine could be applied; after that period, and when the Transvaal became occupied by people of European descent, the area upon which these forces could be expended became more and more circumscribed, and it is now cut off altogether.

... But the engine has not ceased to exist or to generate its forces, although the reason or excuse for its existence has died away; these forces have continued to accumulate and are daily accumulating without safety valve or outlet.

... War is the universal cry among the soldiers, who are anxious to live up to their traditions and are disappointed in their early expectations.

... Had Cetywayo's thirty thousand warriors been in time changed to labourers working for wages, Zululand would have been a prosperous peaceful country, instead of what it now is, a source of perpetual danger to itself and neighbours.

... The question is, what is to be done with this pent-up and still accumulating power?

Shepstone's view became increasingly influential following the annexation of the Transvaal. Even as he had raised the Union Flag in Pretoria, a new British proconsul had arrived in southern Africa with specific instructions to implement Confederation. Sir Henry Edward Bartle Frere was an experienced Imperial diplomat who was reaching the end of his career. He had cut his administrative teeth in India in the difficult years following the Mutiny, and he was by rights too senior for the post of High Commissioner at the Cape. He had been persuaded to take the job on the premise that by successfully confederating southern Africa he would end his career on a glittering note. Typical of his type, Frere was energetic, able, and an uncritical believer in the Imperial vision, and within weeks of his arrival he had reached an accurate assessment of the problems which faced him. Not only were the newly annexed Transvaal Boers at best sullenly acquiescent, but the Cape, as the senior British colony, showed a marked reluctance to be shackled to its less established and more backward neighbours. Frere became convinced that a firm demonstration of the advantages of British rule might both rally supporters of Confederation and intimidate waverers.

One obvious area which required immediate attention was the endemic friction with African groups across the region. In the late 1870s, a wave of unrest had swept across southern Africa, a common reaction to decades of political and economic dispossession. With no previous experience of local politics, Frere inevitably relied upon men like Shepstone for an insight into these disturbances, and Shepstone argued that there was a common thread behind disturbances among the Pedi in the Transvaal, among the BaSotho north of the Cape Colony, and among the Xhosa on the Eastern Cape Frontier. For Shepstone, that thread was the influence of King Cetshwayo and his tireless engine of war.

Frere accepted this interpretation of the Zulu King's motives without question, and indeed very soon came to the view that a short, sharp and successful war against the Zulu would be hugely beneficial to the Confederation plan. By reducing the most powerful independent African group south of the Zambesi, it would open Zululand to settlement and commercial exploitation and at the same time send a clear message to other groups that the British could not easily be defied. Among those he hoped to intimidate were not only black Africans but also the republican Boers, whom he hoped would be suitably overawed by this display of British sabre-rattling, thereby sparing him the embarrassment of making war on a white population who were technically the Queen's subjects. By opening up post-war Zululand to Christian missions and to the civilizing influence of labour, Frere took the view that such a conflict was even in the best interests of the Zulu people themselves.

Throughout 1878, Frere began to prepare his superiors in London for the inevitability of an Anglo-Zulu War. In a despatch to the Colonial Office dated 5 November 1878 – by which time he had already embarked on a policy of direct confrontation – he revealed both his wider aims and the extent to which he had been influenced by the negative views of the Zulu monarchy held by men like Shepstone:

It may possibly occur to Her Majesty's Government, that a settlement of the Zulu question may be deferred to a more convenient season. I cannot think that this can safely be done as regards the Zulus.

... Cetywayo is in no respect superior in character to his predecessors. Since his coronation placed him firmly on the throne he has had ample opportunity for showing that in cruelty and treachery he is no degenerate representative of Chaka and Dingaan. I have met persons who agree that there is no ground to fear an unprovoked attack from the Zulus, but I have never met a man who, having had dealings with him, professed to have any trust in Cetywayo's word, or who believed that anything except fear would restrain him from acts of the most revolting cruelty and bloodshed. As long as a large force is maintained in Natal, it is possible that fear might continue to preponderate over cupidity, pride, or passion; but with Chaka as his avowed model, we can never have any better security for peace than an armed truce while he rules in Zululand.

... But even if there were any hopes of real peace by deferring a settlement with the Zulus, it is quite impossible to hope for a solution to our difficulties in the Transvaal till the people of that country are assured that we have some better reason for abstaining from coercing the Zulus than a sense of our own inferiority and weakness.

This was a position which was not entirely shared in London. Lord Carnarvon's successor, Sir Michael Hicks Beach, fully accepted that the threat of force was implicit in the Confederation programme, but the Government was, on the whole, keen to avoid another war in southern Africa. This was not entirely due to humanitarian or even financial concerns, for the Government was preoccupied with a more serious crisis which was then brewing elsewhere in the Empire. Threat of Russian interference in Afghanistan had made the British once again nervous of the vulnerable North-West Frontier, and British intervention had resulted only in the slaughter of a British envoy to Kabul, and a full-scale war seemed unavoidable. With British troops needed in India, the Government had neither the will nor the resources to deal with a conflict in Africa, and Frere was instructed to come to an amicable agreement with King Cetshwayo.

He had no intention of doing anything of the sort, however, and indeed had decided to embark on a Zulu campaign without the express support of the Home Government. He deliberately exploited the delay in communication between London and the Cape to present them with a *fait accompli*, gambling that by the time he had provoked the Zulus into a war, British troops would have defeated them in the field before the Colonial Office had time to object.

Throughout 1878 he cast about for an issue upon which to force a confrontation with Cetshwayo. The disputed border with the Transvaal provided one obvious point of conflict, and Shepstone's assurances that the Zulu claims were largely bogus seemed to legitimize his aggressive stance. At the last minute, however, the Lieutenant-Governor of Natal, Sir Henry Bulwer, who was worried about the long-term effects of a war on the colony, intervened and suggested that an independent Boundary Commission be set up to look into the dispute. Confident that it would back Boer claims, Frere agreed. The Commission met at the mission station at Rorke's Drift on the central Zulu border, and for several weeks painstakingly researched the history of the dispute and interviewed the claimants on both sides. When it finally presented its report on 20 June, it came unequivocally to the conclusion that 'no cession of territory was ever made by the Zulu nation, and that even had such a cession been made by either King Umpanda, or after him King Cetywayo, such would have been null and void unless confirmed by the voice of the Chiefs and people, according to the custom of the Zulus'. The Commissioners took a pragmatic view of their findings, and merely suggested that, while the Zulu title should be recognized, Boers living in the area should be allowed to remain on their land, pending a suitable rent agreement with Cetshwayo.

The findings were not what Frere had expected, but while he pondered his next move, a group of Zulu living opposite Rorke's Drift played into his hands. Rorke's Drift was one of the few established entry points into the Zulu kingdom, and the land facing it had been given by the King into the care of one of his most trusted *izinduna*, Chief Sihayo kaXongo. In the middle of 1878, two of Sihayo's wives had fled from his homestead and moved in with lovers living on the Natal bank. Sihayo himself had been reluctant to pursue the matter, but while he was visiting the King at the royal homestead of oNdini (Ulundi) in July, his sons decided to act. On the 28th, a Zulu *impi*,* led by Sihayo's senior son, Mehlokazulu, and accompanied by other members of his family, crossed the Mzinyathi river below Rorke's Drift and surrounded the homestead of a black Natal border policeman, Mswagele, where one of the women had taken refuge. Mswagele had been inclined to resist, but the sight of Mehlokazulu's followers, armed with shields, spears and firearms, was sufficient to intimidate him, and the woman was dragged out. She was taken across the river and executed. The following day, Mehlokazulu again crossed the border and sought out the second woman, who was dealt with in the same way.

Such treatment was acceptable under Zulu law, particularly given the embarrassment his wives' behaviour had caused Sihayo's family. Nor was it entirely unknown for one side or the other to pursue fugitives across the border. Against the background of the growing tension between Natal and Zululand, however, Mehlokazulu's actions were held as proof of the innate savagery of the Zulu people and the aggressive intentions of the King. This view seemed to be supported by an incident on the Transvaal border which took place in October, when a Zulu *impi* raided

* The Zulu word *impi* denotes a body of men gathered together for war, or in a broader sense, matters relating to warfare.

Swazi homesteads along the Phongolo river, attacking a number of
African settlements close to Luneburg and causing the Luneburg farmers
to take refuge in their church. On this occasion the raiders were followers
of a disaffected Swazi prince, Mbilini waMswati, who had left Swaziland
following an unsuccessful attempt to claim the throne and had given his
allegiance to Cetshwayo. Cetshwayo had given him lands on the far
north-western borders of the kingdom, to shore up Zulu support along
the Phongolo, but in fact Mbilini had proved a problematic subject.
Shrewd, ambitious and aggressive, he regularly raided both black and
white inhabitants in the region in an attempt to restore his prestige and
build up followers, counting on his remoteness from the centres of
power to protect him from retaliation. The unsettled situation which
had prevailed on the Transvaal–Zulu border in the aftermath of the
British annexation had simply provided him with a fresh opportunity.
It is unlikely that King Cetshwayo had known of the planned raid in
advance, let alone authorized it.

Nevertheless, Mehlokazulu and Mbilini had between them provided
Frere with the *casus belli* he had been searching for. He had not to that
point made known the findings of the Boundary Commission report,
but he now invited Cetshwayo to send his representatives to a meeting
to be held at the Lower Drift on the Thukela river on 11 December
1878. Here he intended to make public the Commission's recom-
mendations – and to demand redress for the actions of Mbilini and
Mehlokazulu.

The meeting took place beneath a large wild fig tree, which grew on
the Natal bank. The Thukela here is near its mouth, and the spectacular
gorges which mark the progress of one of the region's most important
river systems have by then given way to a broad expanse of brown
water, framed on either side by undulating grasslands. Frere's party
was headed by John Shepstone – brother of Theophilus – who had
succeeded him as Natal's Secretary for Native Affairs. The Zulu party
consisted of a number of important Zulu *izinduna* and royal messengers
but, the whites noted with some disappointment, did not include any of
the leading chiefs of the nation. A tarpaulin was strung over the tree to
provide some shade, and a photographer had travelled up from Durban
for the occasion.

From the first, the British stance was apparent. British troops had
already established a camp overlooking the drift, and a detachment of

sailors were lined up nearby, ostensibly as a guard of honour. The presence of two field-guns and a hand-cranked Gatling machine-gun provided an unmistakable air of menace. The report of the Boundary Commissioners ran to several pages, and it was explained in detail to the Zulu, who expressed approval of its findings. Then came the bombshell. Frere had added to the report a long complaint against the recent border violations, which evoked Shepstone's coronation expedition to justify interference in purely internal Zulu affairs:

Her Majesty's High Commissioner has now, therefore, to require that the Zulu King will forthwith send in to the Natal Government, for trial under the laws of the Colony, for the offence committed by them in the Colony, the persons of Mehlokazulu, Inkumbikazulu, and Tyekwana, the sons of Sihayo, and also Zuluhlenga, the brother of Sihayo ... [they] must be sent in and delivered over to the Zulu authorities within 20 days of the date that this demand is made ...

There is also the case of Umbelini, a Swazi refugee living in the Zulu country, who is charged with having recently made a murderous raid into the country north of the Pongolo, which is claimed as British territory by the Transvaal Government. It will be necessary for the offenders in this case to be given up to be tried by the Transvaal Courts for the offence of which they are accused ...

It is necessary that the military system which is at present kept up by the King should be done away with, as a bad and hurtful one; and that the king should, instead, adopt such military regulations as may be decided on after consultation with the Great Council of the Zulus and with representatives of the British Government.

It is necessary that the Zulu army, as it is now, shall be disbanded, and that the men shall return to their homes ...

Let every man, when he comes to man's estate, be free to marry. Let him not wait for years till he gets permission to do this ...

... the Queen's High Commissioner, on behalf of the British Government, will appoint an officer as his deputy to reside in the Zulu country, or on its immediate border, who will be the eyes, and ears, and mouth of the British Government towards the Zulu King ...

He desires, also, that all missionaries be allowed to teach as in Panda's time, and that no Zulu shall be punished for listening to them.

... These are the conditions which Her Majesty's High Com-

missioner, in the name of the British Government, considers necessary for the establishment of a satisfactory state of things in the Zulu
country, and for the peace and safety of the adjoining countries. Let,
therefore, the King and the chief men of the nation consider them,
and let them give an answer within 30 days from the day on which
this communication is made to the Zulu representatives . . .

The Zulu deputation listened to the unfolding ultimatum with
concern. When told that Cetshwayo had broken the promises supposedly
made at his coronation, one asked sharply, 'Have the Zulu complained?'
Clearly realizing the gravity of the situation, they asked for some points
to be explained in greater detail and for the time allowed for compliance
to be extended; they were curtly told that Shepstone had no authority to
debate the issue, and that thirty days was considered ample.

That afternoon the Zulu party crossed back over the river with heavy
hearts. Frere had pitched his demands well; he knew, just as the Zulu
knew, that the King could never consider the destruction of the military
system, upon which so much of his power rested, without a fight, nor
would his people allow the indignity of a British representative at his
court.

Frere's decision to embark on an armed confrontation without the
full support of the Home Government reflected his confidence in his
military commander on the spot. Frederic Augustus Thesiger, who
became 2nd Baron Chelmsford shortly before the war began, shared the
prevailing opinion that any British expedition to Zululand would be
both short and successful. Lord Chelmsford, who was fifty-one when the
war began, was a typical product of his background and class. The eldest
of seven children, he was the son of a former Lord High Chancellor of
England and had bought a commission in the Army in 1844. Since then,
he had amassed a typical array of experience in the very varied wars of
the mid-Victorian era. He had served as a captain in the Crimea, where
he was mentioned in despatches, and throughout the Central Indian
campaign during the Mutiny. In 1868 he had been selected as Deputy
Acting Adjutant of the Abyssinian Field Force, in an expedition which
proved a triumph over inhospitable terrain as as much over the Abyssin-
ians. Staff appointments in both India and England followed, and
in February 1878 Chelmsford had been sent out to replace General Sir
Arthur Cunynghame as Commander-in-Chief in southern Africa. He

arrived to find a messy little war against the Xhosa in progress on the Eastern Cape Frontier, and despite a shortage of troops and the difficulties of controlling colonial volunteers in an inhospitable terrain, he had managed to reduce the pockets of Xhosa resistance and bring it to a successful conclusion. A tall man, with a pleasant, rather reserved manner, he was very much a Victorian gentleman, with an innate confidence in the superiority of British values and aims and a rather conservative approach to his profession. At a time when the British Army was increasingly under attack from within by junior officers advocating reform, Chelmsford remained firmly within the establishment framework. Personally courageous, he had proved a good administrator and a competent rather than inspired commander, who preferred to rely on techniques which had been proved elsewhere. Under pressure he could be stubborn and unusually terse with subordinates who disappointed him, and, raised in the days before training in staff work became the norm, he had a marked reluctance to delegate. The events of 1879 were to test his character to an entirely unexpected degree, and it cannot be said that he always rose to the challenge.

Nevertheless, even before Chelmsford left Cape Town for Pietermaritzburg in July 1878, he expressed himself perfectly content that Frere's confrontational policy was not only the right one, but militarily practicable;

> If we are to have a fight with the Zulus, I am anxious that our arrangements should be as complete as it is possible to make them – Half measures do not answer with natives – They must be thoroughly crushed to make them believe in our superiority; and if I am called upon to conduct operations against them, I shall strive to be in a position to show them how hopelessly inferior they are to us in fighting power, altho' numerically stronger –

Once in Pietermaritzburg, Chelmsford began a thorough assessment of the military situation in Natal. Against the background of the unfolding political crisis, he collected information on the Zulu military system, debated the merits of the various routes into Zululand, assessed the number of troops he might require for the task, and pondered Natal's defence capabilities. A Natal Border Agent, F. B. Fynney, who had long taken an interest in the Zulu army, was asked to produce a report which was later published for the benefit of officers under

Chelmsford's command. It provided an admirable description of the main characteristics and strengths of the *amabutho* system, although Fynney shared the prevailing misconceptions about the nature of Zulu society. He strained to make comparisons between recognizable British formations and Zulu ones, and failed to grasp the fundamental difference between the two institutions. Whereas the British Army was a full-time professional body, governed by its own laws and traditions, the Zulu army was no more than a part-time civilian force, the males of the nation assembled temporarily for war. Nevertheless, Fynney's report was thorough, and should have left Chelmsford in no doubt about the nature of the enemy he was facing:

The method employed in recruiting its ranks is as follows: – At short intervals, varying from two to five years, all the young men who have during that time attained the age of fourteen or fifteen years, are formed into a regiment, which, after a year's probation, during which they are supposed to pass from boyhood and its duties to manhood, is placed at a military kraal or head-quarters. In some cases they are sent to an already existing kraal, which is the head-quarters of a corps or regiment, of which they then become part; in others, especially when the young regiment is numerous, they build a new military kraal. As the regiment grows old, it generally has one or more regiments embodied with it, so that the young men may have the benefit of their elders' experience, and, when the latter gradually die out, may take their place and keep up the name and prestige of their military kraal. In this manner corps are formed; often many thousands strong, such, for instance, as the Undi.

Under such a system, then, the Zulu army has gradually increased, until at present it consists of twelve corps, and two regiments, each possessing its own military kraal. The corps necessarily contain men of all ages, some being married and wearing the headring, others unmarried; some being old men scarcely able to walk, while others are hardly out of their teens. Indeed, five of these corps are now composed of a single regiment each, which has absorbed the original but practically non-existent regiment to which it has been affiliated.

Each of these fourteen corps or regiments have the same internal formation. They are in the first place divided equally into two wings – the right and the left – and in the second are sub-divided into companies from ten to two hundred in number, according to the numerical strength of the corps or regiment to which they belong, and which is estimated ... at sixty men each, with the exception of the Nkobamakosi regiment, which averages seventy men to the company.

Each corps or regiment, possessing its own military kraal, has the following officers: one commanding officer (called the induna yesibaya 'sikulu), one second in command (called the induna yohlangoti), who directly commands the left wing, and two wing officers (called the induna yesicamelo yesibaya 'sikulu, and the induna yesicamelo yohlangoti). Besides the above there are company officers, consisting of a captain, and from one to three junior officers, all of whom are the same age as the men they command, while in the case of a corps the C.O. of each regiment composing it takes rank next to its four great officers when he is himself not of them.

... The chief distinction is between married and unmarried men. No one in Zululand is permitted to marry without the direct permission of the King, and when he allows a regiment to do so, which is not before the men are about forty years of age, they have to shave the crown of the head, and put a ring around it, and then they become one of the 'white' regiments, carrying white shields, &c., in contradistinction to the 'black', or unmarried regiments, who wear their hair naturally, and have coloured shields.

The total number of regiments in the Zulu army is thirty-three, of whom eighteen are formed of men with rings on their heads, and fifteen of unmarried men. Seven of the former are composed of men over sixty years of age ... so that in practical purposes there are not more than twenty-six Zulu regiments, able to take to the field, numbering altogether 40,400. Of these 22,500 are between twenty and thirty years of age, 10,000 between thirty and forty, 3,400 between forty and fifty, and 4,500 between fifty and sixty years of age ...

Drill – in the ordinary acceptation of the word – is unknown among the Zulus; the few simple movements which they perform with any method, such as forming a circle of companies or regiments, breaking into companies or regiments from the circle, forming a line of march in order of companies, or in close order of regiments, not being deserving of the name. Their skirmishing is, however, extremely good, and is performed even under heavy fire with the utmost order and regularity. The officers have also their regulated duties and

responsibilities, according to their rank, and the men lend a ready
obedience to their orders.

As might be expected, a savage army like that of Zululand neither
has nor requires much commissariat or transport. The former consists of three or four days' provisions, in the shape of maize or millet,
and a herd of cattle, proportioned to the distance to be traversed,
accompanies each regiment. The latter consists of a number of lads
who follow each regiment, carrying the sleeping mats, blankets, and
provisions, and assisting to drive the cattle.

Since the time of King Shaka, the Zulu army had fostered an
essentially aggressive outlook. As it was difficult to release the men from
their civilian roles for more than a few months at a time, Zulu strategy
was framed by the need to bring them into decisive combat as soon as
possible. Shaka had placed great emphasis on personal courage, and had
insisted that his men fight at close quarters with a long-bladed, short-
hafted stabbing spear known as the *iklwa* – the sound it made on being
withdrawn from a deep body thrust. This was wielded under-arm in a
practised technique which included an aggressive use of the great cow-
hide war-shields, battering the enemy off guard and exposing him to the
fatal thrust. To deliver his men to the point of contact as efficiently as
possible, Shaka is said to have devised the tactic known as *izimpondo
zankomo* – 'the beast's horns'. A central body, known as the *isifuba*,
or 'chest', and composed of more disciplined, senior warriors, made a
frontal assault on the enemy, while flanking parties – 'horns', *izimpondo*
– made up of young, energetic warriors rushed out to surround them
on either side. A reserve known as the 'loins' – *umuva* – and usually
consisting of elderly warriors or cadets not yet fully trained, was kept
back to plug any gaps in the assault.

The fifty years since Shaka's death had led to only cosmetic changes
in the Zulu military system. The great *izihlangu* war-shields, nearly five
feet high, had become unfashionable, and most of the younger *amabutho*
preferred to carry a lighter variant, the *umbhumbulosu*, which was just
three feet long. Throwing spears – relegated to hunting weapons in Shaka's
time – had made a widespread reappearance, as they offered at least some
retort to enemy musketry, particularly in the early conflicts with whites
armed with smooth-bore flintlocks which were themselves accurate to
only thirty or forty yards. Indeed, in the 1850s and '60s large numbers of

firearms were traded into Zululand, and on the eve of war King Cetshwayo had made a determined effort to equip his troops with guns. British estimates suggested that there were at least 20,000 firearms in Zululand at the outbreak of war, and there may have been more. Most, however, were hopelessly obsolete by contemporary British standards, weapons forty or fifty years old, dumped by rival world powers on unsophisticated markets around the globe. With poor-quality powder reserves and often equipped only with home-made bullets, the untrained marksmen of the Zulu army were to prove woefully inadequate for the challenge ahead of them. With the exception of a few hunters, who had been trained by the white hunting parties who operated in Zululand in large numbers before the war, most Zulus had so little faith in their guns that they regarded them as barely more than exotic throwing spears, to be fired at close range and cast down before the final rush with the stabbing spear.

In their failure to adapt to the possibilities afforded by new technologies, to rely on close-quarter weapons against an enemy armed with modern breech-loaders and artillery, the Zulu army effectively accepted battle on British terms in 1879.

Faced with an enemy that was highly mobile and likely to outnumber him – Fynney's list suggested a theoretical Zulu strength of 40,000 men – Chelmsford decided that an element of containment would be necessary in any British invasion plan. He was well aware that his greatest asset was the firepower of his regular infantry – 'I am inclined to think', he wrote to one of his subordinates, 'that the first experience of the Martini Henrys will be such a surprise to the Zulus that they will not be formidable after the first effort' – but by concentrating his regular troops together he would have to leave large tracts of the country unguarded. Instead, he opted to invade in a number of self-contained columns, which would start at different points along the border and converge on King Cetshwayo's principal residence at oNdini. As he explained to the Secretary of State,

> In conducting operations against an enemy like the Kaffir or the Zulu, the first blow struck should be a heavy one, and I am satisfied that no greater mistake can be made than to attempt to conquer him with insufficient means. He has the advantage of being able to march in one day at least three times as far as the British soldier, and has no commissariat train to hamper him.

Unless, then, his country or stronghold is attacked by several columns, each strong enough to hold its own, moving in from different directions, he has always the power to evade the blow and prolong the war to an indefinite time . . .

Chelmsford had few doubts that he would win a pitched battle in the open, when it came. In shaping his invasion plan, he was heavily influenced by the limited availability of existing tracks. No roads as such existed in Zululand, but over the years, traders and hunters had pioneered a number of wagon-tracks which did at least meander towards the principal areas of Zulu settlement. From the first, Chelmsford planned to exploit these to the full, and he identified five potential invasion routes – by way of the Lower Drift on the Thukela, the Middle Drift further upstream, Rorke's Drift on the Mzinyathi, across the Ncome east of Utrecht in the Transvaal, and from the hamlet of Derby, which lay near the confluence of the Zulu, Transvaal and Swazi borders. His plan was to despatch a column along each route. The basis of each column would be a battalion or two of British infantry, supported by artillery and, in the absence of regular cavalry, Mounted Volunteers. He also hoped that the African population of Natal could be mobilized to provide a force of auxiliaries.

Here, however, Chelmsford became aware for the first time that the colonial authorities in Natal did not entirely share either his own or Frere's priorities. The head of the Natal administration, the Lieutenant-Governor Sir Henry Bulwer, was reluctant to sanction the creation of such a force. He was both unwilling to hand over the colony's scant military resources to the direct control of the British Army and nervous about the long-term repercussions of arming Natal's African population. In a letter to Frere, written as early as August 1878, Chelmsford described the emerging pattern of his relationship with Bulwer:

I am getting on very well with Sir Henry and I am doing all I can to put quietly but firmly the military requirements of the present situation.

He is I think a very self-opinionated man, he has, I should say, a bad temper and is inclined to be obstinate. On the other hand he has very good abilities, an evident desire to do his duty towards the Colony and to protect its interests, and a very keen desire to gain a reputation for strict justice. I do not think he has fathomed the

intricacies of the native character, nor does he, I think, fully realize
the exceeding cleverness with which men like Cetywayo . . . can throw
dust in the eyes of those whom they are anxious to have on their
side . . .

This disagreement was to have profound consequences for the
formation of the black auxiliary forces. It was not until 23 November
1878 that the raising of the corps was authorized, just six weeks before
hostilities began. Three regiments of infantry were assembled, the 1st
Regiment consisting of three battalions, each of 1,000 men, and the
2nd and 3rd Regiments of two battalions each. While men from certain
chiefdoms predominated in some battalions, no attempt was made to
organize them along traditional lines, and each battalion consisted of
men from a number of disparate groups. Only one man in ten was
provided with a firearm, and the only equipment issued consisted of a
blanket, a cooking pot and a red rag to serve as a distinguishing mark.
Most of the men carried their own spears and shields. Moreover, by that
stage many of the best settler volunteers had been appointed to other
units, and the black troops – collectively known as the Natal Native
Contingent (NNC) – received those who remained as officers and
NCOs. Many of the NCOs, in particular, were recruited from the ranks
of unemployed adventurers on the Eastern Cape Frontier, many of
whom had no knowledge of the Zulu language and little interest in Zulu
customs. Six troops of mounted auxiliaries – of roughly fifty men apiece
– fared rather better, since they were regarded as superior soldiers and
were issued with a yellow cord uniform and a carbine. Throughout the
war, they would serve as a reminder of the squandered opportunity
vested in the rest of the NNC.

Bulwer was reluctant, too, to allow Chelmsford direct control over
Natal's established Volunteer forces. Since the 1850s, Natal had raised a
number of small Volunteer units from amongst the settler population.
Drawn largely from the families of the colonial elite, these units met
once a year to train, the men providing their own uniforms and horses
and the Government supplying weapons and equipment. In 1878 there
were fifteen such corps in Natal, three infantry, one artillery and eleven
mounted units, a total strength of 753 men. By the terms of their
enlistment, however, they were required to serve only in defence of the
colony and could not be compelled to fight outside it. Bulwer refused to

pass control of these units over to Chelmsford, insisting that he needed some at least to protect Natal. However, since there were no units of British cavalry in South Africa, Chelmsford was chronically short of mounted men and could not afford to ignore the Volunteers' potential. In the end, Bulwer sanctioned their employment in Zululand only so long as the men themselves agreed, and eight of the mounted units were added to the columns assembling on the borders. As their numbers were still not sufficient for the task, Chelmsford authorized the raising of a number of irregular units – Volunteer Cavalry serving for a fixed term – on the Eastern Cape Frontier and in the Transvaal.

Most serious, however, was the shortage of regular troops. Chelmsford's initial plan required a minimum of five Infantry battalions – one for each invading column – and this allowed no spare troops for garrison or escort duties. At full strength, a battalion consisted of eight companies of 100 men each, but in wartime sickness, natural wastage and detached duty often reduced the total to a field strength of 600 men. Such a number was clearly inadequate if each column was to be self-sufficient, so instead Chelmsford decided that the backbone of each column should be two battalions. Yet in the middle of 1878 he had just six infantry battalions available in South Africa – the 2/3rd, 1/13th, 1st and 2nd, 24th, 80th and 90th. These amounted to little more than a total of 4,500 redcoats at field strengths, and they were scattered in detachments across the newly annexed Transvaal and the Cape Frontier. A further battalion, the 88th, was arriving piecemeal from Mauritius. There were just two batteries of artillery – N Battery 5th Brigade and 11 Battery 7th Brigade – and a solitary company of Engineers. Moreover, Chelmsford's Commissary General, Edward Strickland, had only nineteen officers under his command, and he despaired at the prospect of a new campaign in Zululand. 'As regards Commissariat work in Natal and the Transvaal,' he wrote to Chelmsford,

> I beg respectfully to remind your excellency that of necessity it must be carried out over a vast extent of country; at isolated posts, separated from each other by great distances, and in wild impracticable country almost destitute of Commissariat resources.

All provisions would have to be carried by the columns themselves, a fact which required hiring or buying large numbers of civilian transport wagons to augment the few military wagons available. In September, Chelmsford had admitted to Frere that

> Transport is our greatest difficulty and the District Commissary General has brought to my notice that he can neither hire nor purchase it except at rates which must be considered prohibitive. I have brought our wants in this respect to the notice of the Lieut. Governor; and should a sudden emergency arise I can see no other course but to proclaim Martial Law and to impress all available private transport, paying for the same at a fair and equitable rate.

As the probability of war with the Zulus increased, Chelmsford became increasingly concerned that he had insufficient troops for the job. Yet his application to London for reinforcements was rewarded with only two further infantry battalions – the 2/4th and 99th – two companies of Royal Engineers and a handful of special service officers. Some of these would inevitably be tied to the unglamorous but essential work of guarding the lines of communications towards the front, so according to the careful count in the official history, Chelmsford began the invasion with an offensive capability of just 5,128 British infantrymen.

Moreover, there was one further aspect which troubled him – the vulnerability of the Natal border to counter-attack. Apart from a few small earthworks built during the tension which followed the Zulu succession dispute in the 1850s – most of which were in any case in disrepair – Natal had made little effort for the defence of its white settler population, and none at all for its Africans. Chelmsford had been appalled:

> The possibility of resisting a sudden raid into Natal by the present machinery for defence appears to me to be almost hopeless; and I am afraid this fact must now be known to the Zulus.
>
> The danger which threatens Natal appears to me, therefore, very great; and will be increased should it be decided to take a firm stand against the claims and encroachments lately made by Cetewayo.

He made a hasty attempt to rectify the situation. Chiefs living along the borders were required to supply contingents to watch the principal drifts, while defensive posts, known as 'laagers', after the Boer word for a defensive wagon-circle, would be provided as places of refuge for white civilians living on exposed parts of the frontier. The Africans, however, would be expected to fend for themselves. It was hardly an ideal solution, and it strained Chelmsford's military resources as well as his relationship with the Natal administration.

Under the circumstances, he had little option but to amend his strategy. Three of his original five columns – those at the Lower Drift, Rorke's Drift, and on the Ncome – would remain offensive, while the remaining two were reduced and given a defensive role. By late 1878, Chelmsford had appointed his column commanders. The Lower Drift column, designated No. 1, or the Right Flank Column, would be commanded by Colonel Charles Knight Pearson of the 3rd Regiment, while No. 2 Column at Middle Drift was commanded by Colonel Anthony Durnford. The Centre Column – No. 3 – was commanded by Colonel Richard Glyn, 24th Regiment, and the Left Flank Column, No. 4, by Colonel Henry Evelyn Wood of the 90th. The northern column, No. 5, was commanded by Colonel Hugh Rowlands VC, of the 34th. Rowlands's situation was particularly delicate, as he was expected not only to watch for Zulu movements to his front, but also to keep an eye on Boer dissidents to the rear. His position close to Swaziland also meant that he was ideally placed as a channel through which Chelmsford hoped to persuade the Swazis to enter the war. They were traditional rivals of the Zulu, and were in a position to threaten the Zulu borders, but in the event, despite intense diplomatic activity, they adroitly refused to commit themselves while the fighting lasted.

Chelmsford had scarcely more success with the Boers on the Transvaal border. Although the old Republic had also been deeply wary of the Zulu, the idea of serving with the British was anathema to most Boers. While Chelmsford hoped that self-interest would persuade some of the farmers living in the Disputed Territory to join Wood's column, he also realized that the report of the Boundary Commission undermined his bargaining position, and in the event, only one Boer patriarch of note, Petras Lefras Uys (known as Piet), agreed to serve with Wood. Uys's family had something of a blood feud with the Zulu – his father and brother had been killed by King Dingane's warriors in 1838 – and his farm lay in the heart of the disputed territory. Uys brought with him a commando of fifty men, most of whom were relatives, friends or dependants; many of them seemed to have been lured into service by the promise that they would be allowed to keep looted Zulu cattle.

Finally, Chelmsford placed great faith in the assurances of Shepstone and others that the Zulu kingdom was held together only by the tyranny of King Cetshwayo himself. Once the fighting began, he hoped that large numbers of ordinary Zulus would defect to the British and that a number of important chiefs would place self-interest above their loyalty to the House of Shaka. As early as 30 October, he had noted,

> In the event of an advance being made into Zululand it is I consider very probable that a large number of Cetewayo's subjects may wish to avoid fighting, and may desire to come across our Border for protection –
>
> Every reliable account from that country shows conclusively that Cetewayo is most unpopular, and those who are best informed regarding the state of feelings in Zululand are of the opinion that an internal revolution is not only possible but probable –
>
> It would seem well therefore to be prepared for a considerable exodus of Zulus from either their own country into British territory, or into that of friendly natives to the North, South and West and to lay down beforehand instructions as to their disposal –
>
> Even supposing that I am too sanguine regarding the numbers that will desert Cetewayo, it is certain that singly, or in small parties, refugees will come across and will have to be provided for, as it would clearly be undesirable to allow them to remain near the border line –

In the event, the hope that Cetshwayo's subjects would desert him in droves proved to be as unfounded as many other of Chelmsford's expectations.

December 1878 ticked away without any apparent response from the Zulus. Indeed, the King and his royal council were at a loss how best to proceed. The extent of Frere's demands had shocked them. While Cetshwayo was prepared to offer reparations for the border incidents, he was reluctant to hand over the sons of Sihayo, who was his personal representative on the Mzinyathi border. To have done so would have meant acquiescing in a calculated slight to royal prestige. Moreover, while opinion was divided among the great men who advised the King, the young men who made up the Zulu army were indignant at the apparent arrogance of the British demands. The best Cetshwayo could do was prevaricate, sending messengers across the border to ask for more time. Chelmsford would have none of it:

> I told them plainly that I believed the only desire of Cetywayo was to gain more time until the mealie crop was ripe, that I knew there was no food in the country now, and that it was useless their talking any more...
>
> ... I am satisfied in my own mind that Cetywayo is doing all he can to gain time, knowing full well that he could not fight us at a more inconvenient time...

By the end of 1878, Chelmsford's preparations were largely complete, and the columns began to assemble at their specified bases. Among them was Lieutenant Julius B. Backhouse of the 2/3rd ('the Buffs'), whose regiment was appointed to Pearson's coastal column, and who recalled the his first experience of the hardships to come:

> ... paraded at 12 noon, and marched off, but as I was bad with dioreah all day, I was compelled to fall out, and was carried in the ambulance: we marched about 12 miles and halted for the night, but owning to the badness of the roads and the oxen only a few of our waggons came in, and most of the men had to sleep under the waggons...
>
> ... Inspection parade at 7.30 a.m., just as it began to rain, which lasted during the whole of our march to the drift, where we arrived about 7 [p.m.] after about 11 miles march at a very good pace...

The sudden change in the weather provided a miserable backdrop to the last of Chelmsford's preparations. The summer months – December to February – are usually wet in Natal, the baking heat of the day giving way to fierce electrical storms in the evening and heavy downpours at night. At the end of 1878, moreover, a drought which had gripped the region for several years broke with a vengeance, turning the wagon-tracks to muddy quagmires and making life unpleasant for men living under canvas. As officers on detached service scurried up to join their men on the border, they found the weather a serious encumbrance. Lieutenant Nevill Coghill, of the 24th (2nd Warwickshire) Regiment, had been in southern Africa, on and off, since 1876. For much of that time he had been detached from his battalion, serving as ADC first to Chelmsford's predecessor, General Cunynghame, and then briefly to

Frere himself. Bright, ambitious, a lover of field sports and, like many
of his fellow junior officers, short of cash, Coghill had been anxious
to serve in the new campaign, and had been offered a post as orderly to
Colonel Glyn, the commander of the Centre Column. With just a few
days to go before Frere's ultimatum expired, Coghill had ridden to join
his regiment at the camp at Helpmekaar, above Rorke's Drift, and his
description suggests something of the sheer physical difficulties faced by
an army working in such an environment;

> The next morning, the 7th, I was on the road at 5.30 a.m. and
> having off-saddled for 2 hours and had breakfast at Sterks Spruit
> reached Seven Oaks about 12. Having given the horses time to rest
> I started for Grey Town . . .
> A regular deluge fell that night preventing my starting till 10 the
> next morning, the 8th.
> When I did start I found the little Grey Town stream so swollen
> that I was unable to cross it and had to go back some 2½ miles to a
> bridge. I arrived at Burrups at the edge of the thorn country at about
> 2 o'clock and having fed the horses started again. Up to this I had
> been travelling along ridges of high land. I now dropped into a basin
> thickly studded with thorn. This thorn country extends for about
> 24 miles and through it flows the Mooi and Tugela Rivers. I reached
> the Mooi river that evening and crossed it by means of a pont. Here
> I found Huntley and Smith-Dorrien superintending the Transport
> Duties, and very arduous work it was and a more abominable locality
> than the 'Thorns' to live in I cannot well imagine. Toothache, a
> complaint which I am not much given to and a close atmosphere
> left me awake the greater part of the night and the next morning at
> 4 a.m. (9th) woke up with a 'head' that considerably took away from
> the pleasure of my ride down the Thugela cutting where there is
> some fine scenery. Arrived at this river we were delayed some two
> hours owing to some breakdown of the pont arrangements but
> eventually got across and had breakfast. After breakfast we started on
> our road again accompanied by our landlady who took advantage of
> our escort to go to Helpmekaar. We stopped two hours at Sandspruit
> just outside the limit of the Thorns and at 7.30 got to Helpmekaar. I
> found my Regiment had started now for Rorke's Drift on the Buffalo
> River. I was, however, hospitably put up and fed by the General, and
> his Staff, and next morning, the 10th, descended to Rorke's Drift.

Helpmekaar (on the Biggarsberg) the proper translation of which is I believe 'Help one another', so called because there was a difficulty in the olden days in crossing the berg and the old foretreckers combined to make a cutting, a proceeding rarely resorted to in those primitive folk, is situated on the broad green flat on top of the Biggarsberg. Until made a Military Depot it consisted of two houses. Now there is a Govt. Store and white tents now dot the hill top. It is cold at night with as far as I have experienced it hot sun and cool breezes by day. It is more free from that bane of South Africa, Horse Sickness, than most other places which greatly influenced the Military Authorities in the selection of this situation.

At the border itself, preparations were under way to cross into Zululand. For Colonel Pearson's men, this meant crossing the Thukela river at its widest point, now swollen by the constant rain. It was hard and dangerous work, carried out against a background of mounting excitement as it became apparent that King Cetshwayo was unlikely to comply with Frere's terms. According to Backhouse,

The Tugela rose very much during the night, and carried away the arrangements for working the pontoon, which is to carry us over the river, this will involve another three days delay on this side, I expect. Parade at 5.30 a.m. Privates Craney H Company & Bowman G Company flogged for drunkeness 25 lashes each, it did not affect either of them at all. On a fatigue party of 4 companies, to assist at the drift in hauling out the anchor, out of the river, at the end of the hawser, which was carried away during the night, after a great deal of difficulty, and to the tune of fifes and drums, we hauled it out, and landed it safely on this side: this delay was due to the Naval Brigade not having fixed the hawser firmly on the Zulu side of the river. Went down to Smith's Store with Mason in the afternoon; no parades as all were on fatigue. A sailor belonging to HMS 'Active' was drowned in the river today, while they were getting the pontoons etc., ready, he had not much chance as a flood is on the river, and his body was never recovered. It cleared up in the middle of the day, but rain came on again about 4 p.m. . . .

On the 10th, Pearson's men noticed a group of about fifteen Zulu on the low hills beyond the river, apparently watching British movements.

It was the only obvious response to the fact that King Cetshwayo's time had run out; at dawn the following morning, the Anglo-Zulu War began.

The British entered Zululand in high spirits. Lord Chelmsford had no idea what the Zulu response might be, or whether Cetshwayo would choose to confront him as soon as he crossed the border. Nevertheless, as Nevill Coghill's description of the crossing at Rorke's Drift suggests, an air of confidence prevailed in the British camp, despite the dreary weather:

> On the morning of the 11th the rouse went at 3 a.m. and at a little after 5 the crossing commenced. It was a raw misty morning, the mist rising every now and then and disclosing the position of our forces as they were pushed across, but there was no sign of an enemy whom we had been confidently assured by the best authorities on such matters would certainly oppose our crossing. Two ponts were kept constantly at work on the swollen river for the transport of European troops and supply waggons, the natives crossing at the drift. The latter were a curious sight, these people amusing to look at at any time, now with their shields, sticks, blankets, feathers and other paraphernalia entering the cold water which must certainly have reached as far up as their waists and this without the shouting which usually accompanies them when moving but with a kind of low whistle as they felt the cold water rising up their naked bodies the further they advanced into the stream.
>
> The camp pitched, all the necessary precautions taken we lay down for the night after a long tho' satisfactory day. The General and the mounted men had been out and had met Colonel Wood but had not observed any of the enemy and picking up some 200 head of cattle . . .

The next day, the shooting would begin in earnest.

Chapter Two

'They shot us down in numbers . . .'

Dawn on 11 January 1879 brought respite from the recent rain and the promise of a hot day. For the troops camped at the Lower Drift, however, it was also to bring disappointment: No. 1 Column was not yet ready to advance.

In many respects, the terrain which faced Colonel Pearson enticingly across the Thukela was perhaps the easiest of any through which a British commander would have to advance in the coming campaign. The high weathered ridges and deep rocky gorges which characterized much of Zululand's interior gave way in the coastal strip to corrugated downland, covered after the recent rains with tall green grass and scattered with mimosa trees. Here and there, and in the hollows along the banks of twisting streams, there were patches of tangled, almost tropical bush, while further north a rising upland was crowned with a primordial forest, known to the Zulus by the evocative name of Dlinza – 'the grave-like place of meditation'. The country was more open and less at risk from surprises than much of the rest of Zululand, and it boasted, moreover, one of the best 'roads' in the country.

For thirty years, hunters and traders had crossed the Thukela river at the Lower Drift, and the country opposite was perhaps the part of Zululand most exposed to white influence. In the 1860s, King Mpande had allowed a number of mission societies into the kingdom and had granted them permission to build stations in the coastal strip. To regulate his own dealings with the whites, King Cetshwayo had appointed a white adventurer as chief over the district, with powers to vet all white movements in the area. This man, John Dunn, had adopted a lifestyle which had effectively straddled two very different cultures, and the coming conflict would present him with some stark choices.

Dunn's history was a curious one. His family had settled at Port Natal in the anarchic years before the arrival of British authority, when it was a haven for adventurers and elephant hunters. His father had died at an early age, and Dunn had become disillusioned with the settler way of life; while still a teenager he had moved to Zululand and taken up the Zulu lifestyle. For a while he was lured back to Natal under the protection of a Border Agent at the Lower Drift, but in 1856 he had become embroiled in the Zulu civil war between Princes Mbuyazi and Cetshwayo. The decisive battle of the war had taken place on the banks of the Thukela, opposite the Lower Drift – the killing had raged across the very country where Pearson's troops would enter Zulu territory – and Dunn had offered his services in support of Mbuyazi. Mbuyazi, however, had been spectacularly defeated, and Dunn barely escaped with his life, although he had fought sufficiently well to impress even Prince Cetshwayo. Dunn made his peace with the new heir apparent, and Cetshwayo subsequently offered him a position as white *induna*. Dunn accepted, and found himself chief of a large district between Eshowe and the border. He served Cetshwayo as an adviser on the peculiarities of white politics, vetting those who made their way through his territory en route to the King, and his trading contacts proved invaluable: it was Dunn who had been largely responsible for the importation of the thousands of firearms which had re-equipped the Zulu army on the eve of war.

Dunn's lifestyle was a source of constant amazement to colonial visitors. He lived in a European house, dressed in tweeds, imported fine guns and furniture from London, and entertained passing European hunting parties. At the same time, he took forty-nine wives in the Zulu fashion, allying himself to most of the powerful families in his area and making himself wealthy in cattle and followers. For Dunn, the rift with the British was a personal tragedy; he had done his best to urge Cetshwayo to placate British demands but had been unable to divert the crisis. He found himself the subject of suspicion and hostility from the King's counsellors, although Cetshwayo privately sympathized with his predicament and advised him to remain neutral. In the tense months before the British ultimatum Dunn found it impossible to stay in Zululand, and at the beginning of January he had crossed into Natal with hundreds of his followers and thousands of head of cattle.

So great had been Dunn's influence in the coastal region that the traders' track which Pearson would follow was known, rather grandly, as Dunn's Road. It ran northwards for perhaps thirty miles then divided, one branch continuing up the coast towards the Mozambique border and the other striking inland, rising through the hills on the far side of the Nyezane river and passing the Norwegian mission station on the Eshowe heights before continuing on towards the Zulu heartland. From the beginning, Chelmsford intended that Pearson should advance by this road. The Norwegian missionaries at Eshowe had fled Zululand at the end of 1878, but with a shortage of permanent walled structures inside the country, Chelmsford had recognized that the post might make a serviceable supply depot. On 31 December he wrote to Pearson outlining his strategy, suggesting that Durnford's column upstream at Middle Drift might play a supporting role;

... your columns should advance as rapidly as possible, and occupy Ekowe, so as to prevent the buildings being burnt – Having occupied that post, unload all your waggons and send them back for supplies – Ekowe should be filled up as quickly as possible with as much commissariat stuff as you can cram into it – Place Ekowe in a state of defence, so as to be safe against any attack that may be made upon it. The men of the 'Active' should be placed in it as garrison with such an addition of redcoats and natives as you may consider desirable – The remainder should accompany the waggons back to the drift as an escort and the men should be allowed to ride in the waggons and the return journey should be made if possible in two days – I have told Mr Strickland that I wish him to accompany your column, so as to make sure Ekowe is perfectly filled up, and that the transport along the Durban–Tugela line is kept in proper working order –

... You will probably have to remain some time at Ekowe, or rather between that place and the Lower Tugela, as your column must not advance from there until the two left columns have made some progress – You will have plenty to do however and the troops, European and native, should be kept hard at work entrenching, or escorting supplies, or improving the roads – The latter duty is most important, as it will facilitate the supplies coming up –

As regards Col. Durnford's column crossing the Tugela, I will leave the time entirely to you – Until you are quite certain that no large body of the enemy is between Intumeni and Middledrift, he had better remain watching the latter point – But, as soon as that part of the country is clear, he will be more useful at Intumeni –

Clearly, the mobility and proper coordination of his advance preoccupied Chelmsford at this stage rather more than the risk afforded by the enemy, and not without justification. The effects of the recent bad weather had not only torn the hawser from the Zulu bank, necessitating repairs on the flat-bottomed ferries, known as ponts, which were to ship the troops into enemy territory, but had delayed some of Pearson's transport wagons en route to the border. Moreover, Pearson had been allocated one of the battalions sent out from England in response to Chelmsford's request for reinforcements – the 99th – and they were still on the road from Durban. With a sense of frustration, the best the men of No. 1 Column could do, on the day war broke out, was to harass parties of Zulu scouts who had gathered on the opposite bank to watch proceedings. As Lieutenant Backhouse observed,

> About 8 a.m., some Zulus were seen on the opposite side of the river, some distance off, so the sailors fired 2 shells from the 12 pounder Armstrong gun at them, making very fair practice, for the shells went most unpleasantly near to 2 or 3 of them and they ran off as hard as they could. About 9 a.m., six Zulus came over the river, they could give no account of themselves, so were put down as spies and handed over to the Police; they will not be allowed to return to Zululand. The Mounted Volunteers (Stanger, Victoria and Durban Corps) came in about 11 a.m., this will bring our cavalry force up to about 300 strong. I hear it is settled that the crossing is to begin at 4 a.m. tomorrow. I expect it will take 2 or 3 days to get the waggons and all across ... Four companies of the 99th marched in about 6 p.m., a very young lot of men ...

A long crossing would inevitably expose the column to the risk of attack. While Pearson's position on the Natal bank was secure – he had built an earthwork redoubt* on a high bluff above the drift, which dropped 300 feet straight into the river – the countryside on the Zulu bank was open, and a secure bridgehead was desperately needed. It meant an early start on the 12th for the Naval Brigade, to whom the task of supervising the transport fell. According to Lieutenant Hamilton of HMS *Active*,

* Fort Pearson.

Everything was ready for work on Saturday night; we turned out at 3.30 a.m. on Sunday morning, had an early breakfast, and crossed the river in the boats at 4.30 a.m. We hauled the 1st company of the Buffs over at five, next came 100 of the native regiment, who relieved us on the hauling line; we then kept the boats going, leaving a party of blue-jackets to show the natives what they had to do. By 8 a.m. the whole of the Buffs were across, then came the mounted volunteers, baggage for the Buffs, and four companies of the 99th regt. We were to have crossed before the 99th; but the programme was altered at the last moment, and although we had struck all our tents and made all our gear up, we were obliged to pitch our camp again. We are now encamped close to the Buffs, and we are working away at the punt day and night. All the troops are across, and the waggons will be over by tomorrow if the work goes on as at present ... The centre column is already on the march, the General is with them; our transport has delayed us very much ...

Lieutenant Backhouse, who was signalling from the top of Fort Pearson until late afternoon, had a spectacular view of events. 'I never saw such a scene as the crossing was,' he confided to his diary, 'a picture should have been taken of it.' That evening, he spent

my first night campaigning in Zululand. A body of Zulus was seen about four miles off and we expect they will come down tonight or early tomorrow: until this campaign is over, we have to sleep in our clothes ... The 99th started an alarm at 3 a.m., which proved to be nothing much, they said a party of about 300 Zulus were near us. Rainy at night ...

Despite the nervousness on the Zulu bank, however, there was no sign of an attack that night, nor the following morning. There was no possibility of continuing the advance until the column was complete, and elements continued to struggle up from Natal throughout the following few days. The sense of frustration felt by the men waiting on the Zulu bank was heightened by the arrival of news from elsewhere in the war, and on the 16th Backhouse noted,

News, by telegraph, that Colonel Glynn's Column has had a skirmish with the Zulus, and killed about 24 of them, our loss, only

two native levies killed and 12 wounded, also that Wood and his
column have met. Nearly all the waggons and oxen are now across
the River, and I hear it is decided that we shall start on Saturday, but
I doubt whether we shall move by then. We are hard at work building
a fort . . .

Backhouse was overly pessimistic; in fact, Pearson was indeed ready
to move forward on the following Saturday, the 18th. The force under
his command was now impressive, but mixed. He had eight companies
– a full battalion – of his own regiment, the Buffs, who, having been in
southern Africa since 1877, were acclimatized to the extremes of weather
and the strange sights and sounds of the continent. By contrast, the six
companies of the 99th Regiment attached to the column were newcomers
who had landed at Durban only a few weeks before. Most of them,
moreover, were recruits, and they struck the 'old salts' of the Buffs as
very young indeed. For artillery Pearson had just two 7-pounder guns
and a rocket trough belonging to 11/7th Battery RA, although this was
to some extent offset by firepower put ashore by the Navy. Some
290 sailors from HMS Shah and HMS Active, all under the command
of Captain H. J. Fletcher Campbell, had been placed under Pearson's
command, and brought with them two heavy 24-pounder rocket tubes,
and a Gatling gun. The Gatling was a hand-cranked, multi-barrelled
machine gun which had yet to be used in action by British troops and
would receive its baptism of fire in this campaign. The Navy had also
landed two 12-pounder Armstrong guns, which had been emplaced in
the redoubt at Fort Pearson to protect the crossing. For cavalry, Pearson
had the services of a squadron of Mounted Infantry – a scratch force,
raised from men in the infantry battalions who knew how to ride – and
no fewer than five of the small Natal Volunteer units, in this case drawn
from the towns and villages between the border and Durban – the Natal
Hussars, Durban, Victoria, Stanger and Alexandra Mounted Rifles. The
mounted contingent were all placed under the command of Major Percy
Barrow of the 19th Hussars, a resourceful and energetic officer who
had once been Commandant of the School of Instruction for Auxiliary
Cavalry. For Engineers, Pearson had the No. 2 Company, Royal Engineers, under Captain Warren Wynne, and a company of the Natal Native
Pioneers, who were considered among the best of the African auxiliary
units. The rest of his force was made up of the 2nd Regiment, NNC,

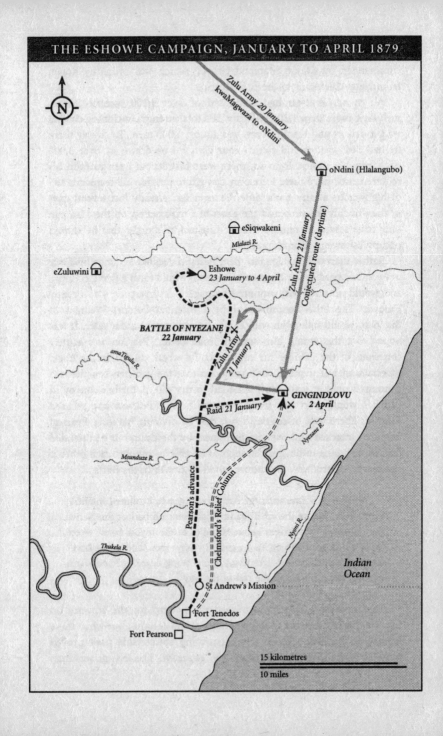

THE ESHOWE CAMPAIGN, JANUARY TO APRIL 1879

Zulu Army 20 January
kwaMagwaza to oNdini

oNdini (Hlalangubo)

eSiqwakeni

Mlalazi R.

Zulu Army 21 January
Conjectured route (daytime)

eZuluwini

Eshowe
23 January to 4 April

BATTLE OF NYEZANE
22 January

Zulu Army
21 January

amaTigulu R.

GINGINDLOVU
2 April

Raid 21 January

Nyezane R.

Msunduze R.

Pearson's advance

Chelmsford's Relief Column

Nyoni R.

Thukela R.

Indian
Ocean

St Andrew's Mission

Fort Tenedos

Fort Pearson

15 kilometres

10 miles

commanded by Major Shapland Graves, which was primarily drawn from Natal chiefdoms in the coastal strip.

All in all, Pearson had command of over 4,200 combat troops, including more than 1,200 redcoats. His total strength, including civilian wagon drivers and team leaders, was almost 5,000 men. To supply them he had 384 wagons and twenty-four carts, to be drawn by over 3,000 oxen and 121 mules. Even so, there were insufficient oxen to fulfil his requirements, since there were only enough to provide full teams for 195 of his wagons at any given time. Pearson had already lost several days in the difficult crossing, and the news of Glyn's action on the 12th can only have served to remind him of Chelmsford's order that he should occupy Eshowe as soon as possible.

Rather than wait any longer, then, Pearson decided to divide his force in two. One part, under his own command, would form a flying column, and would advance with minimal baggage – fifty wagons – to occupy Eshowe. The other, commanded by Lieutenant-Colonel Welman of the 99th, would follow on with eighty supply wagons a day later. It was hoped that this would also suit the road better; Pearson was acutely conscious of the damage his column could wreak on the fragile track, especially in wet weather, and he hoped that the gap between the two columns would at least allow the road to dry out. A further convoy of supplies would start out from the border once Pearson had secured Eshowe. There was, of course, a risk that by dividing his force Pearson might be attacked and overrun piecemeal by the Zulu, but he intended the two columns to be close enough to be able to support each other if necessary. Accordingly, Backhouse noted on the 18th, the Buffs

> Paraded at 5 a.m. with the Artillery (2 guns), Mounted Infantry, Volunteers, 'Active' Naval Brigade, Engineers and part of the Native Contingent, and marched about 10 miles to the Inyoni river, where we encamped for the night ... country very open, and a few kraals scattered about, but no sign of any Zulus being near. Fine and warm starting, but it rained all the rest of the way ...

That first day's march established the pattern for the advance on Eshowe. Barrow's patrols scouted ahead of the column, but while there seemed to be little sign of the enemy, the countryside itself proved more of a challenge than Pearson had expected. The iNyoni was little more than a stream a few feet wide, one of dozens of small rivers which crossed his line of advance, but it was in flood, and the high, narrow banks meant that the crossing was painfully slow. That night Pearson camped in a sea of long wet grass just 200 yards beyond the iNyoni, while the track behind him was such a quagmire that he decided to allow Welman's column to close up behind before continuing his advance.

The following day brought the first intelligence of the long-awaited Zulu response, as Backhouse recalled:

> An alarm last night, which proved to be a false one, although I believe some Zulus were about. A despatch came from Mr Finney, the Border Agent, to say that Cetewayo has sent one regiment to oppose us at Ekowe, and that he won't send more men, as he says one Regiment will be sufficient to drive us into the sea: 'I doubt it' ... Marched at 1.30 p.m. to the Umsindusi River where we halted for the night after having to ford the river, which was up to our waists. I was on outpost duty all night, which luckily was fine, although we had rain nearly all day. Zulu spies about, I saw about 50 on a hill as we marched into camp before dark, my Company being on Rear Guard. No alarm at night, but our Native Levies burnt a large kraal not far from the Camp about 1 a.m. Had a lively night of it as I was wet through, and had to patrol in front of the sentries during the night, into thick bush, not a wink of sleep.

The information supplied by Fynney, the Border Agent – the same man who had compiled Chelmsford's report on the Zulu army – was surprisingly accurate, a rare occurrence in a war characterized on the British side by an almost total ignorance of Zulu movements. King Cetshwayo and his council had been unable to decide on a defensive strategy until the invasion convinced them that the British were in earnest. The main army had already been assembled at the complex of royal homesteads at oNdini, in the heart of the country, which constituted the national capital. There were perhaps some 28,000 men gathered at oNdini, undergoing the rituals necessary to prepare them for battle, but Cetshwayo was determined to wait to see which of the British columns would prove the most dangerous before committing his troops. When news reached him that Glyn's column had gone into action on

the 12th, he decided to despatch the main army to confront the Centre
Column. To harass Pearson's column, however, he detached some 3,500
men under the elderly Chief Godide kaNdlela of the Ntuli people
and ordered them to march to the coast. Godide's force consisted of
the uMxapho *ibutho*, 2,600 men in their mid-thirties, and a number
of companies from the izinGulube and uDlambedlu regiments, which
comprised men in their fifties. The army had left oNdini on the 17th,
Godide's contingent moving off to the south-west, heading towards the
royal homestead of Hlalangubo, north of Eshowe, which was to serve as
their base. They arrived there on the night of the 20th, having been
joined by local elements along the way. These were men from a variety
of regiments – the iNsukamngeni, iQwa, uDududu and iNdabawombe –
who lived locally and had stayed in the region to watch Pearson. At full
strength, the *impi* numbered close to 6,000.

The feeling that the enemy was nearby added an air of excitement
to Pearson's otherwise painfully slow advance. On the 21st, he heard a
rumour that the Zulus had concentrated at another royal homestead,
kwaGingindlovu, which lay about five miles off to his right, and he
detached two companies of the Buffs, with artillery support, to investigate. This action reveals something of the overconfidence which prevailed
throughout the British camp, since had the Zulu been present at
kwaGingindlovu in any strength, this force would have been woefully
exposed. As it was, the homestead proved to be deserted apart from an
ancient Zulu woman, whom the troops brought away with them before
gleefully setting the complex on fire. That night Pearson camped on a
grassy ridge north of the amaTigulu river.

In the morning, Pearson's men found that large swathes of grass
around their camp had apparently been trampled flat during the night.
It was a disconcerting discovery, but there were no Zulu in sight, and
the column continued its advance. Ahead, the track descended a gentle
slope before crossing the Nyezane river some four miles off. The
Nyezane, too, was a narrow river, just a few yards wide, but the water
was waist-deep, and the banks were choked with reeds and thick bush.
On the far side, the track continued along a grassy flat for a few hundred
yards before turning to the left and rising up through a line of hills
beyond. This was the first of a series of terraces which lay between the
Nyezane and Eshowe, and an obvious place for attack. The track wound
up a sloping finger of land, flanked on either side by hollows, which

rose up to steeper spurs beyond. Pearson sent the mounted men under Barrow to scout the road, and according to Pearson's own report,

> . . . I received a note from him to say that he had selected a fairly open space for a halting place, which he had carefully videtted. I at once rode forward to reconnoitre, and found the ground covered with more bush than seemed desirable for an outspan, but there was no water between the Inyezani [and Eshowe], and with several steep hills to climb – I decided upon outspanning for a couple of hours to feed and rest the oxen, and to enable the men to breakfast.
>
> It was just then eight o'clock, and I was in the act of giving direction about piquets and scouts required for our protection, and the waggons had already begun to park, when the leading company of the Native Contingent, who were scouting in front – personally directed by Captain Hart, staff officer to the officer commanding that regiment – discovered the enemy advancing rapidly over the ridges in our front, and making for clumps of thick bush around us . . .

Pearson's suspicions about the site had proved correct. Chief Godide's troops had come within striking distance of the British the day before. Thinking that Pearson had not yet advanced so far, Godide had intended to occupy the kwaGingindlovu homestead, and indeed it was probably the arrival of his advance guard which had given Pearson his hint of the Zulu presence there. But the advance guard had abandoned the homestead as the British approached, and had not been detected; that night Godide moved to intercept the column before it crossed the Nyezane. His warriors had actually surrounded the camp in the darkness, but the sound of the sentries calling to one another had convinced the Zulu that Pearson was prepared for an attack, and Godide had withdrawn before dawn. He took his men north across the Nyeazane and they had bivouacked behind the hills overlooking the river. They had hoped to catch Pearson on the march, and might well have succeeded, had not the NNC patrol blundered into scouts hidden in the long grass on the forward slopes of the summit. The result was electric, as Captain Hart – the 2nd NNC's Staff Officer – recalled:

> Suddenly a mass of Zulus appeared on the hilltop on our left, and opened a fire of musketry upon us at a distance of about 400 yards. I saw at once that we had almost fallen into a trap, and I instantly gave the order 'Retire.' At the same moment the Zulus poured down

the hill by hundreds at the top of their speed, with a tremendous shout, while others above kept up the fire over the heads of those descending the hill. The kloof [ravine] was not far behind us, and we reached it, as far as I could perceive, without any loss, although the bullets whistled among us and struck the earth all about us as we went. There only remained to cross the kloof and we should be safe. I was at the end of the company next the enemy – the end next the hill – and I even had to ride some little way towards the Zulus, to reach the track by which I was certain my horse could cross. So it seemed to me that as I had got safely over the kloof, all the others, who were further from the enemy, must necessarily have done so too, and it was not until the close of the general engagement which followed that I found that one of the lieutenants, two sergeants, and two corporals were killed in the kloof, evidently with assegais. I have never been able to make out how this occurred . . .

The loss of these men would prove to be the worst British casualties of the day. According to Pearson,

The Zulus at once opened a heavy fire upon the men of the company who had shown themselves in the open, and they lost one officer, four non-commissioned officers, and three men killed, almost immediately after the firing began.

Unfortunately, owing to scarcely any of the officers or non-commissioned officers of the Native Contingent being able to speak Kaffir, and some not even English (there are several foreigners among them), it has been found most difficult to communicate orders, and it is to be feared that these men who lost their lives by gallantly holding their ground, did so under the impression that it was the duty of the contingent to fight in the first line, instead of scouting only, and, after an engagement, to pursue.

. . . As soon as the firing commenced, I directed the Naval Brigade, under Commander Campbell, Lieutenant Lloyd's division of guns, and Captain Jackson's and Lieutenant Martin's companies of 'The Buffs', to take up a position on a knoll close by the road (and under which they were halted), and from whence the whole of the Zulu advance could be seen and dealt with.

Within minutes of the first clash, the uMxapho *ibutho*, which had been lying behind Wombane, a round hill which rose up steeply on the spur to the right of the road, streamed into view, running down the slope and into the hollow which separated them from Pearson's column. As the uMxapho rushed out to form the left 'horn', a second body of warriors – the 'chest' – appeared at the head of the central spur, blocking the road, while a third – the right 'horn' – moved tentatively round to occupy the spur on Pearson's left. 'Meanwhile', Pearson reported,

> The waggons continued to park, and as soon as the length of the column had sufficiently decreased, I directed the two companies of the Buffs, which were guarding the waggons about half-way down the column, to clear the enemy out of the bush, which had already been shelled and fired into with rockets and musketry by the troops on the knoll.... These companies, led by Captains Harrison and Wyld, and guided by Captain Macgregor, D.A.Q.M.G., whom I sent back for the purpose, moved out in excellent order, and quickly getting into skirmishing order, brought their right shoulders gradually forward, and drove the Zulus before them back into the open, which again exposed them to rockets, shells, and musketry from the knoll.
>
> This movement released the main body of the mounted infantry and volunteers, who with the company of Royal Engineers, had remained near the Inyezana, to protect that portion of the convoy of waggons. The Royal Engineers happened to be working at the Drift when the engagement began.
>
> When thus released, both the Engineers and mounted troops, under Captain Wynne and Major Barrow, respectively moved forward with the infantry. Skirmishers on the left of the latter, the whole being supported by a half-company of 'the Buffs' and a half company of the 99th Regiment, sent out by Lieutenant Colonel Welman, 99th Regiment, who with the rear of the column, was coming up.

Lieutenant Backhouse's company had been in the second division, but was among those sent forward to support Pearson. 'We heard Lloyd's guns firing at some hills about 2 miles from us,' he noted in his diary, and his detachment

> marched as hard as we could, but we were not in time to have any firing, however, we did some good as we went into the bush and drove back about 300 Zulus who were making for our waggons, we skirmishing along the right of the road, it was just as well that the

Zulus turned back on seeing us for we got into some awful bush, and could not see a yard in front of us . . .

While the Zulu who were left continued to try to dislodge Pearson's position on the road, the 'chest' began to move down the centre spur, directly towards the head of the column. According to Pearson,

> About this time the enemy was observed by Commander Campbell to be trying to outflank our left, and he offered to go with a portion of Naval Brigade to drive away a body of Zulus who had got possession of a kraal about 400 yards from the knoll, and which was helping their turning movement. The Naval Brigade was supported by a party of officers and non-commissioned officers of the Native Contingent, under Captain Hart, who were posted on high ground on the left of the Ekowe road, and who checked the Zulus from making any further attempt on our left.

The Zulu homestead lay directly up the slope from Pearson's position, and by occupying it the Zulu had effectively denied him the road. It was imperative that it be cleared, as Captain Hart recognized:

> The enemy now began to fire upon us from a kraal that stood close by the road, about half-way up the hill . . . This fire was coming into the backs of our troops who were engaged near the gun. I accordingly marched the company I had rallied together, with another company of the natives who had been on the advanced guard, against the kraal; but the courage of our natives utterly failed, they crouched down under any cover they could find, and after fruitless efforts to make them advance, I called upon the white men of the two companies to go with me without them. We advanced steadily against the kraal by the main road, the officers, except myself, dismounted; and the little party used their rifles well, and did as I directed, halting to fire, and advancing again when I gave the word. Thus we approached the kraal. It was a small kraal, but it occupied a very advantageous position; the enemy covered by it could fire a quarter of a mile down the road; and the road up to it, and the ground about it, was under the fire also of both Majia's Hill [Wombane] and the hill on the other side of the road. As we approached, the enemy retreated from the kraal, except a few who remained almost until we reached it. Not one of our party was killed or wounded in taking the kraal; but several dead bodies of the enemy

there showed that our fire had been more effective. I at once set the kraal on fire, and as the flames shot high into the air, we gave a loud cheer all together, and I trusted that flames and cheer would as much dispirit the enemy as they would exhilarate our men. The Zulus, who had retired from the kraal, now made a stand, a few hundred yards farther back, upon the road, the ground still rising towards them. I ordered my party to advance again, but found they had not a round of ammunition left. I knew that our ammunition reserve was a long way off, so fearing that there might be a difficulty, I rode back myself to where Colonel Pearson was still engaged with the guns and the 'Buffs' . . . and I got leave to take ammunition from the first supply, no matter to whom it might belong. I thus got a supply at once, and got some of our natives who were crouching about to carry it, but so great was their dread of the fire upon us as we went, that it was only by pointing my revolver at their heads, and threatening to shoot them on the spot, that I could manage to get them up to the kraal with their loads . . .

When my party had replenished their ammunition pouches, some minutes were spent by ourselves, the sailors and the 'Buffs', in replying to the enemy's fire, directed upon us from in front, from right and left.* I tried to push my party on, but found the enemy's number so great that we could make no impression on them.

The crisis of the battle was clearly at hand, as Lieutenant Hamilton of the Naval Brigade described in a letter to his father:

The Zulus were all round us, and finding it impossible to do much where we were, we moved to the rear, and extended along the road. A kraal on the left of the road was at first occupied by Zulus, but before we came up it was taken by two companies of the natives under Capt. Hart, our rocket party having sent a rocket right through the place first. Along the road we were exposed to fire from both sides, as the high ground on each side was occupied by the enemy.

* These comments are particularly interesting in the light of the controversy which has dogged the question of the 24th Regiment's ammunition supply at Isandlwana later that same day. Having secured the necessary authority, Hart clearly had no problem in obtaining ammunition from a unit other than his own, nor in opening the boxes and distributing rounds. In the author's opinion the difficulties of ammunition supply at Isandlwana have traditionally been exaggerated to excuse the British defeat, and are not supported by a close reading of the evidence.

Whilst there I had five men wounded in my company, two very
seriously. As there appeared to be no chance of our fire driving the
Zulus from their position, we kept on advancing with a view to
charging along the ridge and forcing them to retire. Before doing
so we were reinforced by one company of the Buffs, under Colonel
Parnel, and Captain Hart's natives. Captain Hart was most anxious
to advance at once; he and Captain Campbell finally rode on, almost
alone. I followed, bringing up my company as fast as I could, followed
by the Buffs. Two of the Buffs were killed there, and Colonel Parnel's
horse was shot under him; our other company of bluejackets was
some distance behind. The Zulus did not wait for us; they bolted to
a man, and we advanced and took the heights without any further
resistance.

For Captain Hart, the Zulu collapse offered an uncharacteristic
moment of almost chivalrous personal combat:

    I urged my men to their utmost speed, and charged forward
on horseback at the group of Zulus on the summit. They fled – all
but one man. He stood leaning forward, watching me intently, his
left hand on his knee, and his rifle ready in his right. I could see
glistening on his head the black ring that signifies in Zululand a
married man ... I was rapidly approaching him, he was now only
a hundred yards distant, and in a few moments I should use my
revolver, but just then he dropped quickly on one knee, took very
deliberate aim at me for a couple of seconds, and fired. He seemed
scarcely to believe he could have missed his prize, for he waited to
take one eager look at me, as his smoke cleared away, and then
seeing me still coming on, he bolted away and disappeared. Directly
afterwards I was on the summit, and saw hundreds of Zulus crowding
down the opposite side of the hill in full retreat. I fired my revolver
into the crowd, and looked around for my men to open fire, but it is
one thing to ride up a hill, and another to walk up! It was some
minutes before they reached me. Then up came the 'Buffs' and the
men of the Naval Brigade. We stood on the key of the enemy's
position. We commanded the whole country around ...

As the Zulu 'chest' retired, the left 'horn' began to withdraw in the
face of the heavy fire from the companies sweeping out from the wagon-
train. Only the right 'horn' remained largely intact, but – to the disgust

of the rest of Godide's men – it failed to launch a committed attack. As they moved down the spur to the left of the road, the men of the right 'horn' came under fire from a handful of mounted men placed to watch for such a movement. Thinking that the British position was defended on all sides, the right 'horn' retired back over the skyline. It was now about 9.30 a.m., and as Pearson put it, 'the Zulus now fled in all directions, both from our front and left, and before the skirmishers on the right'.

The battle had been fierce while it lasted, and Pearson's light losses reflected the fact that the Zulus had been unable to charge home, rather than any lack of determination in the attack. A total of just twelve men had been killed on the British side – many of them officers and NCOs of the NNC, killed in the first encounter – and twenty more wounded. The Zulu, by contrast, had suffered heavily. It was impossible to get an accurate picture of the number of Zulu dead, since many were concealed in the bush and long grass, and Pearson made no effort to collect them for burial. Pearson's own estimate of 300 Zulu casualties was a conservative one; accounts based on Zulu sources put the true figure at 600. Certainly, a Zulu named Sihlala, who fought with the uMxapho *ibutho*, was impressed by the destructive capabilities of the British weapons:

> We fought hard but we could not beat the whites, they shot us down in numbers, in some places our dead and wounded covered the ground, we lost heavily, especially from the small arms [rifles], many of our men were drowned in the Nyezane river, in attempting to cross at a part of the river where it was too deep for any but a swimmer, in the rush made for the river several were forced over trees and dongas, and killed that way, the 'Itumlu' [rockets] killed people, but the small guns are the worst.

Pearson confirmed that the carnage was very evident on the ground: 'The dead were lying about in heaps of seven or eight, and in one place ten dead bodies were found close together. At another 35 were counted in a very small space.'

Lieutenant Backhouse 'saw about 10 dead Zulus' when the column later continued its advance up the track, and noted that 'they were mostly oldish men', a fact which reflected the Zulu practice of deploying senior regiments in the 'chest' and allocating younger, more energetic men to the 'horns'. Pearson's mounted men were too few to give an effective pursuit over such terrain, and as a result the Zulus were able to carry away many of their wounded.

The battle of Nyezane was the first full-scale engagement of the war, and the British were delighted at the result. Despite the premature Zulu attack, during which Pearson's column had remained highly vulnerable, he had nevertheless reacted quickly and firmly. The elation felt by the troops was, however, tempered by the realization that they had under-estimated their enemy. As Hart put it,

> The Zulus fought well, showing judgement and courage quite equal to their enemy, but although they outnumbered us greatly, they could not hold their ground against our artillery and superior rifles. We had the best rifles in the world; they, for the most part, merely muskets, weapons of the past . . .

One aspect of the battle which caused some interest among the victors was the performance of HMS *Active*'s Gatling gun. Although the Gatling had been carried into the field by British troops in an earlier campaign,* this was the first time it had been used in combat. Commanded by eighteen-year-old Midshipman Lewis Coker, the gun had been towards the rear of the column when the Zulus had attacked. Coker promptly

> placed my gun on a knoll in a good position for firing if necessary. I brought my gun into action, but through the clumsiness of my driver the disselboom carried away. I repaired it as quickly as possible; no natives appearing I moved on with the waggons, owing to the disselboom I was much delayed.
>
> On arriving at the foot of the hill where the Head Quarters were I was ordered by Colonel Pearson to bring the gun up and place it opposite a hill, where some natives had taken up a position. I immediately opened fire on them, they retiring into the bush I ceased firing having expended about 300 rounds, and stationed my men to try and pick off a few natives who were annoying us considerably.

The gun must indeed have been devastatingly effective at suppressing Zulu fire, but 300 rounds represent only a short burst, and Lieutenant Hamilton merely remarked that 'it was too late to be of much effect'.

By mid-morning the temperature on the battlefield was soaring,

---

* The 1873/74 Asante ('Ashanti') campaign in West Africa.

and the Zulu dead were beginning to bloat. Pearson was determined to give the Zulu no suggestion that their attack had delayed his progress, and once his own dead were buried he ordered his men to make ready to advance. The column climbed slowly up the track away from the battlefield, leaving behind as evidence of the fight a small wooden cross over the British grave, and a circle of Zulu corpses strewn through the long grass. From the top of the heights, the British could see long lines of Zulu in retreat, several miles away in the distance. That night the column bivouacked on the ridge-tops, and the following morning they occupied Eshowe.

Their arrival at Eshowe, under such circumstances, had an air of unreality about it. The mission, built by the Norwegian missionary Ommund Oftebro in 1860, was one of the most established in the country. It consisted of a solid church, built out of home-made bricks and topped with a corrugated-iron roof, and three thatched outhouses which had served as living quarters, a store and a school. Oftebro had cleared a patch of adjacent bush and had painstakingly cultivated an orchard of fruit trees. The site was eerily deserted but had not been touched by the Zulu, and Pearson's engineer, Wynne, immediately began to plan for its defence.

The buildings were not ideally placed from a military point of view. Although built on a high, breezy upland, they were overlooked by low rises a few hundred yards away, while the ground fell away to both east and west into the beds of marshy streams. Here and there patches of bush grew quite close to the mission and would provide cover for an attacking enemy. Pearson's original instructions merely called for him to make the post secure as a supply depot; he expected to resume his advance within days. Since the column's wagons would be needed to ferry supplies back and forth to the border, Wynne had little option but to turn the mission into a fort by digging an entrenchment around it. Both he and Pearson anticipated that it would be held by a few hundred men at most, and Wynne laid out a perimeter just large enough to surround the buildings. Since the orchard fell outside the defensive area, Wynne reluctantly persuaded Pearson to order the trees to be cut down.

With his first objective in hand, Pearson unloaded his supply wagons, and sent some back under escort to collect supplies stockpiled at the Thukela. Lieutenant Backhouse was among those detailed to accompany them:

Left Ekowe at 5 a.m. [25 January], with 'B' and 'H' Companies, 2 companies of the 99th, and two of the Native Contingent, and a few mounted men, all under the command of Major Coates, 99th Regt., conveying 50 empty waggons to the drift; we marched about 7 miles, and halted for breakfast, then marched about 10 miles further and halted for the night, on our camping ground of the 21st instant; passing through the battlefield at Inyezane, where, as may be supposed, there was an awful stench, and the unburied Zulus something too awful to see. On our way over the place, we picked up a wounded Zulu, who had his leg smashed by a shell, poor wretch he had been lying there for 3 days without food or drink and was starving, we gave him some biscuits, and took him on the waggons with us; I believe two others were heard calling out in the bush, but they were too far off and we had to leave them to their fate. Thunderstorm just as we outspanned and as we have no tents it was a most wretched night for us, all wet through and lying in the long wet grass, to add to this my company was on Picquet. Fine except for the storm. The wounded Zulu told us that a number of regiments had been sent against the other columns, also that 5 regiments were against us on the 22nd and that 12,000 Zulus would await us in the bush about 12 miles beyond Eshowe. On our way we fired at some Kaffirs about a mile off, luckily we did not hit any of them, as they proved to be some messengers returning from the drift.

The following day, while still on the march, Backhouse noted that a curious rumour reached the column – 'news, but not yet confirmed, that Colonel Durnford's column had been smashed up by the Zulus'. This was the first hint to anyone in the coastal theatre that fighting might have occurred elsewhere in the country. At Eshowe, Pearson was largely isolated from the rest of the war and was dependent on runners to carry messages to and from the Thukela. That same day, however, some of the Volunteers on vedette duty, who spoke Zulu, reported hearing Zulu shouting news from hill-top to hill-top. They were calling out that they had won a great victory. Neither Pearson nor his officers took the reports seriously, but the following morning a runner arrived with a curt despatch from Bartle Frere. The news it contained was shocking and bewildering. According to Lieutenant Hamilton, 'we heard that Colonel Durnford, R.E., had been attacked, and his column, composed entirely of native troops, cut to pieces. Colonel Durnford himself has been killed – that we know for certain; but the rest of the story is very unintelligible.'

The news was particularly disturbing because as far as the garrison knew, Durnford's column was still stationed at Middle Drift and was supposed to advance to support Pearson. By implication, Pearson had now been outflanked, and it was entirely possible that a Zulu force had crossed into Natal upstream of the Lower Drift, threatening not only his own line of communication but the civilian population in Natal as well. Frere's note gave Pearson no clue as to what was expected of him, but the following morning – the 28th – a runner arrived with a message from Chelmsford himself. Written from Pietermaritzburg on the 27th, it gave no further details of Durnford's demise, but was stark in its implication of defeat:

> Consider all my instructions as cancelled and act in whatever manner you think most desirable in the interest of the column under your command. Should you consider the garrison of Ekowe too far advanced to be fed with safety, you can withdraw it.
>
> Hold however, if possible, the post on the Zulu side of the Lower Tugela. You must be prepared to have the whole Zulu force down upon you. Do away with tents, and let the men take shelter under the waggons, which will then be in position for defence, and hold so many more supplies.

The note of despair which pervaded this despatch added to the confusion of the Eshowe garrison. A note added by a border magistrate hardly helped to clarify the situation, as Lieutenant Hamilton recalled:

> With this telegram came a letter from a man named Barton (a magistrate on the border) to the colonel, in which he said that the General's camp had been attacked by the Zulus, that after four hours' hard fighting the Zulus overpowered the 200 men guarding the camp, and killed every white man.
>
> How only 200 men came to be in camp we are not told, so you can see we had only the vaguest instructions to work on, and we have not heard a word since; all communication is stopped.

Hitherto, Pearson had operated entirely within the framework of Lord Chelmsford's plan of campaign, but it was immediately apparent that that plan had now been abandoned. Pearson was thrown on his own resources and would have to rely on his own initiative to secure the safety of his column. No sooner had Chelmsford's despatch arrived than he called his officers together in a council of war. The options before them were to retire on the Thukela or to try to hold their advanced position. After some debate, it was decided to stay. Worried about the limited supplies, however, Pearson ordered Barrow's mounted contingent and the NNC to return to the Thukela. This was probably a wise decision – there was in any case no room to house either the NNC or Barrow's horses, and both units would be of more use on the border – but the retreat, which began that afternoon, was somewhat disorderly. Barrow, well aware that his men were vulnerable to a Zulu ambush, pressed on quickly for the border, leaving the NNC trailing behind. Feeling abandoned by their allies, morale among the NNC collapsed, and the regiment broke up into small groups who made their own way back to the Thukela. Both parties reached Fort Tenedos without incident, although Captain Hart found the march through the Nyezane battlefield trying:

> As we approach Majia's Hill, I noticed our natives eagerly gathering the leaves of a shrub and stuffing them into their nostrils. This was in prospect of the stench from the battlefield, and I was glad to follow their example. The leaves chosen had a very pleasant smell . . .

A few days later, Pearson explained his decision to remain at Eshowe in a letter to Lord Chelmsford:

> now that we are here it would be a fatal mistake, in my opinion, to abandon the post, which, as I have already said, will be required as a forepost when you are ready to advance again. Indeed, if we retired to the Tugela, we should most likely have all the Zulu army at our back, and be obliged either to destroy all our ammunition and stores before we left Ekowe, or abandon them on the march if attacked, as in all probability we should be by overwhelming numbers.
>
> We have 1,365 Europeans here, all told, and about 100 natives, including pioneers, but exclusive of leaders and drivers, the number of whom I don't quite know. We have in round numbers 1,200 rifles and 332 rounds of ammunition for that number, also 127,000 rounds Gatling, 37 naval rockets, 24 pounders (shot, not shell rockets), 46 rockets (shell) for 7 pdrs, also for 7 pdrs 200 Shrapnel, 254 common shell, 20 double shell, and 33 case. It is almost impossible to get an

accurate return of food, but I think we must have over 3 weeks'
supply; the cattle, however, may be swept away at any moment, as
of course they have to be kept in the waggon laager outside. I am
keeping a small reserve in the ditches, where we stable the horses
also. Although commanded, the ground is perfectly open round here,
except for one or two patches of wood, which would give cover, but
which are being cut down as fast as we can do it; the brushwood,
however, is all destroyed . . .

Indeed, once the news of the disaster spread throughout the garrison,
the men took to building the entrenchments with renewed energy. Two
mission outbuildings, a few hundred yards away, were blown up to
prevent the Zulus from using them as cover, and a deep ditch, with the
earth piled up inside to form a parapet, was dug around the remaining
complex. Since there was now no immediate hope of further wagons
returning to the Drift to fetch supplies, these were dragged within the
perimeter and incorporated in the defences. All outside camps were
abandoned; from now on the garrison would have to sleep inside the
fort each night. There was no room for tents, so the men had to find
shelter where they could. By 6 February, Pearson could write:

We are now very strongly entrenched. Good thick parapets,
ditches nowhere less than seven feet deep and ten feet wide. In places
they are both deeper and wider; the ditches are partly flank as well,
either by flanks, stockades, capponieres or cuttings in the parapet.
Enfilade and reverse fire have been well considered and traverses have
been constructed to protect us from both. The batteries are masked
and spare sand-bags provided to protect the gunners from the fire
upon any point from which the gun is not actually firing.

Trous-de-Loups are being made on the glacis, and a zig-zag will
be made to the watering-place about 60 yards from the fort, to
ensure the safety of the watering party. We have three entrances,
a main entrance over a drawbridge, over which carts or unloaded
waggons can pass; this is drawn back at night; a small foot-bridge to
the watering place which is topped up on the alarm sounding, and a
trestle-bridge, also a footbridge which is dismantled at retreat. Near
the main entrance is a sally port leading into the ditch where at night
we have some earth-closets, as, of course, the day latrines are some
distance from the fort. In a hollow below this face are two cattle-
laagers built of waggons chained and reimed together. The circular

one holds the slaughter cattle, and the other most of the trek oxen. These are protected by an L shaped work, nevertheless, the cattle are a constant source of anxiety to me, as they might be taken away during a dark night, if the Zulus should be enterprising, at least so it seems to me. I trust I may be wrong. We are better off for food than I thought we were, and, if our cattle are left to us, we shall be able to get along for over three weeks from this day, and, with many essentials, for some time longer . . .

As it is, it is highly probable, I suppose, that Cetewayo may make a supreme effort to drive us out, and bring the bulk of his army this way. I trust he may do so, and he will find it a very hard nut to crack indeed. We have got all the distances measured, and this after-noon a table of ranges will be issued to the troops. If we have time, the distances will all be cut on the hills which slope our way, and the cuttings filled in with white clay, which we get out of the ditches, so as to make the figures visible.

For the first few days after news of Isandlwana had reached Pearson, the threat of a Zulu attack seemed very real. In fact, however, Pearson's men had no clue of the true price paid by the Zulus in defending themselves against the invasion. On the same day that Pearson had defeated Godide's men at Nyezane, the Zulus had fought actions on both the central and northern front. Total Zulu losses in these actions amounted to between 2,000 and 3,000 men killed, with many hundreds more wounded. Among them were dozens of important chiefs and commanders. Indeed, this one day was to prove the most costly twenty-four hours of the war for the Zulus, and they were exhausted by it. Across the country, the warriors dispersed to their homes to recover and undergo the necessary post-combat purification rituals.

King Cetshwayo, unable to follow up his advantage immediately, grew increasingly indignant during the first week of February that Pearson had apparently made himself at home. Cetshwayo refused to sanction a direct attack on the entrenchments, for fear of the losses, but instead urged them to isolate Pearson and draw him out from his fort. As a result, over the next few weeks the Zulus developed a sophisticated strategy for containing the Eshowe garrison. Several thousand warriors were assembled at royal homesteads in the region, and detachments of them took turns to occupy temporary camps close to the mission. From these camps scouts watched the garrison on a daily basis, harassing

Pearson's patrols in the hope of provoking him into making a sortie. These men were under the control of a council of chiefs who lived locally and knew the terrain. Among them were Prince Dabulamanzi and Mavumengwana kaNdlela, both of whom had been involved in the victory of 22 January.

Within a few days, Pearson noticed that Zulu patrols dominated the country between Eshowe and the Thukela, and it became impossible for British runners to get through. Pearson could neither advance nor retreat and was effectively under siege; a waiting game had begun.

At first, morale amongst the garrison remained high. Lieutenant Hamilton described something of the daily routine of the naval contingent:

> In the meantime, life here is dull enough; we have working parties at the works all day, commencing at 6 a.m., finish at 4.30 p.m. No one is allowed to go out of sight of the fort, so our walks are rather limited. We all live inside; tents have been done away with, but we are fortunate in having a house in our part of the fort, in the verandah of which 10 officers sleep at night; the men have rigged up a shelter for themselves with a waggon cover, under which half of them sleep at night, the other half sleep on the ramparts, and are ready at a moment's notice, in case of night attack . . .
>
> This is a very healthy place, the men are all well, and all we want are some vegetables to make the rations very good.

Yet this last comment was optimistic. With so many men and animals cooped up at night in such a confined area, it became increasingly difficult to keep the fort sanitary and the men healthy. The men drew their water from streams draining off the slopes outside the fort, and these soon became contaminated. The weather continued much as it had since the war began, heavy, humid heat giving way to torrential downpours, and the interior of the fort soon became a quagmire. As early as 1 February, Private Kingston of the Buffs succumbed to fever, the first of a steady stream from the garrison to die of disease over the following months. Nevertheless, Pearson remained optimistic, and on 18 February commented that

> Our sick remain very steady and no sign of typhoid or anything of that kind. We have 30 in hospital including the wounded [from

Nyezane]. Three men died . . . last week of diarrhoea and fever. They were always weakly men and had been ailing for some time.

The band of the Buffs or 99th play every afternoon in the fort, which affords some pleasure. We found some cricket gear in the Volunteer baggage, also a number of books which of course I have jumped . . .

We have no news here. We have not been molested in any way and are beginning to fear that the Zulus don't intend to attack us here – at any rate as long as we are strong. They are all round us, however, and exchange shots pretty often with the vedettes . . .

The dead were buried on a slope to the west of the fort. Despite the efforts of the senior medical officer to persuade them otherwise, the men continued to fill their water-bottles from the stream below, and the incidence of sickness continued to rise.

Once the novelty of their situation wore off, the garrison became increasingly prone to boredom. Constantly aware of the Zulu presence, the men had little to do beyond adding increasingly sophisticated improvements to the fort, and the sense of isolation began to tell on their nerves. A month after their arrival, there was still no sign of a major Zulu attack, contact with the outside world had been cut, and the only excitement was provided by periodic raids to loot food from nearby deserted Zulu homesteads. On 23 February, Lieutenant Hamilton wrote,

Although there is no immediate prospect of sending a letter, still as I suppose this state of siege cannot last much longer, I think I may write something, if it is only just to keep my hand in. We have had no news whatever since the 11th; on that day, a letter was brought up from the General, to which a reply was sent; and since then we have been looking out every day, for either a force sent to relieve us, or else for orders for some of us to go down. However, we have heard nothing, and can only suppose our messengers have been caught and killed by the Zulus. We know there is a large force of Zulus between us and the Tugela, and I am afraid we shall have to wait some time before they attack us here. They know a great deal more about our movements than we know about theirs; they could not well know less, and will probably attack the convoy, which must be sent sooner or later to provision the place. Of course a strong escort will be sent with the waggons, and I have no doubt they will give the Zulus a lesson. If we could only find out when they start, we could cooperate from this end, but, in the absence of all news of what is going on, it is impossible to know what to do. The fort is finished, and is as strong as a very bad position can possibly be made; at any rate it is quite strong enough ... You can imagine that it is dull enough, being cooped up here. The excitement of supposing we are going to be attacked has dried out; the only thing out of the common that happens, is when a party go out to burn some of the Zulu kraals on the hills about us. Yesterday, we sent out a party consisting of 30 of our men, and a company of the 99th. I was not in charge of any of our people, but walked out with them to look on; we saw about 200 Zulus, but all a long way off, out of range. We burnt a kraal and captured one fowl, the latter very precious in these hard times. You would have been amused, and I think horrified, at the prices given a few days ago for some preserves found in one of the waggons, and sold by public auction. Here are a few of the items: – one tin of preserved milk, 17s; a bottle of curry powder, £1; tin of sardines, 112s 6d; and a few other things in proportion; a ham of twelve pounds weight, £6. The stores in our mess have lasted pretty well; we are not quite out yet. I am caterer, and know the ration pretty well. We are on short allowance of some things, but in case this letter should get into the hands of the Zulus, I must not tell you how much longer we can last out. You will be glad to hear that there is not a drop of wine or spirits to be had anywhere, except in the hospital, and I cannot say anyone seems the worse for it, although on some of the wet nights we have had lately, a glass of grog would be very comforting ... One of our sub-lieutenants has lost one stone weight, and looks all the better for it. My weight is 10 stones 11 pounds; not been so light for a long time. We get on very well with the Buffs and 99th. At first there were continual alarms, stumps of trees being mistaken at night for the whole Zulu army advancing, and so turning the whole camp out. The weather is abominable, very wet and cold; it set in with the new moon, and the weather-wise people say it will last a whole month. At this present moment the rain is beating all over this paper, so you must excuse the ink running ... I have never felt better in my life, not withstanding the short commons. There are a number of cases of dysentery in hospital; one of our men, the shoemaker, died a few days ago, and we have one or two others who are not so well as they might be; but with those few exceptions our men are very well indeed.

Despite such optimism, Pearson was forced to admit a few days later that

> The wet weather brings diarrhoea with it, and although our official sick list has diminished rather than increased yet I fear there are a good many cases of diarrhoea here, which of course may turn to dysentery at any moment.
>
> We now have so little grass in the immediate vicinity of the fort that we are obliged to send the cattle a considerable distance – guarded of course. Nevertheless, it is a continual source of anxiety to me.
>
> I went out with a foraging party this morning and we 'drew' more Zulus than usual, but they kept at a safe distance. Some of them were heard to shout, 'You are eating our mealies today, but we will drink your coffee tomorrow.' I wish to goodness they would come and try. They will get no quarter from us. 'Remember No. 3 Column' will be our war-cry, and I long for nothing better than to see the country laid waste and the ground strewn with black carcasses . . .

It was probably this feeling of frustration which prompted Pearson to order the biggest foray of the siege on 1 March. A small royal homestead by the name of eSiqwakeni lay a few miles north of Eshowe, across the Mlalazi river. Prince Dabulamanzi was a commander of this homestead, and it was widely held that he was directing the siege from there. At 2 a.m. on the 1st, Pearson set out at the head of a scratch force of 500 men, including one of the RA's 7-pounder guns. After a night march across difficult terrain, the column reached a ridge overlooking eSiqwakeni at dawn the following morning. The move had clearly caught the Zulus by surprise, but as Pearson deployed his men into a firing line, his troops were spotted by a lone Zulu emerging from a hut. Immediately the Zulu shouted the alarm, and warriors tumbled out of the huts, rounding up their cattle and driving them off with them. The artillery fired a shell into the homestead and then shelled the retreating warriors, killing or wounding some ten men. By this time it was light, and Pearson, considering that he had achieved his objective, ordered the retreat. The Zulus immediately rallied and set off in pursuit. Several times Pearson's rearguard was forced to stop and fire volleys to drive the Zulus away, but the warriors kept pace and occupied every tactical feature as the British passed on. They continued the pursuit until within just two miles of the fort. Although Pearson declared himself well pleased with the foray, there was an uneasy feeling amongst the garrison that it had merely revealed the extent to which the Zulus entirely dominated the countryside away from the immediate confines of the camp.

It was probably as a result of this sortie that the Zulus stepped up their harassment of British patrols. Each day it had been the habit of Pearson's last remaining mounted men – who ironically had dubbed themselves 'the Uhlans', after the dashing Prussian lancer regiments – to place a vedette on a knoll about half a mile from the camp. This knoll was on the edge of the Eshowe upland, and the ground fell away steeply in front of it, giving a panoramic view of the countryside towards the Thukela. As such, it was considered important as a possible signalling site, and Pearson was determined to remain in control of it. There had, however, already been skirmishes around the spot, and the Zulus had tried to ambush the British patrols several times as they arrived to take up their positions. On 7 March, a Mounted Infantryman of the 99th, Private Carson, had a lucky escape, as Lieutenant Hamilton described:

> some Zulus made a rush at him from a piece of bush, in which they were concealed, as he was riding past, fired, and hit him in 4 places, one shot disabling his right hand; one of the Zulus seized the horse by the mane, the animal reared, but the rider held on, and badly wounded as he was, stuck his spurs in and got away, the horse received an assegai wound as he galloped off. The man rode into camp and is doing very well, but has lost the best part of his right hand, and has a gunshot wound in both legs, and a wound in his back.

A few days later, a party sent out by Pearson to make a short-cut in the road also came under heavy Zulu fire. A Lieutenant Lewis of the Buffs – who had carried one of the Colours at Nyezane – was hit in the head and seen to fall. The bullet had passed through the peak of his sun-helmet, and his face was covered with blood, but miraculously it turned out to be no more than a flesh-wound. Apart from two black eyes and a cut across his forehead, Lewis was uninjured. That same day, however, the Zulus mounted another attack on the vedette post. The vedettes scattered, and a Private Brookes of the 99th fell from his horse.

He was saved only by the gallant action of Captain Shervington of the NNC, who rode his horse between Brookes and the approaching Zulus, and kept them at bay with his revolver. Shervington was later recommended for the VC, the only man during the siege to be nominated; he was refused, however, on the grounds that no senior officer had witnessed the deed. A week later Private Kent was not so lucky: in yet another attack on the same post, he too was thrown from his horse, and speared to death before anyone could save him. The Zulus made off with his carbine and ammunition.

Despite these attacks, the morale of the garrison had risen at the beginning of March. On the 2nd, a vedette patrolling the escarpment had noticed an unnatural light flickering from the direction of the Thukela. He had reported it at the fort, and, as Lieutenant Hamilton put it,

> there was great excitement in the afternoon, when it was known that flashing signals were to be seen in the direction of Fort Pearson. The distance is 27 miles in a straight line, so you can imagine it is not easy work to signal in. The flashes were made, we suppose, with a heliograph, which I believe is simply a large looking glass, on which the sun's rays are concentrated, and short and long flashes are made.... After two hours' work we made out the following message: – 'Prepare to receive 1000 men on the 13th'. Next day, flashing went on for 5 or 6 hours, but we could make nothing out of it...

None the less, the message was the first news of the outside world the garrison had received in nineteen days, and the excitement was intense. All the lurking fears that the Zulus had overrun Natal and destroyed the Thukela bases were dissipated, and the garrison had some concrete hope of relief. In fact, however, Hamilton had overestimated the technology at the disposal of the Fort Pearson garrison, for there were no heliographs in southern Africa at that time, and the men on the Thukela had been forced to improvise signalling equipment. Pearson's garrison now found themselves in the same predicament. In the euphoria of that first message, everyone in the garrison who could lay their hands on a mirror or a flat piece of metal or glass had rushed out to the escarpment to try their luck – most of them without the first idea of the principles of signalling or Morse code.

1. King Cetshwayo's 'coronation' on 1 September 1873. A European armchair substitutes for a throne, and the King wears the theatrical crown provided by Theophilus Shepstone, who sits to the right, shaded by an umbrella. To the left of the king stands Major Anthony Durnford RE.

2. *Below, left.* A posed studio photograph purporting to show a young Zulu warrior. Although Natal Africans were often passed off as subjects of the Zulu King, to satisfy the public demand for souvenir images of the war, this man is at least typical of the appearance and weapons of the younger *amabutho* in the field.

3. *Below, right.* Marriage was an important rite of passage within Zulu society, marking the onset of full adult status and a reduction of obligations to the state; it was signified in men by the wearing of a head ring known as *isicoco*.

4. Confrontation: James Lloyd's photograph of John Wesley Shepstone reading Frere's ultimatum to King Cetshwayo's envoys at the Lower Thukela Drift on 11 December 1878.

5. Imperial muscle: a naval contingent from HMS *Active*, lined up to overawe the Zulu envoys at the presentation of the ultimatum. Note the Gatling gun prominently displayed on the right.

6. *Above, left.* Lieutenant-General Lord Chelmsford, the senior British commander in Zululand in 1879.

7. *Above, right.* King Cetshwayo kaMpande. Carefully composed to suggest that it was taken in Zululand, this picture was, like most photographs of the King, actually taken in Cape Town during his exile.

8. *Below, left.* Colonel Henry Evelyn Wood VC. Experienced in colonial warfare, Wood commanded Chelmsford's Left Flank Column, and was one of the few British commanders to emerge from the war with his reputation enhanced.

9. *Below, right.* General Sir Garnet Wolseley, who was sent to southern Africa to supersede Lord Chelmsford. He arrived too late to command at Ulundi in July, but supervised the highly destructive post-war settlement of Zululand.

10. A detachment of the 2nd Battalion, 1st Regiment Natal Native Contingent, photographed at Fort Bengough. The only thing that distinguishes these men as being in British service is a red headband.

11. An unidentified battalion of the Natal Native Contingent, drawn up with their white officers seated in front.

12. Officers of HMS *Active*, photographed at the Lower Thukela before the start of the invasion. Midshipman Lewis Coker – lying left – commanded the Gatling at the Battle of Nyezane, and later died at Eshowe.

13. Invasion: a company of the 99th Regiment attached to Pearson's column crosses into Zululand by pont at the Lower Thukela Drift on 12 January 1879.

14. Pearson's first camp in Zululand, photographed from the Natal bank of the Thukela on 14 January 1879.

15. The Mzinyathi river at Rorke's Drift, where the Centre Column crossed into Zululand on 11 January. The pont was moored in a deep pool upstream to the left; Rorke's original crossing was downstream to the right. The skirmish with Chief Sihayo's followers took place among the hills to the left, while the ominous peak of Isandlwana is clearly visible on the horizon.

16. A pencil sketch by Lieutenant William Fairlie of Isandlwana hill, 'from the Zulu side'. The camp was placed along the foot of the hill and the battle raged across this open slope; note the dongas that featured prominently in the fighting.

18. The Isandlwana battlefield, photographed during the burial expeditions of June 1879. Many of the more serviceable wagons had been removed during the expedition of 21 May, but those left behind remained a feature of the site.

18. Isandlwana, June 1879. One of the burial detail, a trooper of the King's Dragoon Guards, stands with a spade at the head of a patch of disturbed ground where he has presumably interred human remains.

19. The grave of Lieutenants Melvill and Coghill of the 1/24th, who died attempting to save the Queen's Colour of their battalion at Isandlwana, and were later posthumously awarded the Victoria Cross.

It fell to the Engineers to provide a solution. The indefatigable Captain Wynne, who had designed the fort's defences – and by working long hours in all weathers had undermined his health in the process – now applied himself to making means of reply. His first attempt involved a large paper balloon, which he hoped to inflate with hot air and, on a day when the wind was blowing towards the Thukela, set it free with a message attached. This he duly did; but at the last minute the wind changed direction and the balloon was lost. Next, Wynne tried to fix a large black tarpaulin on to a wooden frame to make a screen, attached to a horizontal pivot. He hoped that by swinging the screen up and down for long or short 'flashes' he would be able to send a message by Morse. After several days' labour, he raised the screen – only to see it blown down by a sudden squall and smashed.

In the event, it was another of Pearson's staff officers, Captain Macgregor, who solved the problem. A search of the officers' baggage had turned up a shaving mirror, which proved large enough to reflect the light properly. To direct it, Macgregor used a length of old gas pipe which was found in the mission church. A signal post was established on the edge of the escarpment, and a support for the apparatus improvised from sacks and boxes. It was crucial that the pipe was aligned correctly so that the sun's rays were directed down the entire length of the pipe, and to this end one unfortunate Volunteer had to look down the pipe until the reflected flash shone straight in his eye! It seemed that the risk of blinding would be an inevitable part of the process, until someone suggested that by fixing paper at both ends of the pipe, the operators could clearly see if both ends were illuminated. Once the beam was concentrated in the right direction, the signallers could spell out a message by obscuring the mirror with a board fixed to the operator's hand. Throughout the remainder of the siege, this apparatus proved cumbersome and slow, but it worked; and from that day onwards the garrison had a means of contacting the outside world.

Yet the optimism generated by those first messages dissipated when it became clear that the Thukela garrison was not yet ready to march and that the Zulus were, in any case, aware of their intentions. Large parties of warriors could be seen in the distance, making their way through the hills to concentrate between Eshowe and the border; when no advance was attempted, they could be seen a few days later marching back to their camps. The delay was frustrating for the garrison, among

whom disease had now firmly taken hold. Among those who succumbed
was one of the heroes of Nyezane, as Lieutenant Hamilton wrote on the
21st:

We are not off yet. All was ready to go on the 13th. What little
we were going to take was packed on the pack oxen, when a signal
was made: 'Relief postponed, 4,000 whites and 2,000 natives leave
on April 1st.' Later on they made 'Be ready to leave with the whole
of the garrison and waggons; 60th Rifles to replace you.' So here
we are still waiting. Sickness has increased very much, I am sorry
to say; we have lost poor Coker, midm., who died of dysentery on
Sunday last. Poor fellow! We miss him greatly; he was a general
favourite of everybody. He had been ill for a long time, but we all
hoped he was getting over the attack, but there was a sudden change
on Sunday morning, and he never rallied. The fact is, the doctors
have no medicine left. It is a very trying time for them, as they can
do very little good. The church here is used as a hospital, and makes
a very fair one. Including Coker, we have had four deaths in our
force since we entered the fort. Altogether, 23 have died, which I
suppose is a large proportion, out of 1,200 men in 9 weeks. The Buffs
have lost one officer, Captain Williams, and have another very ill.
The days slip by quickly enough; always something going on. One
day it is cattle guard, another road making, and so on. The guard
for cattle consists in taking out a party of men when the cattle
are feeding, and posting sentries all round on the lookout for the
wily Zulu coming up to seize the animals. Well, when one is out for
5 hours watching for these gentlemen, and they don't come, it is a
trifle wearisome; however, it is a great thing to be able to go out,
which is more than a good many people are. On Tuesday last, two
Zulu messengers arrived from the king's kraal, with a message from
his Majesty, requesting us 'to go away'. The King also says 'he does
not know what the fighting is all about, but that if we will leave this,
and not do any mischief in the way of burning huts, etc., he will give
his chiefs orders not to attack us'. He is very kind, but I am afraid
matters have gone too far, and we want some satisfaction for the loss
of the 24th. Colonel Pearson did not believe they were from the
King at all, and made prisoners of them for being spies, which they
probably were. They tell us we are surrounded by 3 armies, numbering in all, 35,000 men. If so, the force coming up will have a fight . . .

Over the last two weeks of March, while the garrison waited anxiously for some sign of activity from the Thukela, the bad weather continued, and deaths from disease averaged one every two days. The road party continued to build its short-cut, hoping to reduce the time the relief garrison would take to ascend the Eshowe heights. A sudden message from Lord Chelmsford himself on the 29th injected a sense of urgency: 'Come down with 500 fighting men when I am engaged. Four thousand men will leave Tugela today or tomorrow, and arrive at Eshowe on 3 April. Expect to be hotly opposed.'

Reluctantly, Pearson replied that he could not comply. Sickness and shortage of food had so affected the garrison that he felt he would not have sufficient fit men to hold the fort while he was away. Chelmsford would have to take his chances on his own.

On 1 April, all those who found an excuse to do so left the fort to look out from the escarpment across the undulating green countryside towards the border. To their intense delight, they spotted parties of British horsemen on the road, ten miles below Eshowe. By late afternoon, those with good telescopes or field-glasses could see Chelmsford's column itself, preparing to laager for the night on a grassy rise on the far side of the Nyezane.

Early the next morning, 2 April 1879, as the mist lifted from the Nyezane valley, they heard the distant thud of artillery firing in earnest.

Chapter Three

'They died in one place . . .'

The war had begun well enough for the Centre Column. The crossing point at Rorke's Drift had proved easy to negotiate, despite the depth of the water, and by the evening of 11 January 1879 Chelmsford had moved most of his combat troops across the border, although it would be several days before his transport wagons could follow. There had been no sign of the enemy; the only Zulu the column encountered was a solitary and rather astonished herdsman whose charges were promptly appropriated by the Mounted Volunteers.

Chelmsford established a new camp on the Zulu side of the river, leaving a company of the 2/24th to guard the supply depot which had been established at the mission station close by on the Natal bank. Although the column was nominally under the command of Richard Glyn of the 24th, Chelmsford's decision to accompany this column in person had effectively robbed Glyn of much of his authority, and it was Chelmsford's command decisions which shaped the column's movements. Chelmsford's own standing orders specified that permanent camps were to be partially entrenched or protected by wagon-laagers, but he did not intend to remain long on the border, and made no effort to secure either the post at Rorke's Drift or the sprawling camp which had sprung up on the Zulu bank of the Mzinyathi. With the war only a few days old, he clearly had no great fear of a Zulu attack.

Ahead of him, the road pioneered by the hunter and trader Jim Rorke – who had given his name to the crossing – passed through several miles of undulating, rocky terrain before descending into the valley of the Batshe stream. The Batshe ran no more than a few inches deep for most of the year, but like every other river in Zululand the recent rains had made it more formidable, and the banks were strewn with the large boulders that had earned it its Zulu name. While the hills on the near side of the Batshe consisted of nothing more than low, open ridges, the ground rose up steeply to the wall of cliffs which framed the Ngedla hills beyond.

The Batshe was the first physical and military obstacle on Chelmsford's line of advance. It was the territory of the Qungebe people, whose chief, Sihayo kaXongo, maintained an impressive homestead – kwaSoxhege, 'the maze' – nestling in the folds at the foot of the cliffs at the northern end of the valley. Sihayo's sons had been mentioned in the British ultimatum for their participation in the border raid of the previous June, and Chelmsford was determined to demonstrate his serious intentions by taking punitive action against them. Moreover, once he had moved forward, the Batshe would lie across his line of communication, and he could not in any case allow Sihayo's followers to pose a threat to his rear, especially as kwaSoxhege was widely rumoured to be both fortified and occupied by a large number of warriors.

No sooner was Chelmsford across the border, therefore, than he decided to make a foray into the Batshe. It was timed for dawn on the 12th, much to the delight of Lieutenant Coghill, who accompanied the expedition as Colonel Glyn's orderly officer,

> a party consisting of the 1/24th and 2/3 N.N.C. were to start at 5 and the 2/24th and 1/3 N.N.C. to leave at 8 by another route and join the first party at a certain point. This arrangement was however changed as in approaching within a mile or so of the Krantz* near Sirayo's Kraal we heard the lowing of cattle and the Zulus chanting their war song and as it was evident that resistance would be made I was sent back to bring up the 2/24th and the 2/3rd N.N.C. When I returned from the performance of this duty I found that the only response to our demand that they should give up their arms was a volley which necessitated coercion to carry out our request. The first volley delivered by the enemy had the effect of wounding several of the N.N.C. who were rather in advance and of producing a momentary check, but the 1/24th coming up they followed them and the Krantz was taken the Zulus expelled from their caves with a loss which is difficult to estimate, but somewhere between 12 and 15 killed and in the meantime the mounted men had moved round to the flat ground above the Krantz and there met 40 or 50 of the enemy. A

* Cliff face.

sharp exchange of fire took place resulting in the rout of the Zulus leaving 18 dead bodies on the ground. While this was going on the 2/24th and 2/3rd N.N.C. were being moved round to attack the Kraal itself which was reported to be strongly fortified and loopholed. The position was strong had it not been that it was completely commanded from a cliff above under whose shelter Sihayo had in the innocence of his heart erected an impregnable fortress. Its strength and the metal of its defenders were not to be tested for on arriving at the Kraal it was found to be deserted and we were informed by some old women who still remained that they had only left the previous day. The Kraal was burnt and we returned home with the cattle we had captured in a thunderstorm accompanied by torrents of rain. Our loss was 2 Native Contingent privates killed, 18 wounded, 2 N.C. Officers N.N.C. wounded.

Chelmsford himself was delighted with the result of his first action of the war, and wrote to Frere,

> The British soldiers and natives skirmished or rather clambered up the steep mountainside and entered all the caves which were found empty – I ordered Sihayo's Kraal to be burnt but none of the other huts were touched – The Native Contingent behaved very well & not a native touched a woman or child or killed a wounded man – Lt. Colonel Russell was sent along the Isipezi Hill road with order to get onto the high ground above the kraantz. As he was nearly at the top about 60 of the enemy came down & fired at his men at a distance of about 100 yards fortunately without hitting anyone – His men dismounted and managed to kill 9 or 10 of the enemy amongst whom was one of Sihayo's sons, distinctly recognized – I have not yet received a correct list of the enemy's losses but I fancy it will be about 30. . . . I am in great hopes that the storming of Sihayo's stronghold and the capture of many of his cattle (about 500) many have a salutary effect in Zululand & either bring down a large force to attack us or else produce a revolution in the country – Sihayo's men have I am told always been looked upon as the bravest in the country, and certainly those who were killed today fought with great courage. I have visited two wounded Zulus who are in our hospital & have seen that they are well looked-after – Directly they are well enough I shall let them go, so that they may tell their friends how the British make war –

Yet the air of self-satisfaction which settled over the expeditionary force as it returned to the camp at Rorke's Drift that afternoon served to obscure the reality of the exchange. The British had noted with some disappointment that Sihayo had made little serious attempt to defend his property, yet they do not seem to have drawn any ominous conclusions from the fact. In reality, neither Sihayo nor his senior son Mehlokazulu had been present at the action; they were at oNdini, attending the King's general muster. Sihayo had left another son, Mkhumbikazulu, and just two or three hundred of his followers to defend their homes and cattle. The skirmish had been one-sided from the start, but even so the Zulus had resolutely held their ground before being overcome, and Mkhumbikazulu was among the dead. So far from reassessing the capabilities of the Zulu in the light of the action, Chelmsford and his staff merely noted the ease with which their own men had defeated a courageous enemy. As a result, Chelmsford did nothing to address a sense of complacency which pervaded the column, and which deepened after the skirmish. This was to have terrible consequences when the repercussions Chelmsford had wished for were indeed visited upon him.

There was little hope of following up the first brush with the enemy by a further advance. The weather and its impact upon the transport system had hampered Chelmsford as much as it had Pearson on the coast, and the day following the attack on Sihayo's homestead, Chelmsford wrote to Evelyn Wood:

> I see no chance of our advancing for 7 days – Road near camp over a swamp must be drained, and supplies must be stored at Rorke's Drift – at present there are scarcely any there –
> The rain latterly all over Natal has been incessant and the roads are reported impassable . . .

That same day, he wrote with uncharacteristic irritability to Commissary-General Strickland:

> I have been across the Buffalo R. today to see how the depot was going. I find that there is absolutely nothing there and this column cannot move until there is a months supply with the column. Mr Dalton is the only representative of the Commissariat Dept. at Rorke's Drift, and for the first time today he has been given a

sergeant of the 24th to assist him. Mr Dalton is too young to take the weight of responsibility which the charge of a column represents, altho I am sure he would do well under another. You must send up one of the new Assist Commissary Genls who are on their way out, at one to Helpmekaar, or we shall have a breakdown. There is no one here like Colonel Wood to keep everyone up to the mark and Helpmekaar appears to me to have been sadly neglected. Look after the interests of this column before you advance with No. 1 Column, & leave PMBurg to be, what it is, merely a forwarding station. This column will advance very shortly, and it will be a sad disgrace to the Commissariat, if it is obliged to halt short of its destination for want of supplies.

While he fretted at the delay, Chelmsford planned the next step of his advance. He was already reconsidering the role he had originally given to the No. 2 Column, under Brevet Colonel Durnford, which was stationed at Middle Drift, between his own command and Pearson. Chelmsford had intended Durnford to guard Pearson's left flank, but on 13 January Durnford, acting on his own initiative on information received from local spies, had taken his column down from their encampment on the hills above the Thukela to the river in anticipation of a rumoured Zulu attack. Chelmsford had been surprised by Durnford's independence, which seemed to threaten the coordination of his overall strategy, and revealing the same sense of frustration he had let slip to Strickland, he wrote tartly to Durnford:

Unless you carry out the instructions I give you, it will be my unpleasant duty to remove you from your command, and to substitute another officer for the command of No. 2 Column. When a column is acting separately in an enemy's country I am quite ready to give its commander every latitude, and would certainly expect him to disobey any orders he might have received from me, if information which he obtained, showed that it would be injurious to the interests of the column under his command – Your neglecting to obey my instructions in the present instance has no excuse. You have simply obtained information in a letter from Bishop Schroeder, which may or may not be true, and which you have no means of verifying – If movements ordered are to be delayed because report hints at a chance of invasion of Natal, it will be impossible for me to carry out

my plan of campaign – I trust you will understand this plain speaking
& not give me any further occasion to write in a style which is
distasteful to me –

As a result of this incident, Chelmsford began to plan instead for
Durnford to work more closely with his own Centre Column. Beyond
the Batshe valley, the road passed through increasingly broken country,
and on the 16th Chelmsford outlined his new thinking in a letter to
Wood:

> Russell made a reconnaissance as far as the Isepezi hill yesterday
> about 22 miles – Road at present quite unfit for convoys to pass –
> Our first move must therefore be to the Isanblana hill where
> there is wood and water – I shall from there clear the Equidini forest
> or receive the submission of the chiefs and Headmen residing in that
> district. Having settled that part I shall move on to ground between
> Isepezi and Umhlabumkosi but nearest to the latter, where there is
> wood . . .
> From Isepezi I should at first work towards the mission station
> close to the little Itala, where I shall hope to establish Durnford's
> column –

This is one of the earliest references in Chelmsford's correspondence
to a name which would haunt the rest of his career – Isandlwana. The
hill itself – it is not large enough to be called a mountain – is clearly
visible from Rorke's Drift, and had caught the eye of the troops even
before they had crossed the border. It lies a few miles beyond the Batshe
valley, its peak rising up immediately to the left of the track, a seeming
pointer to the way ahead. Even without the terrible events which were
to be played out there, Isandlwana seems a brooding and mysterious
place, and from a distance the rocky crag appears to hang just above the
horizon in the haze. An isolated outcrop of the iNyoni ridge, which
frames it to the north, the weathered face of Isandlwana shifts its moods
with the changing light, casting a long shadow across the plain before
it. Literally translated, the name means 'it looks just like a little hut',
a complex allusion among a people obsessed with cattle to the second
stomach of a cow; to the British, who brought to it their own romantic
imagery, it resembled a crouching lion, or the Sphinx of Egypt. There
was an appropriate symbolism in this, too; the regimental badge of the

24th was the Sphinx, a battle honour won fighting Napoleon at the other
end of the African continent nearly eighty years before.

Isandlwana was an obvious objective for the next stage of the advance,
and for the troops camped at Rorke's Drift the delay was tedious and
frustrating. As Coghill noted in his diary,

> The following week was spent getting our stores, etc., etc., down
> to Rorke's Drift and in repairing and making good the roads between
> Helpmakaar and Sanhlwana which was destined to be our next
> encampment. This was very arduous work as the road to the drift
> was bad and beyond hardly deserving of the name passing over soft
> marshy ground where the waggons would inevitably stick. Mounted
> patrols went out every day sometimes capturing cattle, never meeting
> opposition. The general feeling of the natives seems to indicate that
> those in this particular part of the country do not care about fighting
> and wish to 'come in' with their families and cattle . . .

By the 18th, however, the preparations were nearly ready, and Coghill
wrote home optimistically to his family:

> We have done nothing beyond making patrols and capturing
> cattle to the value of £1,500 since last Sunday. Talking of that there
> are a string of curious coincidents. The most expensive action the
> 24th ever was in took place at Chillianwallah what day of the week
> I don't know, on 13 Jany. On 13 Jany last (1878) the 24th were
> engaged at Numaxo* on a Sunday. Nearly all the engagements in the
> old Colony took place on a Sunday. This January 12th, also a Sunday,
> the 24th was engaged, and I should not be surprised if tomorrow
> (Sunday) we should not have an engagement of some sort, for last
> night we received information that as soon as Cetywayo heard that
> we had burnt Sihayo's Kraal that he despatched four regiments to
> wipe out the disgrace. . . . According to tradition the Zulu tactics are
> to attack 'in the horns of the morning', i.e., when the tips of the
> horns of the cattle in the kraals are just discernible from the general
> mass against the sky . . .

Coghill's comments reflect not only the eagerness of the column to
fight a major action, but also a surprisingly good understanding of the
general strategic situation. Chelmsford's wish, made in the euphoric

---

* On the Eastern Cape Frontier.

aftermath of the attack on Sihayo's homestead, had indeed come true. King Cetshwayo had assembled his army at oNdini once it had become clear that the British had crossed the border, and for several days the *amabutho* had undergone the necessary preparatory rituals at the great royal homesteads on the Mahlabathini plain, in the heart of the kingdom. The King and his commanders were resolved not to commit the army until they were sure which column posed the most immediate threat, however, and Chelmsford's action on 12 January naturally attracted their attention. On 17 January, the army left oNdini, and climbed the high uplands beyond the White Mfolozi river. Here it divided, the portion under Chief Godide striking off to the south-east, towards Pearson's column, while the remainder moved slowly westwards towards Rorke's Drift.

The army was perhaps the largest ever assembled during the kingdom's history. It is difficult to be precise about its exact strength because of the Zulu habit of assessing the size of an army according to the number of companies – *amaviyo* – rather than by individuals, and the strength of the companies often varied considerably. Many elements of regiments present in the main army had stayed in the coastal districts to harry Pearson, but if few of the *amabutho* were at full strength, they were joined along the line of march by local elements who had not attended the local muster. There were perhaps 24,000 men altogether, and all the great regiments were present in strength. For the most part, the army consisted of young men in their twenties and thirties, the unmarried warriors of the uVe, iNgobamakhosi, uKhandempemvu, uMbonambi, uNokhenke, iMbube, uDududu and iSangqu regiments. Yet it was a reflection of the crisis facing the nation that the middle-aged, married men attached to the King's oNdini homestead – the iNdluyengwe, uDloko, iNdlondlo and uThulwana – had also been mobilized and had marched with the column. There was a handful of men, too, from even older regiments, some of them veterans of King Dingane's war against the Voortrekkers forty years before. Most of the younger men had laid aside their regimental regalia when marching out, and they wore little beyond their loin coverings and necklaces of charms to ward off evil. Cetshwayo did not lead his army in person, but entrusted command to his leading general, Chief Ntshingwayo kaMahole. A stocky, powerful man in his sixties, Ntshingwayo was a skilled tactician, deeply imbued with the traditions of the Zulu Royal

House, and a natural leader. As co-commander Cetshwayo had appointed Mavumengwana kaNdlela Ntuli, a close personal friend, and, like himself, a member of the uThulwana *ibutho*. Many of the great chiefs of the nation were present with the army, including Zibhebhu kaMaphitha, who would later emerge as the greatest Zulu commander since King Shaka, and several of the King's brothers, the Princes Ndabuko, Dabulamanzi, Sitheku and Magwendu. Morale was high; the warriors were indignant at the British invasion and confident of their ability to defeat the redcoats in open battle.

The rumours of the approach of a Zulu force did not deter Chelmsford from making his forward movement to Isandlwana. The move was scheduled for the 20th, and Chelmsford had already ordered Durnford's column to move on to the Biggarsberg heights, behind Rorke's Drift, to be ready to support his advance. On the 19th, Chelmsford outlined his plans to Durnford, identifying as his next target two chiefs, Matshana kaMondise and Matshana kaSitshakuza, who lived beyond Isandlwana:

> No. 3 column moves tomorrow to Insalwana Hill and from there, as soon as possible to a spot about 10 miles nearer to the Indeni Forest.
>
> From that point I intend to operate against the two Matyanas, if they refuse to surrender.
>
> One is in the stronghold on or near the Mhlazakazi Mountain, the other is in the Indeni Forest. Bengough ought to be ready to cross the Buffalo R. at the Gates of Natal in three days time, and ought to show himself there as soon as possible.
>
> I have sent you an order to cross the river at Rorke's Drift tomorrow with the force you have at Vermaaks.
>
> I shall want you to operate against the Matyanas, but will send you fresh instructions on this subject.
>
> We shall be about 8 miles from Rorke's Drift tomorrow.

The move to Isandlwana, when it at last occurred, proved difficult. Despite the best efforts of the Engineers, the ground remained waterlogged in places, and then shortly before the column reached the mountain, it had to cross a difficult drift across the Manzimnyama river. The band of the 1/24th played the march along, but three times it was interrupted on the road, which some of the men considered a bad omen. Coghill noted in his diary that they started 'at 6 and not getting the last waggons in till late in the evening two or three "sticks" of waggons occurred, but on the whole it may be considered satisfactory'.

The column pitched camp on the forward slope beyond Isandlwana hill, on gentle grassland which faced out on to the open plain beyond. Chelmsford was much criticized later for his choice of campsite, but in fact it was as good as any in the region. There was plenty of water in the Manzimnyama stream behind Isandlwana, and in a network of dongas in front, while patches of bush in the valley behind provided ample firewood. A long, low ridge, known as the iNyoni, rose up less than a mile away and limited visibility on the left, but this could be picketed, and to the front the country was open as far as the Magogo and Silutshana hills, some twelve miles away to the east. On the right, however, to the south, the view was shut a few miles away by a steep rocky hill known as Malakatha, and by a long undulating ridge leading away from it, Hlazakazi.

Chelmsford's immediate concern lay with this difficult country to the south. While the open plain would give him ample warning of any Zulu advance coming directly from oNdini and the east, the wall of Malakatha and Hlazakazi would mask any movement towards the Natal border which might try to slip round his right flank. On the Cape frontier, he had frequently found that the Xhosa had preferred to avoid a direct attack, and despite warnings to the contrary, he remained convinced that the Zulu would do much the same. At the far end of the Hlazakazi range, moreover, the Mangeni river had cut a deep gorge through the hills, and this feature was widely rumoured to be a stronghold for 'the two Matyanas'.

Even as the column arrived at Isandlwana, and the men began to unload their tents and equipment, Chelmsford and his staff rode out along the road to investigate the country beyond Hlazakazi. Chelmsford gave no orders to entrench the camp; the ground was hard and stony, and in any case he did not intend to remain there long. As he wrote to Frere,

At 1 p.m. I started off to reconnoitre what is called the Zulu stronghold which is almost ten or twelve miles from here.

Our road lay over a hard rolling plain, cut up at long intervals by deep watercourses which however will not be difficult to get waggons over. It ran at first almost North, then North-East and finally due

East when we got round the Malakata range (vide Durnford's map). The so-called stronghold is a precipitous valley with krantzes on each side in which there are caves. The river which runs through it tumbles over a precipice at the upper end, and the valley is thus closed on three sides. The fourth opens out into lateral valleys some three miles down and the main valley continues on until it reaches the Buffalo river, close under the Indeni bush.

No sign of Zulus or cattle could be discovered. We mounted up onto the Malakatha range which is fairly level and open, and from the distant spurs we could see a long distance into the main valley. A few kraals were visible and from some we saw a few women running away with bundles on their heads, but otherwise the country was deserted. Some natives say that the inhabitants have gone to the King, others say they are in the Indeni bush ...

Lieutenant Coghill accompanied the party, and in youthful high spirits: 'On the way home we found some fowls at a deserted Kraal and in capturing them I put my knee out which kept me in my tent for some days.' By such threads do personal fortunes hang. Coghill's injury would keep him in camp for the next two days, when his duties might otherwise have taken him elsewhere, with tragic consequences.

As a result of this patrol, at first light on the 21st, Chelmsford

sent two parties of mounted men this morning to explore the country more thoroughly than I was able to do yesterday, and I have sent Lonsdale and his two battalions Native Contingent round the west side of the Malakata range with orders to climb up to the top and make a position with the mounted men. I shall know by evening therefore whether anybody is left in the country ...

This foray consisted of some 150 Mounted Volunteers, under the command of Major Dartnell of the Natal Mounted Police, and almost all of Chelmsford's available auxiliaries. That same day, a small patrol of Mounted Infantry under Lieutenant Edward Browne also scouted due east, towards the Silutshana and Siphezi mountains. Left in camp, Coghill was excited by the news sent back by these patrols:

Browne (1/24th) with 4 mounted men went out towards the Izipezi mountain and on his way home an attempt was made to cut him off by some 30 men on foot and 8 on horseback. Some shots

were exchanged, one of the enemy killed and another badly wounded
and Browne and his men returned safely to camp. A patrol of
mounted volunteers and Police went out under Major Dartnell, Natal
Mounted Police, to the same neighbourhood as visited by the General
the previous day, and saw some 300 men walking off in the direction
of the Koteni bush probably on their way to the King's place, directly
they saw the mounted men they turned back and ensconced themselves in a strong krantz shouting to us to come in. Our party being
weak remained watching them and sent for Lonsdales' Native Contingent who were patrolling the neighbourhood. They all bivouacked
out and sent out to be supported as they had seen a large body of
Zulus on one of the hills in their immediate vicinity.

Dartnell's encounter seemed the more significant. Chelmsford
had intended his patrols to return to Isandlwana before dark, but it had
been dusk when Dartnell's men had encountered Zulus moving near
the Magogo hill, and Dartnell had been reluctant to break contact and
expose his men to the risk of a night attack if they withdrew. According
to Major Clery, Glyn's staff officer, news of this encounter reached
Isandlwana not long after midnight on the 22nd:

About 1.30 a.m. on the 22nd, a messenger brought me a note
from Major Dartnell to say that the enemy was in greater numbers
than when he last reported, and that he did not think it prudent to
attack them unless reinforced by two or three companies of the 24th
Regiment. I took this note to Colonel Glyn, C.B., at once; he ordered
me to take it to the General. The General ordered the 2nd Battalion,
24th Regiment, the Mounted Infantry, and four guns, to be ready
under arms at once to march. This force marched out from the camp
as soon as there was light enough to see the road. The Natal Pioneers
accompanied this column to clear the road. The General first ordered
me to write to Colonel Durnford at Rorke's Drift, to bring his force
to strengthen the camp, but almost immediately afterwards he told
Colonel Crealock that he (Colonel Crealock) was to write to Colonel
Durnford these instructions, and not I. Before leaving the camp I
sent written instructions to Colonel Pulleine, 24th Regiment, to the
following effect: – 'You will be in command during the absence of
Colonel Glyn; draw in (I speak from memory) your camp, or your
line of defence' – I am not certain which – 'while the force is out;
also draw in the line of your infantry outposts accordingly, but keep

your cavalry vedettes still far advanced.' I told him to have a waggon
loaded with ammunition ready to follow the force going out at a
moment's notice, if required. I went to Colonel Pulleine's tent just
before leaving camp to ascertain that he had got these instructions,
and I again repeated them verbally to him.

In fact, the exact wording of this order would be the subject of bitter
dispute later, but at the time the British attention was entirely focused
on the events in front. Nevill Coghill's injured knee prevented him
from accompanying Glyn as his orderly, but a note he scribbled to Clery
in those dark hours before dawn suggests that he was fully involved in
organizing the column's departure:

Dear Major,
    Bloomfield QrMaster came to me just now with his finger in his
mouth saying the light spring waggon would not hold the 2,000
rations so I have requisitioned a larger one from the M.I. There was
no escort so I sent down to the 1/24th to know if they could provide
one. I was waiting for an answer when Pugh came and told me you
had sent an order to the same effect.
    I do not think any waggon can cross the last donga near the
Kraal. Perhaps waggon and escort could take advantage of the store
cattle Kraal, pulling down the huts and wait till the N.N.C. come for
their rations.
    Yours,
        Nevill J. A. Coghill

It was probably the last note Coghill ever wrote.
    Chelmsford was later severely criticized for dividing his force in
enemy territory, but in fact his options were limited. The Zulu had
behaved exactly as he had anticipated, and Dartnell's report suggested
that they were about to slip into the difficult country beyond Hlazakazi.
He could not afford to ignore a hostile force so close to the camp, nor
could he realistically afford to wait until daylight, and the cumbersome
process of breaking camp, before advancing with the column to confront
it. With his experience on the Cape Frontier no doubt in mind, he took
with him a force he considered large enough to bring the enemy to
battle and defeat them. Despite the darkness and a number of dongas
which lay across their path, Chelmsford's men accomplished the march

across the plain in good time and reached the far end of Hlazakazi shortly after dawn on the 22nd.

Here a disappointment awaited them: Dartnell's command, perched nervously on the ridge above the Mangeni gorge, reported that the Zulus had disappeared. There was no sign of the large concentration they had seen the night before, although small groups could be seen retiring through the Magogo and Silutshana hills opposite. Chelmsford ordered the 24th and NNC to fan out and sweep through the hills in an attempt to find out exactly where they had gone.

At Isandlwana, meanwhile, the camp awoke to the day's business. There was a general feeling of disappointment among the men left behind that they had missed out on the chance of action. The atmosphere was relaxed and confident, since no one in the column believed the camp to be at risk. This fact was reflected in Chelmsford's choice of commander. Lieutenant Colonel Henry Pulleine, 1/24th, was an experienced officer who had served through the Cape Frontier campaign, but whose expertise lay as an efficient administrator rather than a front-line commander. Several times during the last war he had been commended for keeping columns moving and well supplied despite the overloaded commissariat system, and Lord Chelmsford, preoccupied with the prospect of a fight at Hlazakazi, had clearly wanted to leave the camp in reliable hands.

According to Captain Edward Essex, the column's transport officer, the first indication that there was a Zulu presence closer to Isandlwana than Hlazakazi occurred several hours after reveille:

> After the departure of the main body of the column nothing unusual occurred in camp until about 8 a.m., when a report arrived from a picquet stationed on a point about 1,500 yards distant, on a hill to the north of the camp, that a body of the enemy's troops could be seen approaching from the north-east. Lieutenant-Colonel Pulleine, 1st Battalion 24th Regiment, commanding in camp, thereupon caused the whole of the troops available to assemble near the eastern side of the camp, facing towards the reported direction of the enemy's approach. He also dispatched a mounted man with a report to the column, presumed to be about 12 or 15 miles distant. Shortly after 9 a.m. a small body of the enemy showed itself just over the crest of the hills, in the direction they were expected, but retired a few minutes afterwards, and disappeared. Soon afterwards,

information arrived from a picquet before alluded to that the enemy
was in three columns, two of which were retiring but still in view;
the third column had disappeared in a north-westerly direction.

At about 10 a.m. a party of 250 mounted natives, followed by a
rocket battery, arrived with Lieutenant-Colonel Durnford, R.E., who
now assumed command of the camp . . .

Durnford's arrival highlighted a question of protocol which Chelmsford's orders had failed to address. Durnford was undoubtedly senior
to Pulleine, and ought by rights to have taken command at Isandlwana.
Yet Durnford was the commander of an independent column, and
the orders despatched to him early that morning had not only failed to
specify his role with regard to the camp, but had implied that Chelmsford required Durnford's support in his action against 'the two
Matyanas'. Durnford had arrived at Isandlwana expecting to find fresh
orders, but was disappointed. While Chelmsford might have expected
him to remain at the camp to await developments, the appearance of the
Zulu on the iNyoni ridge to the left of the camp had clearly changed the
situation. Pulleine, under strict orders to defend the camp, was clearly
limited in the response he could make, but most of Durnford's troops
were mounted, and he was in a position to investigate the Zulu
movements without weakening the camp's defensive capability. Under
the circumstances, Durnford had sufficient grounds not to consider
himself bound by the orders Chelmsford had issued to Pulleine.

That, at least, was how he chose to interpret the situation in which
he found himself. Durnford was a complex man who had spent a good
deal of time in Natal. In 1873, tension between the colonial authorities and a chief named Langalibalele kaMthimkhulu, who lived in the
Kahlamba foothills, had caused Langalibalele and his followers to flee
across the mountains, in the hope of taking refuge among the BaSotho.
Durnford had been despatched at the head of a party of Volunteer
troops to quite literally cut them off at the pass. The action that followed
had been disastrous; several of the Volunteers had been killed, and
Durnford had been so badly wounded in the left arm that he lost the
use of his left hand, which afterwards he was obliged to wear thrust into
the front of his tunic. Moreover, Langalibalele had escaped, and in the
ensuing wrangle Durnford had found both his courage and his judgement ridiculed in the Natal press. He had borne himself well under the

ordeal, but he had carried his sense of frustration and injustice into the Zulu campaign. Still smarting from Chelmsford's rebuke the week before, he was determined to prove himself resourceful and dynamic in Chelmsford's eyes.

Durnford's transport officer, Captain Cochrane, recalled the conversation which then took place:

> On arrival [Durnford] took over command from Colonel Pulleine, 24th Regiment. Colonel Pulleine gave over to Colonel Durnford a verbal state of troops in camp at the time, and stated the orders he had received, viz., to defend the camp; these words were repeated two or three times during the conversation. Several messages were delivered, the last one to the effect that the Zulus were retiring in all directions – the bearer of this was not dressed in any uniform. On this message Colonel Durnford sent two troops of mounted natives to the top of the hills to the left, and took with him two troops [and the] rocket battery, with escort of one company Native Contingent, to the front of the camp about four or five miles off. Before leaving, he asked Colonel Pulleine to give him two companies of the 24th Regiment. Colonel Pulleine said that with the orders he had received he could not do it, but agreed with Colonel Durnford to send him help if he got into difficulties.

Durnford's plan was that two troops of his horsemen should sweep across the top of the iNyoni range, while he took the remainder of his column along the foot. Both groups would reunite at the far eastern end of the range, having caught any Zulu between them. This movement would also prevent any Zulu on the heights from cutting between Isandlwana and Chelmsford's command.

Durnford left the camp at about 10.30 a.m., and, according to Captain Essex,

> a company of the 1st Battalion 24th Regiment, under command of Lieutenant Cavaye, was directed to take up a position as a picquet on the hill to the north of the camp at about 1,200 yards distant; the remainder of the troops were ordered to march to their private parades, when the men were to be down in readiness; at this time, about 11 a.m., the impression in the camp was that the enemy had no intention of advancing during the day-time, but might possibly

be expected to attack during the night. No idea had been formed regarding the probable strength of the enemy's force.

Up on the heights, the two troops of Durnford's men, under the command of Lieutenants Raw and Roberts, had spread out and were moving steadily eastwards. There was no sign of the large bodies of Zulu seen a few hours earlier, but small parties of men were scattered across the undulating grasslands, apparently retiring away from the camp. Lieutenant Raw's troop gave chase, and the rather laconic style of his official report cannot entirely obscure the shock of what happened next;

> We left Camp, proceeding over the hills ... the enemy in small clumps retiring before us for some time, drawing us four or five miles from the camp when they turned and fell upon us, the whole army shewing itself from behind the hill in front where they had evidently been waiting ...

Raw's troop had ridden over a rocky ridge and reined in short as an open valley fell away before them. Sitting in the bottom of the valley were over 24,000 men of King Cetshwayo's main army.

In fact, Chelmsford's intelligence regarding the Zulu army's movements had not been entirely wrong. The previous evening, it had bivouacked at Siphezi mountain, due east of Isandlwana beyond the Silutshana and Magogo hills. Then, instead of moving south-west towards the Hlazakazi range, it had moved north-west, through open country, and into the valley of the Ngwebeni stream. The mounted patrol led by Lieutenant Browne, mentioned by Coghill, had almost intercepted this movement, but had been kept away by the aggressive action of the Zulu scouts, led by Chief Zibhebhu. What Dartnell had seen that evening were local elements moving between the Mangeni gorge and the main *impi*, out of sight at Siphezi. Circumstances had contrived to mislead Chelmsford completely about the army's whereabouts. The Zulus had not intended to attack on the 22nd, because the coming night was the night of the new moon, a time when dark spiritual forces were known to interfere with human enterprise. As soon as Raw's men appeared on the heights above them, however, every warrior who saw them knew in an instant that there could be no more waiting.

According to a warrior of the uNokhenke regiment, the impact on the uKhandempemvu (also known as the uMcijo) regiment was electric:

> a small herd of cattle came past our line from our right, being driven down by some of our scouts, and just as they were opposite the Umcityu Regiment, a body of mounted men on the hill to the west evidently trying to cut them off. When several hundred yards off they perceived the Umcityu, and, dismounting, fired one volley at them, and then retired. The Umcityu at once jumped up and charged, an example which was taken up by the Nokenke and Nodwengu on the right, and the Nkobamakosi and Mbonambi on the left . . .

According to Raw,

> The enemy had already opened fire upon us, we then opened fire upon them, and retired skirmishing on to the camp. Before this, my troop had been joined by Roberts with a Company of Lonsdale's footmen – Lonsdale's men at the sight of the enemy at once ran back towards the camp leaving their Officers with us . . .

The army spilled out of the valley in some confusion, the *amabutho* mixed up together. There had been no time to undertake the last-minute pre-battle rituals, or for the commanders to address their men, and it says much for the determination of the regimental officers that they managed to impose some order on their troops in the time that it took them to cover the five miles to the camp. Indeed, for all their insistence that they had no intention of attacking the camp that day, the Zulu generals would have been well aware of the position at Isandlwana, and had probably already discussed options for an assault. The right 'horn', closest to Isandlwana, rushed towards the escarpment, while the 'chest' shook itself into shape on their left. The left 'horn', camped further away from the incursion, moved out to descend the heights further to the east. Only the senior men attached to the oNdini homestead, camped at the far end of the valley, were not sucked into the attack, and were held back by Ntshingwayo to form a reserve.

Durnford's staff officer, George Shepstone – son of Theophilus – had accompanied Raw, and leaving the mounted men to their fighting retreat, rode back to Isandlwana to warn the camp. On his arrival, he met Captain Alan Gardner, who had just returned from Hlazakazi with a

message from Lord Chelmsford ordering Pulleine to break up the camp.
According to Gardner, Shepstone had

> a message from Colonel Durnford that his men were falling back,
> and asking for reinforcements. We both went to Colonel Pulleine, to
> whom I delivered the order. Colonel Pulleine at first hesitated about
> carrying out the order, and eventually decided that the enemy being
> already on the hill on our left in large numbers, it was impossible to
> do so.
>
> The men of the 24th Regiment were fallen in, and the artillery
> also ...

Pulleine's actions in those first few minutes were crucial to the
eventual outcome of the battle. Like most of the officers under his
command, it is clear that at that stage he did not appreciate the full
extent of the Zulu threat, and rather than deploying his men in a secure
defensive screen from the start, he was apparently motivated by the need
to support Durnford's scattered units. Rather than recall Lieutenant
Cavaye's company, which had been sent up into the hills when Durnford
left and was now out of sight beyond the skyline, he sent a second
company to support it. Captain Essex, the Transport Officer, decided to
see for himself what was going on;

> At about 12 o'clock, hearing firing on the hill where the company
> of the 1st Battalion 24th Regiment was stationed, I proceeded in that
> direction. On my way I passed a company of the 1st Battalion 24th
> Regiment under command of Captain Mostyn, who requested me,
> being mounted, to direct Lieutenant Cavaye to take special care not
> to endanger the right of his company, and to inform that officer
> that he himself was moving up to the left. I also noticed a body
> of Lieutenant-Colonel Durnford's Mounted Natives retiring down
> the hill, but did not see the enemy. On arriving at the far side of the
> crest of the hill, I found the company in charge of Lieutenant Cavaye,
> a section being detached about 500 yards to the left, in charge of
> Lieutenant Dyson. The whole were in extended order engaging the
> enemy, who was moving in similar formation towards our left,
> keeping about 800 yards from our line.
>
> Captain Mostyn moved his company into the space between the
> portions of that already on the hill, and his men then extended and
> entered into action. This line was then prolonged on our right along

the crest of the hill by a body of native infantry. I observed that the enemy made little progress as regards his advance, but appeared to be moving at a rapid pace towards our left. The right extremity of the enemy's line was very thin, but increased in depth towards and beyond our right as far as I could see, a hill interfering with extended view.

From his position at the foot of Isandlwana, Pulleine could still see nothing of the developing attack, but ordered the two guns of N5 Battery to take up a position a few hundred yards to the left front of the camp, supported by two companies of the 24th. This position offered commanding views of the escarpment facing them, and of the hollows and dongas which drained off the foot of the ridge.

Durnford, meanwhile, had advanced about five miles from the camp, following the foot of the heights. His mounted troops were well to the fore, and his rocket battery – carried on mules and escorted by a company of the NNC on foot – had fallen behind. The spurs of the iNyoni escarpment hid both the rocket battery from Durnford, and Durnford himself from the camp. He had scarcely noted the sound of distant firing when a messenger arrived from the heights to warn him of the Zulu approach. The news irritated him, and for a minute or two he refused to believe it, until a long column of warriors – the left 'horn' – suddenly came into view, heading directly towards him just a few hundred yards away. Durnford immediately deployed his men into line, ordered them to dismount and fire a volley, and then began to retire steadily towards the camp.

In the meantime, the Zulu had scored their first success of the battle. Major Russell, in charge of the rocket battery, had also heard the sound of shooting, and had led his men up the escarpment on his left. He was perhaps half-way up the slope when a line of skirmishers, screening the advance of the iNgobamakhosi regiment, suddenly appeared on the skyline above him. What happened next was described by Captain Nourse, in charge of Russell's NNC escort:

> Before nearly reaching the crest of the hills on the left of the camp, we were attacked on all sides. One rocket was sent off, and the enemy was on us; the first volley dispersed the mules and the natives, and we retired onto the camp as well as we could.

In fact, Nourse rallied a handful of his men to make a courageous stand to allow the survivors of Russell's crew to escape. The Zulus, who were clearly waiting for the main body to support them, did not press their attack, and Nourse's men were eventually met by Durnford in his retreat.

By this time the Zulu 'chest' was beginning to appear along the length of the iNyoni ridge, to the right of Mostyn and Cavaye, who were then in danger of being outflanked, and Pulleine was sent to recall them. According to Essex,

> I was informed by Lieutenant Melville, Adjutant 1st Battalion 24th Regiment, that a fresh body of the enemy was appearing in force in our rear, and he requested me to direct the left of the line formed . . . to fall slowly back, keeping up the fire. This I did; then proceeded towards the centre of the line. I found, however, that it had already retired. I therefore followed in the same direction, but being mounted had great difficulty in descending the hill, the ground being very rocky and precipitous. On arriving at the foot of the slope I found the two companies of 1st Battalion 24th Regiment drawn up about 400 yards distant in extended order, and Captain Younghusband's company in similar formation in echelon on the left. The enemy was descending the hill, having rushed forward as soon as our men disappeared below the crest, and beyond the right of the line with which I was present had even arrived near the foot of the hill. The enemy's fire had hitherto been very wild and ineffective, now, however, a few casualties began to appear in our line . . .

Raw and Roberts's troops had lingered on the escarpment near Mostyn and Cavaye, but with the British withdrawal they too fell back, together with the last NNC elements on the heights; Raw's *induna*, Nyanda, recalled that there was some confusion as they descended the slope, and 'we retreated to the bottom of the hill, mixed up with the company of red-coats that had advanced with us'.

Pulleine's command was now formed up in a line facing the foot of the ridge, separated from it by a few hundred yards of hollows, scarred by dongas which carried water off the heights in summer. Once the Zulus had descended from the hills and moved to occupy the dongas in large numbers, their assault began to bog down. The gulleys afforded them some shelter from the fire of the 24th, sweeping across them, but

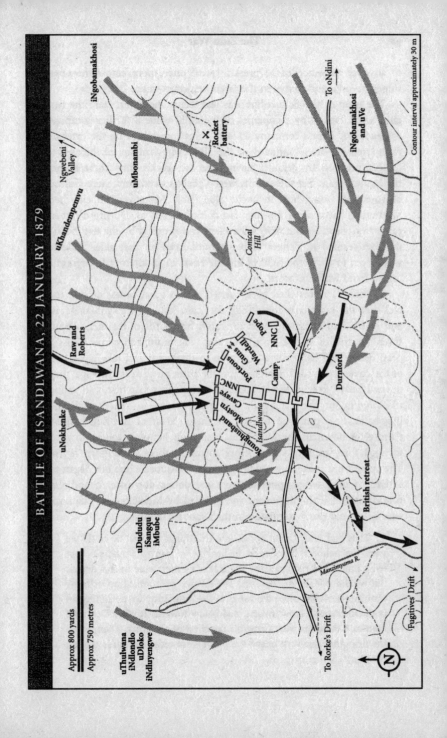

BATTLE OF ISANDLWANA, 22 JANUARY 1879

Contour interval approximately 30 m

iNgobamakhosi

To oNdini

iNgobamakhosi and uVe

Ngwebeni Valley

uMbonambi

Rocket battery

uKhandempemvu

Conical Hill

Raw and Roberts

Pope

NNC

uNokhenke

Wardell

Guns

Porteous

Durnford

Camp

Cavaye

NNC

Mostyn

Isandlwana

youngHusband

uDudu
iSangqu
iMbube

British retreat

Manzinyama R.

To Rorke's Drift

'Fugitives' Drift'

uThulwana
iNdlondlo
uDloko
iNdluyengwe

Approx 800 yards

Approx 750 metres

N

to advance they needed to press forward once more across the open slopes beyond, and that even they were reluctant to do.

The right of the British line was less secure, however. Here the two guns were flanked by companies of the 24th, while a further company – Lieutenant Pope's company, 2/24th – was somewhere on the extreme right. Nearby was a company of the NNC who had found themselves in that position by default, having been on picket duty there before the battle began. Yet these units were widely spaced, and there was no obvious point on which to anchor the flank. Moreover, Pulleine had begun the battle with his line facing north, but as Durnford's men came into view, far out across the plain and pursued by the left 'horn', the line seemed in danger of being outflanked on that side. Pulleine was forced to curve the right of his line back, in an attempt to present a united front with Durnford.

Durnford's retreat had been carried out in good order, despite the fact that the regiments composing the Zulu left – the iNgobamakhosi and uVe – had at times closed to within fifty yards of his men. About three-quarters of a mile from the camp, Durnford had come across a deep donga and had ordered his men to dismount and take advantage of the cover it afforded. Nestling into the bank on the eastern edge, they opened heavy fire on the warriors pursuing them. At first, the young uVe *ibutho*, in the vanguard, had been forced-to retire, until the iNgobamakhosi came up to support them. Most of the Zulus threw themselves down in the long grass, rising up between volleys to rush forward forty or fifty yards before throwing themselves down again. They could not make any headway against Durnford's line but began to extend to their left, hoping to cross the donga downstream and slip round his left. This movement was recalled by Mehlokazulu kaSihayo, who held a company command in the iNgobamakhosi:

> They had drawn their horses into this donga, and all we could see were the helmets. They fired so heavily we had to retire; we kept lying down and rising again. The Edendale men were in this donga, but we did not see the Basutos. The former were mixed up with the Carbineers. At this time the wings of the Zulu army were running on both sides above Isandwhlana, and below towards Rorke's Drift; the men in this donga were firing on the chest of the army. Then, when the firing became very heavy – too hot – we retired towards the left wing . . .

Nor was Durnford's left secure. Here, the uMbonambi, on the left of the 'chest', had occupied the hollows above Durnford's men, and the more courageous elements were already trying to slip between them and the nearest of Pulleine's companies, several hundred yards away.

With the Zulu attack fully developed, the British position was now dangerously overextended. What happened next has often been attributed to ammunition failure among the 24th's companies, but while Durnford's men – on both sides of the field – were undoubtedly running short, the evidence of survivors, supported by recent archaeological work on the site, suggests that this was not the case with the infantry. There was no regulated system of ammunition resupply in 1879, it being considered the duty of bandsmen and unemployed camp personnel to carry rounds to the line. Captain Essex was emphatic that this procedure worked perfectly well at Isandlwana:

> The companies 1st Battalion 24th Regiment first engaged were now becoming short of ammunition, and at the request of the officer in charge I went to procure a fresh supply, with the assistance of Quartermaster 2nd Battalion 24th Regiment and some men of the Royal Artillery. I had some boxes placed on a mule cart and sent it off to the companies engaged, and sent more by hand, employing any men without arms. I then went back to the line, telling the men that plenty of ammunition was coming.

But if the 24th's line remained secure, Durnford's position on the right had become untenable. From the camp Captain Gardner saw Durnford's men cease firing, mount up, and retire towards the camp. This was clearly a critical movement, and Gardner rode out to investigate:

> And, in reply to my question as to why they were retiring, was told that they were ordered by Colonel Durnford to retire, as the position taken up was too extended. This same remark was made to me by Colonel Durnford himself immediately afterwards.

Durnford's withdrawal exposed the flank of the nearest of Pulleine's companies – Pope's 2/24th and the NNC – who had tried to support him. Members of the uMbonambi began to follow Durnford up, some driving cattle before them to mask themselves from the British fire. Essex too saw the danger, and

On looking round to that portion of the field to our right and rear, I saw that the enemy was surrounding us. I rode up to Lieutenant-Colonel Durnford, who was near the right, and pointed this out to him. He requested me to take men to that part of the field and endeavour to hold the enemy in check; but while he was speaking, those men of the Native Contingent who had remained in action rushed past us in the utmost disorder, thus laying open the right and rear of the companies of the 1st Battalion 24th Regiment on the left . . .

Within minutes, the British position collapsed. Durnford was seen to ride into the camp, presumably to confer with Pulleine, and shortly bugles sounded the ceasefire and recall. If Pulleine intended the 24th to take up a more secure position closer to the camp, however, it was too late, for the British dilemma was all too apparent to the Zulu commanders. Ntshingwayo and Mavumengwana had taken up a position on a rocky outcrop on the iNyoni escarpment which had effectively given them the best view on the field of the unfolding battle. Seeing the 'chest' pinned down at the bottom of the slope under fire from Pulleine's line, Ntshingwayo had already sent an *induna* of the uKhandempemvu regiment, Chief Mkhosana kaMvundlana of the Biyela people, to rally them. The warriors were crouching behind the banks of the watercourse, and Mkhosana strode among them, apparently impervious to the bullets striking around them, calling out phrases from King Cetshwayo's praise-poem to encourage them. Stung by this reminder of their honour and duty, they began to press forward up the slopes beyond the donga; as they did so, Mkhosana, one of the great Zulu heroes of the battle, was shot clean through the head and killed.

As the Zulu renewed their advance, the 24th abandoned their positions and began to retire towards the tents, turning to fire every few yards as they did so. Lieutenant Curling of the Artillery described the speed with which events overtook them:

The enemy advancing still, we began firing case, but almost immediately the infantry were ordered to retire. Before we could get away the enemy were by the guns, and I saw one gunner stabbed as he was mounting on the axle-tree box. The limber gunners did not mount, but ran after the guns.

The uMbonambi regiment, on the left of the Zulu centre, rushed forward with such speed, past Pulleine's right flank, that they reached the tents before the 24th. Those auxiliary elements who had so far held their positions in the line now fled in disorder towards the rear. According to Malindi, a member of the NNC,

> Our ammunition failed once but we got more from the camp, and remained firing until the Zulus were within 100 yards of us. We were then ordered to retire as we were also threatened to our rear by the advancing left of the Zulus, and fall back on camp, which we did, crossing the watercourse opposite the camp of the Lt. General. The company of soldiers was with us and on nearing the tents knelt down and commenced firing at the enemy. Below them, some distance to the west, was another company or more of soldiers, also kneeling down and firing. Our Captain now got off his horse and gave it to me, telling me to take it to the ammunition wagons, and, turning back . . . he joined the red soldiers who were firing and I never saw him again. After this I know nothing; the Zulus surrounded us on all sides, and I thought of nothing, save my own escape . . .

Nyanda, who was with Raw's mounted troop towards the British left,

> looked round and saw the guns retreating. We were then chased into the course of the camp – and saw a large number of soldiers being assegaid on the right centre and on their right were the mounted men. Then the Zulus drove in the right wing, and the whole of the force – white and black – foot and horse were mixed up together and being assegaid.

Essex, too, was struck by the speed of the collapse. 'In a moment', he recalled,

> all was disorder, and few of the men of the 1st Battalion 24th Regiment had time to fix bayonets before the enemy was among them using their assegais with fearful effect. I heard officers calling to their men to be steady; but the retreat became in a few seconds general, and in a direction towards the road to Rorke's Drift. Before, however, we gained the neck near the Isandula Hill, the enemy had arrived on that portion of the field also, and the large circle had now closed in on us.

'A rush was then made for the neck', said Nyanda, 'and we were met by the Zulus on the other side, and everyone who could save himself tried to do so.' According to Mehlokazulu,

> When the soldiers retired on the camp, they did so running, and the Zulus were then intermixed with them, and entered the camp at the same time. The two wings then met in the rear of the camp, and those who were in the camp were thus blocked in, and the main body of the Zulu army was engaged in chasing and killing the soldiers. When the Zulus closed in, the English kept up a strong fire towards the Buffalo. They were concentrated near the rear of the camp, and the fire was so heavy as to enable them to make an opening, and thus a great many of the mounted men escaped through this opening. The attention of the Zulus was directed to the killing of men in the rear, and so they did not attend to the closing of this opening, and thus let the mounted men out. There was a mixed medley, of white men, Edendale Kafirs, and others, who managed to get out in the direction of the Buffalo . . .

It was this failure of the Zulu 'horns' to complete the circle behind Isandlwana – the only flaw in an otherwise perfectly executed manoeuvre – that allowed survivors like Curling to escape. 'The gunners were all stabbed going through the camp', he recalled flatly,

> with the exception of one or two. One of the two sergeants was also killed at this time. When we got to the road to Rorke's Drift it was completely blocked up by Zulus. I was with Major Smith at this time, he told me he had been wounded in the arm. We saw Lieutenant Coghill, the A.D.C., and asked him if we could not rally some men and make a stand, but said he did not think it could be done . . .

Indeed, the pressure of the Zulu attack had broken up the 24th companies as they retired through the tents. They tried to regroup on the nek,* but with the Zulus already between them, it was impossible to re-form a line. One group, which had fallen back above the tents, made a stand below the southern end of the mountain, providing a focus of resistance that drew others to it. Younghusband's company, which had been on the left of the line, retreated across the foot of the mountain

---

* Nek is a southern African term denoting a saddle of land connecting two higher hills.

and made a stand on a rocky shoulder which provided a bastion against Zulu attack. But, when their ammunition was expended, there was no hope of replenishing it and nowhere to go, and they charged down off the mountain to join the groups struggling below. 'The resistance was stout where the old Dutch road used to go across,' said Mehlokazulu,

> It took us a long time to drive back the English forces there; they killed us and we killed them, and the fight was kept up for a long time. The British troops became helpless, because they had no ammunition, and the Zulus killed them.

Pulleine himself is thought to have died amongst this group. On the right, a group of Natal Volunteers under Captain Bradstreet and Lieutenant Scott, who had retired from the donga, dismounted and took up a position on foot above the 1/24th's tents, next to the road. Here Durnford, emerging from the camp again, found and joined them. They too held out while their ammunition lasted, according to Mehlokazulu, who was among the Zulus facing them:

> The Carbineers on entering the camp made a strong stand there, and their firing was very heavy. It was a long time before they were overcome – before we finished them. When we did get to them they died in one place all together. They threw down their guns, when their ammunition was done, and then commenced with their pistols, which they used as long as their ammunition lasted; and then they formed a line, shoulder to shoulder, and back to back, and fought with their knives.

Eventually, he said, they were all killed. Months later, Durnford's body was identified among the corpses.

In the closing stages of the battle, as men surged into the camp, the smoke from the heavy firing of both redcoats and Zulu, and the dust thrown up by thousands of milling men and animals, made it almost impossible to see clearly what was going on. There could be no effective command and control on either side, and the battle dissolved into a brutal struggle for survival. Then, with a fine sense of dramatic timing, nature added an apocalyptic touch of her own. The moon passed across the face of the sun in a partial eclipse. Although little more than half the sun was obscured, the eclipse was at its height at 2.29 p.m., just as the last British stands were being overwhelmed, and the eerie light seemed all the more unnatural in the chaos of the camp. 'Things were then getting very mixed and confused,' recalled Mehlokazulu, 'what with the smoke, dust, and intermingling of mounted men, footmen, Zulus, and natives, it was difficult to tell who was mounted and who was not.'

Some of the 24th, still rallying to their officers, tried to retire down the road to Rorke's Drift, fighting as they went. The right 'horn' had already slipped into the valley of the Manzimnyama behind Isandlwana, however, and had blocked the road, forcing them off to their left and into country broken with steep dongas and littered with boulders. 'We crossed the road with the crowd', recalled Curling,

> principally consisting of natives, men left in camp, and civilians, and went down a steep ravine leading towards the river.
>
> The Zulus were in the middle of the crowd, stabbing the men as they ran. When we had gone about 400 yards we came to a deep cut in which the guns stuck. There was, as far as I could see, only one gunner with them at this time, but they were covered with men of different corps clinging to them. The Zulus were in them almost at once, and the drivers pulled off their horses. I then left the guns. Shortly after this I again saw Lieutenant Coghill, who told me Colonel Pulleine had been killed.

It was on the banks of the Manzimnyama that the last men on foot were brought to bay. Here, about sixty men of the 24th under Lieutenant Edgar Anstey were trapped against the steep river bank and overrun.

As the camp fell, the killing reached a peak of savage intensity. For days beforehand the Zulus had endured a collective tension, their emotions heightened by pre-battle rituals and a desire to destroy the invaders, and now it was released in the terrible adrenaline rush of combat. In the awful gloom of the smoke-shrouded camp they struck out, killing anything that moved, fighting men, camp personnel and transport animals alike. Mehlokazulu described the end of the last vestiges of the British formations:

> Some Zulus threw assegais at them, others shot at them; but they did not get close – they avoided the bayonet; for any man who went up to stab a soldier was fixed through the throat or stomach, and at once fell. Occasionally, when a soldier was engaged with a Zulu in front with an assegai, another Zulu killed him from behind. There was a tall man who came out of a waggon and made a stout defence,

holding out for some time, when we thought all the white people
had been driven out of camp. He fired in every direction, and so
quickly as to drive the Zulus some in one way, some in another. At
first some of the Zulus took no notice; but at last he commanded
our attention by the plucky way in which he fought, and because he
had killed so many. He was at last shot.

As the Zulus burst into the camp, it seems that Lieutenant Teignmouth Melvill, the adjutant of the 1/24th, had collected the Queen's
Colour of his battalion from the guard tent, where it was kept. After
the battle, the 24th circulated a story that Melvill was ordered to save
the Colour by Colonel Pulleine, to avoid the disgrace of it falling into
enemy hands, but there is no survivors' evidence to corroborate this. It
is more likely that Melvill intended to use it to rally the battalion, which
was the primary function of Colours on the battlefield in the 1870s.
Such was the speed of the collapse, however, that there was no time to
organize a rally, and instead Melvill rode out of the camp with the cased
Colour across his saddle. Somehow, he managed to run the gauntlet of
the Manzimnyama valley and to urge his horse up the steep, rocky slopes
of Mpethe hill beyond. For a mile or two, across the summit, the pursuit
slackened as the Zulus were distracted, finishing off the last knots of
resistance in the valley, and this allowed the mounted men a respite to
flee pell-mell across the high ground. This then dropped down steeply
into the narrow valley of the Mzinyathi, five or six miles below Rorke's
Drift. This was the border, and it offered some hope of salvation, but for
most of the wretched fugitives it would prove to be cold comfort indeed.
The descent lay through a jumble of steep boulders, and at the bottom
the river itself was in flood, a surging brown torrent roaring over its
rocky bed. Some of Chief Sihayo's followers, keen to avenge the attack
of ten days before, had already cut across country and were harassing
the fugitives on the river bank, spearing the horses and killing any men
whose exhaustion or wounds caused them to delay too long. Then, just
as the last cluster of survivors, Melvill among them, descended into the
valley, a fresh wave of Zulus appeared on the heights above them. The
iNdluyengwe *ibutho*, part of the reserve, had been despatched to cut
them off, and they streamed down the rocky slope, stabbing at the panic-
stricken soldiers who scattered before them. After the battle, Colonel
Glyn of the 24th pieced together Melvill's fate;

Lieutenant Melville reached the bank of the Baffalo, and at once plunged in, horse and all; but being encumbered with the colour, which is an awkward thing to carry even on foot, and the river being full and running rapidly, he appears to have got separated from his horse, when he was about half-way across. He still, however, held on resolutely to the colour, and was being carried down stream when he was washed against a large rock in the middle of the river. Lieutenant Higginson, of the Natal Native Contingent, who had also lost his horse in the river, was clinging to this rock, and Lieutenant Melville called to him to lay hold of the colour. This Lieutenant Higginson did, but the current was so strong that both officers were again washed away into still water. In the meantime, Lieutenant Coghill, 1st Battalion 24th Regiment, my orderly officer, who had been left in camp that morning when the main body of the force moved out on account of a severe injury to his knee, which rendered him unable to move without assistance, had also succeeded in gaining the river bank in company with Lieutenant Melville. He too had plunged at once into the river, and his horse had carried him safely away; but on looking round for Lieutenant Melville and seeing him struggling to save the colour in the river, he at once turned his horse and rode back into the stream again to Lieutenant Melville's assistance.

It would appear that the enemy had assembled in considerable force along their own bank, and had opened a heavy fire on our people, directing it more especially on Lieutenant Melville, who wore a red patrol jacket. So that when Lieutenant Coghill got into the river again, his horse was almost immediately killed by a bullet. Lieutenant Coghill was thus cast loose in the stream also, and not withstanding the exertions of both these gallant officers, the colour was carried off from them, and they themselves gained the bank in a state of extreme exhaustion.

Indeed, the survivors who emerged on the Natal bank were all bedraggled, traumatized, and at the limit of their endurance. Some of Durnford's men had managed to keep together during the rout, and once across they paused long enough to fire a volley or two over the water at the Zulus beyond, driving them away from the bank and allowing a last few to complete their escape. There were many acts of individual heroism, too; a Private Samuel Wassall of the 80th Regiment, attached to the Mounted Infantry, had swum his horse safely across to the Natal bank, but was attracted by the shout of a colleague, Private Westwood, from behind him. Westwood had come off his horse in the water and was struggling to stay afloat in the current. Wassall coolly put his horse back into the water and swam across to the Zulu bank, where he dismounted and tied his horse to a bush. He dived in, dragged Westwood out, and hauled him on to his horse. By now the Zulus, attracted to the conspicuous red coats, were only a few yards away, and Wassall urged his horse back into the water with its double load. Both men survived, and in due course Wassall would be awarded the Victoria Cross for the incident.

Melvill and Coghill had been among the last to get across. Coghill was still suffering from his twisted knee, and they made slow progress up the ridge on the Natal side, away from the river. Most of the survivors were ahead of them; somewhere near the top, Durnford's men halted again to cover the retreat. It was left to Higginson, writing later to Coghill's father, to describe what happened next:

> when we had got 100 yards up the bank we saw two Zulus following us and when they got within 30 yards of us Melvill and Coghill fired and killed them both. I was without arms of any kind having lost my rifle in the river and I had not a revolver.
>
> When we had gone a few yards further Melvill said he could go no further and Coghill said the same. (I don't think they imagined at this time there was anyone following us). When they stopped, I pushed on reaching the top of the hill I found four Basutos with whom I escaped by holding a horse's tail.

Higginson himself did not see the end; Melvill and Coghill were overtaken, and their bodies were found lying close together a fortnight later. A question mark hangs over the identity of the men who killed them; few Zulu had crossed the Mzinyathi at that point, and it may be that they were killed by men living on the Natal bank. Certainly, local lore today suggests that members of the Natal border community, who were attracted to the river by the approaching commotion of battle, were spotted and hailed by Zulu *izinduna* on the far side. Under threat of retribution, it is conceivable that the last strugglers struggling up from the valley were actually killed by citizens of the colony of Natal.

Melvill and Coghill were probably killed about 3.30 p.m. Perhaps they were among the last whites to die in the battle, but it is equally possible that individuals held out among the wagons at the camp, or in secure crevices among the boulders, until much later in the day. Here and there men feigned death, hoping to be overlooked in the general carnage, only to be discovered when the Zulus prepared to strip the corpses of their equipment and uniforms.

Any Zulu who had killed in battle was considered ritually polluted by the blood he had shed. To free himself from the taint, it was necessary for him to slit the stomach of his victim in the belief that this allowed the dead man's spirit to pass to the afterlife. A failure to do so could result in all manner of misfortune, and the killer's own body might bloat like a corpse. Occasionally, too, body parts which were associated with strength and courage were removed by specialist war-doctors, since the essence of a man who had been killed while fighting bravely might be harnessed to assure supernatural ascendancy in future conflict. A victorious warrior remained unclean until he had passed through complex cleansing rituals on his return home, and to mark his state he was also required to wear some of the clothing of his victim. It was not always possible to perform these rituals correctly in the ebb and flow of battle, but after Isandlwana the Zulu were left in possession of the field, and could accomplish them at leisure. 'As a rule we took off the upper garments', recalled Mehlokazulu,

> but left the trousers, but if we saw blood upon the garments we did not bother ... all the dead bodies were cut open, because if that had not been done the Zulus would have become swollen like the dead bodies. I heard that some bodies were otherwise mutilated. There was a man whose head was cut off at the entrance to the camp, where the white people held out, and formed back to back.

One Zulu source suggests that the last man of the 24th to die had hidden himself in a cave at the foot of the crag of Isandlwana itself, and had defended it 'until the shadows were long on the ground', shooting or bayoneting every warrior who approached him. Finally, the Zulu fired a volley into the cave, and killed him.

Even as the final resistance was being overcome, those Zulu who had carried the camp turned their thoughts to plunder. According to the warrior of the uNokhenke,

The portion of the army which had remained to plunder the camp did so thoroughly, carrying off the maize, bread stuffs . . . and stores of all kinds, and drinking such spirits as were in camp. Many were drunk, and all laden with their booty; and towards sunset the whole force moved back towards the encampment of the previous night . . .

The Zulu captured perhaps 1,000 Martini-Henry rifles in total, together with the column's entire reserve supply of ammunition. Everything of military value was carried away, together with whatever trinkets each man took a fancy to. The bodies lay scattered thickly across the slopes at the foot of the hill, mixed up with the carcasses of hundreds of transport oxen, horses, mules and dogs, which had been caught up in the fury of the attack. Where they could, the bodies of the Zulu dead were collected together by kinsmen and friends, and tumbled into the grain-pits of deserted homesteads or dragged into dongas. There were so many, however, that some were merely covered over with war-shields in a symbolic burial – 'Zulus died all around Isandwhlana', recalled Mehlokazulu sadly. By late afternoon, the camp at Isandlwana, from which Lord Chelmsford had marched out in such high expectation just twelve hours before, resembled a charnel-house.

According to the official history, fifty-two officers and 806 white NCOs and men died on the British side at Isandlwana, and 471 Africans, including non-combatant servants and wagon-drivers. Since most of the column's military records were lost in the camp, neither figure is entirely reliable. Although the NNC subsequently received much of the blame for the disaster, their front-line losses were scarcely less staggering than those inflicted upon the redcoats. Two companies of the 2/3rd NNC had found themselves in the centre of the British line; they were mostly men from the amaChunu chiefdom in the Msinga district of Natal, and according to their magistrate's careful count, they suffered 243 casualties out of a total of 290 men. Among them was Chief Pakhade's son and heir, Gabangaye. European survivors of Isandlwana numbered scarcely sixty men.

The Zulu losses can only be guessed at. According to the warrior uNokhenke, 'the Umcityu suffered very severely, both from artillery and musketry fire; the Nokenke from musketry fire alone; while the Nodwengu [the right horn] suffered least'. Perhaps 1,000 Zulu were killed outright in the area around the camp, while as many again might have suffered wounds which were beyond the skill of their herbalists to heal. They faced a long and painful journey to their homesteads across the country, and many arrived there only to die from the effects of shock and infection.

For the most part, Lord Chelmsford's force had remained entirely unaware that the battle was in progress. Once he had arrived at the far end of the Hlazakazi heights early that morning, Chelmsford had deployed his men to sweep through the surrounding hills in search of the enemy seen by Dartnell the night before. Small bodies of warriors were seen retiring towards the north-east, where they appeared to be rallying on Siphezi mountain, and throughout the morning Chelmsford's men skirmished with parties of stragglers. Nevertheless, if the main *impi* had ever been in the area, it was clearly not there now, and by mid-morning Chelmsford had sent a note to Pulleine by Captain Gardner, telling him to break camp and advance the column to join him. Pulleine's response – that he could not do so, because there was heavy firing in the hills above Isandlwana – aroused curiosity amongst Chelmsford's staff, but no alarm. No one seriously expected the Zulu to have outflanked Chelmsford's command in any numbers, nor did they think the camp vulnerable. According to one of Chelmsford's ADCs, Captain Gosset, the truth dawned slowly:

Lt. Milne, Naval A.D.C., was sent to the summit of an adjoining hill with a large Naval telescope. He could plainly see the camp and reported all quiet. At about midday I met Captain Lonsdale, who said his Native Contingent had been without food for 24 hours and he wanted to ride to the camp to make arrangements for them. I rode with him for a short distance and pointed out the camp and left him. Soon after this Lord Chelmsford came up where the force was collected, except Harness's battery and two companies of the 2/24th under Captain Church who were waiting for orders about a mile to the north. Cecil Russell and his mounted infantry was also away patrolling our L Flank. The General had decided on moving his camp to this point, which was about 12 miles from Isandlwana and rode over the ground with Col. Glyn to select a suitable position. When thus engaged a native came with a report from Commandant Browne who was with his native battalion watching the road between us near Isandhlwana. We at once rode to a hill from which we had a clear view but noticed nothing, the tents were standing and all was apparently as we left it. However, there was little doubt that an engagement had taken place and the General so far moderated his plans, as to order Glyn to bivouac where he was for the night, while he rode in with his escort to Isandhlwana. I was ordered to go to Harness's battery with orders to join Glyn. I rode up to Harness with the orders and was told by him that the fire of his two guns which had been left at Isandhlwana had been heard.

While talking to him Church of the 2/24th rode up in a very excited state and said the camp had been taken. I did not believe the report, but at the same time felt uneasy and saw that those around me shared the feeling. Harness on hearing Church's report said, 'I presume, under the circumstances I had better move towards the camp.' I said, 'I do not know, but send an officer back with me and he can carry to you the General's instructions.' The General and Staff were some distance behind. I made my report. Harness was ordered back, and the General mounted and rode towards the camp. I preceded him and found that Harness had moved on. I stopped him, and while talking to him, Cecil Russell rode up and asked for the General, saying that one of his troopers had been trying to find him with a note from Pulleine saying that Durnford was engaged to his Front. The General himself rode up and I sent Russell to him. We soon after started for the camp, a distance of about 10 miles. It was then as far as I remember about 2 o'clock. We moved rather leisurely as the horses had had a hard day's work.

When about 4 miles from the camp, Lonsdale, who as stated above had ridden in to arrange about food for his battalion, rode up to us and said, 'the Zulus have the camp.'

The General's reply was, 'but I left 1,000 men to guard the camp', and turning to his Staff said, 'Glyn must return at once.' I said, 'Shall I go?' and galloped off, followed by two Md. Infantry. Not wishing to cause alarm to Glyn's men I slackened my pace as I rode up, and said 'you are to march back to the camp.' 'Hoorah,' cried some of the men, little knowing the reason for the change of orders.

The way in which Chelmsford and his officers had remained unaware of a pitched battle taking place just twelve miles away still seems curious today. Yet they were undoubtedly deceived in part by the landscape, for from Magogo and Silutshana Isandlwana appears to lie below the horizon, no more than a dark smudge against the hills beyond. Moreover, on a hot summer's day like 22 January 1879 the heat would have risen off the plain, causing the mountain to shimmer in the haze. Even with a good naval telescope, Chelmsford's staff could probably see little more than the blur of the white tents, which had not been struck, as they routinely were in action. More important, however, was the fact that Chelmsford's column were looking for signs of normality, and allowed themselves to be reassured too easily by what they saw.

Even once Chelmsford had decided to return to Isandlwana, it took time to assemble his men. His infantry were scattered in companies throughout the hills – they would, incidentally, have been acutely vulnerable had they found the Zulu army they were looking for – and had to be recalled. Most had been on the move since 2.30 that morning, and they were now tired and hungry. Although, once the rumour that something terrible had befallen the camp spread among them, their pace quickened, it was still evening by the time they approached Isandlwana. In the gloom large bodies of warriors could be seen retiring over the iNyoni hills in the distance to the right; it was not at all clear whether the Zulu still occupied the camp, and what exactly had happened to the defenders. According to Gosset,

> Lord Chelmsford made a short and soldierlike address to the men, which was received with cheers, and we moved on. Two miles from the camp we formed into fighting order with the guns in the centre, flanked by a wing of the 2/24th and a native battn. with the mounted men on the extreme flanks. We longed for a couple of hours of daylight, but darkness had set in and when we arrived near the camp but little was to be seen save the hill which frowned against the star-lit sky and the nek which separated it from a stony kopje on the left. On this nek we saw figures moving and as it was necessary to establish ourselves there, fire was opened by the guns and Major Wilsone Black, 2/24th, was ordered to move forward and occupy the kopje and having gained it a cheer was to be our signal to advance. The kopje was reached without opposition and we moved on. The enemy had disappeared and whether they were in the vicinity or not we could not tell. So the force was drawn up in a square on the nek where we had perforce to remain until daylight...

It is hard to fault Chelmsford's decision to bivouac on the battlefield on tactical grounds – he could neither afford to allow the Zulu to retain the camp, nor march on with his tired command and the enemy around him in unknown strength in the darkness – but it condemned his men to a night of horror among the freshly dead. The foetid smell of blood and decay hung over the field, and everywhere men stumbled over bodies lying in the grass. A few wounded or drunken Zulu cried out throughout the night, while a terribly injured mule whinnied in pain. Far off, jackals howled. Fires flickered here and there amongst the ruin of the tents and wagons. Ghastly rumours spread like wildfire, fed by horrors which seemed all the worse because they could be no more than glimpsed in the moonless blackness. In this fraught atmosphere, it was easy to believe the stories of decapitated corpses, and 'little drummer boys' – the average age of the drummers killed at Isandlwana was twenty-four – hung up on butchers' hooks. The night passed without sleep in a series of false alarms.

There was, moreover, one more element to complete Chelmsford's nightmare. From the nek below Isandlwana, looking back towards Natal, the outline of Shiyane hill could be seen silhouetted against a rosy glow of fire. The mission station at Rorke's Drift was burning; the Zulu had crossed into Natal.

*

Since the flurry of excitement which greeted the departure of the main column on the 20 January, and the passage of Durnford's men, life at Rorke's Drift had been quiet. Chelmsford later claimed that he had instructed Glyn to prepare a defensive position to guard the crossing at the Drift, but if so the order had gone astray, for nothing had been done. A single company of the 24th Regiment – B Company, 2/24th – had been left to guard the post. The 2nd Battalion had arrived in southern Africa only during the closing stages of the Cape Frontier War, and, coming fresh from the depot in Brecon, they included a higher proportion of younger men than the more seasoned 1st Battalion. A number of B Company's men had been recruited in the Welsh borders, although by far the majority of the men reflected the Victorian army's traditional recruiting grounds in the slums of the English industrial cities or among the agricultural poor of England and Ireland. Despite their comparative youth – their senior NCO, Colour Sergeant Frank Bourne, was just twenty-four – the company had seen desultory action in the Cape, and had grown acclimatized to both the southern African environment and local warfare. Their original company commander, Captain Alfred Godwin-Austen, had been wounded accidentally by one of his own men during fighting in the bush, and command had devolved on his subaltern, Lieutenant Gonville Bromhead.* Known to his fellow officers as 'Gunny', Bromhead was popular among his men despite a rather retiring personality and slight deafness.

Bromhead's company was responsible for the security of a post which had been appropriated by Lord Chelmsford as a supply depot and hospital. The post itself, built by Jim Rorke in the 1840s, had changed little since his day; it consisted of two long, single-storey buildings built of local bricks, stone and thatch, which had been placed on a terrace of flat land at the foot of the Shiyane hill. When the site had been bought by the Swedish mission society after Rorke's death, the incumbent, the Reverend Otto Witt, had occupied Rorke's old house and used his trading store as a church. Witt was still living at the mission on 22 January, although he had made his home available to a small medical detachment, under the command of Surgeon James Reynolds, who had turned it into a makeshift hospital. About thirty men slept on beds improvised from planks raised a few inches above the hard earth floor on bricks. Only a handful of them were suffering from wounds incurred in action during the fighting on 12 January; the rest were suffering from the assorted fevers, dysentery and injuries which inevitably accompanied life on campaign in Africa.

Witt's church had been taken over by the military as a store for the supplies stockpiled to go forward to the column. Ironically, thirty wagons had been due to return from Isandlwana during the morning to collect provisions; they had never set out, and the store remained overflowing with heavy wooden crates of biscuit and tinned meat, and sacks of local corn, known as mealies. There was not room in the building to hold them all, and two large pyramids of mealie bags stood neatly in front of the veranda, watched over by a small commissariat staff commanded by Commissary Walter Dunne and Acting Assistant Commissary James Dalton.

There was one further element in the post's garrison, although the regulars, with their traditional disdain of auxiliary forces, had taken little notice of them. A company of the 2nd Battalion 3rd NNC, under

* Pronounced 'Brumhead'.

Captain William Stephenson, was also based at the post. These men were late arrivals, abaThembu from the Natal's Klip River district who had only joined the column on the 14th and had been detailed to remain on the Natal bank. Probably as a result of this, they were extremely short of white officers – they seem to have included no lieutenants or sergeants and just three corporals – and had had little opportunity to train in the duties expected of them. Like most NNC units, they were armed principally with their own weapons, and at best only one in ten carried firearms.

On the 19th a small detachment of Royal Engineers had arrived at the Drift in advance of the 5th Company, RE, which was marching up from Durban. Under the command of Lieutenant John Chard, the party – a corporal, three sappers and a driver – had pitched camp by the river, and had been kept busy repairing the overworked ponts, which by the time Durnford's column had crossed into Zululand were beginning to show the strain.

Late on the evening of the 21st, Chard had received an ambiguous order from Isandlwana ordering his men forward to join the column. Unsure whether this included himself, he had set out early on the 22nd with his men in a wagon. In fact, only the services of his men were required, and Chard was directed to return to the Drift with his driver and the wagon. While he was present in the camp, he saw something of the first appearance of the Zulus on the iNyoni heights, and on his return he reported this to Major Spalding. Spalding was the senior officer at Rorke's Drift and was responsible for the line of communication extending from the border to Helpmekaar. Chard's news prompted them to discuss the safety of the garrison, and Spalding decided to ride to Helpmekaar to hurry along a further company of the 2/24th, which should have already moved up to the border to reinforce the garrison. Before he left, Spalding gave some thought as to who should command in his absence; consulting an Army List, he found that Chard was the senior officer, and Spalding rode off with the immortal remark, 'I see you are senior, so you will be in charge, although, of course, nothing will happen, and I shall be back again early this evening.' With no men to work on the ponts, Chard returned to his tent and passed the morning writing letters home.

About lunchtime, the garrison at Rorke's Drift heard the distant crackle of gunfire from the direction of Isandlwana. Three men with no particular duties to perform – Surgeon Reynolds, Otto Witt and a chaplain attached to the column, the Reverend George Smith – took the opportunity to climb the Shiyane hill to see if they could observe anything of the battle. The view from the top of the hill is spectacular, commanding stunning views of the Mzinyathi valley, with Isandlwana squarely on the horizon. Yet Isandlwana itself blocked the view of the battle taking place beyond it, and all the spectators could see was something of the early movements to the left of the hill, and, later, of fierce fighting on the nek. They watched fascinated as one body of men emerged on to the ridge above the river, downstream on the Natal side, and sat down to rest, while another took a more direct route from Isandlwana, crossing the Mzinyathi much closer to Rorke's Drift. Both parties were clearly Africans, and for a while the observers assumed they were NNC, returning to the post. Only when the men were near enough for it to be clearly seen that the officers among them, too, were black, did the truth dawn. The men were Zulus, and they were coming to attack Rorke's Drift.

In fact, King Cetshwayo had ordered his army not to cross the border and carry the war to Natal. Not only did he fear that this would provoke the British to greater acts of retaliation, but he felt strongly that he was the victim of British aggression and did not want to compromise his position of moral strength in any subsequent peace negotiations. Indeed, when some of his warriors, in the heat of the chase, had shown themselves willing to pursue the survivors from Isandlwana across the river, their *izinduna* had restrained them by reminding them of the King's commands. Nevertheless, for men who had been close to exhaustion, had already taken part in the fighting and, moreover, had the looting of the camp to look forward to, this had perhaps been an easy order to obey.

The same could not be said for the regiments who had made up the reserve. These were senior men associated with the royal homestead at oNdini, a cluster of regiments linked to the uThulwana *ibutho*, to which King Cetshwayo himself had belonged. For the most part they had hardly been engaged at Isandlwana, swinging wide of the right 'horn' to cut the British line of retreat. One section, the younger men of the iNdluyengwe, had been detached to catch the fugitives at the drift, and had then beaten through the broken terrain on the Zulu side of the river, moving upstream and crossing in a narrow gorge a mile above the survivors.

The remaining regiments – the uThulwana, iNdlondlo and uDloko, all married men in their forties – had struck the river closer to Rorke's Drift. They had begun the battle under the command of the energetic and resourceful Chief Zibhebhu kaMaphitha, but he had been wounded in the hand during the pursuit and had taken the opportunity to retire from the field. Command had devolved upon Prince Dabulamanzi kaMpande, a younger brother of the King and a royal favourite. Dabulamanzi had not been appointed to a specific command, but exercised authority by virtue of his royal status and strong, aggressive personality. After the war, Dabulamanzi admitted that he had been irritated by the fact that his men had missed out on the glory of the victory at Isandlwana, and had decided to cross the river to allow them an opportunity to redeem themselves. The existence of the supply depot at Rorke's Drift was well known to the Zulu, and in the aftermath of Isandlwana it must have seemed a prize well within their reach. The small size of the garrison and the prospect of looting the supplies stockpiled there must have made it doubly tempting. By about 3.30 p.m., both Zulu groups had crossed the river, and some broke away to ransack deserted African homesteads on the Natal bank. The rest, about 3,500 strong, began to move in a leisurely manner upstream towards Rorke's Drift, with the iNdluyengwe some distance in front.

What followed was destined to become legendary in British military history. For the Zulus, the battle of Rorke's Drift was little more than a border raid, a mopping-up exercise which was to prove a costly failure in the aftermath of the far more significant victory at Isandlwana; for the British, it was an epic of courage and endurance. Chard's official report provides a remarkably clear account of the events of the next twelve hours:

> At about 3.15 p.m. on that day I was at the ponts, when two men came riding from Zululand at a gallop, and shouted to be taken across the river.
>
> I was informed by one of them, Lieutenant Ardendorff of Lonsdale's regiment (who remained to assist in the defence) of the disaster at Isandula camp, and that the Zulus were advancing on Rorke's Drift. The other, a carabineer, rode off to take the news to Helpmakaar.
>
> Almost immediately I received a message from Lieutenant

Bromhead, commanding the company 24th Regiment at the camp near the commissariat stores, asking me to come up at once.

I gave the order to inspan, strike tents, put all stores, &c. into a waggon, and at once rode up to the commissariat store and found that a note had been received from the 3rd column to state that the enemy was advancing in force against our post, which we were to strengthen and hold at all costs.

Lieutenant Bromhead was most actively engaged in loopholing and barricading the store building and hospital, and connecting the defence of the two buildings by walls of mealie bags and two waggons that were on the ground.

I held a hurried consultation with him and with Mr Dalton, of the commissariat (who was actively superintending the work of defence, and whom I cannot sufficiently thank for his valuable services) entirely approving of the arrangements made. I went round the position, and then went down to the ponts and brought up the guard of 1 sergeant and 6 men, waggon, &c. I desire here to mention the offer of the pont-man, Daniels, and Sergeant Milne, 3rd Buffs, to move the ponts in the middle of the stream and defend them from their decks with a few men. We arrived at the post about 3.30 p.m. Shortly after an officer of Durnford's Horse arrived and asked for orders. I requested him to send a detachment to observe the drifts and ponts and throw out outposts in the direction of the enemy and check his advance as much as possible, falling back upon the post when forced to retire and assist in its defence.

I requested Lieutenant Bromhead to post his men, and, having seen his and every man at his post, the work once more went on.

About 4.20 p.m. the sound of firing was heard behind the hill to our south. The officer of Durnford's returned, reporting the enemy close upon us, and that his men would not obey his orders, but were going off to Helpmakaar, and I saw them, apparently about 100 in number, going off in that direction.

About this time, Captain Stephenson's detachment of the Natal Native Contingent left us, as did that officer himself.

I saw that our line of defence was too extended for the small number of men now left us, and at once commenced a retrenchment of biscuit boxes.

We had not completed a wall two boxes high when, about 4.30 p.m., 500 or 600 of the enemy came in sight around the hill to our

BATTLE OF RORKE'S DRIFT, 22/23 JANUARY 1879

south, and advanced at a run against the south wall. They were met by a well-sustained fire, but, notwithstanding their heavy loss, continued the advance to within 50 yards of the wall, when they were met with such a heavy fire from the wall and cross-fire from the store that they were checked, but, taking advantage of the cover afforded by the cookhouse, ovens, &c., kept up a heavy fire. The greater number, however, without stopping, moved to the left, around the hospital, and made a rush at our N.W. wall of mealie bags, but after a short but desperate struggle were driven back with heavy loss into the bush around the work.

The main body of the enemy were close behind, and had lined the ledge of rock and caves overlooking us about 400 yards to our south, from where they kept up a constant fire, and, advancing somewhat more to their left than the first attack, occupied the garden, hollow road, and bush in great force.

Taking advantage of the bush, which we had not time to cut down, the enemy were able to advance under cover close to our wall, and in this part soon held one side of the wall, while we held the other. A series of desperate assaults were made, extending from the hospital, along the wall, as far as the bush reached; but each was most splendidly met and repulsed by our men with the bayonet, Corporal Scheiss, N.N.C., greatly distinguishing himself by his conspicuous gallantry.

The fire from the rocks behind us, though badly directed, took us completely in the reverse, and was so heavy that we suffered very severely, and about 6 p.m. were forced to retire behind the retrenchment of biscuit boxes.

All this time the enemy had been attempting to force the hospital, and shortly after set fire to its roof.

The garrison of the hospital defended it room by room, bringing out all of the sick who could be moved before they retired. Privates Williams, Hook, R. Jones, and W. Jones, 24th Regiment, being the last men to leave, holding the doorway with the bayonet, their own ammunition being expended. From the want of interior communication and the burning of the house it was impossible to save all. With most heartfelt sorrow I regret we could not save these poor fellows from their terrible fate.

Seeing the hospital burning and the desperate attempts of the enemy to fire the roof of the stores, we converted two mealie bag heaps into a sort of redoubt, which gave a second line of fire all round; Assistant Commissary Dunne working hard at this, though much exposed, and rendering valuable assistance.

As darkness came on we were completely surrounded, and, after several attempts had been gallantly repulsed, were eventually compelled to retire to the middle, and then inner, wall of the kraal on our east. The position we then had we retained throughout.

A desultory fire was kept up all night, and several assaults were attempted and repulsed; the vigour of the attack continuing until after midnight, the men firing with the greatest coolness did not waste a single shot; the light being afforded by the burning hospital being of great help to us.

About 4 a.m., 23rd instant, the firing ceased, and at daybreak the enemy were out of sight over the hill to the south-west.

We patrolled the grounds, collecting the arms of the dead Zulus, and strengthened our defences as much as possible.

Chard's cool official style belies the ferocity of the fighting, which had lasted intermittently for the best part of twelve hours. When dawn broke on the 23rd, his men held only the storehouse and a few square yards in front of it. The roof of the hospital had caved in, and a heavy pall of smoke hung over the field. The yard was littered with spent cartridge cases, spears, helmets, shields and torn uniform and equipment; dead Zulu lay in heaps around the barricades and were thickly carpeted on a few feet of ground in front of the hospital veranda, where the fiercest hand-to-hand fighting had taken place. Most of Chard's men were nearing exhaustion, and had fired off the best part of a company reserve of 20,000 rounds of ammunition. Many of them had cuts and bruises, contused shoulders from the recoil of their rifles, and burnt fingers from the overheated barrels. Just fifteen of them had been killed in the battle, however, and two more mortally wounded; an extraordinary testimony to the effectiveness of their barricades, which for the most part had kept the Zulu at arm's length.

At about 7 a.m. a large body of Zulu appeared from behind Shiyane hill and took up a position on the slopes of kwaSinqindi opposite. Chard hurriedly called his men in and prepared for another attack, though he knew that their chances of surviving it were slim.

The Zulu, too, were drained by their ordeal. Their exertions since noon the day before had been extraordinary. They had crossed fifteen miles from the Ngwebeni valley, and some of them, at least, had been involved in a running fight along the way. They had crossed the swollen Mzinyathi before embarking on hours of exhausting fighting, much of it at close quarters. Although Chard's first impression was that the Zulu had lost about 350 men during the attack, he later admitted that, taking into account the bodies later found some distance from the site, the figure was closer to 500. Some Zulu accounts suggest it was as high as 600. Many of the survivors were wounded. Some elements had already retired during the hours of darkness, and for those who remained the cold, harsh light of day revealed that the white men were still as secure behind their barricades as ever. Moreover, from their position on the hill, the Zulu could see movement on the road to Isandlwana, across the river.

Wearily, the Zulu rose up and quietly retired behind Shiyane, to cross the river downstream. Some were so tired they could only drag their shields behind them; the two sides had fought one another to a standstill.

The Zulu retreat raised the spirits of the garrison. In the distance, a long line of men could be seen approaching the drift on the Zulu bank. For a moment the rumour passed amongst the garrison that this was the main Zulu army, come from Isandlwana to finish them off, and indeed there seemed to be many Africans and few enough redcoats among them. Then, to their intense relief, a handful of mounted infantrymen rode up from the river. It was the remains of Chelmsford's command, fresh from the terrible night at Isandlwana.

For Lord Chelmsford himself, the meeting was a time of conflicting emotions. He was delighted that the garrison had held out, but until that point he had hoped some of the men from Isandlwana had fallen back on the post. When told there were none, he was crushed.

The column marched up slowly, marvelling at the extraordinary evidence of the fight. There were wounded Zulu lying out in the bush in front of the post, and members of the NNC, joined by a few redcoats, walked over the field and killed them. They were in no mood to be merciful, and to save ammunition they stabbed or clubbed most of them to death. Then there was nothing to do but drag away the bodies and prepare to bury them. For Chelmsford, there lay ahead the unpleasant duty of riding to Pietermaritzburg to break the news of the disaster to the colonial authorities, and to prepare for a Zulu counter-attack. For the survivors of the Centre Column, there was little option but to secure themselves as best they could. They could not afford to abandon Rorke's Drift now; and there was no telling what move the Zulu army might make next.

Chapter Four

'They did great execution . . .'

For Colonel Wood's column, too, the third week of January had seen the start of the war in earnest.

The Left Flank (No. 4) Column, some 2,300 men, mostly from the 1/13th and 90th Light Infantry, had assembled at the Transvaal border town of Utrecht in September 1878. From the beginning, it was clear that Wood's war would be different in character from that in other parts of Zululand. He was, of course, expected to advance towards oNdini, to the south-east, in support of Chelmsford's broader invasion strategy, but the complex political situation in the northern sector inevitably meant that war would be shaped by a tangled web of local rivalries and alliances to a greater extent than elsewhere.

In many respects, Wood was perhaps the most ideally suited of Chelmsford's column commanders for such a task. A dapper, rather slight man with a heavy beard, his personal appearance and tendency towards hypochondria belied an extraordinary range of combat experience which in the couse of a colourful career would see him rise from the rank of Midshipman in the Navy to the dizzy heights of Field Marshal in the Army. Like many of his generation, he had cut his teeth in the Crimea and Indian Mutiny, but it was in the forests of Asante in West Africa in 1873 that he had first distinguished himself and revealed an unusual flair for colonial campaigning. Capable and self-reliant, he was undaunted by the challenges associated with such warfare, and proved consistently resourceful and dynamic. Thorough and organized, he was an aggressive tactician, and he was highly popular with both officers and men under his command. Not that he was without faults: his approach to staff matters was cliquish, and he was sometimes over-optimistic to the point of rashness. He was ambitious and intuitively political, and knew how best to remain on good terms with his superiors while distancing himself from their misfortunes. He was known to the Africans as *Lukuni*, after a hardwood from which they made their knobkerry war clubs – an association which was as much to do with Wood's reputation for swift and decisive action as it was a pun on his name. Throughout the war, Wood would rely heavily on his cavalry commander, Brevet Lieutenant Colonel Redvers* Buller, with whom he had served in the Cape. A gruff bulldog of a man whose famously abrasive manner concealed a very real sympathy for his men, Buller was tireless and impressively fearless. On the Cape Frontier he had emerged as a natural leader of the mounted irregular units who constituted Wood's cavalry command. At a time when many regular Army officers struggled – usually unsuccessfully – to apply the principles of conventional cavalry warfare to the command of irregulars, Buller had instinctively grasped their unique characteristics, and played to their strengths rather than their weaknesses. Under his nurturing, one of the Cape units, the Frontier Light Horse (FLH), had emerged as perhaps the most effective mounted unit under British command in South Africa. The FLH had followed Buller to Zululand, and became the yardstick by which Wood's other mounted units would be judged.

A flexible approach would certainly be needed in the northern sector, where a frontier situation had prevailed long before the outbreak of war. Geographically isolated, a long way from the centre of any metropolitan authority, white or African, the swathe of land which lay between the upper Ncome and Phongolo rivers had been subject to conflicting claims from the Zulu and Swazi kings for a generation, a situation which had been given a further twist with the advent of colonial rivalries. The original inhabitants had been largely dispersed by King Shaka during the warfare of the 1820s, and the area remained thinly populated. The survivors had been brought together under appointed *izinduna* who exerted a fragile authority on behalf of the Zulu kings. Indeed, in an attempt to secure his hold on the region, Shaka had established a royal homestead east of the Ncome and Mfolozi headwaters to serve as a centre of royal control. It was known as ebaQulusini, and the king had placed it under the command of one of his most powerful female relatives, his aunt Mnkabayi; a generation later the descendants of the regiment attached to ebaQulusini had settled in, and come to dominate, the surrounding area. They had become known as the abaQulusi and they were regarded not as a local chiefdom, but as a section of the Zulu

* Pronounced 'Reevers'.

Royal House, ruled over not by hereditary chiefs, but by *izinduna* appointed directly by the King. The abaQulusi territory lay about forty miles immediately to the east of Wood's base at Utrecht, and their settlements were concentrated around the Zungwini and Hlobane mountains. The abaQulusi cherished a fierce loyalty to the Zulu throne, and Wood expected them to be among the most diligent supporters of the Zulu cause.

Other local groups, however, had a more ambivalent attitude to political loyalties, which had been shaped by years of local instability and violence. North of the abaQulusi area the terrain became more broken as it extended towards the beautiful, rugged valleys of the Ntombe, Phongolo and Bivane rivers which marked the borders with Swaziland. Here Swazi and Zulu groups intermingled, and lived uneasily in the shadow of both kingdoms. Most of the regional chiefs, like Manyanyoba Khubeka, who lived in the upper Ntombe valley, owed their allegiance nominally to the Zulu, but had long since been used to exercising a degree of independence which would have been impossible closer to oNdini. Wood hoped that such chiefs might be prised from their loyalty to Cetshwayo, and before the war began he had opened clandestine channels of communication in an attempt to persuade them to defect.

One significant individual who was unlikely to adopt the British cause, however, was Mbilini waMswati. Mbilini was a Prince of the Swazi Royal House, the eldest son of the famous King Mswati, and he had fled the kingdom following a succession dispute in 1865. With just a handful of followers, he had sought the protection first of the Transvaal Boers and then of Prince Cetshwayo. Cetshwayo, who was attempting to build his power-base in the last years of King Mpande's rule, had accepted Mbilini's allegiance and had allowed him to settle in the Ntombe valley as a bastion against both Swazi and Boer ambitions on the border. A young man, whose slight physique and pleasant manner concealed a ruthless and ambitious nature, Mbilini was said by missionary propaganda to have been sewn into the fresh pelt of a particularly savage dog as a child, in the hope that he might absorb some of its fierce nature. Certainly, he was renowned for his restless and aggressive spirit and had earned himself the praise-name 'Hyena of the Phongolo'. No sooner had he arrived in the Ntombe than he set about raiding cattle from both the Boers and the Swazis in an effort to rebuild his prestige and following. He was widely regarded as a bandit, who had learned to use both the broken terrain and local loyalties to good effect. He maintained a homestead on the Tafelberg hill, overlooking the Ntombe, which offered him a hiding place among the caves and boulders when he was faced with the threat of reprisals, and he had cultivated links with the abaQulusi, who had allowed him to build a second homestead on the slopes of Hlobane mountain, further south. When hostilities began, Mbilini would quickly emerge as the most dynamic guerrilla leader in the Zulu cause.

The volatile situation on the northern border had been further destabilized by the infiltration of whites into the region from the 1840s. During the exodus of Boer settlers from Natal, which had followed the advent of British rule, a number of Boer groups had persuaded King Mpande to allow them to graze their herds in the open country above the headwaters of the Ncome. In the years in between, many had not only put up farm buildings but had begun to press their claims deeper into Zulu territory. This had, of course, been the basis of the territorial dispute which had been a cause of the war, and it had created a situation in which patterns of settlement overlapped. Wood had hoped that these frontier Boers would see the advantages of supporting the invasion, but with the exception of Piet Uys and his followers, most had preferred to abandon their properties for the safety of Utrecht. Indeed, so ingrained was the Boer distaste for the British that some of those who remained had preferred to maintain links with the Zulu.

The most vulnerable settlement along the frontier was the German Lutheran mission village at Luneburg, in the Ntombe valley. The settlement had been established in the 1860s, and the hard-working and devout Germans had taken the precaution of securing permission from both the Transvaal authorities and King Mpande before marking out their property. By 1878, however, King Cetshwayo had come to see the village as symbolic of the wider struggle for control of the area, and he had ordered the abaQulusi to build a small royal homestead within a few miles of Luneburg to reinforce his claims. In a sense he was right, for the Germans were determined not to abandon their property, and in October the British had established a garrison and an earthwork to protect them in the centre of the village. Nevertheless, while the white inhabitants of Luneburg could count themselves relatively secure, their black Christian farm-workers, scattered on farms along the Ntombe valley, remained exposed, the more so because of the proximity of Mbilini's Tafelberg stronghold.

The need to protect Luneburg and the vulnerable frontier, had pre-occupied both Chelmsford and Wood. Chelmsford's solution had been to straddle the most dangerous area with two British concentrations. Wood's column was to advance from Utrecht and establish a base on the banks of the Ncome, which would place it squarely to the south of Luneburg. A similar distance to the north lay the hamlet of Derby, which was the most southerly outpost of Colonel Hugh Rowlands's No. 5 Column. Rowlands's column, like Durnford's at Middle Drift, had been reduced to the status of a defensive force early in the planning, but even as such it was stretched. With scarcely 1,500 men – just one battalion of infantry, the 80th, and Swazi auxiliaries raised among the tenants of white farmers along the frontier – Rowlands was expected not only to hold his section of the border but also to keep an eye on the Swazi kingdom to the east of him and the republican Boers in the Transvaal behind him. The twin strategic objectives – to protect the border and prosecute the invasion – would not only necessitate careful cooperation between Wood and Rowlands but would also require Wood to use considerable initiative. As Chelmsford himself wrote to Wood from Rorke's Drift on 18 January 1879,

> You will see that in order to strengthen your left flank I have authorized Rowlands to bring the 250 of the 80th now at Derby down to the Pongolo, always provided that he can feed them there and that the Swazis accompany him – If they move down, I leave the question of their future movements entirely in your hands – Rowlands is of course long senior to you as a Colonel and there-fore cannot serve under you, but you can place his force wherever you think it will help your left flank most, sending him the order in my name –
>
> As you now have a roving commission and are not tied down to any particular line, I hope you will be able to rub on without diffi-culty –

Wood had begun the campaign with typical resolve. On 6 December 1878 – five days before Frere's ultimatum officially expired – he crossed the Ncome into Zulu territory, and established a camp on the Zulu bank. On the 11th, the day specified for the invasion, he rode down the Zulu side of the border with an escort, and met Chelmsford close to Rorke's Drift to discuss strategies. By the 20th, Wood had moved his column eastwards and established a camp at Nseka hill, on the White Mfolozi. This was the territory of Chief Thinta of the Mdlalose people, and to Wood's delight, Thinta, intimidated by the arrival of so large an enemy force, promptly surrendered with a number of his adherents.

If this defection reassured Wood that the royal hold on the borders was indeed fragile, however, it soon became clear that the greatest hindrance to further surrenders was the presence of the loyalist aba-Qulusi under arms further to the north. The abaQulusi, under their principal military *induna* Sikhobobo, had called out their fighting men as soon as the invasion began in earnest. They had assembled around a chain of mountain strongholds – Zungwini, Hlobane and Ityenka – which lay directly north of Wood's new position. From here they not only posed a threat to British movements in the region but served to intimidate Zulu waverers. Although their strongholds lay away from the line of his projected advance on oNdini, Wood clearly could not afford to ignore the threat posed by them, and from the 19th – just as Lord Chelmsford prepared to advance to Isandlwana – he began to feel out the enemy position around Zungwini.

Zungwini lay about twelve miles from Nseka, and Wood's men would be required to operate a considerable distance from their base. It is interesting to note that, at this stage of the war, Wood had no more qualms about this than had Chelmsford. On the 20th, Buller and the irregulars were despatched on a reconnaissance to the area and met with an immediate response, as Buller's report describes:

> Crossing the Umfelosi River by an indifferent drift, about two miles above Mount Iseki, I moved towards Mabomba's Kraal, round the south-east spur of Zingan. About seven miles from the river Mr Uys' men, who were reconnoitring the left, found about 50 armed Zulus in a kraal of Seketwayo, under the side of Zingan; leaving the kraal, the Kafirs at once took to the rocks.
>
> An engagement ensued, during which I reinforced the burghers with 20 dismounted men under Captain Brunker.
>
> Twelve Kafirs were, I know, killed, and I would think a few more. One man, F.L.H., was wounded by an assegai thrown by a wounded

Kafir, and another had a narrow escape. We found four guns and a good many assegais, all of which I had broken, but I did not search the ground thoroughly as I did not think the risk of getting men stabbed by wounded Kafirs worth the result.

About this time two of Mr Uys' men came to us and reported a commando of Kafirs on the top of Zingan. Ascending the mountain by a difficult stony cattle track, we found the report was quite true, as the rocky ridges were lined with Kafirs.

I endeavoured to cross the upper plateau in order to get a view of Mabomba's kraal from above, but the hill was too strongly held for us to force it. With the view of ascertaining the full strength of the enemy, who were coming down to attack us in three columns, I seized a small stony koppie and commenced an engagement with the centre column. Our fire soon drove them to cover with a loss of about eight dead (seen, and a good many more reported), but meanwhile we were completely outflanked on our right by some 300 Kafirs, who crept round among the stones and kraantzes of the ridge, and our left by some 400 men, boldly moved in tolerable order across the open ground about a mile off.

I accordingly decided to withdraw. In doing so one man of the Frontier Light Horse was wounded, and two men hit by spent balls, and the horse of Mr Raymond, a burgher, was hit. The Kafirs pursued us to the Umvelosi River in force, and about 100 crossed the drifts; but having then secured my retreat I turned on the flats and drove them back. As far as we could see, they all returned to the top of Zingan.

The Zulu showing had impressed even Buller, but this did not deter Wood from making a stronger sortie the following day. After dark on the 21st – shortly before Lord Chelmsford was to march out of Isandlwana, thirty miles to the south – Wood set out from camp with the majority of his column. He left just two companies behind to guard the stores and wagons – a good deal less than Chelmsford was to leave at Isandlwana. Wood marched across country and at dawn the following morning attacked Zungwini in a pincer movement on three sides. The full weight of the British response clearly caught the Zulu by surprise, and they abandoned Zungwini after a skirmish, retiring across the valley to rally on Hlobane. From the summit of Zungwini, Wood could see about 4,000 Zulu being prepared for war on the northern slopes of Hlobane. They were mostly abaQulusi, but Zulu sources confirm that Mbilini had brought his followers south to join them. It was too late to attack them that afternoon, but Wood ordered his men to bivouac at the foot of Zungwini and be ready to attack Hlobane on the 23rd. At first light, his men passed over the saddle of land between Hlobane and Zungwini and spread out along the slopes of Hlobane, searching for the men they had seen the night before. They found them; but even as the subsequent skirmish unfolded, Wood was to receive some disturbing news:

> About 7.30 a.m., when the column had marched about eight miles, some Zulus ran forward towards a stony hill on our front, but were anticipated by Colonel Buller and a troop of the Frontier Light Horse. The morning was misty and apparently our advance was unperceived, as the Zulus were only forming up when the two guns opened on them and caused them to disperse in all directions. Finding we could not advance where our guide thought the track existed, I ordered the column to turn to the left and pass round a high hill on our left and there outspan. Before I reached this position, however, the 90th Light Infantry and two guns moved down into a valley and up the opposite hill, the Frontier Light Horse and Mr P. Uys pursuing them. It was at this time I received the first intimation of the attack of the Zulus on No. 3 column camp. I therefore retraced my steps towards the Umvolosi, where the column arrived at 7 a.m. this day . . .

This message had an interesting history. It had originated with Captain Alan Gardner, who had had a busy day on the 22nd. Originally out with Chelmsford, he had been sent back to Isandlwana with the order to Pulleine to break camp. He had been present throughout the battle and had run the gauntlet of the fugitives' trail. Gardner had arrived at Helpmekaar late that evening, and it occurred to him that Wood's column, just thirty-five miles away, might be vulnerable if the Zulu chose to follow up their victory. Since he could find no one willing to carry a message for him, he set off on horseback in the dark, arriving utterly exhausted at Utrecht at dawn. Here he found a volunteer to take the message to Wood in the field. His dedication did Gardner little good, however; an over-enthusiastic suggestion that he should be awarded the Victoria Cross earned the derision of his fellow survivors and the unwarranted contempt of Wood.

It was immediately clear to Wood that, like Pearson on the coast, his own situation had completely changed with the disaster at Isandlwana. Not only was his advance unsupported, and his right flank now open to a Zulu counter-assault, but he could also expect to be attacked by the whole Zulu army at any time. Moreover, news of the victory could only encourage local Zulu groups and offset the effect of the recent successful skirmishes around Zungwini, which had undermined support for the abaQulusi. Indeed, the advent of the eclipse on the 22nd was, combined with Wood's attacks, generally held by Zulu in the northern districts as a sign that the ancestral spirits were foretelling a decline in Mbilini's fortunes.

Wood's response was to abandon his camp at Nseka hill and move his column north to a more secure spot in the shadow of the Nqaba-ka-Hawana mountain. Known as Khambula, this position lay directly between the abaQulusi strongholds and the border town of Utrecht, and was much closer to Luneburg. It was, moreover, a much better defensive position. Wood pitched his camp on a narrow, open ridge, which fell away steeply to the south into the streams which provided the source of the White Mfolozi river. The northern approaches sloped gently towards several miles of unbroken grassland, which afforded no more cover to an attacker than a scattering of ant-hills. At Nseka, the countryside was littered with boulders, which Wood had used to construct a series of sangars in key points around the camp; the ground at Khambula was not so rocky, however, and Wood protected his positions with wagon-laagers and shallow trenches. A low knoll in the centre of the ridge was ideally situated for conversion into a stronghold by the addition of an earthwork redoubt to the summit.

When no Zulu attack materialized in the aftermath of Isandlwana, however, Wood returned to harassing the abaQulusi. King Cetshwayo had retained a version of the ebaQulusini homestead, which served the abaQulusi as a headquarters and mustering point. It was situated at the far end of the Hlobane range, about thirty miles from Khambula, but on 1 February at 4 a.m. Buller set out with a mounted force to attack it. The attack caught the Zulu completely by surprise;

> We ... scrambled down the hillside into the basin, in the centre of which the place is situated, and then galloped up to it at 12.30 p.m.
> The Kafirs in it fled in all directions, we took 270 head of cattle

and entirely destroyed the kraal, which contained about 250 huts. About six Kafirs were killed. We had, I am happy to say, no casualty.

If Wood thought that by taking the war to the Zulu he would overawe them, he was wrong, for just ten days later the Zulu retaliated with a spectacular raid on the outskirts of Luneburg. Since the beginning of the war, there had been constant scares and alarms around the settlement, but the defences there had been strong enough to discourage a direct attack. The fact that local Zulu elements lacked the strength to try their luck against the main British positions, however, merely tempted them to seek out softer targets. While the white inhabitants of outlying farms had deserted them for the safety of the village laager, many had left them in the care of their African labourers. On the night of 10/11 February, Mbilini himself travelled north from Hlobane with a large force of abaQulusi and called upon Luneburg's black adherents to pay the price of their loyalty. According to Commandant Frederick Schermbrucker, an irregular officer in charge of the Luneburg laager,

A Zulu war party led by Umbelini crossed last night the Pongolo, and was joined on this side (north) by a strong force of Manyanyoba's people led by Manyanyoba himself. The combined forces of the enemy numbered about 1,500 men. Umbelini was on horseback, and rode a brown horse. By first cock's crow (about half-past 3 a.m.) this morning the enemy had arrived at the Rev. Mr Wagner's mission station, situate about four miles from here almost due north, slightly inclining westward, where they commenced with the most barbarous and most atrocious massacre of men, women and children which it is my painful duty to record. At Wagner's they burnt down three of the Christian natives' houses, killed two men, six women, and burnt seven children alive. Next they went to Nomapela's kraal, a native in the employ of the farmer Benneke, where they killed two men, 11 women, and 15 children, burning down all the huts; one man, Mangala, a friendly native who resided at Benneke's farm, succeeded in killing three enemies and still escaped.

Next the enemy proceeded to Luhlanya's kraal, where they murdered one man, two women, and two children, burning the huts; next they arrived at Kluigenberg's farm, where 'Ncela', a loyal native, resided, they killed here six women, wounded one man, and took away a number of children; from here they came to 'Makolo', killed two women and one child and burnt the huts, and then turned to 'Petros" kraal, where, however, Petros received them with a few shots, and then escaped. From this place they turned back to Kluigenbergs', killed one man and one women at Laarse's, burnt down Kluigenberg's house, and it being then already full daylight, made off with the spoil of several hundreds of cattle, and thousands of sheep and goats, in the direction of Manyanyoba's caves. The great war-party on first arriving at the Rev. Mr Wagner's house divided into two divisions, which afterwards sub-divided again into two sub-divisions each, and it was the last of these sub-divisions upon which my patrol came just when the enemy had succeeded in getting the cattle across the Tombe River.

... The bodies of the women and children were frightfully mutilated, and at Mr. Wagner's house my patrol found a woman still alive who bore 37 assegai wounds on her body. I had her carried into the laager, where she is now under treatment ... but little hope of recovery.

As soon as news of the raid reached Luneberg, Schermbrucker hastily despatched a mounted patrol of six men of the Kaffrarian Rifles, under Acting Lieutenant Schwartzkopt and Sergeant-Major Pogge, to investigate. According to Schwartzkopt,

coming close to Mr. Wagner's mission station, a distance of about four miles from here, I met about 50 armed friendly natives, by whom I was informed that about 400 Zulus were making towards the Entombe's caves. Following their direction, I sent two men as videttes to the top of a hill, from which a large view was obtainable, whilst I went with the remainder of the men round the bottom. Hearing several shots fired, I hurried up to the hill, where I found the two men with a small party of friendly natives, and our native police, engaged with a body of about 300 Zulus.

As soon as my men arrived on the top my men took up the firing and drove the Zulus towards the Entombe, after inflicting on them a loss of about 15 men. Our natives followed them up (when brought to laager they were found to be nearly 700), and took some sheep and goats from the retreating enemy, covered by the fire of my men, no casualties occurring on our side. From my position I could see in the distance beyond the caves large bodies of the enemy, and saw also some droves of cattle ...

Despite Acting Lieutenant Schwartzkopt's gallant sortie, the attack paralysed the country around Luneburg – as it was meant to do. As soon as a report reached Wood, he despatched the indefatigable Buller to reinforce the garrison. On the 15th, Buller led a combined force of mounted men and auxiliaries in a punitive raid through the Ntombe valley. They attacked Manyanyoba's homestead, driving out a number of his surprised adherents, who fled up the slopes of the valley and took refuge among the boulders and caves. After a stiff skirmish, in which the British lost two auxiliaries killed, and Zulu losses were estimated at thirty-four men, Buller withdrew, carrying away 375 head of cattle and 254 goats.

Buller's action had retrieved something of British prestige in the region, but in fact the war had reached a stalemate. The Zulu dared not attack the main British concentrations, but Mbilini's mastery of the countryside meant that it was almost impossible for Wood's men to bring him to open battle. He moved freely between his stronghold in the Ntombe and his homestead on Hlobane, conferring with his allies on how best to prosecute the war.

At the beginning of March, however, the British in the northern theatre scored their biggest diplomatic triumph of the war. Since the beginning of November, they had been trying to persuade one of the most influential chiefs in the region to defect. Prince Hamu was a biological son of King Mpande and a brother to Cetshwayo, although by complex laws of genealogy he was regarded as heir not to Mpande, but to Mpande's brother Nzibe. As such, he was debarred as a candidate for the Zulu throne, but he was one of the most important lords in the northern marches, and he was widely held to resent Cetshwayo's ascendancy. Before the war he had cultivated close links with colonial traders and had installed a white man, Herbert Nunn, to advise him at his principal residence, and he had been a leading member of the peace party. Hamu's defection would be deeply embarrassing to the King and would greatly strengthen the British position in the north. On 17 February, two days after Buller's attack on the Ntombe, messengers arrived at Khambula to say that Hamu was indeed encouraged to throw in his lot with the British.

Hamu's followers, the Ngenetsheni, lived to the north-east of Hlobane, abutting the Swazi border. In order to reach Wood's camp at Khambula, they therefore had to run the gauntlet of Mbilini and the abaQulusi, who lay in between. Hamu had no intention of fleeing alone; he hoped to bring his wives, children, adherents and cattle with him, but the King, hearing whisper of his intentions, sent an *impi* to prevent his escape. Harassed, Hamu crossed north over the Phongolo river and took refuge in a homestead on the Swazi side of the border. When the British agent in Swaziland, Norman MacLeod, heard of his whereabouts, he hurried to find him and assure him that the British were more than prepared to protect him. On 2 March MacLeod wrote with delight to Wood from Derby that

> I have the honour to report that 'Oham' is now in my house here; I found him at a Swazi kraal on the border late on the 2nd, brought him on to another Swazi kraal yesterday, and in here in a waggon to-day. He has about 300 men with him, and a white man, Rorke, and a man who gave his name as Fyn, otherwise I am told Calverley. Mr Nunn joined me yesterday, and will bring 'Oham' with all possible despatch to your camp; 'Oham' is most anxious to get there, and his wives out. He says 2,000 of his people will come too. I was informed at first that there was an impi after him, so not to run any risk of his being taken when almost in our hands I called for volunteers, and got all that could be got, four white men and a few kaffirs, six I think . . .

MacLeod sent Hamu to Luneburg, and then under escort to Khambula. Wood had his followers disarmed, and it was noted with interest that they surrendered three Martini-Henrys which had been taken from the 24th at Isandlwana. Most of Hamu's fighting men were drafted into Wood's auxiliary unit – Wood's Irregulars – while the prince and the remainder of his followers were relocated near Utrecht.

Hamu's defection was undoubtedly a coup, leading the British to speculate on whether the hoped-for disintegration of the Zulu kingdom was happening at last. Yet the troops in the northern sector had little time to bask in their success; it was followed almost immediately by a new disaster.

Following the raid of 10/11 February, five companies of the 80th Regiment, under Major Charles Tucker, had been despatched from Rowlands's headquarters at Derby to reinforce the garrison at Luneburg. Although Rowlands himself was involved that same month in a number of skirmishes around the Eloya and Talaku mountains, east of Luneburg,

20. Prince Dabulamanzi kaMpande, photographed c.1882. The Prince led the unsuccessful attack on Rorke's Drift, and later commanded the right wing of the Zulu army at the battle of Gingindlovu, where he was wounded.

21. A group of Royal Engineers, photographed in the field at the end of the campaign; Major John Chard, the senior officer at Rorke's Drift, wears the VC that Wolseley had presented to him on 16 July.

22. The mission station at Rorke's Drift, photographed six months after the battle. The original storehouse still stands in the centre of the photograph; the hospital has been demolished, but part of the endwall was incorporated into the defensive stone walls – built after the battle – and can be seen behind the trees on the right. The rocky terraces around Shiyane hill, occupied by Zulu snipers during the battle, are clearly visible.

23. Rorke's Drift. The storehouse is on the right; the stone walls built after the battle enclose the area of the original yard, and include the surviving end wall of the hospital (left). The first Zulu attack took place across this ground. The British dead are buried in the walled cemetery in the foreground; the river is visible in the distance.

24. Men of the 2/24th build a memorial at Rorke's Drift some months after the battle. The mission station is visible on the horizon; the memorial is that of Lieutenant R. W. Franklin, 2/24th, who died of disease at Helpmekaar on 20 February – where this memorial now stands.

25. In the aftermath of the British collapse at Isandlwana, the settler population of the central border rushed to defensive laagers. This stone fort, Fort Pine, not far from Rorke's Drift, was unusually impressive.

26. *Above, left.* Lieutenant Fairlie's sketch of Colonel Richard Glyn of the 1/24th, the commander of the Centre Column.

27. *Above, right.* Colonel Redvers Buller, Wood's energetic cavalry commander, who won the VC during the rout at Hlobane. Buller's practical civilian clothes reflect the hard-riding reputation of the irregulars.

28. *Below, left.* Lieutenant Fairlie's jaunty sketch of Louis Napoleon, the Prince Imperial of France, captures something of his engaging personality. The Prince habitually wore a Royal Artillery officer's uniform, although he held no official rank during the campaign.

29. *Below, right.* Major-General Sir Frederick Marshall, who commanded the Cavalry Brigade during the later stages of the war, and who was present when the Prince Imperial's body was recovered on 2 June.

30. The ruins of the mission station at Eshowe, photographed in late 1879. The trenches on the left suggest the impressive nature of the fortifications built by Colonel Pearson's engineers during three months of siege.

31. Officers of the 91st Regiment, the only Highland battalion to serve in the campaign. The 91st played a prominent part at the battle of Gingindlovu. Note the typical Zulu trophies on the ground in front of them – and the ubiquitous dog.

32. An Imperial battalion in Zululand – the 91st Highlanders formed up by companies, pipers to the fore.

33. An impressive trophy of Zulu weapons, taken by the 91st Highlanders. It includes a full-sized regimental war-shield, headdresses, body ornaments of cow tails, and a magnificent waist kilt. The percussion firearms on either side reflect the widespread use by the Zulus of trade guns during the war.

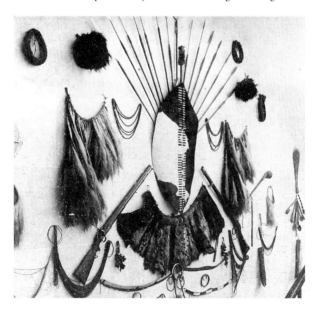

34. The romance and reality of Victorian colonial warfare: a carefully posed study of a 'dead' Zulu warrior, and . . .

35. Zulu skeletons lying on the ground covered by the Zulu right wing at the battle of Gingindlovu.

36. The war in northern Zululand was characterized by a greater degree of low-intensity skirmishing than in any other theatre. Irregulars from Raaf's Transvaal Rangers and auxiliaries from Fairlie's Swazi Police march out from Rowlands' column to attack a Zulu outpost at Talaku mountain on 15 February.

37. Captain Rowland Bettington (right) and a member of his troop of the Natal Horse. The Natal Horse was formed from the white NCOs of the disbanded 3rd NNC, and their appearance was typical of the irregular cavalry units in Zululand.

his column was being increasingly sucked into the volatile situation
further south, where in fact it was most needed. When, on 26 February,
a Republican declaration in the Transvaal prompted Rowlands to return
to Pretoria to calm the situation, Wood took the opportunity of bringing
his remaining troops directly under his control. The garrison at Luneburg, however, though physically much closer to Khambula, continued
to draw its provisions by Rowlands's old line of supply, which began at
the Transvaal town of Lydenburg and travelled via Derby.

Late in February, a convoy of eighteen ammunition and supply
wagons set out from Lydenburg, destined for the new garrison at
Luneburg. They began the journey without escort, but this was clearly
not ideal once they had reached the border, the more so because close
to its destination the track crossed the Ntombe river just a few miles
from Mbilini's Tafelberg stronghold. On 1 March Major Tucker sent
D company of the 80th under Captain Anderson to Derby to meet the
convoy and bring it in. Progress was painfully slow owing to the onset
of bad weather; heavy rain turned the track to mud and bogged down
the wagons. On the 5th, Tucker, becoming irritated, ordered D Company
to return to Luneburg by nightfall. Assuming that they were required for
other duties, the company promptly abandoned the wagons on the road
and marched into Luneburg without them. This was clearly a highly
dangerous situation, and at dawn on the 7th Tucker despatched Captain
David Moriarty and a company strength detachment of the 80th to
gather in the convoy.

They found the first of them at the Ntombe river, just four miles
from Luneburg. The Ntombe is not a wide river, less than fifty yards
across, and at most times of the year it flows no more than a few inches
deep across a sandy bed, between steep banks six or seven feet high.
Following the recent heavy rains, however, the river had swollen right to
the top of the banks, and indeed over the following days it would burst
them completely several times. Seven of the convoy's wagons were
stranded on the northern bank, unable to cross; the rest were scattered
down several miles of road behind. They had not had a comfortable
time since D Company had left them, for their obvious vulnerability had
encouraged local Zulu to attack them. They had suffered no casualties
but had lost forty-six oxen.

Moriarty pitched camp on the south bank of the Ntombe and set
about building a raft to ferry the wagons across. Once it was working, he

crossed the river with the escort and rounded up the wagons, but with too few oxen and in pouring rain, he did not bring the last of them to the Ntombe before the evening of the 9th. During his absence, two of the wagons had succeeded in crossing the river, but the water-level was still rising and it was too dangerous to continue the attempt. The best that Moriarty could do was form the remaining wagons into a defensive laager on the north bank. He positioned them in an inverted 'V', the base resting on the river. Presumably because of the poor state of the ground, the wagons were not placed closely together, and little attempt was made to seal the gaps between them, although the ammunition wagons were placed inside the perimeter. The site was hardly ideal, however, since it sloped down towards the bank, and much of the enclosed area was in a hollow. Moriarty pitched his own tent at the apex of the 'V', on a high point which gave him some view of the road back towards Derby.

It continued to rain throughout the 10th and 11th, during which time the river rose at one point, and flooded half the laager. It was impossible to attempt to move any more wagons across, and the men were wet through for days on end, with no opportunity to dry their clothes. The concentration of so many men and oxen on the north bank had churned it into a sea of mud. On the 11th, Tucker, increasingly concerned at the lack of progress, rode out from Luneburg to confer with Moriarty. By the time he arrived, the river level had fallen by four feet, and the two legs of the laager were now several yards short of the banks. Tucker pointed out that the defences were inadequate to stop an attack, but Moriarty blamed the river. Generally, the men seemed disheartened and miserable. Tucker returned to Luneburg after urging Moriarty to come in as quickly as he could.

Throughout this time, the column had been clearly visible to any Zulu on the nearby heights, and to Mbilini himself. Indeed, on the 11th a party of unarmed Zulu approached the camp offering to sell vegetables, and were allowed into the laager. One of the civilian wagon drivers claimed to have recognized Mbilini among them, though when he pointed this out to the soldiers, they took no notice.

The evening of the 11th saw seventy-one men under Moriarty on the northern bank, and thirty-five under Lieutenant Henry Harward and Sergeant Anthony Booth on the south bank. Harward had only arrived at the spot with Tucker earlier that day, and he had spent the afternoon rounding up strayed cattle. When he returned that evening he had fallen asleep in Moriarty's tent, but Moriarty had woken him up and ordered him to cross the river and take command of the detachment there. Most of the soldiers were asleep in the tents; Moriarty had posted just two sentries outside the laager on the north bank, only ten yards from the wagons. The white civilian wagon drivers slept in their wagons, while the black *voorloopers* – team leaders – took what shelter they could underneath them.

Sometime during the early hours, a single shot shattered the quiet night, fired out in the darkness on the northern bank. According to Booth,

> At about 4.30 a.m. . . . we were alarmed by the firing of a shot apparently from the other side. Lt. Harward called me, and we went together to the river but saw nothing; the sentry reported that the shot was fired at some considerable distance. I went back to where I was sleeping . . .

Lieutenant Harward himself

> . . . ordered the sentry to rouse the detachment on the side of the Intombi Drift nearest Luneburg, and to appraise Captain Moriarty of the fact, and ask for his orders; these were that the escort should remain under arms . . . I retired to my tent close by, where I waited, dressed . . .

It seems that Moriarty allowed his men to remain asleep on the north bank. It had been raining for much of the night, and a heavy mist had risen from the river, limiting visibility to fifty or sixty yards. Suddenly, about 4.30 a.m., the whole camp was woken by a frantic shout of 'Sergeant Johnson!' from one of Moriarty's sentries. Harward, looking out of his tent, saw to his horror 'as the fog lifted, a dense mass of Zulus about 200 yards from the waggon laager, extending all across the valley with a front of some 2 or 3 miles apparently'. The Zulu had approached undetected to within fifty yards of the wagons, screened by the mist. As soon as they were spotted they fired a volley into the wagons at close range, threw down their firearms and rushed into the laager.

The prize had proved far too tempting for an experienced marauder like Mbilini to ignore. Although the British later put the number of men at his command as high as 9,000, Zulu sources suggest that it was closer to 800 warriors. These included not only Mbilini's and Manyanyoba's followers but abaQulusi, and indeed a number of Zulu belonging to the King's regiments. The royal *amabutho* were then dispersed among their own homesteads, and a number of men who lived in the northern districts joined the attack on their own account. On the north bank one of the survivors, Private Deacon, realized to his consternation that the defences were far too inadequate to withstand the charge:

> About 4.40 a.m. I was awakened by the report of a rifle. I at once rushed out [but] I found the laager full of Zulus, in addition to numbers still outside, they came in under and over the wagons; as I saw there was no chance of resistance I made for the river and got across followed by large numbers of Zulus . . .

Most of the men on the north bank were cut down as they stumbled out of their tents, half-awake, unarmed, and in many cases naked. Moriarty himself emerged to find himself in the thick of the slaughter. Private Hogan saw him

> . . . come out of his tent, he was immediately stabbed with an assegai by a Zulu. Captain Moriarty came inside the laager, and was then shot, he fell on his face, but did not speak. Finding that a number of our men were killed, I with others made the best of our way to the river . . .

On the south bank, Private Lewis had been on sentry duty when the attack began;

> I saw a large body of men approaching the camp on the opposite side of the river, I at once fired and gave the alarm, I retired on the guard, the Zulus were then in the laager; and about 200 or 300 Zulus commenced to cross the river from both sides of the laager, which was completely surrounded, when the Zulus commenced climbing the bank . . .

Neither Harward nor Booth had gone back to sleep after the first alarm, and the sudden terrible commotion on the north bank brought them and their command hurrying out to form up. According to Booth,

> . . . the sentry on my side of the river fired a shot, and called out 'the Kaffirs are on us', everyone then turned out. I saw the kaffirs on the opposite side of the river, they were then crowding on the tents

and wagons. We at once opened fire, and kept the fire up for about ten minutes or ¼ of an hour; the kaffirs were then in the river, in great numbers coming towards us, and at the same time assegaing the men from the other side who were attempting to cross; about 200 Zulus came to our side of the river, and as we saw no more of our men crossing the river, we commenced firing and retiring, having received the order from Mr Harward. The Zulus followed us to the farm known as Raby's, a distance of about 2 miles, trying to surround us. At Raby's farm the Zulus left us, and I with my party made the best of our way to Luneburg (2 miles from Raby's). From the time of leaving the Intombi River to arrival at Raby's Farm not one of my party was wounded, although several shots were fired at them.

Harward agreed that it had not been possible to do more than cover the retreat of a handful of men from the north bank before the entire position was overrun:

The enemy were now assegaing our men in the water, and also ascending the banks of the river close to us; for fear, therefore, of my men being stabbed under the waggon, and to enable them to retire before their ammunition should be exhausted, I ordered them to retire steadily, and only just in time to avoid a rush of Zulus to our late position. The Zulus came on in dense masses and fell upon our men, who being already broken, gave way, and a hand to hand fight ensued. I endeavoured to rally my men, but they were much scattered, and finding re-formation impossible, I mounted my horse and galloped into Luneburg at utmost speed, and reported all that had taken place.

Major Tucker was in his tent at Luneburg when

about 6.30 a.m. Lieut. Harward arrived ... from the Intombi River reporting that the camp and waggons were in the possession of the enemy ... As I have no mounted men under my command, I at once ordered all the horses belonging to the officers of the regiment to be saddled, and proceeding to the camp at the Intombi River. Leaving orders for 150 men of the 80th Regiment to follow. On approaching Myers' Mission Station we observed, extending for about two miles under the brow of Umbeline's Hill, a long thick line of Zulus making eastward. I computed the body of the enemy in view at not less than 4,000; there were undoubtedly many more;

as we could see no cattle being driven, these Zulus were evidently making a hurried retreat. Arriving at Intombi River, I found the laager completely wrecked, the cattle being taken and the contents of the waggons strewn about the place, and from the bank of the river we could see the dead bodies of our men lying about on the opposite side. On arrival of the 80th from Luneburg, the bodies were collected and interred on this side of the river. I regret to report that Captain D. B. Moriarty was killed, together with Civil Surgeon Cobbin. Out of a total of 104 Officers and men of the 80th Regt. 40 are known to be killed, 20 are missing, and 44 have escaped to Luneburg – 1 man slightly wounded. In addition to the above Mr Whittington, waggon conductor, a volunteer named Campbell, late of Ferreira's Horse and a native driver, have been killed. With regard to the 20 men reported missing of the 80th Regiment, I fear most of them have been drowned or assegaid in the river, which was running swiftly, and was exceedingly high at the time. A list of the waggon employees will be sent as soon as possible.

Tucker's fears were correct; the final official toll of casualties was sixty-two of the 80th killed, together with two white wagon conductors and fifteen black *voorloopers*.

The Zulu force scattered to avoid reprisals, and while Mbilini returned to his home on Hlobane with the spoils, the garrison at Luneburg was left to apportion blame for the disaster. Clearly Moriarty had been most at fault, for the bad position of the laager, and for failing to ensure that it was properly secure. Moriarty, however, was dead, and could not be called to account. Sergeant Booth, the senior surviving NCO, had acquitted himself so well that in due course he was awarded the Victoria Cross for the incident.

That left Lieutenant Harward. Harward's actions in the opening stages of the battle had clearly been creditable, and indeed Chelmsford himself commented that he had appeared 'to have done his utmost to assist his comrades in their unequal struggle'. Tucker was moved to observe in his official report that 'The small party under Lieut. Harward ... rendered to a hopeless cause valuable assistance.' Harward argued that he had stayed with his men until their position had been overrun, and then, being the only man with a horse on the southern bank, had ridden off for assistance. None the less, there was clearly room for other interpretations. As Sergeant Booth put it in a letter to his wife, 'Lieutenant Harward saddled his horse and galloped away leaving us to do the best we could.' Harward continued in his duties for a year, serving throughout much of the rest of the Anglo-Zulu War and the subsequent campaign against King Sekhukhune, and there is nothing to suggest during that time that he experienced anything other than the support of his fellow officers. Then, in February 1880, he was tried by Court Martial on a charge for misbehaviour before the enemy. By that time Lord Chelmsford had long since resigned his command in South Africa, and his successor, Sir Garnet Wolseley, had been determined to draw a line under a number of unfortunate lapses in discipline which, in his view, had characterized the war.

Harward was tried on two counts, namely that he had deserted the men under his command and had failed to take proper precautions for the defence of the laager. His defence regarding the second point was robust and difficult to refute; he had only arrived in the laager the day before the attack, and it had been his superior, Moriarty, who had been responsible for constructing the camp. The first charge was more problematic, but Harward argued that by the time he rode off, the position had deteriorated to the extent that he could no longer exert any authority, and the only hope of survival was to hurry reinforcements out from Luneburg. Clearly the Court had some sympathy for him, and he was acquitted.

Wolseley, however, who had not experienced the general demoralization which had prevailed after Isandlwana, took a different view when the decision was passed to him for review, and he refused to confirm the verdict:

> Had I released this officer without making any remarks upon the verdict in question, it would have been a tacit acknowledgement that I concurred in what appears to me to be a monstrous theory, viz., that a regimental officer who is the only officer present with a party of soldiers actually and seriously engaged with the enemy, can, under any pretext whatever, by justified in deserting them, and by so doing, abandoning them to their fate. The more helpless the position in which an officer finds his men, the more it is his bounden duty to stay and share their fortune, whether for good or ill . . .
>
> It is to this faith of the British soldier in his officers that we owe most of the gallant deeds recorded in our military annals; and it is

because the verdict of this Court-Martial strikes at the root of this
faith, that I feel it necessary to mark officially my emphatic dissent
from the theory upon which the verdict had been founded.

Harward was released from arrest and returned to duty, but of course
his career was ruined; he resigned his commission in May 1880.

The Zulu victory at Ntombe had inflicted on the British the heaviest
casualties of the war since Isandlwana. For Lord Chelmsford himself,
it was a further grim reminder that the Zulu held the upper hand on
all fronts. In the north, there was a severe setback to the ascendancy
which Wood had tried hard to establish in the wake of Hamu's defection. While the nervous garrison and civilians huddled into the laager
at Luneburg, Wood immediately ordered Buller to raid the homesteads
in the Ntombe valley in retribution. In fact, however, the Zulu force
had already dispersed, and the only concentrations which remained were
secure on the Hlobane stronghold.

By this stage in the war, as he had anticipated, Hlobane had indeed
come to pose a major problem for Wood. Although Buller's men had
patrolled the length of the foot of the mountain, and had skirmished
several times with warriors on the slopes, they had made no attempt to
seize the heights. Hlobane was all the more formidable because it was a
plateau, three or four miles long, and its undulating, wind-swept surface
was almost entirely cut off by a line of sheer cliffs. These rose for two or
three hundred feet from the steep lower slopes, and at their feet lay a
dense jumble of huge boulders, which had split away from the sides over
the centuries and collapsed. For the most part the summit was accessible
only by a few cattle tracks, which wound up across loose stones between
the rock walls. It was too exposed to the elements to allow the abaQulusi
to live there in comfort, but in times of danger they drove their cattle up
on to the plateau, sealing the paths behind them with dry stone walls.
By this simple expedient Hlobane was turned into an effective natural
fortress.

Only at the western end did the terrain suggest a more readily
accessible route. Here Hlobane is connected to a smaller plateau, known
as Ntendeka, a triangular feature whose point jammed up against the
bulk of Hlobane. Although steep, Ntendeka lacks the crown of cliffs
which characterizes the bigger mountain, and its surface lies about 200
feet below the summit of Hlobane. A steep, narrow pass connects the

two; having examined it through field glasses from the slopes of Zung-wini mountain opposite, Wood concluded that this pass was no more than a grassy slope.

Throughout early March, Wood fretted at the possibility of attacking Hlobane. On 3 March, a week before Ntombe, he had written to Chelmsford:

> [Buller] wanted to 'try' the Hlobane before raiding past it. 'Tis a double mountain joined by a narrow nek, and has precipitous sides on all but two or three spots. I am against 'trying', or fiddling at a place. If we try I say we must go up if it costs half a battalion, and I think we can't spare half a battalion at present . . . I should like to clear it before we go forward, but I don't think we ought to attempt it just now . . .

The Zulu success at Ntombe underlined the threat posed by the complex, however, and over the following week Wood was given a prod by the events unfolding elsewhere in the war. From as early as mid-February, Chelmsford had begun to receive reinforcements at Durban, in response to his urgent appeals following Isandlwana. By the middle of March, he had begun to accumulate sufficient fresh troops to contemplate a new offensive. His first objective was to extricate his existing commands. Wood was still capable of limited offensive action, and while the remainder of the old Centre Column was shut up at Rorke's Drift, it was not directly under threat. Not so with Pearson's column, however, which was still cut off inside Zululand with no form of communication with the outside world. With no detailed information available, Chelmsford could only ponder the extent of Pearson's vulnerability. He had little information, too, on the condition of King Cetshwayo's army, although reports from inside Zululand suggested that the warriors had recovered from their ordeal at Isandlwana, and that the king was preparing to order a general call-up. There was at least a possibility that Pearson would be the subject of a concerted attack; and that in his weakened state he would have been unable to resist it. The political consequences of Eshowe becoming a second Isandlwana were too dreadful to contemplate.

By the third week of March, therefore, Chelmsford was actively preparing to use his new troops to march to the relief of Eshowe. As

early as the 17th – less than a week after Ntombe – he hinted broadly to
Wood,

> If you are in a position to make any forward movement about
> the 27th of this month, so that the news may reach the neighbour-
> hood of Eshowe about the 29th, I think it might have a good effect –
> I shall tell the border commandants to make demonstrations all along
> the border also . . .

This directive – which fell short of an order – left the exact means of
carrying out a diversion to Wood's discretion, a freedom Wood himself
clearly relished. Along the central Thukela, the garrisons on the Natal
border would seek to confuse the Zulu as to Chelmsford's true intentions
by crossing the river to burn homesteads and carry off Zulu cattle. To
Wood, it provided an opportunity to reconsider the clearing of the
Hlobane complex. Suggestions that the abaQulusi were sheltering as
many as 2,000 head of cattle on the summit of the plateau may also have
influenced his decision. Wood and Buller had become adroit cattle
thieves, and Buller and his mounted men clearly relished the adventure
of such actions. Not only did they strike at the economic base of Zulu
support for the war but they helped, too, to offset British costs as the
cattle were sold on to civilian contractors. Certainly it seems that Piet
Uys's Boers, who were prompted in part by the prospect of loot, regarded
the Hlobane expedition primarily as a cattle raid.

Nevertheless, the timing of the expedition was problematic. On the
27th – the very day that Wood's troops set out – a report reached
Khambula from some of Hamu's people, who had just arrived from
Zululand, that

> Cetywayo has summoned the whole Zulu nation to him at
> Ulundi, and will come in person with them to take Oham from the
> white people, starting from the Hlobane. He intends to attack this
> column, rushing on it in the same way as was done at Isandhlwana.
>
> The impi is to start from Ulundi about the 26th or 27th, but
> Masipula's people are causing delay as they wish to be 'doctored'
> before starting on account of their heavy losses at Isandhlwana.

If this report were true, the Zulu army could be expected in the
vicinity of Hlobane within the next two or three days. Wood, however,
thought it unlikely that any significant force could arrive in time to

threaten his planned foray; as one of his critics later noted acidly, to embark on such an expedition knowing that the enemy might be in the vicinity, but with no clear idea of exactly where they were or what their intentions were, 'was rash'. In the event, however, circumstances would combine to spare Wood the sort of intense scrutiny over his actions at Hlobane that Chelmsford was subject to after Isandlwana.

Wood's plan was not very different from the methods he had successfully employed in January to clear Zungwini. He intended to mount a pincer attack on Hlobane, assaulting the range at either end, with attacks timed to catch the Zulu by surprise at dawn. Despite the fact that Hlobane lay no further from the camp at Khambula than Zungwini had done from the earlier position near Nseka, Wood decided on this occasion not to employ his infantry in the assault. The attacking parties were made up entirely of mounted men, supported by African auxiliaries. One party under Buller, consisting of nearly 400 irregulars with 300 auxiliaries, was to swing round the southern side of the mountain and ascend the eastern end. The other, commanded by Lieutenant-Colonel J. C. Russell, was to attack the western end. According to Wood's orders, Russell's force was intended largely for support:

> It is not intended that the western reconnaissance should force the position against strong resistance – though it will of course advance when it is known when the summit has been gained by the eastern force, or sooner, if not strongly opposed.

Russell's party was weaker in cavalry, just 250 men, a mixture of Mounted Infantry, irregulars and the Native Horse, but included a larger proportion of auxiliaries. In addition to nearly 300 of Wood's irregulars, Russell commanded about 150 of Hamu's Zulu, who were entering into action against their countrymen for the first time. There was an irony in this; Russell himself was a veteran of the Isandlwana campaign – he had been out with Chelmsford at the time of the battle – while many of the Natal irregulars with him had fought in the battle and survived. Numbers of Hamu's warriors, in contrast, had also been present, but fighting for the other side. To give them at least a nominal artillery support, both parties were supported by a rocket trough, carried on mules.

Buller's force had left Khambula early on the 27th, intending to bivouac in the field that night in the hope of deceiving the Zulu as to their true intentions. Russell's force, who were to approach their objective by a more direct route, left in the early afternoon. Wood himself planned to follow in their wake, accompanied by only his personal staff and escort. He had every confidence in Buller's capabilities, and intended to let his field commanders act on their own initiative where possible, realizing that once the attack was under way, he would have very little chance of controlling the assault parties in the difficult terrain.

The geography of the Hlobane complex, indeed, remained problematic. Although British patrols had observed the plateau from a distance many times, and Buller and Piet Uys had ridden on to the lower slopes, no one in the expedition had any experience of conditions around the summit. From a distance, the top of Hlobane had seemed flat, ideal terrain for the tough and self-reliant irregulars to operate in. The narrow ridge connecting the western end of Hlobane to the lower hill appeared no more than a grassy slope, while Buller himself claimed to have spotted a viable cattle track at the far eastern end. Everything would depend on the ability of the cavalry to operate in such country. On the 27th – the same day that Hamu's followers reported the approach of a Zulu army – Wood wrote to Chelmsford:

> Buller has started – Russell goes at 1 p.m. – I at 3 p.m. to try and get up the Hlobane at day-light tomorrow. I am not VERY sanguine of success. We do not know how steep the Eastern end may be, but I think we ought to make a stir here to divert attention from you, altho' as you'll see by our last reports it is asserted you have the coast tribes only against you, and all of Cetywayo's people are coming here. Unless they have started, however, they may move to Ekowe instead, on hearing of your preparation.
>
> I do not plan to do more than attack the Hlobane until the new regiments are ready to take our places if we get cut up. If we fail tomorrow I may try again with infantry . . .

Wood was not daunted by the prospect of a Zulu attack during his absence – Khambula was guarded by his infantry and artillery, and his orders for the day specified that 'Major Leet will leave 50 men [of the auxiliaries] in Camp as Cetewayo is said to be advancing with his whole army'.

That night, Russell and Wood bivouacked about five miles to the west of Hlobane, while Buller's men – who lit camp fires early in the evening, then moved closer to the mountain after dark – were about seven miles to the south-east of it. Before dawn, Buller's party saddled up as quietly as they could and rode through the darkness to the eastern end of the mountain. On the southern face of Hlobane the mountain curled inward, a horse-shoe indentation scalloped by aeons of erosion, and Buller's men struggled up through the long grass and huge boulders while the cliffs seemed to crowd in around them. Just as they followed the last few hundred yards of narrow track up to the summit, a sudden thunderstorm broke deafeningly overhead, illuminating the rock walls around them in the flashes of lightning. Only at this point, it seems, did the Zulu discover their presence; too late, as Buller reported, to stop the attack;

> At 3.30 a.m. on the 28th, we left our bivouac and ascended the Hlobana mountain. It was luckily a misty morning and our attack was practically a surprise. This was fortunate as the position was an extremely strong one, and had the Zulus had time to prepare we could not have got up without heavy loss.
> The men led by Mr Piet Uys, Commandant Raaff, and Captain Barton carried the position with a rush, our loss being two officers, the Baron von Stietencron and Lieutenant Williams, Frontier Light Horse, who were killed in the assault and while occupying the kranz which was the key of the position, and one man, Trooper Stewart, Frontier Light Horse, mortally wounded.

'The ascent', confirmed Major Knox Leet, commanding the 2nd Battalion, Wood's irregulars,

> ... was very steep, the ground being rough and stony, when a sharp fire was opened on the head of the column from the left of the mountain in our front and the caves and rocks on both flanks. The horsemen got off their horses and climbed up the ascent, which was here very steep and rough, and I brought up the 'Irregulars' as rapidly as possible, and they swarmed up the hill with praiseworthy courage and rapidity ...

Once on the summit, Buller's men found themselves in an eerily beautiful lost world. The surface of the plateau, which was about three miles long, had seemed flat from a distance, but was in fact a gently undulating table-land topped with a layer of boulders worn almost flat by erosion. Grass grew up in the narrow gaps between them, making it difficult for even the hardy horses ridden by the irregulars to place their feet, while here and there streams meandered through marshy beds before tipping themselves over the sides. Such was the lie of the land that, just two or three hundred yards in from the edges, all sight was lost of the world below. As a result, the battle of Hlobane remains the most confusing and least understood of the war, a running fight in which small groups of men moved about across the plateau with only the haziest sense of direction, and isolated from events going on around them.

It was now light, and as the mist cleared Buller could see hundreds of head of cattle grazing on the summit, guarded by small parties of warriors. These, he found, were easily dispersed:

> ... the natives who occupied it disappeared into the rocks and caves of the side kranzes. These the 2nd Battalion Wood's Irregulars, worked through splendidly, collecting many cattle. To assist them, I placed men all round the edge of the plateau to fire into the rocks below, and I then proceeded to the western edge, beneath which I found Lieutenant-Colonel Russell with a few of his men, the rest being about one mile off, having apparently just ascended the lower Hlobana mountain.

Russell, indeed, had been delayed by the difficult terrain. His party had climbed the steep slopes of the western edges of the lower plateau, Ntendeka, but on reaching the pass which connected it to the main plateau found it completely impractical for cavalry. It was in fact a jumbled staircase of rock about 300 feet high. Some semblance of a cattle track existed down the middle of the pass, but even here it was necessary to jump from boulder to boulder, while on either side the rocks were much larger, and tangled with bush. At the top of the pass, the abaQulusi had built a dry stone wall to keep cattle from straying over the edge. Russell described his progress, and the dilemma which then confronted him:

> I marched from my bivouac about 4 a.m. . . . and arrived at the foot of the westernmost portion of the Hlobana mountain at daybreak.
> I directed the battalion of Wood's Irregulars and Oham's people to move up the hill, following them closely with the Mounted Infantry, Rocket Trough, Basutos, and Schermbrucker's Corps.

I did not take the time on arriving on the plateau, but I think it was about 6.30 to 7 a.m.

It was reported to me by Mr Williams, 58th Regiment, that Colonel Buller's force was already in possession of the upper plateau, and that he and others could be seen upon it.

I at once moved with a small party of the first formed men to try to communicate with Colonel Buller, while the rear of my column was still coming up the hill.

I was fired at and my escort returned the fire. I heard Colonel Buller shout 'Bring your men up to fire,' or words to that effect. I sent back to bring up the rest of the force which quickly arrived.

In the meantime, it had been pointed out that there were large quantities of cattle on the sides of the Hlobana Hill, within easy reach, I therefore directed Commandant White's battalion to go and collect the cattle on the south side of the Nek, and Oham's people, those on the north side of the Nek.

The Mounted Infantry, Basutos, and Schermbrucker's Corps were ready to cover them with fire.

Commandant White brought back a considerable number of cattle to the plateau, but Oham's people drove what they found in a westerly direction, towards the Zunguin. I did not see them again during the day.

Captain Browne, M.I., had been directed to cross the Nek, and to get to the top of the plateau, to find out, if possible, if assistance was required from me by Colonel Buller, and generally what was the situation. Everything appeared to be nearly quiet and the whole object of the reconnaissance to be gained.

Captain Browne remained on the top of the second plateau for some time. He was unable to see Colonel Buller . . .

At this point, the situation across the mountain seemed generally to be under control. On the summit, Knox Leet's auxiliaries were rounding up cattle with little difficulty;

All opposition had apparently ceased on the mountain but looking down into the valley below, about an hour after we had reached the top, I could see a large number of the 'Irregulars' of Lt. Col. Russell's force gathering numerous herds of cattle together, and occasionally hunting a Zulu who was turned out of the rocks.

Yet this appearance of calm was deceptive. Buller now rode back across the summit towards the eastern end to check the situation and supervise the burial of the men killed in the ascent. What he found there was disconcerting. The men he had placed to act as a defensive perimeter were coming under heavy pressure from large numbers of Zulu. Many of the abaQulusi had erected temporary huts below the north-eastern face of the mountain and were moving up through the cliffs in large numbers. Others had moved rapidly round the foot, and had already cut the track by which Buller's party had come up. Buller certainly saw the danger:

> On arrival there, I found that the Zulus had been largely reinforced, and were pressing us hard, and that, owing to the great size of the mountain, and the great difficulty of the path by which we had to retire, there was every probability of the enemy being able to assemble at one end out of fire, then rush upon us as we retired.
>
> I accordingly sent Captain Barton down the hill with 30 men to bury Lieutenant Williams at once and return to camp direct.

In fact, though Buller did not yet realize it, his men were caught in a carefully prepared trap. Although his dawn assault had indeed been a surprise, the frequent British patrols around the mountain had long warned the Zulu of the likelihood of such a move. Knowing every inch of the mountain intimately, the abaQulusi *induna*, Sikhobobo, assisted by Mbilini – whose personal homestead lay high on the southern slopes of the mountain – were clearly prepared. Having got up, it was their intention that Buller would not get down, and to this effect they still had one more dramatic card to play.

The speed with which the Zulu cut Buller's path soon became apparent to parties following in his wake. Wood himself, with his staff, had left Russell early that morning and had ridden along the southern face of the mountain, hoping to pick up Buller's trail to the summit. 'At daylight', he recalled,

> [I] got on Colonel Buller's track, which we followed. Colonel Weatherley met me coming westward, having lost his way the previous night, and I directed him to move on the sound of the firing, which was now audible on the north-western face of the mountain, where we could see the rear of Colonel Buller's Column near the summit.

Wood's encounter with Weatherley is one of the enduring mysteries of the battle. Weatherley's command, a unit of irregulars raised in the Transvaal and called the Border Horse, had started out with Buller's column but had somehow become separated in the dark on the way up the mountain. According to Captain Dennison, one of Weatherley's men, this was because of 'our Colonel not having received orders to march from our first camping ground' – a fact which Buller would later deny. In any case, Wood now urged Weatherley to follow Buller, although the situation was becoming more dangerous by the minute;

It is impossible to describe in adequate terms the difficulty of the ascent which Colonel Buller and his men had successfully made, not without loss however, for horses killed and wounded helped to keep us on the track where the rocks afforded no evidence of his advance. We soon came under fire from an unseen enemy on our right. Ascending more rapidly than most of the Border Horse, who had got off the track, with my staff and escort, I passed to the front, and with half a dozen of the Border Horse when within a hundred feet of the summit, came under a well-directed fire from our front and both flanks, poured in from behind huge boulders and rocks. Mr Lloyd fell mortally wounded at my side, and as Captain Campbell and one of the escort were carrying him on to a ledge rather lower, my horse was killed, falling on me. I directed Colonel Weatherley to dislodge one or two Zulus who were causing us most loss, but, as his men did not advance rapidly, Captain Campbell and Lieutenant Lysons and three men of the 90th, jumping over a low wall, ran forward and charged into a cave, when Captain Campbell, leading in the most determined and gallant manner, was shot dead; Lieutenant Lysons and Private Fowler followed closely on his footsteps, and one of them, for each fired, killed one Zulu and dislodged another, who crawled away by a subterranean passage, reappearing higher up the mountain. At this time we were assisted by the fire of some of Colonel Buller's men on the summit. Colonel Weatherley asked permission to move down the hill to regain Colonel Buller's track, which we had lost, and by which he later gained the summit without further casualties; by this time he had lost three men dead and six or seven wounded.

Mr Lloyd was now dead, and we brought his body, and that of

Captain Campbell's, about half way down the hill, where we buried
them, still being under fire which, however, did us no damage.

I then rode slowly round under the Inhlobana Mountain to the
westward, to see how Colonel Russell's force had progressed . . .

In fact, though Wood never admitted it, it seems that he was badly
shaken by the death of his political officer, Llwellwyn Lloyd, and
Captain Campbell, both of whom were personal friends. Wood seems
to have lost all interest in the battle at that point, and intended to
return to Khambula, leaving his field commanders to make the best of
it. Later, British intelligence reports suggested that it may have been
Mbilini himself who shot Campbell; certainly, he took an active part
in the battle, and received a bullet wound in the shoulder; he may have
been the wounded man who escaped through the jumble of boulders.

On the summit, meanwhile, Buller had been forced to call in his
extended perimeter and retire westwards, towards Russell, and a confused running fight broke out across the summit. Although the British
position was now uncomfortable, it was not yet critical, but Buller was
due for a further shock. As he passed along the southern end of the
mountain, one of his men drew his attention to a large mass, like the
shadow of a cloud, moving across the valley below. It was a minute or
two before the truth dawned; it was a large Zulu army, heading towards
Hlobane.

The reports received so lightly by Wood the day before had been
essentially correct. Well aware of the build-up on his borders, King
Cetshwayo had assembled his main army at oNdini. Although intensely
irritated by Pearson's presence at Eshowe, he had been convinced by
the appeals of Mbilini and the abaQulusi *izinduna* that Wood's column
was the most aggressive and dangerous remaining on Zulu soil. While
a few regiments had been despatched to support the forces operating
in the coastal districts, therefore, the bulk of the army had been sent
northwards. Some 20,000 strong, it was composed of the same regiments which had triumphed at Isandlwana, and the men's morale was
high. It was commanded once again by Ntshingwayo kaMahole, and
accompanied by Chief Mnyamana kaNqengelele of the Buthelezi. Chief
Mnyamana, the King's most experienced and respected counsellor, was
one of the most powerful men in the country, and his presence reflected
the importance the royal council placed on the coming campaign.

Cetshwayo himself had given specific instructions to his commanders, ordering them not to fall upon the British emplacements – having learnt the lesson of Rorke's Drift, he is said to have told them, 'Do not put your face into the lair of the wild beasts, for you are sure to get clawed' – but to feint towards the Transvaal border settlements and draw the British into the open.

The army had left oNdini on the 24th – two days earlier than Wood's informants had suggested – and while its arrival during the attack on Hlobane was coincidental, the abaQulusi had been expecting it. Indeed, they had hoped it might arrive earlier in the day, and had been trying to pin Buller on the summit in the expectation that the main army would appear in time to complete his destruction. The *impi* had been advancing in two columns, and had not expected to fight that day, but even as the left wing drifted westwards towards Khambula, the right crossed the iNyathi ridge a few miles south of Hlobane and was immediately drawn to the battle taking place there. This wing consisted of the young uKhandempemvu, iNgobamakhosi and uVe *amabutho*, who advanced rapidly across the intervening valley, deploying into the traditional 'chest and horns' formation. While the iNgobamakhosi and uVe headed towards the western end of the mountain, the uKhandempemvu swung round to the east.

Russell, still waiting on the lower plateau of Ntendeka, had perhaps been the first to spot the Zulu approach;

> Shortly after 9 a.m. it was reported to me that a Zulu army was seen on the range of hills to the south of the Hlobana.
> At 9 a.m. I sent a message addressed to Colonel Wood to that effect, and I collected my force together.
> I thought that there would be time to get away the cattle.
> The Zulu Army assumed such very large proportions and moved with such extreme rapidity that at about 10 a.m. I thought it necess-ary to abandon the cattle, as I did not see how I was to protect the large number of natives who were driving them. I moved all my force down the hill . . .

By this time Wood had become aware of the danger. Accompanying his staff was Prince Mthonga kaMpande, one of Cetshwayo's rivals for the Zulu throne who had lived in exile in Natal and had joined Wood's column in the capacity of adviser. Mthonga was accompanied

by a handful of his followers, and it had been these men who had dug
Campbell and Lloyd's grave under fire. As the party moved westwards,
round the foot of the mountain,

> We stopped occasionally to give the wounded man stimulants,
> unconscious of the fact that a very large Zulu force was moving on
> our left, across our front. We were about half way under the centre
> of the mountain when Umtonga saw, and explained to me by signs,
> there was a large army close to us. From an adjacent hill I had a
> good view of this force, it was marching in five columns, with horns
> and dense chest, the normal Zulu attack formation. I sent Lieuten-
> ant Lysons to Colonel Russell who, as it appeared, had seen the
> army previously, with the following written order: '10.30 a.m., 28th
> March 1879. Colonel Russell, there is a large army coming this way
> from the south, get into position on Zunguin Nek. (Signed) E.W.'

Russell's response to this order remains one of the most controver-
sial aspects of the battle. According to his own report, 'he moved to
that point', understanding it to mean a saddle of land to the west of
Zungwini, between that hill and Khambula camp. Wood, however,
meant him to take up a position at the foot of the lower plateau,
between Ntendeka and Zungwini, from whence he could cover Buller's
retreat. The fault undoubtedly lay in the hazy British understanding of
the terrain, but Wood, who had been resentful that Russell had been
transferred to his command after Isandlwana, and regarded him as an
outsider, clearly thought otherwise;

> Colonel Russell reports that he moved from the Inhlobana to
> Zunguin's Neck, but this is incorrect, on the contrary, he went away
> six miles to the western corner of the range, and for which Wood's
> Irregulars, the 1st battalion, and Oham's men were making, driving
> the captured cattle. Colonel Russell ordered all the captured cattle
> to be abandoned and made off very rapidly under the western end
> of the range. He thus uncovered the retreat of Oham's people, about
> 80 of whom were killed by the Zulus running down from the
> Inhlobana, they being greatly encouraged by the sight of the large
> army now moving directly on the western end of the range.

There was worse to come on the summit itself. Most of Buller's
command was now drawing towards the western end of the plateau,

under constant attack from the abaQulusi, but the party under Barton, detached to bury those killed in the ascent, was still heading back towards the eastern end. Moreover, unknown to Buller, Weatherley's men had only just reached the summit, following their skirmish along the foot of the cliffs. As soon as he had seen the approaching *impi*, Buller recognized the urgent need to get off the mountain:

> Just after we had seen Captain Barton and his men safely off, we observed a very large number of Zulus advancing in order across the flats on the south-east, and I at once sent two more men after Captain Barton, directing him to drop Lieutenant Williams' body and retreat at once to camp by the right side of the mountain, down which there was I knew a decent footpath, fairly practical for horses in single file, and offering no serious obstacle for this small force.
>
> Just at this time I received a despatch from Lieutenant-Colonel Russell informing me of the advent of the Zulu force. Hastening back to the west end of the plateau, I collected the scattered detachment on my way, and commenced a retreat.

Buller's hasty note to Barton had tragic consequences. It is not entirely clear by which route he intended Barton to descend, although by military convention the terms 'left' and 'right' were relevant to the direction the troops were facing at the start of an attack. Buller may have meant Barton to escape via the north-western edge of the mountain, down the track by which the abaQulusi had come up; or he may, as he was riding westwards, have been referring to a jumble of rocks which provided a possible track on the northern side. Whatever his intentions, however, when Barton received the note, being unaware of the exact position of the approaching Zulus, he seems to have taken it as proof of his original orders to descend by the southern track. Barton had just received this order and was continuing eastwards when, according to Captain Dennison, he met Weatherley's Border Horse coming in the opposite direction:

> Captain Barton, with about 40 or 50 of the Light Horse, came up to us and told Colonel Weatherley that he had received orders to push round the southern side of Thlabana, as a large impi on the enemy had been seen on that side, and that our Colonel was to push on with his corps. We immediately did so, and on getting

to the turn of the mountain, we saw great numbers of the enemy, which I estimated to be 10,000.

Barton and Weatherley had descended the mountain safely enough, but as they started to move west through the valley below, they met the right flank of the Zulu force, the uKhandempemvu regiment, heading straight towards them. With no hope of slipping past them, the irregulars had no choice but to turn about and ride back along the foot of the mountain. Their only hope of escape lay across a saddle of land, known as Ityenka Nek, which lay at the eastern foot of Hlobane, connecting it to the next mountain in the range. As they reached the nek, however, pursued by the uKhandempemvu, the abaQulusi streamed down off the heights to cut them off. As if this situation were not dangerous enough, the ground itself was about to turn against them. 'We were obliged to make a hurried retreat', recalled Dennison,

> . . . as we found our way completely blocked by the enemy. We retreated under a very heavy cross fire to the Nek on the eastern point of the mountain, the enemy following us within a short distance. On getting over the Nek we found the mountain extremely steep with a succession of precipitous ledges, in getting down the enemy rushed down and assegaid our men. Myself, and about 26 of our men, and the Light Horse, reached the bottom of the Nek; several of us kept up a fire for a short time but finding the enemy outflanking us we had to race for our lives across country in the direction of Makatee's Kop, we were followed by the enemy to within three miles of Potter's stores, many of the men were killed on the retreat.

In the terrifying descent through the cliffs of Ityenka Nek, many men simply tumbled over the edge and fell to their deaths. Both Weatherley and his son – a sub-lieutenant in his unit – were killed, while Barton and another officer survived the descent, only to be chased across several miles of the open country beyond by an *induna* of the uKhandempemvu named Sitshitshili kaMnqandi, who caught and killed them.

On the summit, too, the withdrawal had dissolved into chaos. Knox Leet had first noticed the increase in Zulu activity as more and more warriors slipped up through the rocks on to the plateau. He then saw

Lt. Col. Buller with the majority of the mounted men coming along the mountain towards where I was, and followed at some distance by a large number of Zulus who were running rapidly – Col. Buller as he came up said that we had better mount our horses and get down the krantz onto the lower mountain at once. The only possible way of getting down from where we were to the lower mountain was by an almost perpendicular krantz composed of extremely irregular boulders and stones and very narrow. With so many men and horses to go down the operation at any time would have been an extremely difficult one, but with the enemy pressing on it appeared almost impossible.

Indeed, even the carefully controlled tones of Buller's official report cannot entirely conceal the horror of their predicament:

> Our line of retreat was most difficult, descending onto the plateau of the Lower Hlobana Mountain, which had earlier in the day been occupied by Colonel Russell, but which he had now left, by a narrow – almost perpendicular – cattle track down a kranz some 120 feet deep, with scarcely room for three horses abreast, by rocky steps, in many cases only a few inches broad, and with jumps of three, four or even five feet between them; and having crossed that plateau, we then had the mountain itself, very steep, rocky and precipitous to descend. But there are only three ways down, the one at the east end, by which we came up, I considered to be closed by the advancing Zulu force, and the other one is worse than the one I adopted.
>
> In such a descent, a certain amount of confusion was unavoidable, and this was increased by the Zulus crowding on our rear and flanks, and commencing a heavy fire, which killed a large number of the horses.
>
> We should though, I think, have got down with little loss, had not someone called out to the rearguard to cease firing, as a party of natives advancing towards us across the plateau were our own Kafirs, and not Zulus.
>
> They did cease firing, and in a moment the Zulus were among us. In the struggle that ensued we suffered heavily, losing one officer, 15 men, and Mr Piet Uys, who had got down safely but returned to assist his son and was assegaid.
>
> The Zulus pursued us in force, and with so many dismounted

men we experienced great difficulty in descending the mountain, and, but for the experience of a few our retreat would have been a rout, as it was we got down with the loss of those men only who were too badly wounded to be kept on horses ...

With the Zulu crawling among the boulders on either side, throwing spears and firing at close range, the line of struggling men and horses gave way to panic. In the noise and confusion, the so-called pass became littered with dead men and horses, while individual troopers fled on foot or tried to hide among the rocks. Buller and a handful of his officers stemmed the rout as best they could, and Buller personally returned up the slope at the foot of the pass time and again to bring men down. A few tried to escape on the southern side of Ntendeka, only to find that the iNgobamakhosi and uVe regiments were moving across the base, intent on pursuing the captured Zulu cattle towards Zungwini.

Major Knox Leet had managed to survive the ordeal of the pass, though both the horse he was riding and a spare he was leading were killed, and he was forced to mount up as best he could on an artillery pack-horse. While most of the survivors made their way off Ntendeka at the western end of the mountain – the way Russell had come up – Knox Leet decided to try to get away by a more direct route, straight over the edge on the northern face. This nearly proved to be a fatal mistake:

> I began the descent accompanied by Lt. Duncombe, 2nd Bat. W.I. who was on horseback and Lt. Smith, F.L.H., who was on foot, his horse having been shot. We had only gone down a very short distance when large numbers of Zulus appeared on the crest of the hill, and seeing us at once opened fire and pursued us with loud shouts. The side of the hill was extremely steep, and very irregular, with large boulders in all directions, and when we had got down about half way we found we had taken the wrong direction and were over a precipice. There was nothing for it but to turn back in the face of the pursuers and join the right direction again if possible. Fortunately we succeeded, but by this time the Zulus in large numbers were within a few yards of us, firing and throwing their assegais. Lt. Duncombe finding his horse done up got off, and as he ran along occasionally turned to fire. I saw him in this way shoot

three men within fifteen yards of him. At this time Lt. Smith became completely exhausted and sat down, and it was apparent that if I left him he must be assegaid in another minute. I therefore made him get up and run along holding on to the pack saddle, but the ground was so rocky and he was so done up that he could not come on, and I therefore stopped and managed with great difficulty to get him up behind me, the pack saddle having no stirrups. My horse at this time was almost exhausted, and the ground even rougher and steeper than higher up, and the Zulus having assegaid poor Lt. Duncombe were all but on us. At the same time we saw large numbers of the enemy coming up the valley under us from the right and running hard with the intention of cutting us off from Col. Buller's men who were coming down the end of the mountain over on our left, and for whom we were making. The ground now became better less rough and my horse making a final effort brought us to within a couple of hundred yards of Col. Buller's men, and to comparative safety . . .

Fortunately for the survivors, the regiments from the main Zulu army seemed intent on recapturing the looted cattle, and allowed themselves to be drawn away from pursuing the broken horsemen. They chased the auxiliaries from Wood's irregulars and Hamu's people across the southern slopes of Zungwini, killing dozens of them and recapturing most of the abaQulusi cattle. With only the abaQulusi in pursuit, the stragglers from Buller's force reached Zungwini nek, and, covered at last by Russell's force, fell back on Khambula.

The entire attack on Hlobane had been a disaster. According to the official history, Buller's force had lost twelve European officers, with eighty men killed and seven wounded. Of the losses among the auxiliary troops, Wood could only admit that night that 'I cannot be yet sure of the numbers.' That evening, when a report reached Khambula that a handful of survivors from Barton's party were still alive, Buller set out in the darkness and pouring rain to bring them in.

The right wing of the Zulu army chased the survivors for a few miles beyond Hlobane, then gave up the pursuit. Although they were young men, they had crossed many miles of rough terrain that day, and they were happy to give way to their tiredness in the knowledge that they had recaptured most of the cattle and inflicted heavy loss on Hamu's defectors. The left wing of the army, which had taken no part in the fight, had moved to a bivouac a few miles south of Zungwini, along the headwaters of the White Mfolozi river. Here the men of the uKhandempemvu, iNgobamakhosi and uVe joined them, and the entire force camped for the night.

That night was a tense one at Khambula. Many of the survivors of Buller's force were exhausted and traumatized, and the disheartening spectacle of their return to the camp, dishevelled and beaten, cannot have been an encouraging one for the infantry left behind. That night, both the Swazis of Wood's irregulars and Piet Uys's men abandoned the camp, pleading the need to protect their families along the exposed frontier. Nevertheless, while many at Khambula were full of foreboding at events to come, there was, too, a fierce determination to avenge the day's losses. While the objective of the main Zulu army was open to doubt – would they attack Khambula or slip past towards the exposed settlements on the Transvaal border? – the camp would not be surprised, as Pulleine had been at Isandlwana. Moreover, while the lack of infantry support had been felt during the retreat from Hlobane, they were at least fresh to face the challenges to come.

The Zulu army rose early at its bivouac on the morning of 29 March. It was a tradition that the army be formed into a circle to receive final instructions before entering battle, and on this occasion Chief Mnyamana Buthelezi took the opportunity to address the assembled regiments. Mnyamana's reputation within the kingdom was awesome. A powerful orator, he took the opportunity to remind the warriors of the terrible responsibility which lay before them, for it was clear even at this stage that the coming battle might have a decisive effect on the outcome of the war. Already buoyed up by the collective tension of the pre-battle rituals they had undergone at oNdini before setting out, the warriors' emotions were worked to a fever-pitch by his words. It is not entirely clear whether the commanders intended to attack Wood's camp directly – certainly King Cetshwayo had advised them against it – but in the event their strategic considerations would in any case take second place to the powerful need of the younger regiments to attack the enemy wherever they found them.

The army began to move north-west in a leisurely manner and was spotted at about 10 a.m. by British patrols sent out as far as Zungwini mountain. These patrols returned to Khambula with a surprisingly accurate account of the Zulu intentions, for they brought with them one of Hamu's *izinduna*, Mbamgulana, who had spent the night in the Zulu bivouac. Mbamgulana had been present at Hlobane the previous day, and during the retreat had torn off the black and white head-band which was the only sign of his allegiance to the British; he had been lucky enough to fall in with his old regiment, who were unaware that he had defected. After discussing the campaign with his comrades around the camp-fire that night, he had slipped away at first light, on the pretext of scouting, and had made for the nearest British picket. According to Wood, Mbamgulana was able to tell his new allies 'exactly how the attack would be made at "dinner time"'.

In truth, it was perhaps obvious enough that the camp might be attacked, but at least Wood had the opportunity to prepare himself fully. The main wagon-laager, on the west of the camp complex, had been partially entrenched by cutting sods outside the line of the wagons and piling them up between the wheels. The outer buck-rails of the wagons had been further barricaded with sacks of mealies. To the south of the earthwork redoubt, the remainder of the wagons had been formed into a square cattle-laager, which stood on a terrace above a rocky drop of six or eight feet and was linked to the redoubt by a rampart of timber to prevent an attacker moving freely between the two. Most of the tents were pitched on the crest of the ridge, outside the main laager, but Wood had ordered them struck in anticipation of the coming battle. As soon as the Zulu were spotted in the distance, at about 11 a.m., ammunition boxes were distributed from the reserve, opened, and placed behind the lines. Notwithstanding the defections of the night before, Wood had just on 2,000 effective troops within his defensive perimeter, over 1,200 infantry from the 1/13th and 90th Regiments, together with four light 7-pounder guns and at least one rocket trough. It was the strongest force the Zulu had yet faced in open battle.

The Zulu could plainly be seen advancing in five columns from the direction of the White Mfolozi. When they were still several miles from the camp, they halted, and for an hour the anxious garrison watched for their next move. This halt was probably for the war-doctors, the *izinyanga*, to make their last administration of protective charms before the battle, and for the commanders to confer. Cetshwayo had ordered the army to bypass Khambula and its impressive fortifications, and try instead to lure the British into the open. For a while it seemed that this might indeed be their strategy, and Wood had the uneasy feeling that they would march on and strike at Utrecht instead. If that was what the commanders had hoped, however, they were to be frustrated by the young men who made up the bulk of their command, and who had no time for such sophisticated strategies; once they were in sight of the enemy, they simply wanted to attack. When at last the columns began moving again, it soon became clear that they were heading towards Khambula.

It took some time for the regiments to deploy across the final approaches to the British camp. The left 'horn', the uMbonambi, uNokhenke and uKhandempemvu regiments, moved into the valley to the south, while the 'chest' – the men of the senior uThulwana, iNdlondlo, uDloko, uDududu, iSangqu, iMbube and iNdluyengwe regiments – ascended the far end of the Khambula ridge to the east. The right 'horn', the iNgobamakhosi and uVe *amabutho*, moved round to the north. There was considerable rivalry between the uKhandempemvu and iNgobamakhosi regiments who spear-headed either 'horn', which hearkened back to challenges made before the King when the army had first mustered in January, and had been intensified by disputes following the victory at Isandlwana. Both regiments were in high spirits, convinced they could overcome the British if only they could catch them in the open, and each was determined to be first amongst the enemy. In the event, however, the movement of the left 'horn' was frustrated by the streams and marshy ground which lay in the bottom of the valley, and their advance was literally bogged down.

To the British, the spectacle of the regiments deliberately manouvring into position, the regimental masses marked by the uniformity of their shield colours, was mesmerizing. Initially it seemed that the left must be the first in position to attack, but having entered the southern valley, they were lost to sight and failed to re-emerge. To the north, however, the open country gave an unhindered view of the right 'horn' as it marched into position, halted and deployed. Then, suddenly and unexpectedly, it moved rapidly forward, a dense mass of supports screened by a cloud of skirmishers, halting again little more than half a mile from the camp. To Wood, watching from a vantage point on the slope outside the redoubt, this movement was obviously premature, the result, perhaps, of the rivalry between the regiments. Whatever the cause, he saw immediately that it gave him the opportunity to provoke the right 'horn' into an unsupported attack and deny the Zulu the chance to mount a coordinated attack on all sides at once. He ordered Buller to take the mounted men – many of them survivors of the terrible pass at Hlobane the day before – to try to sting the right 'horn' into launching a full-scale attack. It was now around 1.30 p.m., and the battle of Khambula was about to begin:

> . . . the mounted riflemen under Colonels Buller and Russell, engaging an enormous crowd of men on the north side of the camp. Being unable to check them, our mounted men retired inside the laager, and were followed by the Zulus until they came to within 300 yards, when their advance was checked by the accurate fire of the 90th Light Infantry, and the Zulus spread out in front and rear of our camp . . .

As they charged forward, men in the ranks of the iNgobamakhosi and uVe called out menacingly, 'We are the boys from Isandlwana!' So terrifying was their advance that some of the horses panicked, and both Colonel Russell and Lieutenant Edward Browne, attached to the Mounted Infantry, were forced to stop to help men mount. After one such incident, Russell himself got into difficulties, and Browne placed his own horse in front of Russell's until he could mount. It was a risky business, and by the time both officers rode away, the Zulu were only a few yards behind. Browne was later awarded the Victoria Cross for his actions.

Once the horsemen were safely clear of the line of fire, a terrific volley crashed out along the northern faces of the main laager and redoubt. Wood had placed two of his guns in the redoubt, but the remaining four were deployed in the open, between the redoubt and the main laager, in a position that allowed them room to move to meet each attack. There was no cover on the open, bare slopes except for the scattering of ant-hills, and the right 'horn' was exposed to a veritable storm of fire. Some elements pressed forward far enough to threaten the main laager, but they could not sustain their position, and they were at last forced to retire to the shelter of a rocky terrace about 800 yards away. According to a warrior named Sihlahla, the right 'horn' was largely spent by this attack:

The Ngobamakosi could not face the bullets, and every one of
that regiment lay down as the safest, for the bullets from the white
men were like hail falling about us. It was fearful, no one could face
them without being struck.

Mehlokazulu kaSihayo, who had earlier fought at Isandlwana with
the iNgobamakhosi, reluctantly agreed:

> We thought the Zulu army was not far off, but it appears that at
> this time the main body had not yet got up. . . . The horsemen
> galloped back as fast as they could to camp; we followed and
> discovered ourselves almost close to the camp, into which we made
> the greatest possible efforts to enter. The English fired their cannon
> and rockets. . . . Before the main body of the Zulu army came up,
> we, when the Zulu army did come up, were lying prostrate, we were
> beaten . . .

The sudden din which marked the first attack had the effect of
hurrying the rest of the Zulu army forward. The left 'horn', having
negotiated the soft ground at the foot of the valley, was now faced with
a steep slope which rose up to within 200 yards of the British position.
For most of their approach, the Zulu would be hidden from the British
guns, and only as they emerged at the top of the slope would they be
exposed to British fire. In the dry words of Wood's official report,

> The attack on our left had slackened, when at 2.15 p.m. heavy
> masses attacked our right front and right rear. The enemy, well
> supplied with Martini-Henry rifles and ammunition, occupied a hill
> not seen from the laager, and opened so accurate an enfilade fire,
> though at long range, that I was obliged to withdraw a company of
> the 1–13th Light Infantry posted at the right rear of the laager.

The attack of the left 'horn' would prove to be the most dangerous
in a day of sustained and well-directed assaults. Suddenly emerging so
close to the British positions, the Zulu suffered terrible casualties, but
these were not sufficient to prevent them from closing with the western
side of the cattle laager. Moreover, as Wood suggested, large numbers of
warriors armed with Martini-Henrys captured at Isandlwana and Hlobane occupied a low rise on the edge of the escarpment immediately to
the west of the valley. This rise was the site of the camp manure-heap,

and the fecund mix of hot sun and heavy rain over the previous few weeks had encouraged the growth of a dense patch of mealies and long grass. Making good use of this cover, the Zulu were able to pour a heavy and surprisingly accurate fire into the cattle laager in support of the men assaulting it. Wood recognized that the men in the laager were in great danger, and recalled them; the Zulu had gained their first foothold inside the British camp. Those who could not avail themselves of the shelter of the wagons were unable to remain long in the open at the head of the valley, however, and they retired back down it and out of sight to regroup.

Wood realized that he could not allow the Zulu unimpeded use of such crucial dead ground so close to the camp. The only solution was to make a sortie from the main laager, line the lip of the valley and fire down into the warriors gathered below. It was a move that was certainly likely to surprise the Zulu, but the men involved were sure to be exposed to a heavy crossfire from the cattle-laager and manure-heaps on either side. According to Wood,

> I ordered Major Hackett, 90th Light Infantry, with two companies to advance over the slope. The companies moved down to the rear of the cattle laager, guided by Captain Woodgate, and well led by Major Hackett, who with Captain Woodgate standing erect in the open under heavy fire, showed a fine example to the men, as did Lieut. Strong, who, sword in hand, ran on well in front of his company. The Zulus retired from their immediate front, but the companies being heavily flanked, I ordered them back. While bringing them in Major Hackett was dangerously, and I fear mortally wounded; in any case, I doubt his being able to serve again, and he will be a heavy loss to the regiment.

Hackett had been struck in the head by a bullet which passed clean through his temples behind the eyes, severing the optic nerves; he survived, but was blinded. His subaltern, Lieutenant Arthur Bright, was hit by a bullet which went clean through one leg, breaking the bone, and lodged in the other; he bled to death that night.

As Hackett's men rushed out to secure the head of the valley, Wood, who had watched the 13th retreat from the cattle laager from a position on the slopes of the redoubt above it, had an adventure of his own. In his autobiography he recalled:

A 13th man coming away late from the cattle Laager, not having heard the order to retire, was shot by the Zulus lying in the refuse heap, and followed by four men from the cattle Laager. I was running out to pick him up, when Captain Maude exclaimed, 'Really it isn't your place to pick up single men,' and went out himself, followed by Lieutenants Lysons and Smith, 90th Light Infantry; they were bringing the man in, who was shot in the leg, when, as they were raising the stretcher, Smith was shot through the arm. I was firing at the time at a leader ... who, with a red flag, was urging his comrades to come up out of the ravine, and assault the Laager. Private Fowler, one of my personal escort, who was lying in the ditch of the fort, had asked me, 'Would you kindly take a shot at that Chief, sir? It's a quarter of an hour I am shooting him, and cannot hit him at all.' He handed me his Swinburne-Henry carbine, and looking at the sight, which was at 250 yards, I threw the rifle into my shoulder, and as I pressed it into the hollow, the barrel being very hot, I pulled the trigger before I was ready – indeed, as I was bringing up the muzzle from the Zulu's feet. Hit in the pit of the stomach, he fell over backwards; another leader at once took his place, cheering his comrades on. At him I was obliged to fire, unpleasantly close to the line of our officers leading the counter attack. I saw the bullet strike some few yards over the man's shoulder, and, laying the carbine next time at the Zulu's feet, the bullet struck him on the breast-bone. As he reeled lifeless backward, another leader seized and waved the flag, but he knelt only, though he continued to cheer. The fourth shot struck the ground just over his shoulder, and then, thinking the carbine was over-sighted, I aimed on the ground 2 yards short, and the fifth bullet struck him on the chest in the same place as his predecessor had been hit. This and the counter attack so dampened the ardour of the leaders that no further attack was made in that direction ...

Hackett's sortie had temporarily checked the left 'horn', but the regiments forming the Zulu centre now made a determined attack along the length of the ridge. Where possible they kept off the sky-line, streaming down on to the upper slopes of the valley to the south and pressing forward towards the cattle kraal and redoubt. In some places the leading elements almost reached the foot of the ramparts before being shot down, while others fell as they tried to reach the horses of the artillery limbers. The guns, indeed, were crucial to the British success at this stage, and although they were very exposed, the gunners remained in position, firing canister into the warriors at close range. Wood was certainly impressed by their conduct:

> The two mule guns were admirably worked by Lieut. Nicholson, R.A., in the redoubt, until he was mortally wounded; since dead; when Major Vaughan, R.A., director of transport, replaced him and did good service. The horses of the other four guns, under Lieuts. Bigge and Slade, were sent inside the laager when the Zulus came within 100 yards of them, but these officers with their men and Major Tremlett, R.A., to all of whom great credit is due, remained in the open the whole of the engagement.

The Zulu centre proved no more adept at penetrating the British fire zone than had the two 'horns'. By mid-afternoon, the energy of the first concerted attacks was spent, although the regiments continued to mount assaults wherever they suspected there was a weak spot. The iNgobamakhosi and uVe, recovered slightly from the shock of their first attack, streamed out from the cover of the rocky fold and mounted a fresh attack at the north-eastern side of the redoubt. It is here, however, that the approach was naturally steepest, and the attack slowed within easy rifle-range. Again the warriors were subjected to a storm of fire, and fell back. Sihlahla later recalled that he had taken shelter behind a rock placed by the garrison as a range marker: 'I found myself near a large white stone placed there by the white people; behind this I got, and there remained until the force gave way and fled.'

It was late afternoon – four hours after the battle began – that Wood sensed the Zulu were beaten:

> At 5.30 p.m., seeing the attack slackening, I ordered out a company of the 1–13th to the right rear of the cattle laager to attack some Zulus who had crept into the laager, but who had been unable to remove the cattle; and I took Captain Laye's company of the 90th Light Infantry forward to the edge of the kranz to the right of the cattle-laager, whence they did great execution amongst the mass of retreating Zulus. I ordered out the mounted men who, under Colonel Buller, pursued for seven miles the flying Zulus . . .

This stage of the battle was to to involve Wood in some controversy later. Many of the mounted men had been through the fire at Hlobane and were burning for revenge. Commandant D'Arcy of the Frontier Light Horse set the tone when he led his men out shouting, 'No quarter, boys, and remember yesterday!' It was a truism of nineteenth-century warfare that a determined pursuit of a retreating enemy could be far more effective at dispersing and demoralizing them than battle itself, and Wood of course recognized that he was in a position to deliver a devastating blow to King Cetshwayo's principal field army. Most of the Zulu, as Wood freely admitted, were by this time 'too exhausted to fire in their own defence', and the horsemen rode among them with impunity and shot them down without mercy. Some men, finding the work of execution too slow with the carbine, snatched up spears from dead Zulu and used them like lances to ride down the living. Later, Wood would be called to account for this aspect of the battle by humanitarian organizations in London, and while he indignantly defended himself, there is no doubt that the pursuit was utterly ruthless. In the immediate surrounds of the camp, and for many miles along the line of retreat, all the wounded were killed. One young Zulu of the uVe *ibutho*, who was badly wounded in the battle, later recalled that he had managed to evade the pursuit only to be found lying exhausted on the veld by a British patrol a few days later. They questioned him about his regiment and the part he had played in the attack, remarking on his youth – then calmly shot him in the head, leaving him for dead.

Certainly, Sihlahla remembered the pursuit as devastating:

> We were then pursued by the horsemen from the camp, who rode after our retreating army and turned them about like cattle. We were completely beaten, and lost a very large number. Not one of our force doubted our being beaten, and openly said that they had enough and would go home. Umnyamana, the Induna in command, tried to collect the force and march it back to the King, but he could not, and had to go alone and report matters.

Mehlokazulu was among the lucky survivors. 'At the conclusion of the fight,' he recalled, 'we were chased by the English forces over three ridges, and were only saved from entire destruction by the darkness. Night came on, and they left off following us. I myself only just managed to escape . . .'

The pursuit continued as far as Zungwini, and by that time all discipline within the army had collapsed. Many of the abaQulusi had joined the attack on the camp, and the survivors fled back to the safety of Hlobane in disarray. The King's great army, reduced to a dejected mob, simply broke up, most of the warriors heading for their personal homesteads.

Certainly, Zulu losses had been appalling. The dead lay scattered thickly around the camp, particularly at the head of the southern valley, where repeated attacks had been made in the face of close-range fire. Many of the dead here bore conspicuous head wounds, and for days after the bodies were removed the rocky slope was sticky with pools of coagulated blood and brains. All in all, some 785 bodies were collected in wagons from around the camp, and taken for burial in mass graves 500 yards from the British lines. Hundreds more lay out on the line of retreat, their presence revealed over the next few days by clouds of vultures, and by the cloying odour of death carried on the easterly breeze. All in all, it seems that as many as 2,000 warriors may have died in the battle, while up to 1,000 more suffered serious injuries which were beyond the capabilities of their herbalists to cure.

While the full impact of the battle would become apparent only in the following months, it was immediately clear to both sides that the British had won a very significant victory. The Zulu had entered the battle bouyed up with their success at Isandlwana, but they had faced a hard truth glimpsed before at Rorke's Drift – that even the most basic barricade was impregnable when defended by an enemy possessed of devastating firepower, and that raw courage and tactical skill were insufficient to overcome them. As if to underline this point, Wood's own losses were absurdly light, considering the duration and intensity of the fighting. In all, three officers and twenty-five NCOs and men were killed outright or died of their injuries, while five officers and fifty NCOs and men were wounded. A number of black non-combatants in the camp were also wounded, but their exact number went unrecorded. On the whole, Wood had every right to be proud of himself, and the men under his command:

> The Line battalions were very steady, expending in four hours on average 33 rounds a man; though that evening I heard that some of them had thought the possibility of resisting such overwhelming

numbers of brave savages, 13 or 14 to one man, was more than doubtful. I had no doubt, and lost all sense of personal danger, except momentarily, when, as on five occasions, a plank of the hoarding on which I leant was struck. This jarred my head, and reminded me that the Zulus firing from the refuse heap in the right rear of the Laager were fair shots. A few had been employed as hunters, and understood the use of the Martini rifles taken at Isandlwana.

Yet the Zulu on the northern frontier were not entirely stunned by their spectacular defeat at Khambula. Mbilini, that adroit raider, had been wounded at Hlobane, and did not take part in the attack on the camp. Over the next few days he abandoned his homestead at Hlobane and moved northwards, back to the Ntombe valley, taking with him large numbers of abaQulusi who were keen to place themselves beyond the reach of the Khambula garrison. Less than a week after the battles, Mbilini felt confident enough to lead another raid against the black homesteads in the Phongolo valley, and on 4 April over 1,000 Zulu burned huts and carried off cattle. The Luneburg garrison stood to arms in expectation of an attack, but the Zulu were not keen to repeat the mistakes made at Khambula, and they avoided any open confrontation with the British. Indeed, during their retreat the raiders came across two companies of the 4th Regiment, en route to reinforce Luneburg; the British convoy promptly went into the laager, and the Zulu passed them by.

It was in the aftermath of this attack, however, that the British scored another major success. Captain Prior of the 80th Regiment, accompanied by a small party of his men on horseback and the son of Luneburg's Pastor Filter, who served as interpreter, set out from the garrison on the morning of the 5th to harry the retreating raiders. In the Ntombe valley, according to Wood, they came across a small group of Zulu on horseback, driving away captured horses. According to Wood, this party was led by none other than Mbilini himself and one of Sihayo's sons, Tshekwane: 'Captain Prior, 80th Regiment, with seven mounted men 80th and young Filter, followed Umbelini, killed [Sihayo's] son and (we now hear) mortally wounded Umbelini, who is dead.'

Mbilini himself had been attempting to ride his horse down the steep bank of a donga when an auxiliary in Prior's party rushed up to the lip and fired down at him; the bullet had entered Mbilini's right shoulder, passing out below his waist. Somehow he managed to stay on his horse and escape, but he died several days later.

The death of Mbilini was a serious blow to the Zulu cause on the northern frontier. They were not cowed by it, and the abaQulusi and others would remain under arms until the end of the war, but without Mbilini's daring and tenacity they lacked the ability to do more than harass the British, whose presence became steadily more domineering as the war progressed. For the nation as a whole, the news of his death, coming so soon after the defeat at Khambula, seemed to confirm a growing realization that the Zulu were unlikely to win the war in the field.

It came, moreover, hard on the heels of a fresh defeat, for within days of Khambula further fighting had broken out in the coastal districts, at the other end of the country. As a Zulu named Sibalo kaHibana later recalled: 'All this was still fresh in our minds when it was said that the Zulu force had attacked the English camp at Gingindlovu, and had been much beaten, pursued, and killed as the Kambula force had been.'

At the beginning of April, the focus of the war had indeed shifted dramatically towards events in the south, yet there was still one last bizarre postscript to the story of Hlobane to come. On 16 April, a British patrol working through the country near Hlobane encountered a solitary white man on foot. He was bedraggled and exhausted, and dressed in only an irregular's corduroy jacket, ripped with spear-holes, and a pair of infantry trousers, cut off at the knee. He was a Frenchman by the name of Grandier, and he had an extraordinary story to tell. He was a trooper in Weatherley's Border Horse, and by his own account he had been captured by the Zulu during the struggle on Ityenka Nek. He was taken to Khambula, and interviewed by Wood:

> I was taken to Umbelini's kraal, on the south side and about half way up the Inhlobane. He asked me where Shepstone was and who was the leader of this commando. I passed the night tied to a tree. Next day Umbelini riding with two or three companies took me into the middle of a large impi. They all threatened to kill me, but Manyanyana, the leader, a large stout man, said he would send me to Cetywayo. I was taken back to the Inhlobāne and remained there until next day, when I started in charge of four men riding for

Ulundi. I was walking, carrying their food. They had previously taken all my clothes from me.

On the evening of the 4th day we arrived at Ulundi. Messengers went forward to announce our arrival. I was kept tied in the open until about 12 noon the following day, when Cetywayo sent for me.

He asked what the English wanted coming to his country. Asked for Shepstone, and the commander of this commando. Asked where Oham was, and said he would kill him and all the English; said he had plenty of men to do it with. A Dutch-speaking half-caste, with long hair, interpreted . . .

Cetywayo is a very stout man, not tall, and walks with difficulty, apparently about 40 years of age. He had a personal guard of about 100 men. I did not see any large numbers. His kraal is surrounded by a double-row of rough pallisades eight feet high. I saw no other fortifications . . .

I don't think the Zulus knew I was not an Englishman. I heard nothing of any other European being at Ulundi . . .

During my stay at Ulundi I was fed on mealies and kept in a kraal, being frequently beaten by the Kafirs.

Messengers arrived reporting the death of Mbilini. I am certain of this. Cetywayo, on hearing of it, said he would send me to Umbelini's Kafirs to kill.

On the 13th inst. I started in charge of two Kafirs, one armed with a muzzle-loading gun, both with assegais. About midday we were lying down, the Kafirs being sleepy. I seized an assegai and killed the man with the gun, the other ran off. I walked all night by the stars; the next day, the 14th, I had to lie still, as I met a large impi driving cattle towards Ulundi, they took all the morning passing. After this I saw no Kafirs, and walked each night. This morning . . . I was trying to recognize some of the hills when I met our own people, and was brought into camp.

Grandier's story caused something of a sensation, and when the news reached England he was the subject of a number of highly dramatic illustrations in the weekly press. After the war, however, doubts were cast on aspects of his story when Zulu accounts emerged to suggest that Grandier had portrayed himself in an unduly heroic light. The story common throughout Zululand was that he had not been caught at the height of the fighting at Hlobane, but had actually been found hiding among the rocks after the battle was over. It was well known that the King had expressed a wish that a soldier be captured alive, and this had not before been possible, because in the full fury of battle the warriors could not be restrained from killing any enemy they came near. Grandier was sent to oNdini in the hope that he could provide the King with military intelligence; he was generally well treated, but once Cetshwayo realized he was not an officer and had little useful information, he was sent back to Hlobane under guard and released so that the British patrols might find him. After Khambula and the action at Gingindlovu, Cetshwayo was anxious to establish channels of communication with the British, and Grandier afforded him an opportunity to prove that the peace initiative he was about to embark upon was genuine; in the end, though, Cetshwayo was defeated by Grandier's reluctance to admit to his own human frailty.

Nevertheless, however much he might have gilded the lily, Grandier's story remains remarkable, for he was the only white man to be taken prisoner-of-war by the Zulu in the entire campaign.

Chapter Five

'It was a ghastly sight . . .'

Late in the evening of 26 January 1879, Lord Chelmsford had arrived back in the colonial capital of Pietermaritzburg. It had taken him just three days to reach the town from the devastated field of Isandlwana, but news of the disaster had preceded him. On the 24th white towns-folk had awoken to veiled hints full of foreboding from their African servants, and later that day the first breathless survivors of the battle had ridden into town. The High Commissioner himself, Bartle Frere, had come to Pietermaritzburg to keep an eye on the war more closely, and after he had been given the news, his staff had instructed the survivors to tell no one for fear of spreading panic. Yet the news could not be stopped, and by the following morning it was common knowledge. Pietermaritzburg was devastated; the sons of many of the town's gentry had enlisted in the Volunteer Corps, and several of them now lay dead at Isandlwana. Farmers in the outlying districts began to flock into the city, while the town's military commander called for volunteers, and hurriedly began to prepare the government buildings for defence.

Chelmsford's return to the town, in circumstances very close to ignominy, did little to reassure the civilian population, and indeed that last week of January was to prove Chelmsford's darkest hour. His invasion of Zululand, begun just a fortnight before, was in ruins. Although Colonel Glyn still commanded over 1,000 men, cooped up in the cramped and insanitary position at Rorke's Drift, they were clearly demoralized, and the loss of all their transport, camp equipment and reserve ammunition meant that they had ceased to exist as an offensive force. The two flanking columns were left to prosecute the war as best they could, and, numbed by the rapid turn of events, Chelmsford had all but abdicated his responsibility towards them. Large stretches of the border lay open, and Chelmsford could hope for little more than King Cetshwayo's forbearance to prevent a Zulu incursion. Moreover, the defeat was a blow to British military prestige which could only serve to undermine the crucial support for the war among the auxiliary forces. As Chelmsford was forced to admit to Colonel Stanley, the Secretary of State for War, in a despatch dated the 27th,

> The effects of the reverse have already been very serious. Two whole regiments of Natives have deserted and, it is to be feared, that the rest will follow.
>
> A panic is spreading broadcast over the Colony which it is difficult to allay.
>
> Additional reinforcements must be sent out. At least three infantry Regiments and two Cavalry Regiments with horses are required and one more company of Engineers.

In addition to the purely military consequences of the reverse, the political repercussions threatened to derail the entire Confederation policy. The republican Boers in the Transvaal had reacted to the news with ill-concealed glee, as Theophilus Shepstone – whose son, George, was among the dead – reported as early as 6 February:

> The effect of this catastrophe upon the Zulus will to some extent be modified by the gallant and successful defence made by Lt. Bromhead across the river; but the Boers will not look at this at all except as an act of Zulu forbearance. The Boers are exhibiting a very disloyal spirit, and evidently think that a chance of enforcing the return of their country to them has been put into their hands by providence.
>
> They talk loudly and are supplying themselves with ammunition largely and may, most people think, do what they say they will . . .

Although Chelmsford struggled to reassure the white civilian population in Natal, and to stem the desertions among his own auxiliary units, there was little he could do to restore the situation until the first reinforcements arrived. He seemed paralysed by the enormity of the situation, and unable to regain the initiative. As he admitted privately to Wood on 3 February, 'The situation of affairs does not appear to me to improve, and I am fairly puzzled when I contemplate our future operations.' A few days later, he again appealed to the War Office for support:

I consider it my duty to lay before you my opinion, that it is very desirable in view of future contingencies that an officer of the rank of Major General should be sent out to South Africa without delay.

In June last I mentioned privately to His Royal Highness the F.M. Com[mander] in Chief that the strain of prolonged anxiety and exertion, physical and mental was even then telling on me – What I felt then, I feel still more now.

Yet in many respects, King Cetshwayo was to let his enemy off the hook. While both the black and the white population of Natal quivered in their beds in nightly anticipation of a Zulu attack, the Zulu let their opportunity pass. Apart from a few minor incursions, carried out by groups living on the border to take advantage of the rich pickings abandoned by Natal farmers, no serious attempt was made to cross the river. The King had never been in favour of such a move, and the disastrous attack on Rorke's Drift had only confirmed him in that view. Moreover, it is impossible that he could have mounted a fresh offensive so soon after Isandlwana in any case; his army was exhausted, and the regiments had dispersed to recover. The mealie harvest was due to be gathered in, and the men were unlikely to return to their regiments until they had seen their family food-stores replenished. There was a physical obstacle, too, in that the continued bad weather had made the river levels unpredictable, and both the Mzinyathi and the Thukela were too dangerous to cross.

For nearly a month, therefore, the war passed in stalemate, with neither side able to resume the fighting. The truth began to dawn on Chelmsford in mid-February – 'there appears', he wrote to Wood on the 13th, 'so far as we can gather, no present intention on the part of the Zulus to make any raid into Natal' – and his spirits began to rise again. The first reinforcements sent out in response to his appeal might arrive in early March; with each day that passed, the balance of power shifted slowly back in his favour.

The delay could at least be used to limit the damage inflicted on both Chelmsford's own and British prestige. In the weeks since the disaster there had been a growing sense of unease, expressed in the Natal press, about the way that the campaign had been handled. It was hard to believe that an enemy armed primarily with shields and spears had out-generalled the forces of the most powerful Empire of the age, and Chelmsford's actions had become the object of veiled but increasingly persistent criticism. The sense of outrage and humiliation was fuelled by the realization that Chelmsford had made no attempt to bury the dead at Isandlwana when he had returned to the site on the night of the 22nd. In fact, of course, this would hardly have been practical, but as early as 1 February Chelmsford had felt it necessary to say as much in a despatch to the Duke of Cambridge:

> The question will no doubt be asked as to why I made no effort to bury the bodies, and why having gained possession of the camp again I did not retain it – The answer is clear. I had no supplies and no spare ammunition nearer than 10 miles, at a post which was very open to attack & I could not afford to delay as the troops wanted food and rest –
>
> The terrible massacre which had taken place precluded all possibility of my being able to bury those that had fallen, and to do so partially could only have the effect of bringing home to the troops the full extent of the disaster, of which to a certain extent kept in ignorance owning to the darkness – I felt that there was much to lose and nothing to gain by delaying the march, and I consequently did not hesitate –

This was to remain Chelmsford's position until practical necessity forced him to return to Isandlwana in May, four months after the battle. While the delay gnawed at the nerves of the bereaved, particularly the families of the dead Volunteers, Chelmsford's response was nothing if not practical; patrols venturing just a few miles into Zululand along the Rorke's Drift road reported that the stench from the battlefield was overpowering. Chelmsford decided to wait until the worst stages of putrefaction had passed.

In the meantime, he set about answering the specific tactical questions which had been thrown up by the battle. On 27 January a Court of Inquiry was convened at the depot at Helpmekaar. It was chaired by Colonel Arthur Harness, who had commanded the Centre Column's artillery, and who had been present with Chelmsford that day, and its remit was very specific. It was to do no more than inquire into the loss of the camp, to provide information for Chelmsford's use; it was not in any sense an official inquiry into the conduct of the campaign as a whole. Harness himself was a thorough and efficient officer, but he shared the wariness of colonial troops which prevailed among the professionals, and as a result he dismissed much of the information which passed before him as being of no relevance. Instead, he confined himself largely to the opinions of the five surviving Imperial officers – Captains Essex and Gardner, and Lieutenants Cochrane, Curling and Smith-Dorrien – in the hope that they might shed light on the decisions made by the camp's commanders. In fact, however, none of these men had held commands in the infantry, whose actions had been crucial to the course of the battle, and their evidence was inevitably patchy. It was sufficient, however, for Chelmsford to draw comfort from the apparent conclusions, and to absolve himself from any immediate blame:

> From the statements made before the Court of Inquiry it may be clearly gathered that the cause of the reverse sustained at Isandhlwana was that Lt. Colonel Durnford, as senior officer, overruled the orders which Lt. Colonel Pulleine had received to defend the camp, and directed that the troops should be moved into the open, in support of a portion of the Native Contingent which he had brought up and which was engaging the enemy.
>
> Had Lt. Col. Pulleine not been interfered with and been allowed to carry out the distinct order given to him to defend the camp, it cannot be doubted that a different result would have been obtained. As it was, the camp was never defended but the companies and battery were sent forward at long distances from the camp, more or less detached from each other, and were slaughtered in detail, without having been able to offer any really effectual resistance to the enemy.
>
> I would advocate that the proceedings of the Court of Inquiry should be published at once as calculated to remove many erroneous impressions now entertained.

It was convenient, of course, to blame Durnford – he was dead, and could not defend himself – while the Native Contingent were predestined as scapegoats in British eyes by their black skins. Nevertheless, as Chelmsford would discover, the nagging doubts posed by the unquiet dead at Isandlwana could not be silenced entirely.

*

For Colonel Glyn's command at Rorke's Drift, life had remained desperately uncomfortable throughout January and February. The remains of the entire Centre Column were camped around the devastated mission, in a space which had scarcely accommodated 150 men during the battle. With no tents, they slept in the open at night, exposed to the heavy rains which descended each evening with depressing regularity. The first few nights were unnerving, made worse by the recurring vision of Isandlwana and the possibility of Zulu attack. On the first night after the battle, the African soldiers of the NNC had been left to fend for themselves on the hillside while their officers and NCOs huddled together with the rest of the white troops around the ruined buildings; by morning the men were so demoralized that their officers disbanded them. Stray Africans apprehended in the vicinity stood every chance of being shot as spies. An air of decay hung over the site. Although the bodies of the Zulu killed close to the mission during the battle had been buried immediately, dozens more lay hidden in the bush, where they had crawled to die, or out on the line of retreat. Inevitably, the health of the garrison declined, and men began to succumb to dysentery.

In an effort to restore morale, the ruins of the old mission hospital were pulled down, and stone collected from the Shiyane terraces was used to surround the storehouse with a strong loop-holed wall. Some of the more adventurous officers organized patrols to cross tentatively into Zululand, or to sweep the Mzinyathi downstream in search of the bodies of soldiers killed during the rout on the 22nd. In particular, Colonel Glyn, who was deeply affected by the destruction of almost the entire 1st Battalion, was keen to investigate reports that Melvill and Coghill had tried to escape with the Queen's Colour. On 4 February a patrol of volunteers under Major Wilsone Black of the 24th discovered Melvill's and Coghill's bodies high on the slope above the 'Fugitives' Drift'. As Glyn reported,

> I sent a party down to the river to see if they could discover Melvill and Coghill's bodies. They found them lying on a path in a glen about five miles off and about 300 yards from the river on this side. Coghill had been stripped with the exception of his boots and socks, his spurs were lying at his side. Just below him Melvill was lying in his uniform apparently untouched. Below them again was a soldier and a number of the enemy. I think both Melvill and Coghill had been shot as their bodies were not mutilated.

In fact, some of Black's party later disagreed that Coghill had been stripped, while the detail about the dead Zulu was almost certainly added for effect. Nevertheless, the discovery of the bodies brought a sense of closure to the survivors of the regiment. Black had the remains covered with stones, and the following day the party returned to search for the Colour. Leading their horses down the slope to the river they found that the water-level had dropped since the day of the battle, leaving debris stranded among the boulders on either side. A few hundred yards below the crossing, Lieutenant Harford, attached to the NNC, noticed a pole jammed among the boulders and sticking upright from the centre of the river, and another NNC officer scrambled across to pull it out. It was the Colour. It had been swept downstream after Melvill had dropped it during the battle, until the heavy brass crown on top of the pole had jammed between the boulders. The silk was waterlogged and tattered by more than a week's submersion, and as it was pulled out of the water the heavy embroidery in the centre of the Colour fell away. None the less, its recovery was a huge boost to the morale of the Centre Column, and Lieutenant Harford was given the honour of carrying it back to Rorke's Drift where, according to Glyn, 'You should have heard the cheers when the force here saw the Col[our] being brought in. I send it to Helpmekaar tomorrow. We have to thank poor Melvill who so gallantly rescued it from the field of slaughter and who lost his life in trying to save it . . .'

The recovery of the Colour highlighted another issue which had become increasingly pressing in the weeks following the battle. If Isandlwana had been a defeat of unimaginable magnitude, it had at least provided examples of extraordinary courage with which both the army in the field and civilians at home could console themselves. The stand at Rorke's Drift, moreover, while of only limited strategic value, had proved a tremendous propaganda coup. It seemed to nullify the overall impression of defeat, and it provided an example of exactly the sort of sterling courage against the odds which thrilled the public at home. By singling out individuals for distinction, the military establishment could provide a focus for celebration of British pluck and fortitude and restore the army's bedraggled honour.

In truth, of course, there had been no shortage of heroism on 22 January. Yet Isandlwana remained problematic. Although the illustrated papers had been full of heroic images of redcoats standing back to back in the face of savage Zulu hordes, very little was known about the actions of individual officers or men. Details of Pulleine's death were sketchy and contradictory; Durnford had undoubtedly died heroically, in the centre of a stand of Colonial Volunteers, but it was hardly appropriate to single him out for distinction when the official view was that he was responsible for the disaster.

For Glyn, at least, there was no dilemma; Melvill and Coghill had already been eulogized as heroes by the British press, and he had no doubts that they had redeemed the honour of the 1/24th. Chelmsford, however, was uneasy at the prospect of being seen to reward officers who, for whatever reason, had been killed while riding away from the enemy:

> As regards poor Melvill and Coghill the case is even more difficult. The latter was a Staff Officer attached to Col. Glyn, and had every right to leave the camp when he realized the fact that nothing could be done to save it. It is, however, most probable that Melvill lost his life endeavouring to save Coghill rather than vice versa.
>
> Coghill had strained his knee and remained in camp on the 22nd in consequence. He could hardly walk, and any exertion such as walking or riding would have been likely to render him almost helpless. He could not have assisted, therefore, in saving the colours of the 1/24th, and as I have already said I fear he was a drag on poor Melvill.
>
> As regards the latter, I am again puzzled how to reply to your question. I feel sure that Melvill left the camp with the colours under orders received. He was too good a soldier to have left without. In being ordered to leave, however, he no doubt was given the best chance of saving his life which must have been lost had he remained in the camp. His ride was not more daring than that of those who escaped. The question, therefore, remains, had he succeeded in saving the colours and his own life, would he have been considered to have deserved the Victoria Cross? That question can be answered equally as well at home as out here, and I should be glad to be allowed to leave your question regarding Melvill unanswered.

In the event, there were other more practical considerations which prevented Melvill and Coghill from receiving an award; there was no provision in 1879 for the Victoria Cross to be awarded posthumously. Nevertheless, such was the weight of public opinion that Queen Victoria was moved to announce that the pair would have received the award 'had they survived'. In the event, only one survivor – Private Wassall – was honoured for his actions at Isandlwana by the award of a VC.

There was, on the other hand, no ambiguity about the stand at Rorke's Drift, although privately some officers serving in Zululand confessed themselves surprised that the public at home had made so much of the incident. It was all the more laudable because it had been undertaken by a mixed detail of troops, with none of them higher in rank than Lieutenant; it was the perfect example of the qualities of courage and endurance which were expected of the British soldier. Shortly after the defence, it was announced that eight men of the garrison would be awarded the Victoria Cross – Chard, Bromhead, and six men of B Company, Corporal Allan, and Privates Hitch, Hook, Robert Jones, William Jones and John Williams. All of these were men who had been singled out initially by Bromhead. The battle had thrown each man on his own resources, however, and there were clearly many more who deserved to be recognized, so over the following weeks the list of nominees grew to include representatives of most of the units present. Further VCs were later awarded to Surgeon Reynolds, to Walter Dunne and James Dalton from the Commissariat Department, and Corporal Schiess of the Native Contingent. Colour Sergeant Bourne received the Distinguished Conduct Medal, together with Corporal Attwood of the Army Service Corps, Private Roy of the 1/24th, Corporal McMahon of the Army Hospital Corps, and Wheeler Cantwell of the Artillery.

The conclusion of the Isandlwana Court of Inquiry, and the distribution of praise and blame, allowed Chelmsford to put the horrors of January behind him and return to the campaign. As he had hoped, the news of Isandlwana had galvanized the Home Government. The Disraeli administration may not have wanted war in southern Africa, but it could not extricate itself without first restoring military prestige. The response was immediate; two days after Chelmsford's despatch reporting the disaster arrived in London on 11 February, the Secretary of State for War cabled in reply:

The following reinforcements have been placed under immediate orders for Natal. Two regiments of cavalry each 622 men and 480 horses, two field batteries of artillery, 336 men, 220 horses, one field company engineers, 196 men, 44 horses, weapons and equipment, five regiments of infantry from home, each 906 men. Fifty-seventh

Regiment from Ceylon, three companies Army Service Corps 410 men, 380 horses and mules and wagons. Army Hospital Corps 140. Drafts for 57th, 24th, and Royal Artillery. Third Battalion 60 embark on 18 inst. In Dublin Castle, 91st in Pretoria on 19th, remainder will follow as soon as possible, whole force will probably have embarked by the end of this month.

These reinforcements were certainly in excess of those modestly requested by Chelmsford, and they strained the War Office establishment. With large numbers of troops already committed to a war in Afghanistan, those available to meet the Zulu emergency were limited. Officers in the appointed regiments scurried back from leave, while those battalions which were under active strength were hurriedly made good with fresh drafts, many of whom were little more than raw recruits. News of the outbreak provoked a flurry of applications for special service posts from bored officers in garrison duty. Between 20 February and 1 April, no fewer than nineteen transport ships left London docks, Portsmouth or Southampton, heading for the Cape.

The experience of the 94th Regiment was typical. The battalion was stationed at Aldershot on 11 February, and that evening the commanding officer received a telegram ordering it to prepare for active service. In breathless haste, over the next six days, 384 recruits were drafted in to bring it up to strength – twenty-eight officers and 897 NCOs and men. The battalion was inspected by the Duke of Cambridge, and despatched for Southampton, where it embarked on the steam transport *China*.

The prospect of active service evoked mixed reactions among the men. For many, the Zulu War would be their first overseas service, with all the anxiety that entailed, but most were simply excited at the prospect of action and adventure and of avenging the slight inflicted on British honour by the Zulu. Long before the men reached the front, they would have to endure the trials of a month-long sea voyage, in cramped and uncomfortable conditions, around the western coast of Europe and down the length of Africa. The second week of February 1879 was marked by lingering winter gales in the Bay of Biscay, and within a few days of beginning the journey the troops faced seas sufficiently rough to keep them below decks. Then came the gradual slide into the tropics, and 'Crossing the Line' of the Equator. Many of the ships called into St Vincent to refuel, and, as Major Philip Anstruther of the 94th wrote home to his wife, the arrival of so many transports at the same time created something of a festival atmosphere:

> It really was lovely in harbour – we were the centre ship – with 17th Lancers, King's Dragoon Guards & 58th all close round in the 'Russia', 'Egypt', 'France', 'England' and 'Spain', and we played music from 8 to 10 – band and drums – which was immensely appreciated by the gallery of ships. The catcalls and encores from the cavalry were quite alarming.

As the ships approached the Equator, however, Anstruther admitted that the men were beginning to suffer. 'The heat is getting positively awful', he wrote,

> And the men feel it dreadfully being so crowded. The thermometer was at 149 this morning in the stoke hold and the wake of the sea, 84 degrees. The pleasantest time of the day is certainly the morning in our tubs, such nice big ones of tin, and we have about a dozen of them and all tub together and have the hose over us ... today we were only 90 miles from the Equator. The worst of it is that all uniform is only fit for the English climate but we don't wear coats, all day in trousers and shirtsleeves. However, it will soon be over. Within a week we shall be in as good weather as we shall want. The Big Bear is getting very low down in the heavens and the Southern Cross is come up.

For the most part, there was little to do to alleviate the tedium. Like most of the officers, Anstruther fretted about the health of his horse, Armargh, and whiled away the time as best he could:

> When I went to see Armargh this morning just as I got there he began to plunge violently, biting, heaving at the flanks, and lying back on his sling. I think a touch of colic so I gave him a soda water bottle full of hot whiskey & water and warm cloths to his loins, and will give him a warm mash about 1 and some linseed oil after that. I am very glad I got the linseed oil. I hope the poor beast will pull round but we are so cramped, no ventilation and the heat is fearful ... Malthus' horse was seedy in the same way yesterday. Murray's, I think, will certainly die ...
>
> We have got books given to us on the Zulu language and we all had laudable ideas of learning it but it seems impossible. I never saw

such a language, there are 3 'clicks' in it that make a word that means horse, perhaps cow if you put in a different sort of click, and we can't find out how to put in the clicks . . .

Just before lunch Major Tredennick 57 & I went right forward to the bows to get a blow and get out of the smuts but we had not been there ten minutes before a sea came on board and wetted us through and through. Luckily there are a lot of trashy novels on board which I read at intervals but they bore one and I play whist a little but I am unlucky at it and I don't like losing my money . . .

The transports had to stop again at Cape Town or Simon's Bay to take on more fuel, and for the officers this meant a chance to dash ashore, to sight-see and catch up on news of the war. The town was bustling with troops and with Lord Chelmsford's agents, who were trying to raise fresh irregular units. Isandlwana was, of course, the principal topic of conversation, and Anstruther gained the prevailing impression that

. . . there must have been much carelessness as the camp had been there 2 days and they never tried to entrench themselves, treating it as a picnic. When Lord Chelmsford went off reconnoitring he left about a quarter of the troops to defend the camp under Pulleine and the idea is that Durnford came up afterwards and became the senior officer over him and insisted on his sending the companies out.

The first of the reinforcements arrived at Durban in the third week of March. It had not always been an uneventful trip; the 'wild coast' between Cape Town and Durban was a notorious graveyard of ships, and two of the transports – the *City of Paris* and the *Clyde* – came to grief, happily without loss of life. At Durban, the troops were confronted with the realities of colonial life in a setting a good deal more exotic than anything they had encountered thus far. Anstruther thought Durban

One of the loveliest places I ever saw, quite beautiful but the harbour is awfully bare, a terrible bar which any vessels drawing about 6 feet can get over and there are an awful lot of wrecks. There were six wrecks lying within ½ mile of where we landed. We go by train to Pietermaritzburg . . .

Pineapples, sugar canes, and bananas, guavas, oranges etc. grow

here but the place is rather tropical in its climate. I am in hopes
when we get up country a bit it will be nicer . . .

The arrival of the main flow of reinforcements coincided with Wood's
victory at Khambula on 29 March, and with it a significant shift in the
fortunes of the war. Anstruther was confident that the odds were now
decidedly in Britain's favour:

> You see here, as in all barbarous countries, successes are the great
> thing and directly they come savages get demoralized, their more
> decent allies desert them, and so on. I really expect the thing will be
> over in 3 months.

Such optimism had been in short supply along the troubled border
throughout February and March. For the garrison camped at the Lower
Thukela, the long wait had been only marginally more comfortable than
it had been for Glyn's command further north. Despite the undignified
scramble back from Eshowe which had followed the news of Isandlwana,
the British had retained two strong positions at the Lower Drift, gar-
risoned by detachments of the Buffs, the 99th, and the Naval Brigade.
Fort Pearson, on the Natal bank, had been constructed before the
ultimatum expired, and, built as it was on a knoll overlooking a sheer
drop to the river, it was considered impregnable. Fort Tenedos, on the
Zulu bank, had been constructed by Pearson's men during the advance
to Eshowe. It was typical of the many forts built by the British in
Zululand, an irregular earthwork surrounded by a ditch, but despite the
fact that it was overlooked by a low hill a few hundred yards away, it
was considered strong enough to withstand all but the most determined
attack. As a result, the garrison remained secure in the aftermath of
Isandlwana, but life at the Lower Thukela was far from pleasant. The
garrison was preoccupied with Pearson's fate, and despite the fact that
they could maintain only minimal contact, they fretted over the security
of the Eshowe garrison. The occasional appearance of Zulu scouts on
distant hills added a real sense of menace, while the fluctuating state of
the river and the continued bad weather made life unpleasant.

Lieutenant Julius Backhouse of the Buffs was amongst the Thukela
garrison. He had been part of Pearson's advance to Eshowe, but
had returned to the border at the end of January, escorting a convoy
of empty supply wagons, and had arrived in time to hear the news of

Isandlwana. For the next two months he remained in limbo, confiding to his diary his grumbles about the discomforts of life in the field and his exasperation at the stagnation of the war. He fretted, too, about his wife, who had followed him to Durban, and who had recently written to tell him she had suffered a miscarriage. On 2 February, he summed up the state of the campaign as it seemed to the Thukela garrison; Backhouse had endured

> . . . another uncomfortable night, as it rained hard, but I managed to cover part of myself with a piece of tarpaulin (we have no tents at night, but sleep round the parapet of the fort). Church parade at 10 a.m. but only a few prayers read by Lieut. Kingscote, RN, of HMS 'Tenedos' who is the senior officer on the spot, and commands us. About 20 natives came in from Ekowe, which shows us that the road is pretty open, they say plenty of Zulus are about Ekowe, but that no fighting has taken place; we dug a shelter trench around the waggons, afternoon. Began a letter to my girl, as is my custom . . .

By 8 February, however, Backhouse had succumbed to the rumours which spread like wildfire down the border:

> . . . a very disagreeable and wet night, lying with the lower part of my body drenched all night. News from reliable sources that a large force of Zulus is near the Umsundusi, and intend either to attack us or make a raid into Natal. . . . Runners who started to go last night to Ekowe returned, stating that a large force of Zulus is half way between this and Ekowe and that they have barely escaped from them; at the same time, two runners came from Ekowe, all well there, plenty of food, band playing every day, cricket going on, and that one of our men is dead from dysentery. Digging 'Trous de Loup'* all day, we have nearly surrounded the Fort with obstacles now . . .

By the 11th, Backhouse was showing signs of frustration at the inactivity on the border, and his diary reflects the increasing isolation of the Eshowe garrison:

> Bathed in the Tugela River. No digging; a sort of Inspection Parade at 10 a.m., I suppose on account of the General being expected to arrive: a most absurd Field day under Major Coates, 99th

---

* 'Wolf pits' – small holes with pointed stakes placed upright it in the bottom.

Regt., followed, a more absurd farce I never saw. A runner in from
Ekowe, he started with 12 men with letters from Pearson, the others
were killed on the way, and he just escaped with his life, the letters
were lost too, this shows a great many Zulus must be between this
and Ekowe; we shall see some of them in a day or two, I expect . . .

Although the awaited Zulu attacks failed to materialize, the strain of
living in expectation of them had an inevitable effect on the men living
under it. As a result, any lapses in discipline – chiefly falling asleep on
sentry duty, or drunkenness – were greeted harshly. Flogging had been
abolished as a peace-time punishment in the British Army before the
Zulu campaign, but it was still sanctioned as a last resort in the field.
In Zululand, the incidence of flogging among the troops reached such
proportions that later it caused something of a scandal. Backhouse
witnessed several incidents, but was not unduly impressed; on 25 February he

> . . . turned out at once for parade top see Private Woodman of
> 'B' Company get 50 lashes for leaving his post when on sentry.
> Drummers Reilly and White flogged him, a regular farce, they never
> hurt him at all . . .

Even a foray into Zululand by the mounted troops under the
command of Major Barrow failed to provide any diversion from the
gloom:

> Barrow's Mounted Infantry went out reconnoitring about 2 p.m.
> and returned about 5 p.m. bringing two men and some women as
> prisoners, they saw no others, and only burned a few kraals so we
> were disappointed, as we hoped they would have had some shooting.
> Wyld and Mason went out to try and signal by rockets to Ekowe
> last night, there was nothing done . . .
> Private Clarke 'B' Company died of fever . . .

By the middle of March, the arrival of the first reinforcements led to
a general optimism that the war was about to begin again in earnest.
On the 12th Backhouse noted:

> Two companies of the 88th marched in from Stanger, and are
> over this side of the river, they are to come up with us. I hear that it
> is settled that a large convoy is to go up, and not a Flying Column,

and that we are not to start for some time yet. A Zulu gave himself up this afternoon, dressed in uniform trousers, but we found no number on them, he says the Zulus are going to drive us over the river to-night, but I doubt if they will come, and if they do, they come too late, for we have the 88th here now. I believe firing was heard at Ekowe yesterday, also on Monday. The Zulu says an attack on Ekowe was intended to take place yesterday, which may account for the firing, I expect they have been thrashed if they tried it.

The attack on Eshowe proved no more than rumour, and the monotony of life at the Drift was broken only by a bizarre incident on the 13th, when 'a private of the 99th Regiment ran out of Hospital and committed suicide by jumping from Fort Pearson into the river'. A few days later, however, Backhouse received the first tangible proof that a new offensive was brewing when he was ordered forward with two companies of the Buffs to occupy the deserted mission station at St Andrew's. This lay about four miles beyond Fort Tenedos, further into Zululand, but it afforded a better view of the country towards Eshowe and offered an ideal signal post from which to open regular contact with the besieged garrison. On the 15th, Backhouse

Paraded at 4 p.m. and marched off to St Andrew's, being played out of the camp by the penny whistle Band of the 'Shah': arrived at the mission station just before dark, and made ourselves as comfortable as we could in the Mission House, all dining together. I think this is a most absurd mess, and I pity us, if the Zulus come down tonight, for none of us will ever leave this alive ... The room we are occupying here, has been fitted up as a Church, we use the altar as a dining table, which would astonish some of the Exeter Hall people could they see our desecrations. This place is to be fortified, but the sooner we are out of it, the better I shall like it, at present it could easily be rushed by the Zulus if they attacked and there is nothing between us and them except lathe and plaster walls.

The following morning, however, after a good night's sleep in a dry hammock, Backhouse's confidence returned:

On duty; busy all day, clearing grass etc., away round the house and settling down: any amount of snakes and ticks in the long grass, but we don't mind such animals now-a-days ... John Dunn's scouts captured a Zulu this morning, armed with a gun. He says Cetywayo, with the whole Zulu Army is near Inyezane and intends to cross the river at several places, and sweep the whole of Natal, let him try, that's all, it's a bit late for that game. Signalling with Ekowe success- ful, news from there, that they have food up to April 4th. Captain Williams, 'Buffs' dead, we conclude from dysentery, I am awfully sorry, he was a real good fellow, and is a great loss, his poor wife in Durban too. Colonel Law and nearly everyone from the Drift paid us a visit about luncheon time, so we had as much as we could do to entertain them. We have made the place a little more strong than it was last night and more capable of defence.

Yet despite the buzz of activity along the border, it would be two more weeks before the relief column was ready to start. The delay was equally frustrating, both for the Thukela and Eshowe garrisons and for Lord Chelmsford himself. As early as 6 March, Chelmsford had indicated to Wood that the relief of Eshowe was his strategic priority – 'the first two regiments (infantry) that arrive I shall at once send down to Lower Tugela and if necessary a third' – but with Isandlwana all too fresh in his mind, he was not prepared to risk an advance until he was absolutely confident that he could succeed. On 16 March he outlined his plans to the Secretary of State for War:

> None of the messengers sent by us to Ekowe reached Colonel Pearson, so that, for a month, it now appears he was without news of the arrangements being made to relieve him: a messenger, however, reached us from Ekowe on the 11th instant, dated the 9th March, it was in cypher and informed Colonel Law R.A., commanding Lower Tugela, that his flashing signals had been understood. Colonel Pearson instructed that it would be desirable to relieve the whole of the garrison as Officers and men were generally sickly and that any relieving force should bring a convoy and be prepared to fight.
>
> Up to yesterday we were unable however to read their signals, but I am happy to say that last night I received information that communication to and from Ekowe, by means of flashing signals, was quite established.
>
> ... As horse sickness has shown itself in the Lower Tugela valley, I have directed two Companies of the 'Buffs', the 2nd Squadron Mounted Infantry and Native Mounted Contingent to take up a

position, and entrench it, on the high ground by St Andrew's Mission Station, some 3 miles in Zululand beyond Fort Tenedos.

. . . The reinforcements so promptly despatched to our assistance are arriving.

The Naval Brigade, landed from H.M.S. 'Shah', is already across the Frontier near Fort Tenedos. The 'Boadicea' arrived yesterday, and a portion of the Bluejackets and 40 marines will be landed tomorrow.

The 57th Regiment, in the 'Tamar', arrived on the 10th March from Ceylon in 16 days, and were disembarked the following day: they leave for the Lower Tugela tomorrow.

The 'Pretoria' with the 91st has arrived today and the 'Dublin Castle' with the 3/60th leaves the Cape today.

. . . These three Regiments will be pushed on with all speed to the Lower Tugela, and will form a portion of the relieving force, to advance on Ekowe, which will there be as follows: –

'Shah'

'Tenedos'

'Buffs'

'99th Regiment'

'57th Regiment'

'91st Regiment'

'3/60th Regiment'

2nd Squadron Mounted Infantry

& other native details mounted and foot.

The garrison of that place has supplies up to the 15th April, but before that time it will have been regarrisoned, revictualled and will become the pivot of future operations on that line.

. . . I have received no information of value as to the present feeling of the Transvaal Boers, but am inclined to think that the arrival of reinforcements will cause what seemed to be open discontent and threatened rebellion, to disappear.

While the relief column assembled at the border, Chelmsford made a determined attempt to discover the state of the Zulu army. His intelligence, as ever, was imperfect, and for the most part he had to rely on the usual reports from border posts, but in one respect he was particularly lucky with regard to the coastal districts. Since the outbreak of hostilities, the followers of the 'white Zulu Chief', John Dunn, had been settled in a temporary reserve south of the Thukela river. If Dunn had hoped to remain uncorrupted by the war, however, he was to be disappointed. His insights into the inner workings of the Zulu government were unique, and Chelmsford had persistently pressured him to join the British forces. Dunn was nothing if not pragmatic; he realized the probable outcome of the fighting, and in the end he accepted that the only hope of returning to his former way of life was to throw in his lot with the British. It was, perhaps, an inevitable decision, but by abandoning his former patron, Dunn marked himself down as a traitor in the eyes of Zulu loyalists.

For Chelmsford, however, Dunn was a boon. Throughout March Dunn's followers – who were to prove by far the most effective and disciplined of the black auxiliary units – scouted across the lower border, probing the Zulu presence in their former territories. Some measure of their effectiveness can be gained from a remarkably comprehensive report gleaned from one of Dunn's spies on 27 March, just days before the Eshowe relief column crossed into Zululand. One of Dunn's *izinduna*, a man named Magumbi, who had remained in Zululand when the rest of Dunn's followers had crossed into Natal, managed to slip across the border, and his report suggested just how effective was the Zulu containment of Eshowe:

> They now occupy the following positions, their numbers being taken from the number of companies Magumbi was told they consisted of, estimated at 100 each; it is also worthy of note that they do not consist of regiments, but of detachments of regiments mixed up with tribes, and that a large number of men are scattered about among the kraals who would materially increase the force at the disposal of the Zulus had they time to assemble.
>
> Between the Lower Tugela and Etshowe are the men of the Maputo tribe, who come from near St Lucia Bay, and who number about 3,000 men. They are bivouacked at the junction of the Moutyeni and Mkukusi streams about a mile or a mile and a half to the eastwards of the battlefield on Inyezani. Opposite the Etshowe, near the Ntumeni, is a tribal force of about 1,000 men, under Mavumingwana and Dabulamanzi.
>
> At the Hlalangubo Kraal (the old oNdini) on the Umhlatusi are about 2,000 of the Nkobamakosi, 300 of the Nkandempemvu, 300 of the Nokenke, and 400 of the Mbonambi. At the Pousageni kraal, north of the old Undi, is the Ndhluyengwe regt., of which Magumbi

does not know the strength, but which may be estimated at not more than 1,500 at the outside. To the south east of the Etshowe and several miles distant is the Mginginhlova tribe under Mabilwane and Majiya; it also may be estimated at about 1,500 men.

This altogether makes a total of about 10,000 men, but the return of the Umxapu regt. was expected, and also about 600 Undaba-kaombi who went with it, making the strength up to about 13,000. Allowing for scattered men I should therefore say that the Zulus have at this moment not more than 15,000 men available to the south of the Umhlatusi.

Magumbi heard that a force had gone to Northern Zululand, and heard rumours of fighting with Oham. He states that the whole nation is ordered out, even the sick; but that the orders which come from the king are so frequent and contradictory that a state of much confusion prevails . . . The cattle belonging to the lower district on this side of the Umhlatusi are said to be in the Ngoye mountains with the women. The officers commanding at the old Undi, where the principal force is, are Usicwelecwele, Palane, Upetyane, Somopo and Lunguzwayo.

Reports such as these suggested that Zululand was unsettled by the imminence of a new offensive, and that Chelmsford could not afford to delay his advance much longer. He hoped to start on the 28th, and a few days before, while the new arrivals of the 3/60th and 91st Regiments were marching to the border from Durban, Chelmsford moved his headquarters to the Lower Thukela. On the 25th, he outlined his plans in a long despatch to the Secretary of State for War:

As none of the Major Generals ordered out have yet arrived and Colonel Pearson, who at first commanded the column on this line, is shut up in Ekowe and as there is no other senior officer available for the duty, I have decided to take command of the relieving column myself, assisted by Colonel Pemberton 60 Rifles and Lt Colonel Law Royal Artillery.

The column will not advance by the road which Colonel Pearson's column took but by one which runs nearly parallel to it but nearer to the coast: the advantage of this line is that the road runs through an easy open country for ¾ of the distance, whereas by the other line the road runs through bush country the whole way.

The force will advance without tents and with only a blanket & waterproof sheet for each man.

Notwithstanding however this reduction of weight the convoy, carrying one month's provisions for the garrison and 10 days' supplies (without groceries) for the relieving column will consist of 44 carts and about 100 wagons.

With such a length of train, the greater portion of which is drawn by oxen, it will be impossible to do more than about 11 miles in the day; and even this distance according to the calculations of the colonial transport conductors will require nearly all the hours of daylight to be accomplish[ed], if due regard is paid to the interests of the oxen who will not work well in the heat of the day, and who require at least three hours of feeding –

I am desirous of bringing the transport difficulties prominently to your notice, as unless they are fully realized, it will be difficult to understand the apparent slowness which must characterize the movements of the relieving column.

It is probable that the Column will be attacked when moving along the last 10 miles of the road between this place and Ekowe.

The track according to the information of those who know the country, runs along a narrow but open ridge, with deep ravines on each side, and is only wide enough for one wagon; it twists and turns considerably and is reported as being favourable for the attacks of an enterprising enemy.

I have suggested to Colonel Pearson by sun signal that he should be prepared to make a diversion in support of the relieving column with every available fighting man that can be spared from the defence of the post.

I should feel no doubt about being able successfully to convey the convoy and fresh garrison into Ekowe and to bring out the present garrison with its train of empty waggons were the transport of different quality.

A force moving, however, with ox transport through a difficult country is heavily hampered, if attacked determinedly by large numbers, and whilst feeling every confidence in the ability, courage and determination of those under my command I trust that should our efforts fall short of what is no doubt expected of us, circumstances may duly be taken into consideration.

The note of caution upon which Chelmsford ended this despatch reflected not only a greater awareness of the logistical difficulties of campaigning in Zululand than had prevailed in January, but also a lingering dread of the Zulu themselves. Isandlwana had transformed the Zulu in British minds from a disorganized rabble of savages armed with spears to almost super-human bogeymen. In particular, the battalions arriving fresh from England, their ranks filled with young recruits already unsettled by the strangeness of Africa itself, found themselves a prey to exaggerated stories of Zulu prowess which Lord Chelmsford's very proper precautions only tended to confirm. Despite detailed accounts, such as Magumbi's, which suggested that King Cetshwayo could spare no more than 15,000 men to defend the Eshowe front, Lieutenant Backhouse confided to his diary 'that 35,000 Zulus are said to be waiting for us'.

By the time the last elements of the relief column were assembled on the border, towards the end of March, Chelmsford was to command three full infantry battalions – the 57th, 3/60th and 91st – and a total of seven companies from two more, the 3rd and 99th. In addition, the force included detachments from the Naval Brigade, two 9-pounder guns, four 24-pounder rocket tubes, two naval Gatling guns, Barrow's mounted men, and two battalions of the NNC. Altogether, the column consisted of 3,390 European troops and 2,280 auxiliaries; against such a force, the Zulu commander could expect a numerical superiority of no more than three or four to one. Given the devastating superiority of British fire-power, the odds, in real terms, lay decidedly in Chelmsford's favour.

Nevertheless, he took no chances. In case the reports that Cetshwayo had already divided his forces were untrue, Chelmsford issued instructions for his commanders along the borders to mount diversionary attacks. In the event, only one – Wood's foray against Hlobane – had any significant outcome, but Chelmsford was happy that they had apparently served to confuse the Zulu as to his real intentions. Moreover, shortly before the column advanced, he issued a memorandum to his officers which suggested just how closely he had studied the apparent lessons of the Court of Inquiry:

> Companies must be held together in close order – Files must loosen out, but will not be extended.
> Each waggon and cart with the convoy must have some ammu-nition boxes placed on it in such a position as to be easily got at –

The regimental reserve boxes must have the screw of the lid taken out, and each waggon or cart will have a screwdriver attached to one of the boxes so it may be ready for opening when the screw has not been taken out –

The supply waggons containing stores for the garrison of Ekowe must be loaded with a proper proportion of each article of consumption . . .

The two native battalions will act as escort to the waggons and must give such assistance to them as they may require from time to time – A proportion of waggons should be told off to the care of each company . . .

Each regiment must take its proper proportion of entrenching tools, and those with the advanced portion of the column must be so placed as to be easily got at when the road requires repairs –

No tents will accompany the relieving column – except one or two bell tents for hospital purposes –

The force will form a square laager of the waggons every night with a shelter trench round it, 9 ft from the waggons, & will bivouack, as far as possible in the order of march –

The European portion of the force will bivouack between the waggons and the shelter trench; the natives, cattle and horses will be inside the laager –

The troops will be under arms at 4 a.m. every morning; and the column will prepare for its further advance, so soon as it is daylight, and so soon as the scouts (which should be pushed forward when the force gets under arms) have reported that the enemy is not in force in the immediate neighbourhood –

No bugle sound to be permitted, except 'the alarm' which will be the signal for every man to stand under arms –

Combined parties of 6 Europeans and 6 natives will be placed ½ a mile in advance of each face of the laager at night as outlying sentries – Native scouts will however be pushed forward at least a mile.

These parties will remain quietly on the alert – No smoking, no talking above a whisper and only regarding matters of duty – Their duty is to listen – should the enemy be discovered by the native scouts they will fire volleys and fall back on the picquets who will retire quietly and give the alarm, without firing – Care must be taken not to fire upon the scouts when running in – On each face of the laager one company will remain standing on the watch and will be relieved every hour. Sentries however will not move about. On each face of the laager at least one officer should be on duty during the night, with a binocular which is an excellent night-glass –

By 27 March, the elements comprising the new column had assembled at the Drift. 'A most exciting scene going on,' noted Lieutenant Backhouse, 'preparing for the move', and even the ubiquitous bad weather didn't dampen the air of anticipation. 'Poured with rain all night', complained Backhouse, 'so it might be imagined how wretched we all were, but I managed to get into a covered waggon, so kept pretty dry.' At last, on the 29th, the long-awaited advance began. It was the first major offensive in Zulu territory since January, and Backhouse, at least, embarked upon it soberly:

> We made a start about 6.30 a.m., and reached the Inyoni branching off from our old road, as we intend to avoid the Amatakulu bush, by taking a road nearer the sea. Got nothing to eat until 2 p.m. except some bread and coffee before we started. I could see them flashing signals from Ekowe, in a very brilliant manner, they must have seen us I think, and they know we start today. My darling, God grant that I may be brought safely back to you, I feel that it cannot be otherwise. Marched about 10 miles, many men fell out as we carry greatcoats, and they were soaking wet. The General has come in command, I hope we shall not make a mess of it this time. Laagered at night with a trench dug round it, slept under a waggon with the rest of our fellows: we all got a tot of rum, evening, to keep out the cold.

The first night passed without incident, and the following morning the troops were roused at 4 a.m. Backhouse and his men

> Remained under arms at daybreak. Marched off about 9 a.m. and went as far as the Amatakulu River where we arrived about 1 p.m. Laagered as usual, marched about 8 miles. Fine, sunny day, the weather seems likely to keep fine now, so it will not be so unpleasant for us: got all our things dry. Our commissariat arrangements don't seem too good as we get nothing before we start in the morning and one has to smoke to keep down the hunger. Any amount of newspaper correspondents going up with us, so they will be able to read accounts of our doings at home. No men fell out today . . .

The following day, however, the advance slowed, as the column laboured to cross the steep, narrow banks of the amaTigulu river:

> Crossed the Amatagulu River, and were all day doing so, the water being up to our waists, and bivouacked about a mile beyond the river, laagering as usual. Fine, very hot. On outpost duty all night close to the river, a very nasty position if we had been attacked but luckily no one came, the mosquitoes troubled me so much that I could not sleep a wink. Scouting parties of Zulus seen about.

According to Chelmsford, the presence of Zulu scouts, watching the column from distant hills – the first hint of a Zulu response to the advance – had made him especially cautious that day. 'Up to this time nothing had actually been seen of the enemy by my scouts,' he reported to Colonel Stanley,

> But reports reached me from the Border Agents that bodies of Zulus had been seen moving in an Easterly direction from the Indulina range. I fully appreciated I should not reach Eshowe without an engagement and I was only anxious that the long train of waggons should be together so that at any time on the march we might be able to fight without the chance of the camp followers and transport animals suffering: I therefore found it necessary on the 31st March to content myself with only crossing the Amatakulu river and forming a wagon laager one mile and a half beyond: the river was very high and the transport of the train across the stream took from 6 a.m. to 3 p.m. each wagon requiring 32 instead of 16 oxen.
> During this day (31st) the scouts noticed small bodies of Zulus in the vicinity of the Amatakulu bush. Captain Barrow 19th Hussars with a portion of this command pushed on some 12 miles towards the Engoya forest and burnt the kraal of Magwendo, a brother of the Zulu King's.

On 1 April, the column began to emerge from the undulating country close to the border. Ahead of them lay the Nyezane river, and beyond it the hills rising up to Eshowe. This was the country where Pearson had been attacked in January, and where Chelmsford fully expected to be attacked this time. The presence of Zulu scouts was obvious to all and added to an air of anticipation which pervaded the column. With Eshowe

38. Throughout the war, the British made determined diplomatic efforts to persuade members of the Zulu elite to defect. One of their few successes was Prince Hamu kaNzibe – a member of the Royal House – who surrendered at the beginning of March.

39. Lieutenant Fairlie sketched Hamu's arrival at Captain MacLeod's camp on the Swazi border on 4 March.

40. *Below.* Tommy, the grey horse the Prince Imperial was riding on 1 June. This photograph was taken when the funeral cortège passed through Natal en route to Durban; note the Napoleonic 'N' and bee device on the saddlecloth.

41. The donga on the Tshotshosi river where the Prince Imperial was killed; the cairn of stones marks the spot where the body was found.

42. The Prince's body carried on a gun carriage through the camp at Thelezeni on 2 June – the first of many funeral services before it reached its final resting place. The 17th Lancers are lined up in the background, their lances reversed in respect; Lord Chelmsford is the tall officer following the gun to the right.

43. A Naval Brigade camp above Fort Tenedos on the Lower Thukela testifies to the military build-up which preceded the second invasion.

44. An unidentified unit of the Natal Native Contingent – probably the reorganized 4th or 5th Battalion – photographed near the coast during the second invasion. The men have been rearmed with firearms and issued with old British uniforms.

45. Lieutenant Fairlie's sketch of auxiliaries of Shepstone's Horse – veterans of Isandlwana – skirmishing on the slopes of eZungeni hill on 5 June.

46. British artillery shelling Zulu royal homesteads in the emaKhosini valley, 26 June 1879. The emaKhosini was the ancestral heartland of the Zulu kings, and the British attack was a severe blow to Zulu morale.

47. Prelude to Ulundi: British troops and African auxiliaries photographed at Chelmsford's camp on the White Mfolozi in the first days of July.

48. Major J. F. Owen of 10 Battery, 7th Brigade, Royal Artillery with one of the two Gatling guns he commanded at the battle of Ulundi.

49. The opening stage of the Battle of Ulundi on 4 July; British auxiliaries of Shepstone's Horse goad the Zulu into attacking the square. The royal homestead on the left has already been fired as the troops passed by.

50. Lieutenant Fairlie's dramatic sketch of the end of the Battle of Ulundi. Irregulars, following in the wake of the 17th Lancers, ride down Zulu stragglers; Chelmsford's square is on the rise behind, with the kwaNodwengu royal homestead in flames to the right.

51. Perhaps the most historic photograph taken during the war. The view from the British camp on the White Mfolozi, looking towards the battlefield of Ulundi, with oNdini burning to the right.

52. King Cetshwayo: one of a number of rather forced studies taken on board the steamer *Natal* when the King was en route from Port Durnford, on the Zululand coast, to captivity in Cape Town in September 1879.

53. After nearly four years in exile, King Cetshwayo was restored to Zululand. In an ironic twist, the ceremony at Mthonjaneni on 29 January 1883 was presided over by Sir Theophilus Shepstone who had attended Cetshwayo's original coronation in 1873.

54. For the British troops involved, the price of intervention in Zululand in 1879 was paid in the mournful clusters of graves that still dot the African landscape. A contemporary photograph of the Euphorbia Hill cemetery, near Fort Pearson on the Lower Thukela.

less than twenty miles away, the Zulu would clearly have to act soon if they intended to oppose the relief.

In fact, the information collected by spies like Magumbi was unusually accurate. King Cetshwayo had reassembled his army in the middle of March, but had already despatched most of the regiments to attack Wood's column. Many of the men who lived in the coastal area had gone to oNdini to join the regimental muster, but bowing to the pressure of the coastal commanders, Cetshwayo had allowed most of them to return. Once it was clear that the British advance had begun, the warriors left their quarters around Eshowe and began to congregate on the north bank of the Nyezane. They were under the command of Somopho kaZikhala, one of the King's trusted inner circle, and detachments of several of the principal *amabutho* were present – the iNgobamakhosi, uKhandempemvu, iNdluyengwe, uMbonambi and uNokhenke – supported by large numbers of warriors from the client chiefdoms of the Tsonga from the districts around St Lucia Bay. Among Somopho's lieutenants were a number of men who had distinguished themselves in the January battles, including Prince Dabulamanzi – whose personal homestead lay west of Eshowe – Mavumengwana, who had been joint commander at Isandlwana, and Sigcwelegcwele, who had led the iNgobamakhosi at Isandlwana. Nevertheless, Somopho's force numbered little more than 11,000 men, scarcely double the forces at Chelmsford's command.

On 1 April, according to Backhouse,

> we marched to the spot where we burnt the Gingindhlovu Military Kraal, on our march up to Ekowe. Laagered there as usual; just as we arrived, about 5 p.m., an awful thunderstorm came on, so everyone and everything got drenched through. . . . We are now about 18 miles from Ekowe by the road. We'll make Cetywayo pay for all this discomfort when we get hold of him. Saw several Zulu camp fires towards Inyezane in the evening so a good number must be near us. Slept in the open, lying in the mud, as it rained again during the night. I did not enjoy myself very much.

That night John Dunn, accompanied by one of Chelmsford's staff officers, Captain Molyneux, rode out to investigate the Zulu presence himself. In the late evening gloom, made worse by the heavy rain, the pair rode down to the banks of the Nyezane. Leaving his companion to

guard the horses, Dunn stripped off and swam across the river; as he
waited, Molyneux noted that the river rose almost ten feet in the passage
of an hour. At last Dunn reappeared, blue with cold; dodging Zulu
sentries, he had gone far enough to confirm to his own satisfaction that
a large army was bivouacked beyond the river. In all probability, the
column would be attacked at first light the following morning.

Chelmsford was as confident as he could be that he was equipped to
meet it. The laager was built on a good position, cresting a gentle rise
which fell away on all sides and gave a commanding view of the river
beyond. Although there had been no time to clear a field of fire, the
manouevring of so many wagons had effectively trampled the grass for a
hundred yards or so in front of each face of the square, and the troops
were well placed to receive an attack;

> The North or front face was held by the 60th Rifles; the right
> flank by the 57th Regiment; left flank face by the 99th Regiment and
> 'The Buffs', the rear face by the 91st Regiment and each angle was
> manned by the Naval Brigade, Blue Jackets and Marines; the gatling
> of the 'Boadicea' being on the North East corner; two rocket tubes
> on the North West under Lieut. Kerr, 2 9-pounder guns under Lieut.
> Kingscote on the South West; and one Gatling and two rocket tubes
> on the South East under Commander Brackenbury. The night passed
> without any alarm.

The morning of 2 April broke raw and damp, with a heavy mist
hanging in the Nyezane valley. The troops stood to at 4 a.m., and when,
according to Chelmsford,

> ... the sun rose about 6.15 a.m. our mounted men, as usual, were at
> earliest dawn scouting around. At 5.45 reports came in from them
> simultaneously with the picquets of the 60th and 99th Regiments,
> that the enemy were advancing to the attack; no preparation was
> necessary and no orders had to be given beyond saddling up the
> horses of the Officers of the Staff: troops were already at their posts
> and the cattle had not yet been let out to graze ...

Captain Hart of the NNC – who had been sent back from Eshowe
two months before – was standing near one of his men when the alarm
sounded:

. . . his eyes [were] fixed with the look of a hawk, while with one hand he pointed towards the Inyezane valley and said to me, 'Impi', that is 'Army'. I looked there and saw what might have been easily mistaken for a streak of bush, bordering a stream and disappearing back into the distance miles away. But it was not bush; a few instants of observation showed that it was in motion: it was a stream of black men rapidly approaching our position from our left front; it was a Zulu army!

The warriors crossed the Nyezane in columns at two drifts a mile or so apart, and as they advanced up the slope towards the laager they began to deploy into the traditional 'chest and horns' formation, one column veering off to the left to form the left 'horn', the other fanning out into a 'chest'. Another body suddenly came into view around a low knoll on the British left, known as Misi hill; this was the right 'horn'. Chelmsford gave orders for the men in the laager to hold their fire until the Zulu were within 300 yards – the Martini-Henry's most effective killing range – and the troops watched in nervous anticipation as the Zulu advanced rapidly and shook themselves out into open order. 'In a short time', recalled Backhouse,

> the laager was surrounded; we of course took up our positions in the shelter trenches, the men four deep, officers in rear of them. The ground sloped upwards towards the waggons in our rear so only the front two ranks of the men were sheltered, the rest exposed, and awaited their coming: the guns and rockets opened fire on them, but they came very pluckily to within 50 yards of us at some places, in spite of the tremendous fire we kept up. I'm afraid a good deal of ammunition was wasted as the men could not be stopped from blazing away . . .

Captain Hart thought their approach

> the most splendid piece of skirmishing eye ever beheld. No whites ever did, or ever could skirmish in the magnificent perfection of the Zulus. Unencumbered by much clothing, in the prime of life and as brave as it was possible for any men to be, they bounded forward towards us from all sides, rushing from cover to cover, gliding like snakes through the grass, and turning to account every bush, every mound, every particularly high patch of grass between us and them,

and firing upon us, always from concealment. If total concealment were possible, we should not have seen a Zulu till he reached
our trench, but it was not possible, and we could see them as
they bounded from one point of concealment to another, always
approaching. When a Zulu fires from concealment he instantly
throws himself flat, to escape the shots fired to where his smoke
disclosed his place.

On they came. At one part they were about two hundred yards
off, at another they had closed up to forty yards. Our soldiers fixed
bayonets. However, they were not required to use them . . .

In the rather more formal terms of his official report, Chelmsford,
who was riding around inside the laager with his staff, also appreciated
the order of the Zulu attack:

. . . the Zulus advanced with great rapidity and courage, taking
advantage of the cover afforded by the undulations of the ground
and the long grass; the enemy, however, did not succeed in approaching nearer than 20 yards: several casualties took place at this time,
among them Lieut. Colonel Northey, 3/60th, who, I regret to say,
received a bullet wound from which he eventually died. . . . Lieut.
Courtenay's horse was shot as he stood beside him, Captain Barrow
and Lieut Colonel Crealock being slightly wounded at the same time
and Captain Molyneux's horse was shot under him. The Gatling gun
was of considerable value at this period of the defence.

The attack, checked here, rolled round to the West, or left face,
here Lieutenant G. C. J. Johnson 99th Regiment was killed. Whilst
this was being developed, a fresh force came round to the rear,
probably, from the Imisi Hill, anticipating (so prisoners state) that
our force would prove insufficient to defend, at the same time, all
the faces of the laager: here they obstinately held their ground finding
cover in the long grass and undulations.

The first attack on the front of the square had been so determined
that it had unsettled the men of the 3/60th, many of whom were young
recruits in action for the first time. Their officers had managed to retain
control, but it had been this threat which had brought Colonel Northey
to the front line. He had been standing near the right of the 60th's
position, close to the Gatling, when he was hit by a bullet in the shoulder.
He was taken to the makeshift hospital behind the wagons where the

wound was dressed, but when a sharp rise in the din of battle suggested a fresh attack was taking place, Northey struggled up to cheer on his men. In doing so he ruptured an artery; he collapsed, and died four days later.

To the front and left of the British position, the Zulu attacks went to ground in the face of the awesome volleys, the warriors taking what cover they could in the long wet grass, and returning the fire. Much of their shooting was high, and the air above the laager hummed with bullets, striking the wagons with a rattle and making life dangerous for Chelmsford and his staff – the only men who remained mounted throughout. No sooner had the Zulu 'chest' stalled than the right 'horn' came into action, sweeping in a line round towards the rear face of the laager. The Zulu had expected that, as at Isandlwana, the British position would be unprotected at the rear, but as they advanced close enough they were received by controlled volleys from the 91st. Among those injured was Prince Dabulamanzi, who was leading the attack on horse-back, and who received a flesh wound in the thigh. The attack broke up into small groups of skirmishers, who threw themselves down into the grass and tried to wriggle closer. Now and then the British could hear the *izinduna* exhorting their men to charge, and a knot of warriors would break cover, shields held in front of them, only to be cut down a few yards from the trench.

At this point Chelmsford, thinking the attack was spent, ordered Barrow and the mounted men to mount up, ride out of the laager and drive the Zulus away. But the movement was premature, and the Zulus at first refused to give way:

> The Mounted Infantry and Volunteers meantime having left the laager had been engaged in clearing its front face, I now directed Captain Barrow to advance across the right or East face and attack the enemy's right flank. It was now 7.30 a.m. and during one hour and a half the Zulus had obstinately attacked three sides of the laager.

For a while the mounted men seemed in danger of being cut off, and they remained close to the laager, unable to advance. Twenty minutes later, however, the charges had ground to a halt, and Barrow decided to try again. Chelmsford sent out the Native Contingent to support them:

> Even previous to the mounted men appearing on their flank, the Zulu had, I believe, realized the hopelessness of attempting to pass

through the Zone of heavy rifle fire which met them on their
attempting to charge up against the rear face, but on their appearance, the Zulu retreat commenced: on seeing this the Natal Native
Contingent who were formed within the entrenchments on the rear
face, clearing the ditch, rushed forward with loud cheers of pursuit.

It was the moment a professional cavalryman like Barrow had been
waiting for:

> At about 7.15 a.m. the Zulus retired from the rear face and the
> Natal Native Contingent advanced out of the laager. At the same
> time, accompanied by Lieutenant Courtnay, I succeeded in making a
> flank attack on the retreating Zulus with half a squadron mounted
> infantry under Lieutenant Rawlins, who led his squadron with
> considerable dash and to my entire satisfaction.
>
> The half squadron drew swords and charged the Zulus, who were
> in large numbers, but utterly demoralized. The actual number of
> men killed with the sword were probably few, but the moral effect
> on the retreating Zulus as the swordsmen closed in on them was
> very great. In most cases they threw themselves down and shewed
> no fight, and were assegaid by the Natal Native Contingent who
> were following up. A few Zulus showed fight and assegaid one or two
> horses, but the majority did not do so.
>
> The half squadron then rallied and followed up again to a distance
> of about 1¼ miles from camp, when it was at last checked by a
> spruit.
>
> The Natal Horse followed up in support, but they were unfortu-
> nately unable to charge owing to having no arme blanche or revolver.
> They fired however with effect.
>
> I have no hesitation in saying, that had a regiment of English
> cavalry been on the field on this occasion scarcely a Zulu would have
> escaped to Umisi Hill.
>
> The half squadron mounted infantry, under Lieutenant Sugden,
> and the volunteer squadron endeavoured to follow up the front face,
> but were unable to close with the enemy on account of the boggy
> ground, and the fire of the Natal Native Contingent.
>
> The mounted natives followed the enemy for some miles towards
> the Gingindhlovo kraal and Amatikulu, and Thausie's squadron
> succeeded in recapturing some 15 head of cattle, which the Zulus
> had found outside the laager.

As at Khambula a few days before, the pursuit after the battle of
Gingindlovu was severe. The lingering nervousness which had prevailed
among the British found vent in a desire to avenge Isandlwana. Many
of the Zulus were simply killed as they walked away from the battle,
too exhausted to run; large numbers of Zulu wounded were abandoned
on the banks of the Nyezane river and were mercilessly sought out and
speared by the Native Contingent. Even after the first rush of battle
was over, a number of wounded Zulu who had surrendered were shot
in isolated acts of retribution. For many in the British ranks, this was an
aspect of the battle they came to regret, but as Captain Hart explained,
it had seemed inevitable at the time:

> . . . their bravest men had not breath to run away, and they perished.
> Let me draw a veil over that part of the scene. Chivalry ends when
> pursuit begins; but the dire necessities of war oblige that a defeated
> army shall also be dispersed, so that it shall never fight again; it is
> called consummating the victory . . .

For Chelmsford, that victory was a huge relief, and he reported with
some satisfaction that

> Bodies of Zulus were to be seen hurrying away towards the
> Indulinda making a stand nowhere and throwing away their arms to
> assist in the flight.
> Within a short time I directed officers and burying parties to
> count the enemy's loss within 1,000 yards of the entrenchment – 471
> were buried, 200 having been found since near the scene, but from
> the chance wounded men we have found five miles away and the
> execution done at long range by the artillery, I have no hesitation in
> estimating the enemy's loss at 1,000 men.
> . . . Our casualties are small considering the easy mark the laager
> afforded the assailants, and, had it not been for the cover afforded
> the troops by the broad shelter trench, I should have had to report a
> much heavier loss.

The British loss had totalled just 2 officers and 11 men killed, and 4
officers and 44 men wounded. They were buried in the muddy ground
outside the shelter trench. Once the Zulu had disappeared from sight,
Chelmsford allowed the men to stand down, and details passed across
the field collecting Zulu rifles – they gathered 435 in all, including 3

Martini-Henrys with the butt-marks of the 24th Regiment – and drag-
ging away the bodies. As passions cooled, the exultation in the Zulu
defeat gave way to pity and horror as the troops saw for themselves
the effect of their fire on the Zulu bodies. 'I went over the field where the
dead Zulus were lying in the afternoon,' admitted Backhouse,

> It was a ghastly sight, such fine men too, they were as thick as
> peas in some places. Thank God, my darling, I was kept safe, but
> some bullets came unpleasantly near: it was amusing to see the men
> bobbing their heads when the Zulus first opened fire on them.

The battle had been clearly visible through field-glasses to Pearson's
garrison, and the men at Eshowe signalled their congratulations.
Eshowe was still a day's march away – more, if Chelmsford took all
the cumbersome baggage train – and the track rose sharply beyond the
Nyezane, through a corrugation of hills. By noon on the 2nd, the sun
was at its height, and the men were showing signs of fatigue after the
ordeal of battle. Chelmsford decided to delay his advance until the following day, and to leave most of the wagons at Gingindlovu. Among
those ordered to stay was Lieutenant Backhouse, not entirely comfortable
at the prospect:

> The waggons and laager are to remain here, with our 2 companies
> and the companies of the 99th Regt., some sailors and Native
> Contingent, and the rest of the force with the General start for Ekowe
> tomorrow: Ekowe to be evacuated and another fort built somewhere
> nearer the coast: the force hope to reach Ekowe tomorrow evening,
> possibly they will have a fight either going up or coming down:
> I would rather go up with them than remain here, for I should not
> feel too safe if we were attacked by any large number of Zulus, the
> laager being too big for the numbers we shall have to defend it.

Chelmsford set off at about 8 a.m. the following morning, leaving

> . . . Major Walker 99th Regiment with two companies 'The Buffs', two
> of the 91st and five of the 99th, and 400 Naval Brigade together with
> the Natal Native Contingent, as a garrison for the laager, which
> was altered in size to meet the reduced strength. The remainder of
> the column, carrying three days biscuit and meat, with a ground
> sheet between every two men and escorting 58 carts of stores for
> the Etshowe garrison, moved off in compact order for Etshowe. The

distance to be traversed was only some 15 miles but the streams were
deep and the swamps heavy and for the last 8 or 9 miles of the road,
the ascent was steep: in two places the road had been partly destroyed
by the Zulus. It was 11.30 p.m. before the whole relief Column
reached Etshowe. Colonel Pearson and a portion of the garrison came
out to meet us, which would have been of great assistance had the
enemy opposed our advance, but none were to be seen that day . . .

Pearson rode out ahead of his men and met Chelmsford's staff
coming in the opposite direction. 'Here's Pearson,' said Chelmsford
brightly, holding out his hand, 'how are you?'

When the relief column finally marched up to the ramparts, the
garrison turned out to cheer them in. Despite the fact that it was dark,
the men wandered around the fort, chatting excitedly about their
adventures, the newcomers making free with their tobacco. The relief
column were surprised to find that Pearson's men, while looking gaunt,
seemed none the worse for their ordeal; the stiff climb up through the
hills had left many of Chelmsford's men exhausted. They were short of
food, too, having lived on biscuits and tinned meat since the advance
began; to their surprise, the garrison broke open a store of three days'
supplies, which they had been hoarding against the possibility of making
a dash back to the border.

Yet the relief of the garrison was tempered by Chelmsford's decision
to abandon the post. Despite his earlier intention to maintain a fresh
garrison at Eshowe, he had already decided that the extended and
difficult approach made it too exposed to the risk of future Zulu attacks.
With reinforcements arriving almost daily in Durban, he was in a
position to rethink his entire invasion strategy, and he opted instead to
withdraw to a position much closer to the Thukela. This would be easier
to defend and provision until he was ready to begin a new offensive. It
was a decision which caused bitter disappointment among Pearson's
garrison, who for ten weeks had laboured to make Eshowe impregnable
and had endured constant harassment by the Zulu and the ravages of
disease as a result. As one of them, Lieutenant Lloyd of the Artillery, put
it, 'it was too annoying to think that all our work had been done in vain,
that we were to give up the splendid fort on which we had taken so
much pains and time'. Nevertheless, on the morning of the 4th, they
began to dismantle the ramparts and prepared to evacuate the post.

Chelmsford was determined to make one last demonstration before he retired. One of Prince Dabulamanzi's personal homesteads, eZulwini, lay a few miles away, and Chelmsford decided to attack it. The homestead had no military value, but the foray served as a gesture of defiance, a warning that the Zulu should not take the retreat from Eshowe as a sign of defeat. In his official report, Chelmsford confined himself to the bald facts of the expedition:

> I accompanied a patrol under Captain Barrow who, with his mounted force, Dunn's scouts, and a Company of Natal Pioneers of the Eshowe garrison, proceeded to destroy a kraal of Dabulamanzi's some 8 or 9 miles off on the Entumeni Hill, two of the enemy were killed and one prisoner taken. A small body of some 40 Zulus kept up a well-directed fire from a neighbouring hill, but no casualty occurred on our side.

In fact, there was much about the incident to reflect the futility and poignancy of the campaign as a whole. John Dunn himself had accompanied Chelmsford's party, and he recognized Dabulamanzi amongst a group of warriors who gathered on a hilltop overlooking the homestead. As Barrow's men set fire to the huts, Dunn and Dabulamanzi, who had been friends before the war, traded shots at far beyond the effective range of their rifles. No one was hit, though Chelmsford's staff noted with admiration that the Zulu group ducked several times. Then, having made their point, the British withdrew, leaving the Zulu to contemplate the ruin of their possessions.

The following day, the 5th, both Chelmsford and Pearson's garrison abandoned Eshowe. As the column wound down through the hills, they saw smoke rise to their rear; the Zulu had entered the post and set fire to the buildings. The garrison left behind them a small cluster of wooden crosses on an open hillside, the last resting place of twenty-eight of Pearson's men who had succumbed during the siege, mostly to disease. Twelve more lay beneath a spreading mimosa tree beside the track at Nyezane, and fourteen more at Gingindlovu. Nor was the toll of the campaign yet over.

The countryside below the hills still bore the signs of the Zulu concentrations of a few days before – long swathes of flattened grass marking the passage of the *impi* – while the veld was littered with wounded Zulu, some of whom had already crawled several miles since the battle three days before. Even for the victors of Gingindlovu, the obvious signs of the Zulu presence, old as it was, served to instil in them a fresh sense of menace. Indeed, the extent of the Zulu defeat at Gingindlovu was still not entirely apparent to the British. In fact, the Zulu army had been shattered by the battle, and had been particularly demoralized by its inability to penetrate the curtain of British fire. While some had rallied and had remained bivouacked in the Mhlatuze valley, the majority had dispersed to their homes, and they were certainly in no condition to embark upon another fight so soon.

Nevertheless, such was the awe with which the British had come to regard the Zulu by this stage of the war that even in the immediate aftermath of Gingindlovu they remained convinced that a fresh attack was possible. As the war correspondent Charles Norris-Newman put it, the prevailing opinion was that 'they would fight us again and again, no matter how often they were beaten', while in the camp at Gingindlovu Lieutenant Backhouse continued to hope that 'we won't be attacked tonight'. This anxiety would manifest itself amongst Chelmsford's returning command in one of the worst scares of the war. It had been slow progress from Eshowe, and at Dunn's suggestion Chelmsford had decided not to return straight to Gingindlovu, but instead had camped near the deserted German mission station at eMvutsheni. Here the strain of the previous few days found expression in a particularly disturbing incident:

> I regret to report that at 3.30 [a.m.] the following morning (6th April) a sentry of the 91st fired a shot at what he took to be a party of the enemy who did not answer his challenge: on hearing this shot the picquet of the 60th Rifles on the opposite flank of the entrench-ment, retired without orders from its Officer together with Mr Dunn's scouts who had been occupying some mealie fields beyond. It was bright moonlight, and I can offer no excuse or explanation of what occurred beyond the youth of the men of the 60th for it was perfectly well known to Officers and men that these scouts were in their front. It appears that some of the 60th lining the entrench-ment, seeing the picquets running in, fired, probably at the native scouts but 5 of the 3/60th were wounded by their own comrades and I deeply regret to say that some nine of our native allies were bayonetted as they attempted to gain, as they thought, the shelter of

the laager: one man was killed and two natives have since died of their wounds.

The incident provided a suitably sour note on which to end the campaign. Chelmsford decided to abandon the camp at Ginginglovu – made unhealthy by the number of Zulu dead still lying hidden in the long grass – and withdraw the entire command closer to the border. Backhouse for one was delighted:

> On outlying picquet all day, we could see the smoke the Zulus made trying to burn Ekowe. I hope they will leave the graves of our poor fellows, who died there, alone. . . . I hear that we are to start back to the Drift to rejoin our Headquarters as soon as possible, most likely tomorrow; a new fort is to be built and our two companies and those of the 99th will escort a lot of empty waggons back to the drift, with the sick and wounded and rejoin our respective Headquarters.

Yet life on the Thukela outpost was destined to remain far from comfortable. The tension of the previous months gave way to boredom and ennui, aggravated by an increase in sickness brought about by the concentration of troops, and by monotonous food. Dysentery became commonplace, particularly among the unseasoned men of the 60th. There was a bitter irony in this, for more than one man who had stood up to the Zulu charges at Gingindlovu succumbed to typhoid fever. At Fort Chelmsford, an advanced post built on the Nyezane, downstream from the old battlefield, Captain Hart mused on the reasons for the decline in the general state of the troops' health:

> The Inyezane is a small stream, and now in the winter, the dry season, it almost ceases to flow and the water taken from the pools is not good. Added to this, a considerable number of dead Zulus had long been in the river, up-stream of us, some as near as a mile. Whether they were thrown in to poison the water, or whether, as our natives say, they were wounded men retreating from Gingindlovu, drowned in trying to cross the river when it was swollen, I do not know . . .
> . . . The bodies in the Inyezane were almost reduced to skeletons when we found them.
> In the bullet pouch, on the belt of one of them, was a letter from

Colonel Pearson to Lord Chelmsford, written at Ekowe and sent by a native messenger. He must have been killed, poor fellow.

... The letter was still quite legible throughout. Probably the skeleton on which it was found was that of the Zulu who had killed the messenger ...

Nor was there sanctuary at the Thukela, either, for those who had fallen ill at Eshowe; over 200 sick had been brought back on wagons during the retreat, and at least three officers failed to recover. Among them was Captain Warren Wynne, Pearson's chief Engineer, who had planned the defences of Eshowe; he died on 19 April, his thirty-sixth birthday.

Chapter Six

'They got it today . . .'

By the beginning of April 1879, Lord Chelmsford's strategic position was largely as it had been during the first week of January. Eshowe had been relieved, and the concentrations of British troops along the Lower Drift dominated the countryside for a dozen miles across the border. The remains of the old Centre Column were still at Rorke's Drift, and in between, along much of the length of the Thukela river, small outposts watched the drifts for any sign of a Zulu incursion. Further north, Wood's column remained safely entrenched at Khambula.

To his critics, it seemed that in three months of fighting, Chelmsford had successfully occupied only a few miles of enemy territory, and that close to the borders. Yet in fact the progress of the war was not to be reckoned by territorial incursions alone. The tide of Zulu victory, which had thrown back the British offensive in January, had itself been checked. The battles at Khambula and Gingindlovu alone had cost the Zulu as many as 3,000 dead, and the reports of Border Agents spoke of mourning songs heard along the length of the border, and of homesteads full of wounded warriors returning from the front. In the short term at least, the Zulu capacity to resist had been shattered, allowing Chelmsford a few weeks' grace to plan a fresh offensive. Moreover, the nature of the Zulu military system meant that their losses were felt throughout all levels of civilian society, right across the country, and while Chelmsford could ultimately replace the losses endured at Isandlwana, Ntombe and Hlobane, the Zulu could not.

Indeed, by the middle of April the bulk of the British reinforcements had arrived at Durban and were being moved slowly towards assembly points on the borders. Whereas Chelmsford had begun the war woefully under-strength, he now had an embarrassment of riches. No fewer than five Major-Generals had been sent out to share the burden of command, together with two regiments of regular cavalry – the 1st (King's) Dragoon Guards and 17th (Duke of Cambridge's) Lancers – twelve infantry battalions, five artillery batteries, including one equipped with Gatling machine-guns, and a cornucopia of support services – Engineers, commissariat and supply staff, and even veterinary surgeons. Most of the Natal Volunteer Corps and irregular units still remained in the field, while the African auxiliary units – whose morale had been seriously shaken by Isandlwana – had been extensively reorganized. Attempts had been made to instil a greater sense of British military discipline by issuing them with uniforms and firearms, and Chelmsford himself was moved to admit that

> Man for man I believe the Natal Zulu to be quite equal to the Zulu proper, and I am certain that he only requires to be properly armed, organized and disciplined, to make him equal, if not superior to, the enemy we are now fighting –
> ... Altho' I admit that the battalions of the Native Contingent now in the Field, and those at Krantzkop and Sand Spruit, are not as perfectly armed, organized or disciplined as they should be, still there can be no doubt, that owing to what has been done in that direction, they are infinitely superior as regards efficiency...

All in all, Chelmsford faced the renewed invasion of Zululand with over 9,000 regular infantry and 1,000 regular cavalry. Together with all the auxiliary, colonial and support forces, his army totalled over 17,000 men. It now included over twenty field-guns, as well as the first Gatling battery to be fielded by the Royal Artillery. Although just two guns strong, this battery was an impressive addition to Chelmsford's firepower, and indeed, following upon the success of the Navy's Gatling at Nyezane, the Zulu campaign would prove to be the first in which this cumbersome weapon made a significant contribution to the British cause.

It was not an inconsiderable force, when opposed to it were perhaps 25,000 tired, demoralized and hopelessly outgunned Zulu warriors.

The work of reorganizing the auxiliary units had not proceeded without political difficulty, however. The Lieutenant-Governor of Natal, Sir Henry Bulwer, had become increasingly opposed to Chelmsford's attempts to place the black manpower of the colony directly under military control. While Bulwer had been forced to accept that the Natal Native Contingent units were a purely military invention with which Chelmsford could do as he liked, Bulwer continued to insist that the units raised for border defence should remain under colonial authority. In particular, he refused to allow them to be used in any offensive action across the border, and to that extent became embroiled in a row with Chelmsford that came to a head throughout April. 'I have been much annoyed', Chelmsford wrote to the Duke of Cambridge on 11 April,

> by the action of the Lieut Governor of Natal who when I had ordered the Native forces along the border to make demonstrations and if possible raids into Zululand actually sent orders without consulting me or my Staff forbidding any native to cross the border –
>
> When I made up my mind to advance upon Ekowe I felt that I might possibly have to encounter the full strength of the Zulu army and I was anxious to create a diversion in its favour by simultaneously raiding from one end of the line to the other –
>
> The full state of the Tugela prevented this from being carried out, but I consider that the action of Sir Henry Bulwer is quite indefensible & if persevered in must completely prevent my making any use of the large numbers of Natal Natives who are now in arms along the Border ... Sir H. Bulwer from my first arrival in Natal has thrown every obstacle in my way whilst at the same time he has endeavoured by long memoranda, minutes and despatches to make it appear that he has given me all the assistance that I have asked for ...

This disagreement was indicative of a growing rift between the civil and military authorities in the colony, which was further compounded by the perennial difficulties of transport. Supply had been problematic enough in January, but the task of assembling the stockpiles necessary to launch the new invasion was made worse by the reluctance of Natal civilians – black and white – to work for the Army. Furthermore, almost the entire transport for the Centre Column still lay deserted upon the field of Isandlwana, and there were few enough resources to replace it. So serious was the situation that Chelmsford's Commissary General, Walter Strickland, was on the verge of collapse. Chelmsford appointed one of his newly arrived Major-Generals, Sir Hugh Clifford, to replace him in Natal, but despite Clifford's efforts the situation threatened to delay the renewal of hostilities:

> I am not prepared to take so gloomy a view of the Transport situation as that sketched out by Mr Strickland. There can be no

doubt, however, that the difficulties to be overcome are very great, and the advance of the troops into Zululand cannot take place until the Transport has thrown sufficient amounts of supplies into our present advanced depots, and has, moreover, provided the requisite amount of wagons, etc. for that advance.

. . . The Natal Zulu has a horror of continuous service, and, as a rule, no amount of pay will induce him to remain at one particular work beyond a certain time. If, moreover, the work in question takes him away from his own home, or is one that he does not particularly fancy, or should he be to a certain extent tied down by military rules and be subject to Military discipline, no money inducement will persuade him to accept such employ. He must therefore be ordered to perform the duty. The transport service in Natal is therefore absolutely dependent upon the Lt Governor for native assistance without which it is paralysed.

That assistance has been given so far that the several magistrates have been instructed to furnish all the drivers and leaders obtainable in the districts. I have found however that such orders issued to the magistrates through the Secretary of Native Affairs, take a long time in being carried out, and that the Government is unable, or unwilling to put that pressure upon the natives without which no satisfactory result can be expected.

I am quite unable, therefore, to express an opinion as to whether our present want will be met, and I can feel no certainty that, if we obtain the required number of Natives, we should be able to retain them in our service, or whether an Exodus of those natives who are still serving us may not again paralyse the movements of our transport. This actual state of affairs has frequently been brought to the notice of the Lt Governor but His Excellency does not appear to possess any real power to help us.

The paralysis which afflicted Chelmsford's logistical services led to a frustrating delay in renewing the offensive – which found an outlet in the bickering of his transport officers – as throughout April and May the troops were marched to their assembly points. For one of the new arrivals, Major Anstruther of the 94th, the excitement of reaching the Zulu border was tempered by a realization of the challenges which lay ahead:

Yesterday we got in here at our journey's end for some time and
very glad we were of it. We all live in the waggon laager but can get
out in the day time and it is very jolly being able to bathe in the
Blood River. With us from Dundee came Jones' company of Engineers, some native pioneers and about 35 cavalry, just irregular horse,
of which there are a lot about the country – loafers, out at elbow,
hailing from New Zealand, Australia, London, anywhere, Mexicans,
Yankees etc. By the way, Chard is with us as Jones' subaltern . . .

The weather is getting charming, cooler in the middle of the day
and not too cold at night.

The convoy we had to convey is a fearful thing – 112 waggons
and certainly they took 4 miles of road. If they had been attacked
we could have done nothing to save them, except shoot a few
Kaffirs. All the drivers bolt and then you are powerless. People in
England imagine that losing a convoy is like losing the watch out
of your pocket, whereas it is impossible to defend it. You can give
it little more than moral support, i.e. hope that the redcoats will
frighten them by their looks. Oxen are quite as difficult to manage
as geese and if the Kaffirs can't drive them away they assegai them.
I believe 25 of the waggons are to unload and get back tonight
but I should not at all wonder if the Kaffirs had a shot at some of
the others . . .

With the main concentrations largely inactive, it was left to the
border garrisons to maintain some pressure on the Zulu. With the Zulu
army still dispersed in the aftermath of Khambula and Gingindlovu,
Chelmsford was anxious that

Constant patrols and occasional raids, made at different points of
this long line, would of course keep any Zulus that might be living
in that part of the country in a state of perpetual alarm, so they
would never be certain that a general advance from that direction
was not contemplated –

It would prevent them from reaping their crops, it would compel
them to keep their cattle out of reach, and it would most probably
cause eventually the entire evacuation of the Southern border of
Zululand –

I am aware that the objection may be raised to this plan of
operations that it is harassing the Zulu people and not Cetywayo and

that consequently we are not acting up to the announcement which was made, when we first entered Zululand, that our quarrel was with the latter and not with the former –

Since however the commencement of the war our troops have been attacked at different times by the whole available fighting force in Zululand, and it is therefore clear that the Zulu people themselves are not prepared to accept the distinction it was thought advisable to make.

Under the circumstances it would be unwise to neglect any opportunity that may present itself of inflicting substantial injuries upon our enemy . . .

This hope found practical expression in the biggest border incursion of the war, which took place along the Middle Drift sector on 20 May. Ever since the end of March, when Chelmsford had called for border garrisons to demonstrate in support of his march on Eshowe, the garrison encamped on the escarpment high above the Middle Drift had been keen to take him at his word. The flooded state of the Thukela had made any significant raid impossible, but by the middle of May the commanding officer, Major Twentyman of the 4th Regiment, had assembled a sizeable force, consisting of a few Natal Volunteers and a large number of African auxiliaries from the Border Guard and Levies. Both the white officers of the auxiliary units and their men were particularly keen to take an active part in what for them had hitherto proved a rather dull war, the more so because the Zulu seemed demoralized by their recent defeats. When the chance came, they took it with gusto, as the Border Agent J. E. Fannin described:

. . . this morning raids were made into Zululand from three different points.

At the Elibomvu Drift, about one mile above Hot Springs, a force of about 1,000 natives and 100 Europeans crossed and burnt 15 kraals and large quantities of grain. The cattle belonging to them were driven away into a most difficult piece of country, where it was not thought advisable to follow them. Only a few goats were captured. A few shots were fired by the Zulus from a long distance off.

Some miles higher up Captain Walker crossed with 500 of the Ixopo contingent. I hear from the police and natives he burnt

Podidi's and two other kraals, and captured a large troop of cattle. I will forward particulars as soon as I can get them.

Between the Hot Springs and Middle Drift Mangabeza's tribe under Mr Crabb crossed; they burnt two kraals, and then, seeing the Zulus assembling in force, beat a hurried retreat to this side. I will send further particulars of this affair as soon as I get them.

Lomahashe's tribe, under command of Mr Wheelwright, took part in the operations at Elibomvu. Mr Wheelwright did not cross himself, being occupied giving directions on this side.

Major Twentyman was in command, and had a narrow escape; one of the Zulu's bullets passed within a foot of him. I, with several of the border police, accompanied him as far as the huts, giving him all the assistance I could.

The whole force remains in the Tugela Valley tonight. . . . The Zulus were completely taken by surprise; the arrangements were so good that they were not aware of the approach of our force, and first sounded the alarm when it drew up ready to cross the river bank.

Yet the elation felt at the success of the raid was partly dispelled by the willingness of the Zulu to retaliate immediately. That night a force of Zulu crossed the border in the wake of the returning raiders, and destroyed three homesteads on the Natal side. They dispersed before Twentyman's men could return to confront them. The incident was little more than a gesture of defiance, but it was a clear indication that the Zulu were by no means beaten by their recent failures, and indeed it was a hint of further reprisals to come.

Not that Chelmsford needed reminding of the capabilities of his enemy. Despite the successes at Khambula and Gingindlovu, the prevailing opinion within the British force – particularly among those who had yet to face the Zulu in battle – was that the Zulu remained a particularly dangerous foe. This perception, which was increasingly at odds with the strategic reality, had a very real impact upon Chelmsford's plans for the new offensive. Evelyn Wood summed up the situation in a realistic appraisal, written to Chelmsford shortly after Chelmsford's success at Gingindlovu:

I don't know how you felt at your fight, nor how many you had against you – I imagine not more than 12,000. We fought in our intrenched camp about 1,800 whites against as nearly as I can make from 23 to 25,000, of whom I should say 5,000 never came under fire, nor within 2 or 3 miles. We had all chances in our favour, except the previous day's work which had disheartened our mounted men, and with the previous Intombi valley patrol had exhausted the horses.

We were intrenched, tho' by no means in a perfect position, and the following conclusion is in my mind.

1st. – That no mounted Colonial troops who can ride away, will await an attack by say 6 to 1 from Zulus.

2nd. – That I should not like to see you fight in the open or in attacking a position at greater odds than 5 or 6 to 1.

Do not think I am depreciating our men – I am not – but having seen many men under fire, I consider our troops have not forgotten the 22nd of January, nor will they do so for some time. The fact of the Zulu giving no quarter is an enormous advantage to them!

This was sound advice which Chelmsford could not afford to ignore, and it meant that his new invasion would be shaped not only by the need to make each of his advancing columns strong enough to defend themselves if attacked in force, but also to protect Natal against a Zulu counter-attack, which was widely held to be still possible. In effect, he chose to modify his original plan, adhering to the general principle that an attack on more than one front would so challenge the Zulu as to prevent them from attempting a strike across the border. A large concentration of troops – Pearson's old column, together with the Eshowe relief force – now straddled the Lower Thukela, and these Chelmsford brigaded together to form a single division, called the 1st Division. He placed it under the command of one of the newly arrived senior officers, Major-General Henry Crealock, whose younger brother, John North Crealock, was on Chelmsford's staff. With the exception of the Hlobane débâcle, Evelyn Wood's command had performed well throughout the war, and Chelmsford was reluctant to tamper with a successful formula. Rather than reorganize it, he simply gave it a new title which confirmed its independent status – it was now known as the Flying Column. The remaining reinforcements were then formed into an entirely new column, the 2nd Division, which was placed under the command of Major-General Edward Newdigate. Chelmsford himself intended to accompany this column, however, thereby placing Newdigate in the same uncomfortable position which Glyn had experienced in

January. The cavalry regiments were formed into a Cavalry Brigade under Major-General Marshall, which was attached to the 2nd Division.

There still remained, however, the question of the best route by which to advance. Although the 1st Division was already in the field, Chelmsford was concerned by the distance it had to advance towards oNdini, and by the high ridges it would have to traverse on the approaches to Eshowe. As a result, from the beginning, he allocated it a largely supporting role, and directed it primarily to suppress resistance in the coastal belt. As early as 12 April, his instructions to Crealock specified that

> The first objective of this Division will be the Emangwene military kraal, situated on the north side of the Umhlatoosi river –
>
> ... This kraal is said to number 1,000 huts, and is situated in a highly populated District –
>
> The Kraal should be burnt, and the whole district cleared out –
>
> ... When this work is completed the Undi military kraal south of the Umhlatoosi river and about 10 miles distant from the Emangwene, should also be burnt –
>
> ... It is probable that the King will not allow these two Kraals to be destroyed without making an effort to protect them –
>
> ... The road to Emangwene kraal runs through a perfectly open country however, and a road fit for a light carriage exists between that place and the Undi kraal –
>
> ... There are no physical difficulties therefore, in the way of the above mentioned operations –
>
> ... A strong, permanent, entrenched post must be made at some point between the Tugela and Umhlatoosi river from which the advance should be made, and which should be held during the advance by a sufficient force –
>
> ... On the completions of the operations against the Emangwene and Undi military Kraals, the Major-General will have to decide for himself what further operations are possible or desirable –
>
> ... The objective of the Northern force will be Ulundi, and it is to be hoped that the 1st Division will be able to grapple successfully with the difficulties of the Umhlatoosi river between Undi and St Paul's, and establish an entrenched post and supply depot in the neighbourhood – thus assisting in the general advance against the King's own Kraal –

It was, of course, strategically vital that the Zulu living in the coastal districts, who had been so active during the siege of Eshowe, be pacified, but Chelmsford's instructions inevitably relegated Crealock's column to the role of a side-show. Although Chelmsford was cautious enough to suggest that Cetshwayo might yet mount an attack in defence of the royal homesteads, the fact was that the Zulu army no longer retained the capability to fight on two fronts, and after Gingindlovu many Zulu in the coastal sector considered themselves already beaten. For Crealock, what remained of the war would consist of a ponderous and frustrating advance made painfully slow by a continuing shortage of transport – the column soon earned the nick-name 'Crealock's Crawlers' – with little prospect of enemy action to alleviate the boredom. The greatest danger lay in the effects of the humid climate, the monotonous diet, and the insanitary conditions which inevitably accompanied so large a concentration of troops, exacerbated by the presence of the unburied carcasses of transport oxen, worked to death, which soon lay in scores along the road.

In committing the combined 2nd Division and Flying Column to advance towards oNdini from the north-west, Chelmsford had none the less still to decide their exact route. It was clearly neither necessary nor desirable to assemble the 2nd Division too far north, and he hoped instead to cut across country and intersect Wood's projected line of advance. Yet, as he had discovered in January, there were few enough roads into Zululand from northern Natal, especially as he was reluctant to use the best one, which crossed at Rorke's Drift. Ever since Isandlwana, Chelmsford had been under pressure to bury the dead still scattered at the foot of that mournful crag. As he explained on 12 May, in reply to a request from the Bishop of Natal, the Reverend John William Colenso, he had felt unable to comply:

> I need hardly assure your Lordship that the question of burying those who fell so nobly has been continuously in my thoughts, and that I am most anxious to have it done as speedily as possible.
>
> From reports that I have received I do not believe that work could have been done without risking the health of those employed in the task, until quite lately; and now I feel I could not detach the requisite number of troops, without seriously interfering with the operations now going on.

There was another factor, too, in that Chelmsford had no desire to expose troops fresh out from England to the naked realities of Zulu warfare. To take a column of reinforcements past Isandlwana within a day or two of launching a new invasion could only have a detrimental effect on their morale, and he was determined to find another route. If possible, he hoped to strike from the settler village of Dundee, north of Rorke's Drift, avoiding Isandlwana, before rejoining the old Rorke's Drift/oNdini road near Babanango mountain. Such a plan had the advantage, too, of keeping close to the border in the early stages, thus reducing the risk of a Zulu counter-attack into Natal. As he wrote to Wood on 25 April,

> A raiding force must necessarily advance from the King's some-where between St. Paul's and Babanango Mt and would of course have the same line of retreat –
>
> If we advance from the Utrecht base by a road south of the Inhlazatye, we are at once on the line of retreat of any force raiding across the Tugela, and can really give Natal very effective assistance – If however we take the northern road and a raid be made into Natal I feel sure that I should be blamed for my strategy and very properly so – Kindly consider then how we can best work to the South of the Inhlazatye, and yet not leave the frontier North of that mountain completely unprotected.
>
> I am willing to admit that the Babanango road is the worst of the two, but I am certain that I am right in determining that our main line of advance shall be made upon it – and with the force at our disposal, and at this season of the year we ought to have no difficulty in making any line practicable for our convoys –

By the middle of May Chelmsford was committed to this plan, although the exact route was yet to be decided. Wood was still at Khambula but was preparing to advance on a line which would intersect the route of the 2nd Division within days of their crossing the border. In late May, mounted British patrols penetrated deeply beyond the border in search of a viable road. To their relief, they found the country across the border largely deserted, the homesteads empty and devoid of women and cattle. Nevertheless, their movements were sometimes challenged by small parties of Zulu, under the command of local chiefs and *izinduna*, who had remained in the frontier zone to watch British

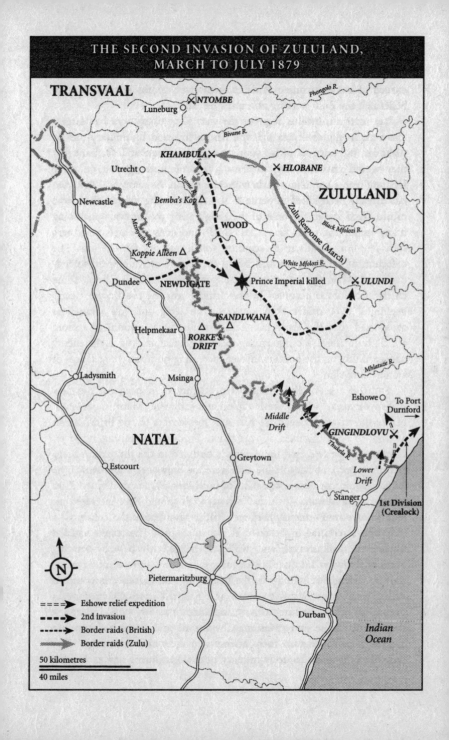

THE SECOND INVASION OF ZULULAND, MARCH TO JULY 1879

TRANSVAAL

Luneburg ○   ✕ **NTOMBE**

Phongolo R.

Bivane R.

KHAMBULA ✕

Utrecht ○

✕ **HLOBANE**

ZULULAND

Ncome R.

Bemba's Kop △

Black Mfolozi R.

Newcastle ○

WOOD

Zulu Response (March)

Mzinyathi R.

Koppie Alleen △

White Mfolozi R.

Dundee ○

NEWDIGATE

★ Prince Imperial killed

✕ **ULUNDI**

Helpmekaar ○

△ **ISANDLWANA**

RORKE'S DRIFT

Mhlatuze R.

Ladysmith ○

Msinga ○

NATAL

Eshowe ○   To Port Durnford

Middle Drift

GINGINDLOVU ✕

Estcourt ○

Greytown ○

Thukela R.

Lower Drift

Stanger ○   **1st Division (Crealock)**

Pietermaritzburg ○

N

Durban ○

Indian Ocean

=====▷ Eshowe relief expedition
▬▬▬▶ 2nd invasion
▪▪▪▶ Border raids (British)
➤➤➤ Border raids (Zulu)

50 kilometres

40 miles

movements and protect abandoned property. The skirmishes which ensued, although inconsequential in themselves, reinforced the prevailing belief that the Zulu were by no means defeated.

Yet in truth, by this stage of the war, King Cetshwayo had largely lost faith in his ability to halt the British invasion by military means. Although the warriors of his younger regiments were still adamant that they would answer a call to arms, the prolonged fighting on three separate fronts had almost exhausted the nation. As many as 7,000 men had already been killed in battle – fit, healthy young men in the prime of life, from whom the bulk of the King's army was drawn – including many important royal favourites, chiefs and sons of chiefs and there were few homesteads in the country which had not felt the loss. The defection of Prince Hamu had raised the spectre of widespread surrenders, and while the majority of the population remained loyal, some chiefs in the areas occupied by the British, near the coast, were clearly beginning to consider their options. The King and his counsellors recognized that the army had sufficient resolve to mount one more attack, but extensive campaigning was impractical, and, with the enemy concentrating on the borders in ever-increasing numbers, the chances of victory were slim.

For this reason, King Cetshwayo attempted to head off the new British offensive with a fresh diplomatic initiative. Many times, even before the invasion began, he had sent messengers to the British in an attempt to open channels of negotiation. From the beginning, however, Cetshwayo was told that the demands outlined in the ultimatum of 11 December were not negotiable, and were the only ones under which the British would consider a cessation of hostilities. Paradoxically, the Zulu success at Isandlwana – which Cetshwayo felt should have increased his bargaining power – merely hardened British resolve, and the Zulu envoys were either rebuffed or detained as potential spies. The results had left Cetshwayo disillusioned, and while he hedged his bets by sending occasional envoys into the British camps, he had continued at the same time to defend his country in the field. This had merely compounded British suspicions of his motives, and had led Lord Chelmsford to dismiss all peace overtures as a cynical attempt to buy time. Indeed, by the eve of the second invasion, Chelmsford and Frere had together evolved a policy to turn these attempts to their own advantage. They refused point-blank to delay military operations during any exchanges, insisting that Cetshwayo should accept the terms of the ultimatum, while at the same time they let it be known that they would negotiate with any regional chiefs who were prepared to abandon the King.

As a result, the stream of messengers despatched by the King in the second week of May were destined to be disappointed. Most set out initially for the nearest British position, which by that time was an earthwork known as Fort Chelmsford, established by Crealock's column on the lower Nyezane river. Indeed, over the following fortnight so many envoys reported to Crealock that he complained in a letter home that he was 'in a state of chronic messengers from the King and his indunas'. He refused, however, to receive them officially, and after listening to their messages merely directed them to report to Lord Chelmsford instead. One of the first of these messages was delivered by Chief Ndwandwe to Fort Chelmsford on 15 May, and both its content and the subsequent response were typical of the exchanges that followed. 'Messengers from King are at this advanced post,' Crealock telegraphed Chelmsford on the 16th,

> King sues for peace. John Dunn sent to see them. Message as follows: 'White man has made me King, and I am their son. Do they kill the man in the afternoon whom they have made King in the morning? What have I done? I want peace, I ask for peace.' King asks for a black man or white man to return with his messengers to say message delivered rightly. Undwana, one of the messengers, states that he has been sent to Dabulomanzi to order him to go to the King. Message had been delivered to him by Undwana, and he ought to have reached the King yesterday. All principal Chiefs have been sent for to the King. He says army is dispersed. Chiefs have been urging peace on King.

Chelmsford promptly telegraphed Frere for a confirmation of his stance, and was told:

> I have received your telegram of the 16th regarding King's message delivered to General Crealock. The King should be told that the second message of the Lieutenant Governor's, delivered to his messengers at the Lower Thukela on the 11th December last, fully explains the grounds of proceeding, and the nature of our first demands; if he wishes now to treat for peace, he must send indunas of a suitable rank, fully empowered by the Great Council, as well as

by himself, to the General's (Lord Chelmsford's) camp; in the meantime the movements of Her Majesty's forces cannot be suspended until they are in possession of what you consider the strategic points, which will ensure complete military command of the country. I agree with you that the terms of peace should be signed at Ulundi in the presence of a British force . . .

To this general rebuttal, Chelmsford added specific requirements of his own, 'which should form part of the terms to be imposed on the Zulu King'. These were the surrender of

a) All the Martini rifles.
b) The 7-lb Guns.
c) And all prisoners taken.
d) Say 10,000 stand of firearms.
e) A minimum of not less than 10,000 head of cattle, and not more than 20,000 to be paid at once. Lord Chelmsford deprecates the payment of a fine by annual instalments.

These terms were clearly designed to be impossible for the King to accept, and indeed by this stage of the war Chelmsford was increasingly confident of victory, despite the fact that the 2nd Division was still not ready to advance. When his disconsolate messengers returned with the British reply, Cetshwayo's response was to send a further envoy to Crealock to ask for clarification. This envoy, Sintwangu, was one of the King's most trusted and senior messengers, a fact which in itself was indicative of the importance Cetshwayo placed on the mission, but Sintwangu was given short shrift by John Dunn, who was serving as Crealock's political adviser:

> Mr Dunn then gave Major-General Crealock's message . . . 'Go to the Great White Chief at General Wood's column, make peace there with him . . . The Great White Chief alone can make peace with you. I am sent here to fight until I reach the Swazi country' . . . This message [was directed] from Cetywayo to Dunn. 'You have all the official correspondence in your possession. You know I was not in the wrong. Can you not help me to make my peace with the white man?' Dunn answered, 'This is idle talk now, you did not take my advice before when I could have done you good. I cannot help you now.' A conversation then ensued with Saintwangu . . . 'The talk of

peace is nonsense you know the king don't want peace.' Saintwangu replied, 'Oh well you will see if it is not true what I have told you.' 'Why then', said Dunn, 'has Cetywayo ordered the people to assemble and attack Wood?' Messenger replied he had not assembled soldiers, they were only district people collected to guard their cattle, the same as the Zulus between the Umlalaz and the Umlatoos, where they were also guarding their cattle. 'Well', said Dunn, 'you can understand, or in two words you can have peace if the king accepts our terms, or war and then we will fight it out to the bitter end.'

It was a painful reminder that Cetshwayo's time had run out. Wood's column had already abandoned Khambula and begun to move south, while Chelmsford had fixed the date for the 2nd Division to cross into Zululand as 1 June. The second invasion was about to begin in earnest.

There was one last unpleasant duty to perform. With a sufficiently strong force on the border, the dead at Isandlwana could no longer be ignored, and indeed there was a rather more pressing practical need to visit the old battlefield. With his transport department so short of supply wagons, Chelmsford could not afford to leave the wagons of the old Centre Column lying on the field. The Cavalry Brigade under Major-General Marshall – the 17th Lancers and King's Dragoon Guards – had recently arrived at the border, and it was to them that Chelmsford entrusted the melancholy task of recovering the wagons and burying the dead. In the event, according to Newdigate, 'Colonel Glyn of the 24th protested so strongly against the burial of the 1/24th on the ground that the regiment wished to do this, that I modified my instructions to General Marshall accordingly.' Marshall set out with a strong reconnaissance force on 21 May, and his official report outlined the stark facts of what was to prove the most macabre mission of the war:

> The left column proceeded at 4 a.m. along the western side of the Bashee valley, and held the head of the valley, whilst Major Bengough's battalion of the Natal Native Contingent pushed up the course of the river.
>
> The right column started at 5.30, and followed the main road towards Isandula with a view of cutting off the retreat of the enemy quitting the Bashee valley.
>
> But few traces of the enemy were found.

In accordance with my order, the two columns combined on the plain to the east of Isandula hill at 8.30 a.m.

Four companies of the 24th Regiment held the ridges to the east of the Bashee River during the reconnaissance.

Protected by vedettes I buried all bodies near the battlefield of Isandula which could be recognized as others than those of the 24th Regiment.

The latter, in accordance with your instructions, were left untouched. Amongst the bodies of the officers buried were those of Colonel Durnford, R.E., and the Honourable Vereker.

I have also to mention that the Army Service Corps detachment, attached to the cavalry brigade, brought into camp three horse waggons, 33 bullock waggons, two water-carts, one scotch cart, all in an excellent state of preservation ... The Royal Artillery brought in one limber.

Yet for all that Chelmsford was pleased with the results of the expedition, the burials had been perfunctory at best. Most of the remains were gathered into shallow holes scooped just a few inches deep into the hard ground, and covered over with stones. It would be another month before the 1/24th could visit the site in comparative safety, and by that time the bodies had long since become unrecognizable. Some of the Zulu dead had been removed by their comrades on the day of the battle and buried in dongas at the foot of the iNyoni heights, but many more still lay on the field, and the British details made no attempt to cover them over. Moreover, with the advent of the first summer rains in late 1879, many of the graves would be washed open, and exposed remains would be a feature of the site for years to come.

*

For the troops concentrated at Koppie Alleen, on the Ncome (Blood) river, the prospect of renewed action had not come too soon. Major Anstruther, for one, had long since exhausted any novelty to be found on the border, despite the healthy climate and daily opportunities to indulge his sportsman's instincts by shooting fowl for the pot:

I go out every day shooting but there is lamentably little. On Monday I got a wild duck and on Tuesday I made a great bag, 2 wild turkeys (small ones) 2 plover and 2 brace of quail – did not miss a shot. The turkeys and wild duck were awfully good eating but I have given up shooting quail as cartridges are scarce and you can't buy them.

Yesterday Brook & I went out stalking what we thought were 3 wild swans but the beasts turned out to be large cranes. This country teems with different sorts of cranes and it is very annoying because they look just like wild geese or swans. The place all round is covered with ponds and I believe I shot the only ducks. It is too disgusting.

This business is getting monotonous.

The delay was all the more frustrating because the objectives seemed tantalizingly near:

> You can see certainly as far as Ulundi from a hill close by and the idea is that we shall go in a few days. Wood goes in by himself and a force from the Lower Tugela. We go – 5,000 infantry, 1,400 cavalry and 24 guns – safe as the Bank of England but, I am afraid, in consequence we shan't see anything of the beasts. It is only 60 miles to Ulundi and we shall just burn it and come away . . . I am afraid it will be an inglorious affair and certainly one good fight would settle the thing. It is much more monotonous and irksome and really more dangerous stopping here.

Chelmsford's eventual plan called for the 2nd Division to cross into Zululand at Koppie Alleen, then strike eastwards below the Thelezeni hill and descend into the valley of the Tshotshosi river. This, he calculated, would be a two-day march, and he hoped then to rendezvous with Wood, who was already advancing towards the Tshotshosi from the north. Then, since

> the 2nd Division and Flying Column have only transport sufficient to carry one month's supplies an entrenched post will be formed near the Babanango, our waggons will be emptied of their contents and sent back to Landman's drift and Conference Hill for a further supply, under strong escort; and the larger portion of the mounted force which will remain at Babanango, will be occupied during this enforced halt in patrolling and reconnoitering the country towards Ulundi, Kwamagwasa, and the Inkandla bush . . .
>
> On the return of the convoy to Babanango, unless the situation alters unexpectedly, a strong force moving without tents with as few

impediments as possible, will advance on Ulundi; a strong garrison consisting of the three arms being left at the Babanango post.

The long-awaited advance began on 1 June. Screened by Lancers and Dragoons, the baggage train of the 2nd Division began its cumbersome crossing of the Ncome. The morning began bright and cool, but by noon the temperature was sweltering, adding to the discomfort of the troops. By evening, however, they had reached their first objective, and had established camp on Zulu soil, on the slopes below the Thelezeni mountain. There, as Lord Chelmsford sat in his tent writing despatches, one of his staff officers burst in to tell him the news that, on the very day that the offensive had resumed, a new calamity had struck. Chelmsford himself telegraphed the bald facts to Colonel Stanley at the War Office at daybreak the following morning:

> Prince Imperial acting under orders of the Assistant Quarter Master General reconnoitered on 1st of June road to camping ground of 2nd June accompanied by Lieutenant Carey 90th Regt. D.A. Quarter Master General and his six white men and friendly Zulus all mounted. Party halted and offsaddled the road about 10 miles from this camp, but as the Prince gave the order to mount a volley was fired from the long grass around the Kraals.
>
> The Prince Imperial and two troopers are reported missing by Lieut. Carey who escaped and reached this camp after dark. From the evidence taken there can be no doubt of the Prince being killed. 17th Lancers and ambulance are now starting to recover the body but I send this off at once hoping to catch mail.
>
> I myself was not aware that Prince had been detailed for this duty.

An extraordinary chain of events had brought Prince Louis Napoleon, the Prince Imperial, exiled heir to the Bonaparte throne in France, to Zululand to fight in the uniform of France's old enemy against a people with whom he had no quarrel. Louis was the son of the ousted French Emperor, Napoleon III, and a grand-nephew of the great Napoleon. In the turbulent decades which followed Waterloo in Europe, France had reverted to a monarchy, and while Napoleon had languished on St Helena, his family and supporters had scattered. By the 1840s, however, the French population was becoming disillusioned with royalty, and in the aftermath of the 1848 Revolution Louis Napoleon exploited a wave of Imperial nostalgia to secure himself a post in the government. Two years later, by means of an efficient coup, he made himself Emperor. For two decades France enjoyed a *belle époque*, emerging once again on to the world stage, and with the birth of the Emperor's son – also Louis – in 1856 it seemed that the great Napoleon's dynastic ambitions had, after all, been fulfilled. Then, in 1870, everything collapsed with terrifying suddenness. The Emperor was manoeuvred into a war by the ruthless ambitions of Bismarck, and French forces proved woefully unprepared for the steely efficiency of the Prussian army. Napoleon III had surrendered at Sedan, and France vented its disillusion upon the Imperial family. The Emperor's wife and son fled to England.

Ironically, they found sanctuary in the very country which had been the great Napoleon's most bitter enemy. Despite a deep-seated suspicion of the French, Queen Victoria had always proved curiously susceptible to the charms of the Imperial family, and she allowed the exiles to settle in England. After a brief imprisonment, the Emperor was released by the Prussians to join them, and the Imperial family passed into life in limbo in the empty luxury of a rented house in Chislehurst in Kent. In 1873 Napoleon III had died, broken in health, if not in spirit, by defeat, and his son assumed the title Prince Imperial.

The collapse of Bonarpartist fortunes had left its mark on Prince Louis. He had become withdrawn and listless, stripped of the purpose for which he had been groomed since childhood, until a chance remark that he might be allowed to train with the British Army brought him out of his shell. As a favour from the Queen, he had been allowed to attend the Royal Military Academy at Woolwich, which trained cadets for entrance into the Royal Artillery and Engineers. The irony of a Bonaparte wearing the uniform of a British officer was not lost upon Louis, but he had flourished with the opportunity to live up to his name, and he had passed through the course on his own merits.

There could be no question of him taking a commission in the British Army, however, as he was not only a foreign national but an Emperor in waiting. He was given an honorary attachment to a Royal Artillery garrison battery, but France was still under Republican rule, and he seemed destined to live out the empty life of a leader in exile, awaiting a call that would probably never come. Then, in February 1879, the news of Isandlwana broke, sending officers scurrying to secure active service appointments. Several of Louis's Army friends were in Africa,

and he begged to be allowed to join them; he was refused, but
shamelessly exploited his influence with the Queen herself. The Government reluctantly relented, and he was allowed to go as an observer, with
no official standing. A private letter to Chelmsford from the Duke of
Cambridge asked that he should be found a safe post on the staff.

Louis was just twenty-three when he arrived in Natal, charming,
boisterous, eager and used to having his own way. Chelmsford, who had
just returned from the Eshowe relief expedition, had more important
things to worry about than the boyhood fantasies of glory of a foreign
pretender, but none the less found him a position as an ADC. When the
Headquarters moved to the border to prepare for the advance of the 2nd
Division, Louis had been attached to the staff of Lieutenant-Colonel
Richard Harrison, who was responsible for reconnoitring the line of
advance. Twice Louis had taken part in extended patrols into Zululand,
and each time had revealed that, for a man obsessed with the profession
of soldiering, he was a dangerous amateur. Whenever he saw a Zulu
scout in the distance, he drew his sword and set off in pursuit, intensely
irritating the troopers sent to recall him. In the end, objections from the
officers in command led Chelmsford to instruct Harrison to confine
Louis to camp – to his great frustration.

On the afternoon of 31 May, however, Harrison had relented. The
invasion was set to begin the following morning, and the country had
been swept by British cavalry for miles in advance. Louis asked for
permission to ride ahead of the column, to inspect the planned camp-
sites, and Harrison allowed him to go, accompanied by one of his staff,
Lieutenant J. Brenton Carey. The true military objectives of the patrol
remain obscure, and in all likelihood Harrison was merely allowing Louis
to see something of the fun. There were no reports of Zulu activity, and
Harrison did not trouble to specify a chain of command. Six troopers
of an irregular mounted unit, Bettington's Horse, were designated to
accompany the patrol, together with six men from Shepstone's Horse –
an African auxiliary unit – and a Zulu guide, but in the confusion of the
advance the men from Shepstone's Horse reported to the wrong place,
and Louis refused to wait for them.

The patrol left camp early on the morning of 1 June. From the
beginning, Louis acted as the officer in command, a position which
Carey accepted without question. They passed Harrison and one of
Chelmsford's staff officers, both of whom were preparing the camp-site

to be occupied that night, and neither of whom questioned Louis' intentions. By midday the patrol had reached the crest of a ridge overlooking the valley of the Tshotshosi river, and at Louis's suggestion they descended to rest at a deserted *umuzi* just a few hundred yards from the river banks. The story of what happened next passed like wildfire through the British camps that night, and Philip Anstruther heard a particularly detailed account from the survivors themselves:

> The Prince Imperial was killed. I first heard the news meeting 4 mounted men coming into camp about 7 p.m. and they told me. They were the 4 survivors. It occurred thus. He is a very energetic active little man and as an outlet for his energies he tried to go with every reconnaissance. Latterly all the reconnaissance nearby has been to allow Carey of the 98th to go about and survey the road in advance, finding water etc. Well yesterday morning the Prince started off early with Carey and 6 men (White) of Bettington's Horse to recconoitre the road we go tomorrow. About 8 miles on they came to what they thought were deserted kraals. Apropos of those kraals I believe they are certain that the Prince got to [them] once before when he was reconnoitering with Bettington and they shot 5 Kaffirs. The Prince was very fond of taking command of these parties and, on this occasion, ordered the party to off-saddle in the middle of some Indian corn fields, about 100 yards from a kraal. From the site what they call a donga, a deep fissure that in the rainy weather the torrents form, ran from the kraal down to the mealie fields. . . . Carey went off sketching close by. All of a sudden there was a tremendous war cry and a volley was poured in – I was forgetting – the Prince had a Kaffir with him who said just before this that he saw a Zulu on which the Prince told them to on saddle but it was too late. The Zulus were on them in a minute and it was 'sauve qui peut!' From all accounts the Prince who is very active always used to vault into his saddle. He was riding a big horse and it is believed that in the hurry he seized the saddle flap which tore. The horse, frightened, went off dragging him with one foot in the stirrup and he was caught and assegaid. Some say he must have been wounded before he tried to get into the saddle. Two of his men were also caught. After Carey had gone about 200 yards he heard one of the men saying that he thought it must have gone hard with the Prince. Carey caught the Prince's horse and they got into camp about 6.20 when I saw them.

By the time the survivors reached the 2nd Division's new camp on the slopes of Thelezeni hill, it was too late to send a recovery force into the dark in the face of an unknown number of the enemy. The following morning, however, Chelmsford ordered the Cavalry Brigade, with Carey as guide, to ride out to find Louis's body. The corpses of the two men of Bettington's Horse – troopers Abel and Rogers – were found first, stripped and disembowelled, while Abel's horse, stabbed during the attack, still floundered close by. It was put out of its misery. A white terrier, a pet of Bettington's Horse, was also found speared nearby.

Louis had almost reached the donga. During the initial stampede he had clung to the saddle of his horse, a grey named Tommy, which had carried him for a hundred yards before he fell. The horse had kicked him as it broke free, and in the flight Louis had dropped his sword. He turned to face his pursuers armed with just his revolver. Interviewed after the war, the Zulu – who were between forty and fifty strong, a scouting party of young men from local homesteads who were watching the British advance – recalled that seven or eight men had rushed forward to attack the Prince. Louis fired at a warrior named Xabanga, who ducked into the grass and threw a spear which caught the Prince inside the shoulder. Louis had pulled the spear out, fired several shots – all of which missed – before turning towards the cover of the donga. Another spear struck him as he ran, but he reached the bottom of the donga before turning on his pursuers. A warrior named Langalibalele threw yet another spear which caught Louis in the thigh, but he pulled it out and brandished it like a sword, keeping the Zulu back. By now, however, there were Zulu all around him, and as he stepped warily backwards, he put his foot in a hole and suddenly sat down backwards. The warriors rushed in and speared him to death.

The body lay where it fell, stripped of all clothing except a single sock, embroidered with the letter 'N', and a religious medallion around the Prince's neck. Chelmsford had sent his staff surgeon, Surgeon-Major F. B. Scott, with the recovery party, and according to Scott's report,

> the body had not been moved before I got there. I think he died where I found him. He was lying on his back, with the left arm across him, in the position of self defence. I counted eighteen assegai wounds, all in front. It is true there were 2 wounds found on his back – but from their nature, I am satisfied that they were the

terminations of wounds inflicted in front. Any one of 5 of the wounds would have proved mortal.

There were no bullet wounds on the body. The reason for believing that the Prince's body had not been dragged is that there were no wounds or abrasions about the body to indicate that it had been dragged . . .

There was a patch of blood, underneath the head and neck, which appeared to me to be caused by wounds received on the side of the neck, and also a wound through the right eye-ball. The Prince's body was entirely stripped.

Scott was being discreet with regard to the wounds found in Louis's back; in the final moments he had undoubtedly been stabbed on all sides. Several of the wounds had been inflicted after death, as members of the attacking party had claimed their share of the victory by stabbing the corpse. The usual cut had been made up the abdomen to release the spirit, but the intestines were not damaged. Once Scott had examined the body, a stretcher was improvised from lances and a blanket, and the corpse was solemnly carried to a waiting ambulance wagon. The senior officers present, including Major-General Marshall himself, were the pall-bearers. The bodies of the two troopers were buried close to the donga.

The whole incident took place in front of the world's media. The news of Isandlwana had catapulted the war to the forefront of press interest, and war correspondents had flocked to the front to cover the renewal of hostilities. Most of them were from the London papers, but among them was Paul Deleage from the Paris *Figaro*, who had been attracted to the story by Louis's presence. The Prince's death gave them their first dramatic story; they hurried to sketch the scene as the body was carried away. Then there was a rush for souvenirs, and several men snatched handfuls of grass which were splashed by Louis's blood – someone carried off the carcass of the dog, in the hope of skinning and stuffing it.

The body arrived in the 2nd Division camp that afternoon. An officer of the 58th Regiment, Lieutenant MacSwinney, described the scene in a letter home to his sister;

. . . the body was brought in and the funeral was ordered for 5. Three companies from each regiment went and formed up three sides of a square – standing with our arms reversed – the body was wrapped in a horse blanket and put on a board and tied to a gun drawn by 6 horses with a tricolour flag over it. The Artillery officers were pall bearers and Ld. C. And his staff following – a R.C. priest in his full stoles etc going before Ld. C. – they halted at the end of the square where the funeral service was read and then moved out again – we giving a royal salute by fixing bayonets and presenting arms. A most solemn affair and I hope I may never see one again – the bagpipes of the 21st played a pibroch or dirge – the body is to be embalmed as well as possible and starts tomorrow morning in an ambulance for Durban. Delache the correspondent of the French *Figaro* came to say goodbye tonight and goes with it, poor little fellow he was awfully cut up and is going home – he said he dared not send a telegraph to the Empress – but he takes back the chain and locket, the pall cover, i.e. the tricolour flag, a lock of his hair and a spur and one of his socks that he found this morning.

Both Stanley and Forbes, correspondents to the *Standard* and *Daily News*, told me that they found in the kraal an old woman who told them that they were her sons that did it and had gone off, as they had heard they had killed a great chief, and the army was coming for the body – so they must have good spies in our camp. Delache wanted to shoot the old woman but they would not let him. He told me that if he had only seen the body before seeing the old woman he would have shot her in spite of them – he can't speak a word of English and is a Legitimist he told me before – he has taken the sod from where the poor Prince's head lay and his hands were covered in blood ... You will hear a good deal in the papers about who is to blame, as both Forbes and Stanley are very wrath. The *Graphic* has taken a very good sketch, and a curious thing just when the gun had halted and the funeral service was being read a man rushed in with a photographic affair and took it – where the thing came from no one has an idea. The Prince's face was very peaceful but Delache said he could not close his left eye – one of the escort that fell had a most fearfully distorted countenance and his shirt covered over it so the Zulus were evidently afraid of it and covered it up otherwise they would have taken the shirt also – the others were not mutilated nor were they at Isandulhawa so the Prince must have fought well. Enough now of such a sad affair and I myself think disgraceful to ourselves.

The Prince's body was carried in an ambulance under escort down the line of communication to Pietermaritzburg, and thence to Durban. At each stage of the journey it was accorded full ceremonial rites, and large crowds turned out in the town to watch it pass. At Durban, it was taken on board ship for England. MacSwinney was right; news of the incident broke long before the body returned home, and created a furore. The illustrated supplements were full of dramatic engravings of the Prince's last moments, and far more was written about this one skirmish than about the wholesale blood-letting at Isandlwana.

For Lord Chelmsford, Louis's death – for which Louis himself had been largely to blame – was merely another sad incident in a persistently unlucky war. Once he had seen the body safely out of camp, he turned once more to his real objective, that of destroying what remained of the Zulu kingdom.

For Lieutenant Carey, however, the ordeal was just beginning. For several days he tried to go about his duties as usual, but opinion was sharply divided in the camp about his own culpability. He had, after all, been the only commissioned officer with the party, and whatever the circumstances of the incident, there was a widespread feeling that he had abandoned Louis to his fate. Lieutenant Frederick Slade, whom Louis had befriended at Aldershot and who was serving with Wood's column, poured out his bitterness in a letter to his mother:

> Neither Carey or his men made the slightest attempt to stand, and in plain words 'ran away', and left the poor dear little Prince to die fighting on foot single handed. I cannot tell you what we all think of Carey's behaviour but will tell you what Buller told him to his face yesterday when they met, 'You ought to be shot' – I think I may safely say that this is the opinion of every man in the column. To think that a British officer would leave any man, even more the Prince Imperial of France, to fall into the hands of the Zulus without making the slightest attempt to save him is too disgraceful. I had rather be lying in the deepest donga in Zululand than in Carey's shoes –

In fact, however, there was a significant body of opinion, particularly among the new arrivals, who were yet to face the Zulu in action, that Carey was no more than a victim of the fortunes of war. The decision to off-saddle at the deserted homestead had certainly been reckless, but the attack itself had been so sudden and so quick that none of the patrol – Louis included – had thought of anything but flight. Louis's death in such circumstances was bad luck, and it might equally have been Carey who had fallen and Louis who had survived. True, Carey had made no attempt to rally the survivors once they were out of range of the Zulu, but four men could have made no worthwhile stand, and by that time Louis was in any case dead. As Philip Anstruther put it,

> Is it not a fearful thing? He was very much liked and, of course, all sorts of people will be blamed and I do not think myself that it was right to allow the Prince to go out with such an escort but he was foolhardy and nothing would stop [him]. Of course there are different opinions as to what Carey and his men might have done but with a sudden surprise like that it was very difficult to know what to do. We are all so sorry. . . . Poor little fellow, it is dreadful but off-saddling in any place where they could not see all round them or, at least, have a man on the lookout is curious.

Three days after Louis's death, Carey was forced to ask for a Court of Inquiry into the incident, in the hope that it would clear his name. By that time the 2nd Division was camped within sight of the ruins of the homestead where the attack had taken place, which the troops had destroyed as they passed. The Court expressed some sympathy for Carey's plight, but the evidence was strong enough to form a prima facie case for misbehaviour before the enemy, and the court recommended that Carey be tried by Court Martial.

Before it could convene, however, the war intervened. Although the 2nd Division and Flying Column had indeed met in the Tshotshosi valley, as Chelmsford had planned – the two columns now advanced in tandem, keeping separate administrative identities, but camping close enough to one another to support each other if attacked – it was already clear, less than a week into the new campaign, that the Flying Column's wagons would have to be sent back for supplies long before they reached Babanango mountain. 'Getting to Ulundi will certainly be a longer job than we thought,' grumbled Anstruther, 'these dreadful oxen can't go, they must feed etc., and we must keep pace with them as they carry our supplies.' Moreover, although the only hostile Zulu encountered since the new advance began had been the group who attacked Louis on the 1st, there were clear signs of sizeable concentrations ahead.

Indeed, King Cetshwayo had responded to the British offensive by instructing his *amabutho* to gather once more at oNdini. The mobilization took time, however, because many of the men were needed at home to gather in the ripening harvest, while others lingered to watch British movements in the hope of protecting their abandoned homesteads. A force of several hundred warriors, gathered under the command of local chiefs and *izinduna*, lay across Chelmsford's line of advance in the hills to the east of the Ntinini stream, and they were to provide the first serious opposition to the British advance.

On the morning of 5 June, Buller's horsemen, scouting ahead of the Flying Column, rode down into the valley of the Ntinini and came under fire from Zulu snipers concealed in the hills opposite. Buller dismounted his men and pushed them through the valley on foot, but despite return fire the Zulu refused to give ground, and some warriors began slipping down into the bush to outflank Buller's men. Buller had just decided that the exchange was not worth the effort and had recalled his men, when the 17th Lancers arrived from the 2nd Division camp. The 17th had hitherto found it difficult to adjust to conditions in the field, and their commander, Colonel Drury-Lowe, was keen to give them the opportunity to test themselves. As Buller withdrew, the 17th passed them, deploying into line, cantering up and down the valley, sweeping through the long grass and mealie fields for Zulu. The warriors had seen them coming, however, and had retired once more to the hillsides to snipe. One particularly good shot struck the 17th's adjutant, Lieutenant Frith, just as he was wheeling his horse next to Drury-Lowe. The bullet hit him in the shoulder and passed through his heart, killing him instantly. Reluctantly Drury-Lowe called off the attack, and his men rode back to camp with Frith's body draped across the saddle. He was buried in the empty veld that night. 'The Lancers', thought Anstruther, 'are doing wonderfully well but, on this occasion, it was certainly stupid halting where they did under fire.'

The incident, coming so soon after the Prince's death, had an unsettling effect on the 2nd Division. A few days before, Lieutenant MacSwinney had noted the unease with which many in the column regarded the prospect of contact with the enemy;

> A Zulu heard of much less seen is quite enough for the whole division to immediately rush into laager, in fact what with Isandula,

Slobane and the way Ld. C. goes about the most minute details to ensure everyone being enabled to run the shortest way into laager, quite a panic has arisen . . .

On the 6th, the column had built a small entrenched earthwork, Fort Newdigate, to protect their camp. Nevertheless, about 9 p.m., sentries in front of the 58th regiment fired three warning shots, and their supports immediately fired several volleys into the darkness. Bugles sounded the alarm, and men scrambled out of the tents to open fire all round the perimeter. According to Bandsman Tuck of the 58th,

> It would take the pen of a Lever or Dickens three hours to describe the confusion that prevails in a tent in about two minutes. I could not describe it to you myself, but if you could imagine yourself in a tent with 16 men all with their arms and belts under their heads. The alarm shots are heard from the outpost, every man in the tent and it is in pitch darkness, then comes the scramble for rifles, belts or other things, no one can see his fingers before his face, and in the darkness everything seems to be suddenly animated with life, eluding your hand as you grope for them. Outside some of the fortunate ones, having arms and belts, are shouting 'down with the tents', the men inside shouting 'stop a minute, where's my rifle', everyone around cursing and swearing, when at last you manage to get hold of a rifle and now you wonder what keeps the gun as firm, little thinking in the darkness that another man has hold of the same gun as yourself, 'What is the matter with the gun?' you keep saying, ditto the other man, until you make a desperate effort pulling it clean out of his hand. Down you go backwards across the tent with your heels in the air knocking down two or three in your journey, 'Who is that?' is shouted from all sides, and if you get off with a couple of kicks you may think yourself lucky. You no sooner pick yourself up than down comes the tent on top of you (for all the tents are struck to leave the ground clear) leaving you to struggle out the best way you can. After you do get out you see some of the most comical sights you could imagine, some without boots, some without helmets, others struggling to get into their belts upside down, others trying to get into a blanket instead of a great-coat, and wondering where the sleeves of the coat had got to. You can imagine this and a great deal more, and then you will have some idea of the confusions that prevail in a tent . . .

One battalion alone fired off 1,200 rounds, while an artillery battery fired several shots of canister – a projectile intended for close-range use against an enemy mass. A picket of Royal Engineers, under the command of the duty officer, Major Chard of Rorke's Drift fame, was caught outside the laager and had to take shelter in a shallow ditch as bullets whistled overhead. Seven men were wounded and several horses were killed before order was restored, and it was found that the entire thing had been a false alarm.

Chelmsford was furious; it had hardly been the most auspicious start to the campaign all round.

The following day, both columns advanced to the banks of the Ntinini, close to where Frith had been shot a few days before. The Zulus still remained in the hills ahead, and it was already necessary to send the Flying Column back to fetch fresh supplies. According to Anstruther,

> We got here on Saturday. Wood who had been encamped Friday night about 3 miles to the right rear of this matched back to the camp ground we left and took over a lot of empty waggons which he is to convey back to Conference Hill and bring stores, about 200 waggons and carts. In the meantime we stay here till he returns, about 10 days in all if, indeed, we are ever to go on ...
>
> A big mountain called Ibabanango is just in front of us but we find we can't go straight to it, but must keep round to the south. This is the place where the adjutant of the 17th was shot last Thursday so yesterday we shelled the bush all round and found that there were a lot of Kaffirs in it, from 500 to 1,000. I believe only one or two were killed, in fact with glasses only one was seen to fall. Then while we were at Church parade the 1st Brigade went skirmishing but met no one. Buller's Horse went off to the left 6 or 7 miles and I believe they killed 5 or 6 poor wretches. At any rate this morning we sent out 5 companies to cut wood and there was not a soul about but there are a tremendous number of kraals and mealie fields and they have all been destroyed. They found 2 gun limbers, a 24th bugle and some Martini rifles that must have been taken at Sandhlwana – alas, one or two 24th uniforms.

The enforced delay provided an ideal opportunity to hold the Court Martial on Lieutenant Carey. Anstruther found himself

appointed Judge Advocate . . . at a general Court-Martial to try Carey
of the 98th for cowardice in not trying to save the Prince. I suppose
you will see it all in the papers. I have been the whole day in court,
among other things there not being a shorthand writer, to write all
the proceedings myself. Poor Carey, it is a bad business for him –
and he has a wife and two children. The nuisance besides is that I
can't get a book of references on court-martials anywhere. There is
not one in camp so I have to do the best I can, in fact bring common
sense to bear on the technicalities.

. . . I am very sorry for poor Carey . . . I expect whatever way the
verdict goes we shall be called fools or rogues as the case may be. I
only know that I thank God that I was not placed in his position.
I hope I should have done differently but really one cannot say. The
whole disastrous affair was over so to speak in a moment. I think
certainly they ought to have gone back when they found the Prince
missing though certainly they would have done no good, they would
have found him dead.

Such sympathies could not alter the bald facts of the case, however,
and after a trial lasting several days, Carey was found guilty. The Court
recommended no sentence, merely passing the verdict on to Lord
Chelmsford, together with a plea for leniency. Chelmsford, too, refused
to pass sentence, merely adding a note supporting the Court's plea.
Carey was sent home to await the decision of the military establishment,
and with that the stage for the last act in the whole unhappy saga shifted
to England.

Louis's body beat Carey home by five weeks. It was put ashore at
Woolwich and drawn on a gun-carriage to Chislehurst, where at Queen
Victoria's insistence Louis was given little short of a state funeral. The
event received saturation coverage in the British press, but to Carey's
surprise, by the time he returned home public anger had begun to shift
away from him in the belief that he had been made a scapegoat for the
wider failings of the high command. Moreover, when the findings of
the Court Martial were passed to the Judge Advocate General, he found
himself unable to confirm the verdict; in their inexperience, Anstruther's
officers had failed to record that they were properly sworn in. Such an
omission made the proceedings technically invalid, and the verdict was
quashed. Carey enjoyed a brief few weeks in the public spotlight, but his
increasingly self-righteous tone dispelled much of the sympathy which

had built up around him. He did not return to Zululand, but rejoined his regiment and served out his time in obscurity. He died of peritonitis in Karachi in 1883.

In South Africa, the war had entered its final phase. On 5 June, Chelmsford had received three Zulu envoys at the camp on the Nondweni river. They had apparently been despatched at the same time as the envoy to Crealock's column, and they received largely the same answer. With the advance gaining momentum, Chelmsford was less prepared than ever to negotiate; as a prelude to any settlement, he demanded not only that the King should surrender the 7-pounder guns captured at Isandlwana, together with all firearms carried by his warriors, but that a Zulu regiment of Chelmsford's choice should surrender to the British wholesale. They were impossible demands, as Chelmsford knew them to be, and the Zulu messengers returned to oNdini with heavy hearts.

Yet at the last minute, it seemed that Chelmsford might be cheated of the victory in the field which he so yearned for to restore his reputation. The British Government, increasingly concerned not only at the successive military disasters but at the prolonged cost of the war and the deterioration of military and civil relations in Natal, had begun to consider replacing Chelmsford as commander in the field. The first hint of this reached Chelmsford in a private letter from Colonel Stanley, the Secretary of State for War, during the wait on the Ntinini river. Chelmsford was indignant:

I have received your private letter dated 8 May, and cannot conceal from you that it has distressed me very much.

. . . I cannot understand what you mean by considerable anxiety existing as to the indefinite prolongation of the War.

Do people at home imagine that a country so large as Zululand, and peopled by such warriors as the Zulus have proved themselves to be, can be conquered off-hand? We have now been 5 months in the field, and looking to all the difficulties which surround military operations in this country, I cannot but consider in spite of the untoward results of Insandlwana, Intombi and Inhlobani affairs, that the forces under my command have made as much progress towards a final result as could reasonably be expected.

I can only look upon the paragraph of your letter which touches on the possibility of an officer of superior rank being sent out to command the forces under my orders should three more regiments still be demanded in the field as a threat. If I am fit to command 17,000 men in the Field I cannot understand by what powers of reasoning I am not equal to command 20,000. Rest assured however that should Her Majesty's Govt and the Duke of Cambridge come to the conclusion that they no longer have confidence in me as Commander of the Forces, I shall be quite ready to serve in a more subordinate capacity under whomsoever may be selected to succeed me.

Chelmsford's protests were in vain; on 28 May Stanley informed him by telegraph that

Her Majesty's Government have determined to send out Sir Garnet Wolseley as administrator in that part of South-Eastern Africa in the neighbourhood of the seat of war with plenary powers both civil and military. Sir Bartle Frere instructed accordingly by Colonial Office. The appointment of a senior officer is not intended as a censure on yourself, but you will, as in ordinary course of service, submit and subordinate your plans to his control. He leaves this country by the next mail.

Stanley's reassurances could not disguise the fact that Chelmsford had been superseded, but there was some comfort in the fact that Wolseley could not reach South Africa before late June. If, for once, Chelmsford was lucky, he might yet reach oNdini and defeat the Zulu army in the field before Wolseley could take command.

Wood's men returned to the camp on the Ntinini with their replenished supply wagons on 16 June, and the following day the advance resumed. The route ahead lay past Babanango mountain, climbing on to a high upland – the Mthonjaneni ridge – which afforded the last geographical obstacle before the descent into the White Mfolozi valley, towards the cluster of royal homesteads which constituted the Zulu capital. The war had finally arrived at the Zulu heartland; on the 26th, British cavalry patrols swept down from the heights to destroy abandoned settlements south of the White Mfolozi, along the valley of the Mkhumbane stream. This was the place where King Shaka's father, Senzangakhona, had lived and died, and it was considered one of the most sacred places in the kingdom. Most of the homesteads destroyed by Chelmsford's patrols had existed in one form or another throughout the kingdom's history; one of them, esiKlebheni, housed the royal *inkatha*, a coil of rope bound in python skin, an artefact of great mystic significance which was said to embody the unity of the nation. The *inkatha* lay unnoticed by the British in one of the huts, and was destroyed when esiKlebheni went up in smoke. For the Zulu, the omen could hardly have been more ominous.

Wolseley reached Cape Town on 23 June, and immediately cabled Chelmsford asking for a report on the state of the campaign. On the 28th Chelmsford replied with a long and detailed memorandum which gave no hint that he acknowledged any expectation to await Wolseley's arrival:

> Two columns under my command, commanded respectively by General Newdigate and General Evelyn Wood are now within 17 miles of Cetewayo's military Kraal, Ulundi – I am now forming a strongly entrenched post, consisting of two wagon redoubts, flanking a central laager, in which I shall leave all spare oxen, horses, mules, wagons and impedimenta – The garrison will consist of two companies 1/24th Regt, 60 volunteers, 100 native contingent, 60 mounted native Basutos, and a number of British Infantry whom it is thought desirable by the Doctors to leave behind as likely to knock up from the exposure of bivouacking. Garrison will number at least 400 Rifles among the regular troops, and there will be in addition some 40 European Conductors who are armed with rifles –
>
> The remainder of the Force ... will move on Ulundi without tents, and with ten days' provisions, and I expect that its advance will be opposed before crossing the Umvolosi River, which is about ten miles from our present position – The road runs through a thorn bush country which gets more difficult as it gets near the river. There is no water between this position and the Umvelosi River, and the road will only admit of one wagon moving along it at a time – As the two columns require 200 wagons to carry their supplies, ammunition, entrenching tools etc. the operation presents some little difficulty, which no doubt however will disappear when we become better acquainted with the grounds –
>
> Three columns of the Enemy were seen to leave Ulundi Kraal this morning, and move in the direction of the Umveloosi River – A certain force is still in Ulundi itself. As this force could only first be seen by the aid of telescopes, it is impossible to form any correct idea of its real strength – All who saw the columns, however, describe

them as being from 8 to 12 men in breadth, and as extending over a
great length of the road in which they were advancing –

This report of movements about oNdini reflected the large numbers
of warriors now gathered nearby. Nevertheless, despite all the evidence
that the British were not interested in a peaceful solution to the conflict, Cetshwayo resolved to make one last effort. On the day that he had
arrived on the Mthonjaneni heights, three of Cetshwayo's most senior
messengers arrived at his camp, carrying as tokens of good faith two
huge elephant tusks, and driving a herd of 150 cattle captured at
Isandlwana. Chelmsford's reply was curt:

> You have not complied with all the conditions I laid down. I shall
> therefore continue to advance as I told you I should, but as you have
> sent me some of the cattle and state that the two cannon are on their
> way, I consent not to cross the Umvolosi River tomorrow to give
> you time to fulfil the remainder of the conditions. Unless all my
> conditions are complied with by tomorrow evening, you must take
> the consequences.
>
> I return the tusks you send, to show you I shall still advance. I
> will keep the cattle a few days to show I am willing to make peace if
> you comply with the conditions laid down.
>
> I am willing that the men now collected at Ulundi whom I have
> seen should, to the number of a regiment – 1,000 – come to me and
> lay down their arms as a sign of submission. They can do so at a
> distance from me of 500 yards and then retire. Their lives are safe
> and the word of an English general is sufficient to ensure it.
>
> The arms in possession of the men around you now, taken at
> Isandlwana, must be given up by them.

For officers like Philip Anstruther, the prospect of a sudden Zulu
capitulation was frustrating:

> We march tomorrow for Ulundi. I don't suppose we shall get
> there until the next day. I believe it is to be peace. Cetch sent in 200
> oxen yesterday and I believe the guns that were captured at Isan-
> dhlwana come in today. Still Lord Chelmsford is not satisfied and
> says we must occupy Ulundi, and I think he is quite right. Otherwise
> afterwards they might say that we had really done nothing. We only

take ten days' provisions so I hope, in a week, we shall be returning
and very glad I shall be as it is getting monotonous.

Anstruther need not have worried. On the morning of 30 June
Chelmsford led the combined 2nd Division and Flying Column down
into the valley of the White Mfolozi and towards the objective which
had eluded him for six bitter months. As they descended the steep slopes
into the belt of thorn-bush which characterized the valley, they were
met once more by two of the King's messengers, Mfunzi and Nkisimana.
The envoys carried a written letter from Cetshwayo, dictated to a white
trader, Cornelius Vijn, who had been detained under the King's protection since the war began, in which Cetshwayo claimed that the two guns
captured at Isandlwana were being brought to him. Yet, unknown to the
King, Vijn had scribbled a message across the letter warning Chelmsford
that in his opinion the Zulu were determined to fight. This merely
confirmed Chelmsford's own opinion, and while he told Mfunzi that he
was now prepared to accept firearms in lieu of a surrendered regiment,
Chelmsford knew that this was an equally impossible demand. He had
boxed Cetshwayo into a corner and left him with no option but to fight.
He gave Cetshwayo until 3 July to comply with his demands, thus
allowing himself a few days to make his preparations for the decisive
confrontation.

That all pretence at negotiation was now at an end was equally
apparent to the Zulu. When Mfunzi returned to oNdini and reported to
the chiefs of the royal council, they bitterly denounced Chelmsford's
conditions and refused to allow Mfunzi to see the King. They would
rather fight than see themselves humiliated further, and indeed this
was the mood throughout the army. For all that the losses endured at
Khambula and Gingindlovu had given rise to a more realistic appreciation of the British strength, the men of the young *amabutho* remained
defiant, as Chelmsford noted when his force advanced to the banks of
the White Mfolozi:

> . . . our advance was continued over a difficult country when the
> wagon track passed through the bush of Cactus and Mimosa trees:
> after considerable labour on the part of the Troops in clearing the
> road and levelling the drifts the Column reached the vicinity of
> the river Umvelosi about 1 p.m. the enemy's picquets fell back on
> our approach and no opposition took place that day to our taking

our positions on the right bank; at one time indeed large bodies of
Zulus were seen to move from Ulundi to certain positions in our
front, which made me anxious to get our camps formed as speedily
as possible. By dark our position was perfectly defensible and our
cattle and horses had been watered at the river.

The two armies were now concentrated just a few miles apart. In
the evenings, the songs sung by the warriors as they went through their
pre-battle rituals drifted across the river, unnerving the waiting British.
By day, watering parties who went down to the river were sniped at by
Zulu posted on bluffs opposite to guard the crossings. On the 2nd,
Chelmsford noted, 'A large herd of white cattle was observed being
driven from the King's Kraal towards us but was driven back again
shortly afterwards.' The cattle were from Cetshwayo's royal herds, a last
desperate attempt to 'ward off the falling tree', but the young men of
the uKhandempemvu regiment, who guarded the fords, had turned it
back in defiance of the King's wishes. The die was cast:

> As no message had been received from Ketshwayo the following
> morning (3rd July) and as considerable annoyance was offered to
> our watering parties by Zulus firing on them, I arranged for a
> reconnaissance to be made by Lieut Colonel Buller C.B. with his
> mounted men, as soon as the time allowed for meeting my demands
> had expired. The cattle sent in by Ketchwayo on 29th June were
> driven across the river to him during the morning.
>
> Lieut Colonel Buller crossed the river by the lower drift to the
> right of our camp, and was soon in possession of the high ground
> on our front and the Indabakaombie Kraal. The object of Lt. Col.
> Buller's reconnaissance was to advance towards Ulundi and report
> on the road and whether there was a good position where our force
> could make its stand if attacked.
>
> I was also anxious if possible to cause the enemy to show his
> force, its points of gathering, and plan of attack.
>
> Lt. Col. Buller completely succeeded in the duty entrusted him:
> having collected his mounted men near Indabakaombi from the
> thorny country near the river, he advanced rapidly towards Ulundi,
> passing Nodwengo on his right: he had reached the vicinity of the
> stream Untukuwini about three quarters of a mile from Ulundi,
> when he was met by a heavy fire from a considerable body of the
> enemy lying concealed in the long grass around the stream –

Wheeling about, he retreated to the high ground near Nodwengo where he commenced to retire by alternate portions of his force in a deliberate manner – the Zulus were checked, but in the meantime large bodies of the enemy were to be seen advancing from every direction, and I was enabled with my own eyes to gain the information I wished for as to the manner of advance and points from which it would be made in the event of our force advancing on Ulundi – though the Zulus advanced rapidly and endeavoured to get round his flank, Col. Buller was able to retire his force across the river with but a few casualties . . .

In fact, Buller's men had narrowly escaped a well-prepared Zulu ambush. Zibhebhu kaMaphitha, one of Cetshwayo's ablest field commanders, who had been placed in charge of the warriors guarding the river, had carefully concealed his uMxapho regiment in a wide semi-circle in the long grass of the open plain near oNdini. The grass had been carefully plaited to trip the horses, and a herd of goats had been left grazing to serve as bait. When Buller's men spotted the goats and gave chase, the herdsmen drove them off through the encircling Zulu lines. The mounted men were only a few hundred yards from the hidden warriors when Buller sensed a trap and ordered them to halt; the uMxapho rose up on three sides and fired a volley, knocking several men out of their saddles. Three of Buller's men – Lord Beresford, ADC, and Captain D'Arcy and Sergeant O'Toole of the Frontier Light Horse – were later awarded the Victoria Cross for attempting to rescue unhorsed men in the face of the Zulu attack. In the event, Buller raced back to the river just yards ahead of the Zulu, leaving three men dead on the field. The closeness of this particular call was not apparent to the troops waiting in the camp, however. 'They made the beggars show themselves,' Anstruther wrote triumphantly, 'in number about 20,000. The cavalry killed a few, a hundred or 150.'

That night, recalled Bandsman Tuck of the 58th, 'Most of our men were awake all night owing to the yells of these savages and we were more amused than annoyed in listening to their war-songs which could be heard distinctly as they were in great numbers and not far off.'

Not all of the men were as nonchalant as Tuck suggests; many found the experience unnerving. Nevertheless, the following morning Chelmsford reported that at '4 a.m. the 4th July the troops were silently roused,

the Bugles however sounding the Reveille at the usual hour, 5-15 a.m'.
Chelmsford had no intention of burdening himself with the baggage
trains of two full columns, and he intended to attack accompanied only
by ammunition and water-carts. Inevitably, and to their disappointment,
part of the force had to be left to guard the camp, and Anstruther was
delighted he was not among them:

> I hope you mark the distribution of the 94th. Of the 4 regiments
> with us the 24th were left in the camp; the 21st have been broken up
> in forts all the way and the 58th have lost 5 companies in the same
> way. We have never been touched. We are certainly the most efficient
> regiment here of the 4 and so everybody owns and it is the occasion
> of jealousy rather. As far as the 24th are concerned it is not to be
> wondered at as their whole regiment except 2 companies is composed
> of drafts from other regiments officered by militia and guardsmen –
> none of their own officers.
>
> Off we went this morning about 6 and marched in a hollow 2
> deep square (Wood and ourselves) – the 94th comprising the rear
> and half the left face . . .

Chelmsford noted his own movements with some precision:

> At 6.45 a.m. the force . . . crossed the river. Lt. Col Buller's men
> going by the lower ford seized the high ground on our front without
> opposition.
>
> Passing over a mile of very bushy ground, the force marching
> in a hollow square – ammunition and entrenching tool carts, etc. in
> the centre, the guns moving also in the square in such positions as
> to enable them to come into action on each face without delay –
> reached the high ground between the Kraals Indabakaombi and
> Nondwengo at 7.30 a.m. The mounted men were now out, covering
> our front and flanks, while the 17th Lancers covered our rear.
>
> By this time our advance from camp was evidently observed and
> dark clusters of men could be seen in the morning light on the hill
> tops on our left and left-front; to our right where the largest number
> of the enemy were believed to be, we could see but little as the mist
> from the river and the smoke from their camp fires hung heavily
> over the bush below.
>
> Leaving Indabakaombi to our left (this Kraal was burnt by our
> rear guard) I advanced to the position referred to by Lt. Col. Buller,

this was about 700 yards beyond Nondwengo, and about the same distance from the stream that crossed the road half way to Ulundi; this was high ground uncommanded from any point and with but little cover, beyond long grass, near it.

At this point I wheeled the square half right so as to occupy the most favourable part of the ground.

The portions of the Zulu army on our left and left front were now formed in good order and steadily advancing to the attack: masses also appeared from the thorn country on our right and passed round to Nondwengo and to our rear, thus completing the circle round us.

The battle commenced about 8.45 a.m. by our mounted men on the right and left becoming engaged: slowly retiring until the enemy came within our range, they passed our square which now opened fire with Artillery and Rifles.

Shortly before 9 a.m. the Zulu Army attacked us on every side.

The Nondwengo Kraal, a vast assemblage of huts probably numbering 400 in number, afforded good cover for concealing the movements of a force which appears to have been the Ulundi, Ngobamakosi, Uve and Umbakalini Regiments; no order was to be seen in their movements, which was caused, (so state prisoners) by these Regiments having been taken by surprise by our early and silent advance; hurrying up from their bivouacs they had no time to form up separately, but, in a cloud advanced to the attack beyond the cover of the kraal; the fire by which they were met however from our right face proved too heavy and the bulk of these Regiments, failing to advance, rapidly passed to their left and joined the Umcityu Regiment which was pressing up to the attack in a determined manner. As the ground here fell suddenly and cover was afforded them in this advance men were killed within 30 yards of the companies of the 21st Regiment forming the rear face at this point.

The fire of the enemy from a few minutes to nine to 9.20 was very heavy, and many casualties, I regret to say, occurred, but when it is remembered that within our comparatively small square, all the cavalry, mounted men, Natives, Hospital attendants, etc. were packed, it is a matter of congratulation that they were not heavier.

The fire from the Artillery and Infantry was so effective that, within half an hour, signs of hesitation were perceivable in the movements of the enemy: I then directed Colonel Drury-Lowe to take out the 17th Lancers, passing out by the rear face he led his regiment towards the Nodwengu Kraal, dispersing and killing those who had not time to reach the shelter of the Kraal or the bush below; Then wheeling to the right charged through the Zulus who, in full flight, were endeavouring to reach the lower slopes of the mountains beyond.

Numbers of the enemy in this direction who had not taken part in the actual attack were now firing and momentarily strengthened by those flying were enabled to pour in a considerable fire on the advancing Lancers below them. Our cavalry did not halt however until the whole of the lower ground was swept and some 150 of the enemy killed: many of those they had passed in their speed, had collected in a ravine to their rear, these were attacked and destroyed by our mounted natives.

For the Lancers, the charge provided the longed-for opportunity to display their true worth. All the difficulties and criticisms regarding their suitability for African warfare which had dogged them since their arrival were swept away in that exhilarating rush, and Drury-Lowe had good reason to congratulate himself on his men's performance:

> The pursuit was carried out in a most determined manner by five troops of the 17th Lancers and 24 men King's Dragoon Guards (one troop remained inside the square unknown to me). The Zulus fled in every direction and were pursued for a distance of some three miles across the slope of the hills before mentioned, very many being killed with the Lances, which proved their decided superiority to the sword in pursuit. It would, I think, be invidious to point out any particular officer or man, when all, I think, showed the same eagerness to reach the enemy, and rode with the greatest determination into the scattered Zulus, for the most time under a galling fire from the hills, where the enemy formed themselves into groups and kept up an incessant fire.

'The flight of the Zulu army was now general,' reported Chelmsford,

the slopes of the hills were however beyond the reach of our already fatigued Cavalry, and having no fresh troops to support him, Colonel Drury Lowe exercised a wise discretion in rallying his men.

Lt. Col. Buller meanwhile had posted the Mounted Infantry so as

to fire into the flank of the retiring army, and the remainder of his
mounted men, making for the country beyond, killed some 450 in
the pursuit.

Our 9 pounder guns were shortly afterwards moved from the
rear and front faces of the square, and made excellent practice on
the enemy retreating over the hills to the East on our left rear, and
between Ulundi and the River Umvelosi.

With the Zulu spent and in full retreat, the British finally had the
opportunity to avenge themselves for Isandlwana. Once the Lancers had
broken up what remained of the Zulu formations, the irregulars rode
among them, shooting down exhausted warriors with impunity. Close to
the square, the Native Contingent passed over the ground, spearing any
wounded Zulu who had taken shelter in the long grass from the curtain
of fire.

Evelyn Wood, who had watched the battle from inside the square,
riding behind the lines of men from his Flying Column, was of the
opinion that the Zulu attacks had been less determined than those at
Khambula:

> The Regiments came on in a hurried, disorderly manner, which
> contrasted strangely with the methodical, steady order in which they
> had advanced at Kambula on the 29th of March, for now not only
> battalions, but regiments, became mixed up before they came under
> fire . . .
> When the attack slackened and our men began to cheer, led by
> men who had not been at Khambula, I angrily ordered them to be
> silent, saying, 'The fun has scarcely begun;' but their instinct was
> more accurate than mine, who, having seen the Zulus come on
> grandly for over four hours in March, could not believe they would
> make so half-hearted an attack.

Perhaps there was some truth in this, for a Zulu prisoner, questioned
after the battle, admitted,

> We had no idea the white force was so strong in numbers till we
> saw it in the open.
> We were completely beaten off by the artillery and bullets.
> The Zulu army was larger today than it was at Kambula, far
> larger. I was at the Kambula battle. All the army was present today.

We had not much heart in the fight when we saw how strong the white army was, and we were startled by the number of horsemen.

Even Mehlokazulu kaSihayo conceded that, 'At the Ondine battle (Ulundi), the last, we did not fight with the same spirit, because we were then frightened. We had had a severe lesson, and did not fight with the same zeal.'

Yet the fact remained that the British square on 4 July represented the largest concentration of firepower yet unleashed by the British Army in southern Africa. At close range, the volleys and artillery fire presented an almost impenetrable barrier, and many Zulu were shocked and stunned by the sheer noise of the firing alone. Bandsman Tuck was of the opinion that 'no living being could possibly come within a hundred yards of us as shells and volleys went into their midst'. Nevertheless, in some places, small groups of warriors had come much closer, as Anstruther noted:

> Ulundi was a very pretty little fight. They are grand skirmishers, took advantage of everything and that, together with the long grass, completely concealed them. I wish they could have caught it hotter but we could not get them into masses. There was one nice little spruit just 28 yards off our rear faces where we were and there were 6 lying behind it. They had died very pluckily and I took one of their shields . . .

Melton Prior, the war correspondent of the prestigious *Illustrated London News*, was deeply sceptical of reports that the Zulu had hung back:

> I have read since various statements as to how near the enemy got to our square, and it was often stated that twenty or thirty paces was the closest, but I can say that I personally went out and reached the nearest one in nine paces, so their onslaught was pretty determined.

It was immediately clear to the men inside the square that the victory had been a decisive one, 'our men being quite satisfied for the day's work', commented Tuck. 'Altogether it was a most satisfactory day', wrote Anstruther, 'and gave the brutes a lesson. They had always been swaggering about our men not meeting them in the open and always fighting them behind entrenchments but they got it today.'

For Chelmsford, the victory meant relief from the months of tension he had laboured under since Isandlwana, and it was all the more sweet because he had been able to accomplish it before Wolseley had arrived to supersede him. He had no doubts that it had brought the war to a successful conclusion at last:

> It appears that Ketshwayo himself arranged the disposition of the forces and that they considered they would have no difficulty in defeating British Troops if they advanced in the open, away from their wagons.
>
> I feel I have a right in saying that the results of the Battle of Ulundi, gained by the steadiness of the Infantry, the good practise of the Artillery, and the dash of the Cavalry and Mounted Troops will be sufficient to dispel this idea from the minds of the Zulu Nation and of every other tribe in South Africa forever.
>
> It is difficult to compute accurately the loss of the Zulus on this occasion as the extent of the ground over which the attack was made, and the pursuit carried on, was so great, but judging by the reports of those engaged it cannot be placed at a less number than 1,500 killed.
>
> The loss of the Zulus, killed in action, since the commencement of the hostilities in January, have been placed at not less than 10,000 men, and I am inclined to believe this estimate is not too great.

Once the firing had ceased and the last groups of Zulu had retired from sight, Chelmsford gave orders for the great royal homesteads on the surrounding plain to be put to the torch, and cavalrymen and mounted officers rode out to set fire to each in turn. With the realization that the war was all but at an end, there was a rush to find souvenirs, but to the disappointment of the troops the *amakhanda* contained no great treasures, only the weapons and utensils of everyday life. 'Our men [picked] up what curiosities they could,' commented Tuck, 'and we witnessed hundreds of dead Zulu bodies lying about.' 'We walked about burning the whole place', recalled Anstruther,

> and picked up shields and assegais. I got 5 shields and 2 assegais – could not carry more. Besides the King's kraal which had about 3,000 huts – so tremendous – there were 5 or 6 other kraals as big. In fact I should think half of Zululand was houseless by this time.

The devastation was complete. After allowing his men an hour or two to rest, Chelmsford ordered them to retire back the way they had come:

> At 2 p.m. the force commenced to return to its camp on the Right Bank of the Umvelosi which it reached about 3.30 p.m. – by sunset every Military Kraal undestroyed up to this time, in the valley of the Umvelosi, was in flames – not a sign of the vast army that had attacked us in the morning was to be seen in any direction.

All this had been achieved, in the end, at remarkably little cost; Chelmsford had suffered just two officers and ten men killed in the battle, and one officer and sixty-nine men wounded, some of them mortally. That night his army slept soundly in their camp south of the river.

Behind them, a fierce glow beyond the bluffs bore witness to the destruction of the Zulu kingdom. A great circle of Zulu dead lay out in the long grass on the silent plain, too many for the scavenging wildlife to dispose of. Over the next few days a few bold women and old men emerged, once the British had gone, to seek out the corpses of loved ones and to drag them into dongas or ant-bear holes, or simply to cover them over with shields. Most of the dead were left where they fell, however, and their bones marked the site for decades to come.

For the living, there was only the shock of defeat. The King himself could not bear to watch the battle and had retired with a few personal attendants to a hill a few miles away. When the thunder of the guns was followed by the first messages of defeat, Cetshwayo covered his face with a blanket and would not speak. Then he silently rose up and walked away, weighed down by the catastrophe which had befallen his people. Some of his fleeing warriors tried to rally to him, but he sent them away, afraid they would only attract British attention. Most of the army simply melted away into the hills, and the warriors made their way to their own homes.

For the most part, the British exulted in the defeat they had inflicted on a courageous and dangerous enemy, but even officers like Anstruther were not immune to the pathos of the tragedy in which they had participated:

> It was very absurd coming up the hill yesterday to see the difference on the plain below. What had been a collection of immense

kraals was simply a bare plain with some blackened circles still smoking or smouldering.

Sir Bartle Frere had got his wish. The terrible cycle of destruction, given vent at Isandlwana, had been brought to its inevitable conclusion.

Epilogue

'Very glad to have finished...'

General Sir Garnet Wolseley, the British Government's new High Commissioner with full military and civil powers in southern Africa, spent the day of the battle of Ulundi in some discomfort at sea. He had arrived in Durban on 28 June and had immediately sought to take charge of events. With Chelmsford at that point poised to strike at the Zulu capital, Wolseley had decided that the quickest way to the front was to travel by sea to Port Durnford – an open beach on the Zululand coast, where General Crealock had established a landing stage – and to join Crealock's column there.

It was an error of judgement which robbed Wolseley of the chance to snatch whatever glory remained in the campaign. The sea was too rough for him and his staff to land, and after a frustrating delay off-shore they were forced to return to Durban. Wolseley hurried up to Fort Pearson, only to hear when he arrived that Chelmsford had beaten him to oNdini the day before. With an attempt at good grace, he immediately telegraphed to congratulate Chelmsford on his success, but his irritation showed in a long letter dated 12 July:

> I have just received a telegram via Landman's Drift purporting to come from you but signed by M. Crealock,* Military Secretary. This irregular mode of correspondence is, I'm sure, without your knowledge. The Military Secretary is in my camp, and as there can only be one General Commanding so there can be only one Military Secretary. No one can be more rejoiced at your brilliant success on the 4th instant than I am, and much as I should have enjoyed being present at the fight, I am sincerely glad that you, who have toiled and worked so hard during this miserable war, should have had personal command at what promises to be the last affair in it. Had I joined

---

* Actually J. N. Crealock.

your column instead of this one, my presence would have prevented your being in command during the action of the 4th instant, and I am as glad as you can be that things have turned out the way they have done.

You can now return home with your halo of success around you, and I am sure you will find all the authorities at the Horse Guards and War Office ready to receive you with the utmost cordiality, for although men may not approve of the way the war has been conducted, all who know anything of what has taken place are well aware that, as far as you personally are concerned, no one could have devoted himself with greater zeal for the public service to the extremely difficult task you had to grapple with, than you have done.

Chelmsford replied, wth obvious self-satisfaction:

I have to thank you very sincerely for your kind letter dated 12th inst. which reached me this forenoon and for the flattering terms in which you speak of our success at Ulundi. I am also much obliged to you for offering to facilitate in every way my wish to get away from S. Africa. With regard to the irregularity (as you call it) of Crealock signing himself 'Military Secretary', I am solely to blame. The view I took of my position (which according to your view is an erroneous one) was that you came out as High Commissioner and Commander-in-Chief replacing Sir Bartle Frere in both capacities, but that I retained the same position as regards yourself as I did to the latter, and that your appointment did not in any way cancel the one I received when I was sent out to S. Africa. This view is apparently embodied in the Secretary of State's despatch to me which I see has been published in the Natal newspaper. I of course expected that you as a general officer would regulate the plan of campaign, and that I should receive instructions from you on the subject, but I did not anticipate that I was to be deprived on my commission as the General Commanding the Forces in S. Africa, and of the services of the chief officer of my personal Staff. Neither from you nor from home have I received any intimation that it was intended to supersede me, and I cannot but think, if such were the intentions of the Government that I ought to have been informed. Crealock will of course cease to sign himself 'Military Secretary', but I think some notification ought to have been sent to me that he had been deprived of his appointment, as the Commander-in-Chief and the Lieut.-General Commanding have hitherto each had an officer on their Staff in that position, and there was therefore no irregularity in Crealock signing himself as such.

With regard to my plan of campaign, it is of course, like any other, fair ground for criticism. I am anxious, however, to let you know that had I to begin operations again, I should make no change whatever in my operations or in the distribution of troops.

I do not wish to claim success as proof that I was right, but am quite prepared to argue out the question on pure military and political grounds.

Chelmsford could afford to stand his ground; he was going home. The official telegram from Colonel Stanley, informing him of Wolseley's appointment, had only reached the camp on the White Mfolozi on 5 July, and there was nothing, now, to prevent Chelmsford objecting to Stanley's assurance

... that this appointment of a senior officer is not intended as a censure upon myself.

I regret that I cannot view the appointment in that light ...

I have therefore to request that, as there are at present more general officers in this part of South Africa than can be conveniently employed, I may be permitted to return to England with my personal staff.

I am satisfied that the power of the Zulu nation has been completely broken, and there can now be no necessity for keeping together even such a force as I have been lately commanding ...

Should Sir Garnet Wolseley offer no objection, I propose to return in anticipation of your sanction.

He had already planned the breakup of the army that had triumphed at oNdini. Both the 2nd Division and the Flying Column had retired from the White Mfolozi valley, and they camped for a few days on the Mthonjaneni heights. From here, the 2nd Division was to march back the way it had come, into Natal via Landman's Drift, while the Flying Column struck off across country to the south-east, towards the deserted mission station at St Paul's. From here it was expected to effect a junction with Crealock's column, but in fact by the time it reached St Paul's Wolseley had countermanded Chelmsford's orders and had begun to stamp his own mark on what remained of the campaign. In his last few days in Zululand Chelmsford had been a changed man, and the strain of the constant disasters, logistical problems and bickering between officers had dissipated, as Anstruther had noted:

> The general can't butter us up enough but he is usually a man of very few words but he was very effusive yesterday – could not say enough about the 94th – said conduct, behaviour, discipline etc., was perfect which was satisfactory, but this morning when he went round the laager and I went out with him he said he wanted to express his satisfaction again to the men which is rather a nuisance. Enough is as good as a feast and I think too much praise is a mistake. I charitably attribute it to the fact that he must have been celebrating the victory and having a good dinner but I suppose it is high treason to say such a thing of a general.

Wolseley and his staff had joined Crealock at the front and rode across country to St Paul's. Here the two generals met, and Wolseley formally assumed command of the forces in Zululand. The following day, Lord Chelmsford and his Staff rode out of the camp for the last time. They arrived in Pietermaritzburg on 21 July, and on the 26th embarked at Durban for the Cape, and England.

Just three weeks had elapsed since the battle of Ulundi; Sir Garnet Wolseley was welcome to what was left of the war.

To the troops in the field, it seemed that it was over. On the coast, Crealock's column, after a painfully slow advance, had destroyed the two *amakhanda* specified by Lord Chelmsford without encountering resistance. Indeed, in the last days before Ulundi, many chiefs living in the coastal districts, faced with the uncomfortable presence of so large an army on their doorsteps, had tentatively begun to negotiate their surrender. Many would not commit themselves to 'come in' openly until it was clear that the power of the King was broken, but the battle on 4 July freed many of them to accept the inevitable. Within a fortnight of the battle, most of the coastal chiefs – including Prince Dabulamanzi, who had led the attack on Rorke's Drift six months before – had formally surrendered.

Certainly, Anstruther noted that after Ulundi ordinary Zulu seemed resigned to the reality of defeat. 'There is no doubt the war is over, the Zulus come in every day bringing guns and cattle and are getting a great deal too friendly.'

Yet, as the British had recognized, by breaking up the apparatus of the Zulu state they had inevitably allowed a great deal of autonomy to pass to the regional chiefs. While many of these were now prepared to accept the new order, content that they had discharged their responsibilities to King Cetshwayo, some remained steadfastly loyal to the old. This was particularly true of chiefs in regions which had been largely untouched by the fighting, and had yet to be occupied by the British. While some parts of the country seemed entirely pacified, there was a very real danger that the young men in more remote areas were still prepared to resist, raising the prospect of a protracted guerrilla campaign.

Some hint that this might yet occur had been suggested by events at the Middle Drift in the Thukela valley, a week before Ulundi. The community on the Zulu bank had been ravaged by Twentyman's raid on 20 May, but while the Natal authorities feared retribution, the border had seemed quiet. Then – having waited until the British had relaxed their guard – the Zulu suddenly struck. On 25 June the Border Agent J. Eustace Fannin reported that

> early this morning a considerable body of Zulus crossed at the Hot Spring's under cover of a fog. The two policemen on guard there discovered them when in the water about 30 yards off. They fired on them, and the Zulus returned it with a volley. The police then turned and encountered another party who had crossed higher up; these rushed on the two police, stabbing one to death, the other escaping.
>
> The Zulus then began firing the kraals, keeping in the direction of Kran's Kop. Mr Crabb and his force went to meet them, and an engagement had ensued, with what result I don't yet know, except that the Zulu were not checked in their advance, they came on rapidly round the eastern end of Kran's Kop, burning all the kraals as they came along. They kept close along under the heights, and then swept back again to Middle Drift, ending with the Ferryman's . . . kraals. About half the kraals of Hlangabeza's tribe are destroyed, and a considerable number of cattle captured.
>
> At the same time another body crossed at Domba's Drift, and they were opposed by the men on guard there, but without effect, they burnt a large number of kraals of Domba's and Homoi's people.
>
> As far as I can ascertain from personal observation and reports the Zulus by this time have probably recrossed. I estimate their number at roughly 1,000 men altogether.

The raid of 25 June had clearly been well planned and efficiently carried out. Over seventy homesteads belonging to the African population on the Natal side of the border were destroyed, thirty people were killed, forty more captured, and nearly 1,400 goats and cattle looted. The raiders were members of the Nthuli and Magwaza chiefdoms, who lived in the broken country just across the river, and while it is possible that the King had been informed of their intentions, it had clearly been a local initiative.

In the light of such incidents, Wolseley regarded Chelmsford's withdrawal from oNdini as premature. The whereabouts of King Cetshwayo was still unknown, and Chelmsford had made no effort to secure the surrender of the important chiefdoms in central and northern Zululand.

Wolseley's solution was to reoccupy oNdini, and to put pressure on those chiefs who had not yet surrendered. Although Chelmsford's army had largely disappeared – many of the battalions were already on the road back to Natal – Wolseley cobbled together two new columns from what remained. One, commanded by Lieutenant-Colonel C. M. Clarke, and consisting of the elements from the old 1st Division, were to march with Wolseley to oNdini, where Clarke summoned the remaining great chiefs to attend him. The other, drawn from Wood's old Flying Column and commanded by Lieutenant-Colonel Baker Russell, was to march north to the Hlobane area, where the ardent royalists of the abaQulusi remained defiant.

For the troops still in the field, these new operations, coming at a time when they were looking forward to going home, were deeply frustrating, as Anstruther recalled:

> The regiment has gone off to a fort near and, I hear, in about 10 days' time we make a move, a few marches on towards a big mountain called Inhlazatye.
>
> Sir Garnet comes up on the 2nd and holds a big Durbar* . . . with the Chiefs at Ulundi and if Cetchwayo comes in and does what is wanted he will be left in possession, if not the country will be divided and, of course, till that comes we must [have] a good body of troops in the country otherwise they would say we were obliged to go – want of food, transport or something.
>
> The 2nd Division is broken up, the 17 Lancers have to walk down

---

* Word used in British India to denote an important meeting.

to Durban. Newdigate has gone home and also the 24th Regiment.
The 58th I met yesterday marching up with provisions for the column
that goes up to the Durbar.

In fact, Wolseley had already determined that Cetshwayo should be
deposed. On 19 July he had summoned the chiefs living in the coastal
districts to a meeting, and advised them that the Zulu kingdom was no
more, and that they would be informed in due course how the British
intended to dispose of it. On 14 August he held a similar meeting at his
new camp, pitched just two miles from the ruins of oNdini. Among
those who attended to offer their submission were Chief Mnyamana of
the Buthelezi, the King's most trusted counsellor, and Chief Ntshingwayo, who had commanded at Isandlwana. Over the following few days,
several of Cetshwayo's brothers surrendered, together with Zibhebhu
kaMaphitha, chief of the powerful Mandlakazi section in the north, and
Wolseley's troops took possession of hundreds of firearms and spears.

For Captain Hart, the spectacle of so many surrenders on the spot
which had once constituted the hub of the old Zulu kingdom, but was
now a scene of apocalyptic destruction, was deeply poignant. Ordered to
survey the site, he found that

> The frequency with which I have come suddenly upon human
> skeletons in the grass has been quite forbidding. When one is not
> alone, the light of one's companion's presence dispels all the gloom
> of horrors, just as the arrival of a lamp spoils a ghost story!
>
> There is nothing so dead and harmless as a skeleton, yet when
> you contemplate them in solitude they appear to possess a life of
> their own, especially when there are so many together. Some look
> angry, some threatening, some foolish, some astonished, and those
> that are on their faces seem to be asleep.
>
> These skeletons were Zulus, killed in Lord Chelmsford's fight on
> the 4th of July.
>
> On arrival here, search was made for the remains of the Hon.
> W. Drummond, a young man not in the army but attached to Lord
> Chelmsford's staff on account of his knowledge of the country. He
> was missing after the action, and so assumed to be killed, for Zulus
> never take prisoners. We heard from certain Zulus who had submit-
> ted to us, that after the action he had ridden forward amongst the
> retreating enemy, who, of course, killed him at once. They indicated

about where this had happened, and after a long search his remains were found, and identified by some hair remaining, but principally by the boots with spurs. His bones alone remained besides, and they were duly interred by our chaplain.

With most of the important chiefs forced to accept the reality of conquest, the King, as Wolseley had intended, found himself increasingly isolated. Wolseley, however, was determined that his capture would provide the final chapter in the whole sorry saga of the war, and from oNdini his patrols swept through the country north of the Mfolozi river, following rumours and reports of the King's movements.

Anstruther, for one, found the wait while these operations were carried out tedious:

> Here we are still, doing nothing. The day before yesterday Baker Russell went off with all the cavalry he could lay hands on to make 2 reconnaisances to the Black Umvolosi, north of Ulundi some distance, with the idea of catching Cetchwayo. They took 3 days' provisions but after going 30 miles the first day they found they were still 40 miles off where Cetch'y was so they returned.
>
> Marter of the King's Dragoon Guards came across yesterday with a squadron of the KDGs from Ulundi just to see what the country was like. I don't know what our next move is to be, of course the great object is to catch Cetchwayo but I don't think it really much matters the thing is really quite over and the Kaffirs are all as friendly as can be desired. Cetchy is away somewhere with, they say, only a dozen followers and I daresay if the Swazies come down on him he will give himself up, prefering to fall into our hands instead of theirs.
> ... Sir Garnet and his people are encamped at Ulundi about 2 miles from where we fought and, of course, they are beginning to say that the numbers of the enemy returned as being killed must be exaggerated – that they can't find the bodies and so on because they are immensely angry at not having been there. Sir Garnet is doing very well but I think it was a mistake sending him here. It has helped to prolongue matters a good deal.
> ... Since I last wrote a lot of Zulus have come, I should think nearly 500 and have given up arms & assegais & cows, I suppose up to this morning about 240 guns and the same number of cattle. I got 6 of the assegais but they are not very good ones and I was late in choosing ...

Anstruther's appreciation of King Cetshwayo's predicament was surprisingly accurate. In the days following the battle of Ulundi, Cetshwayo had made his way north, and had accepted an offer of sanctuary from Chief Zibhebhu, whose territory still lay beyond the reach of British patrols. The King was depressed, resigned to the fact that he had lost his kingdom; when some of the young men from the uKhandempemvu regiment tried to join him, he sent them away. Then, a week after the battle, he had left his family in Zibhebhu's care – an act which was later to have bitter repercussions – and moved south again to Mnyamana's homestead, north of the Black Mfolozi valley. From here he had attempted to open negotiations with Wolseley, but once it became clear that the British were interested only in his unconditional surrender and were prepared to hunt him down, he had taken to the bush. He was accompanied by just a few of his most faithful attendants, and by several girls of the royal household. To Wolseley's irritation, however, neither the recently surrendered chiefs nor the people at large seemed inclined to betray him. 'They all want peace badly,' noted Anstruther, '[they are] tired of war and want to sow next year's crops but they are very faithful brutes and can't make up their minds to give up Cetchwayo.'

In the end, it fell to a patrol of the King's Dragoon Guards, under the command of Major Richard Marter, to seize what last glory accrued to the British cause in Zululand. The hunt for the King had aroused the sporting instincts of Wolseley's officers, particularly those who had arrived too late to fight at Ulundi, and there had been fierce rivalry among those engaged in the pursuit to finally capture him. Lieutenant Amyatt-Burney, attached to the Dragoons, described the excitements – and tribulations – of the chase:

> At 9 a.m. on the 22nd August, 1879, a squadron of the King's Dragoon Guards, with Captain Gibbings and Godson, Lieutenant Alexander, ten men of Lonsdale's Horse under Lieutenant Werge, Lieutenant Burney, Royal Dragoons, the whole under command of Major Marter, KDG, left Ulundi on patrol, the object of which was generally understood to be the attempted capture of the fugitive King Cetywayo. Two patrols were already out under Major Barrow and Captain Lord Gifford, VC; and at the drift on the Black Umvoloose, six companies of the 60th Rifles, with some Mounted Infantry and Natives under the command of Brigadier General Clark, were posted.

. . . none of the officers seemed very sanguine except the Major, who kept his information, whatever it was, quite to himself. We had not been able hitherto to obtain the slightest clue from the natives of the whereabouts of the King. At daylight on the 28th we saddled up, first filling the nosebags with mealies, which the natives supplied with very bad grace. Working round to the north and describing very nearly a horse shoe we came to a steep descent where everyone had to dismount and lead their horses. When half way down a native came up with a note from Lord Gifford to Captain Maurice. He handed it to Major Marter, who read it. The contents were to this effect; 'Have got on the track again, hope to take him tonight, you might have given me the tip before, for "Auld lang syne".' There was much more in the note, but nothing to give the slightest clue about the object of our search. At the bottom of the hill there was a delicious stream where we watered the horses and then let them graze for an hour. As we were about to move off again, a Zulu appeared coming towards us. Major Marter entered into conversation with him through an interpreter, and just as he was going away the Zulu said to the interpreter, 'Which way is the inkos going?' Major Marter said, 'I am going over that hill in front.' The native said, 'I think you had better go round that way (pointing to the right), as the wind blows from there to-day. I have had my say.' He then turned round and walked off. The hint was promptly taken, and everyone became very keen, as Major Marter told the officers that he thought there was a very good chance of their capturing the King. We then worked due east around the hill, and after a steep climb came to a kraal three miles on. We halted a little distance off, and the Major with the interpreter rode up to the kraal, which by the way belonged to Umnyamane, who had surrendered some days before. Major Marter asked for two guides, and two young men got up immediately, and led the way to another kraal about two miles off, situated on the top of a plateau looking down into the valley of the Ngome Forest. The aspect of the country had now changed altogether. Hitherto it had been very monotonous, nothing but a succession of undulating hills covered with rough grass, a good deal of which had been burnt; now the country was green and dotted here and there with clumps of trees, the Ngome Forest forming the back ground. On our approaching this kraal, the guides signed to Major Marter to halt his men close under the edge of the forest, and they then beckoned to him to follow them, and leading the way through a strip of wood, they pointed to a thick bush overhanging the valley about fifty yards on, signing for the Major to go on to it. This he did and perceived a kraal of twelve huts surrounded by a wattle fence, in the valley below. On his return he ordered all the men to draw their swords and leave their scabbards behind with the led horses and mules. This was to prevent the clanking of the swords giving any warning. He also told our natives to strip, so as to appear as much as possible like Zulus, and he left a Sergeant and eight men in charge of everything. This done he told the men 'that from all he could gather the king was in the kraal below in the valley, and that his capture depended on their obeying silently and quickly any order they might receive; that they would have to lead their horses down the side of the mountain, through the forest; and that when they arrived at the edge of the bush they would have to ride about a quarter of a mile. The right troop under Lieutenant Alexander was to extend on the right side; the left troop under command of Captain Godson to extend to the left, and come up on the left of the kraal – the squadron being under the command of Captain Gibbings. The natives were sent round by a circuitous route to the left, to cut off all chance of escape down the valley. When these preparations were completed, Major Marter told the guides to show the way, which proved a very rough one, being simply a kaffir path. We all dismounted and advanced by single files, leading our horses down a very steep incline, strewn with rocks and stones; here and there a huge trunk of a tree barred the path; at another place there was a drop of some feet off a rock with a nasty landing; in fact to men in cold blood it would have appeared almost impossible to have got horses down at all. Eventually all reached the bottom of the hill in safety, and, though several horses slipped up, none were much damaged. The forest extended to within four hundred yards of the kraal, and there was a most convenient knoll between it and us, so that the inhabitants were unable to see anyone approaching from our side until we were quite close. Directly everyone was clear of the forest, Major Marter gave the word to mount, and he then waited for the guides, who had crawled through the long grass to see if all was right. On their return they appeared greatly excited, signing the Major to go on; and he accordingly gave the order to advance at a walk as long as we were hidden by the knoll. On arriving at the top he gave the word to gallop, and led the way himself. The ground between the forest and the kraal was rough and stoney. One man came to grief through his horse putting his foot in a hole and rolling over him. As the cavalry appeared in sight of the kraal, our natives showed themselves in the very nick of time on the other side. One shot was fired, but it is uncertain from which side. Carrying out Major Marter's instructions we rapidly and completely surrounded the kraal. The inhabitants, who numbered twenty-three, were standing at the very narrow entrance to the enclosure and armed, some with assegais, some rifles. Major Marter dismounted and went inside the enclosure with the interpreter. Umkoosana, an induna of the Unodwengo regiment, who had stuck to Cetewayo throughout his flight from Ulundi, was told by the interpreter to show Major Marter in which hut the king was. This he did (it was the third hut to the right of the entrance) and was then told to request his majesty to step outside and show himself. The king at first refused to do so, saying he was afraid that directly he put his head out of the hut he would immediately be shot. When assured that his life was safe, he coolly asked 'What rank does the officer hold to whom I am to surrender?' Major Marter replied that he was the representative of the Commander-in-Chief. Mr Oftebro, the interpreter, and son of the Missionary at Ekowe, who had known Cetywayo since he was a boy, then spoke to him. Cetywayo immediately recognized his voice, and called out to him by name, asking if it was safe for him to come out. On being assured in the affirmative he appeared crawling out of the hut in the usual Kafir fashion, on his hands and knees. He wore a moncha made of otter-skins, and had a ringkop on his head. The upper part of his body was covered with a large red table cloth, embroidered with green flowers, fastened from the neck in front, and hanging over his shoulders. Directly he stood up, all doubts as to his being the king were set at rest, as at a glance we could see his superiority both in appearance and carriage to all other Zulus. He looked round on everyone with the greatest scorn and stalked majestically into the middle of the kraal. Six Dragoons were immediately dismounted and told off as his guard, with loaded carbines. Cetywayo was informed that if he attempted to escape he would be immediately shot, and he was then marched outside the enclosure, while the huts were searched. Amongst the articles found were several Martini-Henry Rifles, nearly all of which belonged to the 1st 24th, a battered bugle, and a private's glengarry cap, a few

very fine assegais, including two barbed ones which belonged to the
king himself, and which were found in his hut, and a double-
barrelled central fire gun, which Major Marter eventually appropriated to himself, to the very great disgust of the officer who found it.
Three of the king's wives and three intombis (young girls) were in
one hut, and they were told that they might accompany the king if
they liked. These women were all young, from twelve to twenty-five
years of age. The three wives and two of the intombis were tall and
well developed, with pleasant looking faces; the third intombi was
quite a child. They were all extremely well dressed in the height of
Zulu fashion, which is easy of description, consisting of little more
than a string of beads. When all the huts were cleared the king's
followers were taken out of the kraal, and with a guard of mounted
men on each side of them., were told to follow the king, whose
women carried his blankets and mats on their heads. Barton's natives
were sent on ahead as an advance guard, and Major Marter rode
alongside the king, with a drawn sword between his leg and the
saddle flap, and a loaded revolver in his hand, the grim features of
the aged major being lit up with a smile of triumph as he gave the
word to march. That evening – for it was not until half-past 4 p.m.
that everything was in readiness for a start – we only advanced three
miles, entirely owning to the reluctance of Cetywayo to move beyond
a snail's pace. In fact, after Major Marter had repeatedly told him to
step out, but with no effect, Cetywayo turned to the interpreter and
said, 'Why does not the officer shoot me? I would have killed a man
long ago if he had not obeyed me better.' This probably gave rise to
the rumour that the king asked to be shot. About dusk we arrived at
a small kraal, and the head man was ordered to provide two huts for
the reception of the king and his followers. Accordingly the two
largest huts were cleaned out, and although the king at first objected
to enter the hut until his own attendants had cleaned it out, yet when
he was once inside he was soon made comfortable. The king and his
six women were put into one hut; Umkoosana and the rest into the
other. A strong guard was posted round the two huts, and Major
Marter himself slept across the doorway of the king's; at daylight
next morning everyone was on the move. Major Marter sent an
officer with a note to Brigadier-General Clarke, who was still at the
Black Umveloose drift, asking for a mule cart and two companies of
the 60th Rifles to be sent to Dnasa Kraal, about five miles from the

drift. This kraal was deserted, and belonged to the king, and Major Marter said he would endeavour to reach it that night. Advancing slowly up the valley we crossed a stream; then turning in a southerly direction over a range of hills, we came up to the kraal where Lord Gifford had halted on the previous day. Here we made a short halt for breakfast. During the rest of the day we made but slow progress, until at dusk we came up to a very steep and rocky pass. We all dismounted and led our horses, and a difficult task it was getting the troop horses up. During the noise and confusion made by the horses slipping and struggling on the rocks, nine men and one woman made their escape, and though several shots were fired at them, owing to the darkness it was impossible to see if any were hit. As soon as it was found that the king was safe, we pushed on and arrived at the Dnaza Kral at 7.30 p.m., having been on the march since daylight. Here we found two companies of the 60th. Just as we came to the kraal another of the king's followers, his cousin, attempted to escape, but was shot by the Farrier-Sergeant of the King's Dragoon Guards. The king and his followers were safely placed in two huts, and a strong guard posted over them. We were off again at daylight next morning, the king riding in a mule-cart, though he showed at first much disinclination to enter it. We reached the Black Umveloose at 8 a.m., and after a halt of three hours, again proceeded on our way, still accompanied by two companies of the 60th Rifles. That night we bivouacked nine miles from Ulundi. On the morning of the 31st, we marched soon after daylight, and on arriving near the camp, received a message from General Colley, CS, ordering Major Marter to wait outside for a short time, as the troops were on church parade, also for him to send out flanking parties two hundred yards on each side to prevent anyone approaching the king. After waiting half an hour the flankers and an advanced guard were sent out under an officer. The officers of the King's Dragoon Guards had the honour of personally guarding the king, this privilege being denied to the other two officers, though they were present at the capture, and with the patrol from the time it started. A large concourse of all ranks had turned out to witness Major Marter's triumphal entry; and the flankers had no easy task to keep everyone outside them. Two tents had been pitched to the left front of the headquarter camp, and to them Cetywayo was brought. The cavalry halted, and the 60th, forming two lines on each side of the tents, the king walked before

them into the tent prepared for him. Two hours later Cetywayo and
all his followers looked for the last time on Ulundi, as they were
taken away in an ambulance drawn by ten mules . . .

For Wolseley, the King's capture marked the real end of the war.
In the fortnight he had waited at oNdini, accepting Zulu surrenders, he
had decided the settlement of Zululand. Ironically, at home the Disraeli
government had fallen, to be replaced by Gladstone's Liberals, and there
was no stomach now for the expense and protracted commitment of
annexation. Wolseley's instructions were to impose a settlement which
would prevent the Zulu kingdom from posing a threat to its white
neighbours, and then to withdraw. His solution was to exile King
Cetshwayo, and to divide Zululand up among the regional chiefs.
In selecting the chiefs to be favoured, he paid lip-service to the idea,
popular in Natal, that Zululand could be broken down into the constitu-
ent parts which had been independent in the days before Shaka. More
important, however, Wolseley's choice was coloured by the need to
choose proxies who either had a vested interest in supporting the British
or were opposed to the Royal House. John Dunn, who had abandoned
Cetshwayo and made himself indispensable as a political adviser to both
Chelmsford and Wolseley, was confirmed as an independent ruler in his
old lands north of the Thukela. Prince Hamu, the only member of the
royal family to defect to the British, was made a ruler in the northern
districts. So too was Chief Zibhebhu, who had fought loyally for the
King throughout the war, but whose independent spirit and commercial
ties with Natal had marked him down as an agent of Imperialism. Chief
Sihayo, who had lived opposite Rorke's Drift, and whose sons had
provided the excuse for the British invasion, was deposed, and Hlubi
Molife, a BaSotho chief who had fought for the British, was given his
border lands instead. When Captain Henry Moore, one of Wolseley's
commissioners appointed to delineate the new boundaries, interviewed
Zibhebhu on 6 October, it was already clear that a new order was in the
making:

> Met Usibebu as we headed towards Ngome Bush. He had a large
> following and seemed to have the air of a man of undoubted position,
> he was young and dressed in a sailor's shirt, Portuguese egg and
> bacon blouse with leather necklace and mounted on a horse, loot of
> course. He confided to Wheelwright that he had brought money to

give the [men] who will come to settle his boundary and pulled accordingly £7 in an old bag out of his pocket. He was of course told it was not the thing . . .

Everywhere, too, Moore found the country alive with tales of the recent fighting, and in particular of Isandlwana:

> One boy showed us the road back; at first he seemed [reluctant] to say he had been at Isandlwana, but afterwards told all about it. [He] was there in the Ngobamakosi regiment, chest failed to advance for long time until the infantry retired, white men in a clump back to back in the camp, there the Zulus really began to be killed in numbers. Same old story, did not intend to attack till next day, did not know of Lord Chelmsford's absence . . .

*

Wolseley's plan was a classic case of divide and rule, and in due course it would produce a crop of bitterness and bloodshed more destructive to the Zulu even than the British invasion.

For Cetshwayo there was only exile. He was taken across country to the beach at Port Durnford – along the way he pointed out to his captors the bush by which his uncle, King Shaka, used to sit when judging cowards in his army – and on 4 September boarded the steamer *Natal*, destined for the Cape. A fortnight later, he and his faithful retainers were securely lodged in quarters at the old Dutch castle in Cape Town.

Most of the lingering resistance in Zululand collapsed when news of the King's capture circulated. Only in the north, in the troubled areas around Luneburg, did the survivors of the raiding bands of Mbilini and Manyanyoba hold out, until at last the British lost all patience with them. According to Anstruther, whose regiment, the 94th, had at last marched out of Zululand towards the Transvaal,

> We left Zululand yesterday, crossed the Pongola, and came here only 2 miles off and are encamped at the mission station where poor Moriarty of the 80th and his convoy were surprised. There has been so little rain that all the marks of the tents and scraps of letters, newspapers etc. are lying about quite fresh and unhurt. You recollect he had his convoy waggons divided on both sides of the Intombi River which had risen and prevented his getting all his waggons and he lost more than half his company. The day before yesterday

we hustled the tribe (Chief Manyobo) who did the mischief. They are outcasts, not proper Zulus or Swazies, and live in caves in the surrounding hills which they won't come out of so they were told to send their women and children away and give themselves up. They did the former but not the latter. The women and children came in in good quantities to our fort in Luneberg, five miles off where four companies of the 4th are so the day before yesterday some of us and the 4th from the Fort went up the hills and set to work to blow up the caves with gun cotton. There were a great many tremendous explosions but, I am afraid, very little damage was done. We got 2 prisoners and blew in the entrance of a lot of caves and the 4th unfortunately lost 2 men, their sergeant-major and a corporal who went into one of the caves and were shot immediately. It was very stupid. We got all their goats and cattle and I fancy they will give one of the prisoners to Mayobo's head man and the other to his son. They are a very small insignificant tribe but have been doing a lot of mischief. An expedition has gone out against them today and they will be harried til they give in.

And on that inglorious note, the war came to an end. Wolseley himself hurried on to the Transvaal, to turn his attention to another African people, the Pedi of Chief Sekhukhune, who had also been steadfastly defying white authority. Baker Russell's column marched to join him. Clarke's column had already left oNdini, and retired by way of the middle Thukela, to intimidate the chiefdoms there.

For most of the men involved, it had been a war of prolonged hardships, of long marches in tough terrain, of extremes of weather, indifferent food, frequent frights, and little enough glory. That was, perhaps, the enduring memory of ordinary soldiers like Bandsman Tuck of the 58th, who left a vivid impression of his company's march out of Zululand:

... it would have done your heart good to have seen us on parade or it would certainly have sent a General Officer into a lunatic asylum to have seen us. We were fully equipped, 70 rounds of ball ammunition etc. Most had helmets but one of our men appeared in a wide awake hat (rather peculiar dress for a soldier). As for trousers, all shapes, sizes and patches. Some square, some oblong, and put on according to the wearer's abilities, as a tailor, or [according to] his taste as a member of Society. It would have puzzled a fashionable tailor in New Bond Street to know whether they were new cut, or some antique fashion renewed. Boots the same, some with soles stitched to the uppers with wire, others with hardly soles at all. No need for the Drill Sergeant to exclaim, 'turn your toes out,' as a great many were turned out to daylight much to the wearer's discomfort. Well not to transgress too much, off we went to the sound of martial music consisting of a small drummer and a large fifer (each company's allowance), and a merry lot we were, joking, singing etc. when we passed Marshall's farm and halted to wish old friends good bye.

Off again and had breakfast along side a branch of the Buffalo River. Distance from start 10 miles. After some coffee and dry bread (for such it was) and any amount of not very pure water, we started again at 10.30 a.m. to finish march. Our band struck up manfully much to the delight of some of the black beauties of South Africa who followed us for a considerable distance in evident delight at our martial appearance. Their dress, which consisted of a string of beads around their waist and a short flowing gauze skirt which did not conceal much of their nether limbs, and would most certainly have sent the Court Milliner off his head. On we trudge like the Duke of York with his thousand men up one hill and down another one again, only to see another appear. No regular road, only a beaten track. No vegetation, nothing but – yes there was, I had nearly forgotten. You must have heard of the charge of the Light Brigade, but instead of guns it was (in S. Africa) ant hills in front of us, ant hills in rear of us, ant hills to the right of us, ant hills to the left of us, if fact it was nothing but ant hills when not employed against an enemy.

We had now travelled 17 African miles and the heat commenced to tell its tale. A few men fell out, some because their soles refused to carry them further, others from fatigue. No joking now, no signing, every man's shoulder to the wheel. Martial music has long since ceased. The small drummer plods wearily on, the fifer has ceased to charm. All is silence except now and then some fellow will have his joke which causes a smile to rise on his comrade's face . . . No water to be got anywhere, nothing but stagnant pools. No Doctor, for our Commandment was for three days thou shalt not be sick, neither shall thou die, for Doctors are scarce, neither have we medicine. On we go over one hill to find another in front of us, no signs of a camp, more falling out for want of shoe leather. Heels left here, soles left there, tips all over the place, til at last after marching from sun rise till long after sunset, we spy the camp having marched 29 African miles in the heat of the day, on about two or three ounces of dry bread and half boiled coffee. I must now tell you that an African mile does not consist of 1,700 yards but they mount their horse, light their pipe and gallop for one hour by the watch, when it is considered that 6 miles have been completed. So much for African miles. Some of our fellows arrived after lights out, and had dinner, tea altogether, but we received a ration of rum which consisted of a table spoonful and a half. How generous of our country, but it is such a rarity to get here, although there are barrels of it in store. Our fellows called it the Rum-less Campaign. Turned in on the ground and slept like a top, stiff as a poker the next morning. So we halted and rested on the seventh day. Started again on Monday and crossed the Buffalo river. Had breakfast at 5.30 and arrived at Utrecht (Transvaal) about 2 p.m. and we were very glad to have finished . . .

Yet for those regiments who were destined to see further service in southern Africa, the Transvaal proved no more welcoming than Zululand. In September, Wolseley, assisted by the Swazi – who, reassured by the destruction of oNdini and the capture of Cetshwayo, finally came off the political fence – defeated the Pedi and captured King Sekhukhune. But rather than secure British influence in the Transvaal, this final reduction of African independence south of the Limpopo had the opposite effect. The Transvaal Boers, who had never been reconciled to British rule, free now from their troublesome black neighbours, rebelled. In December 1880 a rebellion broke out in the Transvaal; in the first pitched battle of the war, a column of the 94th, marching to reinforce the British garrison at Pretoria, was shot to pieces by Boer marksmen at Bronkhorstspruit. Among those wounded was Philip Anstruther, shot through the legs; he died a few days later. British attempts to reimpose their authority came to a bloody end on the slopes of Majuba hill. The Transvaal was given back to the Boers – despite protests from African chiefs who pointed out that the Boers had settled the area only fifty years before – in an unsatisfactory settlement which paved the way for a greater struggle to come.

And the Zulu? Wolseley's settlement certainly achieved his basic objectives, although probably not quite as he intended. Many of the new rulers in Zululand were men regarded, not unnaturally, as traitors by the people placed under them. Scarcely had the British evacuated the country than friction broke out between supporters of the old regime and the British appointees. In particular, members of the Royal House quarrelled bitterly with Chief Zibhebhu. Not a man to be lightly slighted, Zibhebhu promptly allied himself with Prince Hamu and began harassing royalists living in his territories. Deprived of any means of redress, the royalists appealed for succour from the Natal authorities and the British Government. Both clung ruthlessly to the spirit of Wolseley's settlement, refusing to consider the royalists as anything but troublemakers, until by 1881 Zululand was on the brink of civil war.

In an attempt to head off open conflict – a possibility dreaded not for the Zulu' sake, but for fear it might destabilize Natal and the Transvaal – the British Government decided to allow King Cetshwayo a limited role in Zulu politics. The King had been held in relative comfort in the old Dutch castle in Cape Town, and once he had recovered from the immediate shock of his defeat and exile, he took a keen interest in the affairs of his country. He became a popular figure with wealthy tourists visiting southern Africa, many of whom came to question the justice of the war. Championed by influential supporters, he was allowed to visit London in July 1882 to argue his case. He was received by Queen Victoria at Osborne House; the meeting was apparently cool, as the Queen had known several of the officers of the 24th killed at Isandlwana, but as a souvenir of his visit the Queen presented Cetshwayo with a large silver cup.

In January 1883 he was allowed to return to Zululand, in one of the strangest twists of the whole remarkable story. The British had no intention of restoring him to his old position, however, and he was given authority only over the central part of his kingdom. The southern part – John Dunn's territory – was placed under direct British control, to serve as a buffer with Natal, while in the northern districts both Zibhebhu and Hamu retained their independence. The King himself was prohibited from enrolling *amabutho* or rebuilding the *amakhanda* barracks, and was required to accept the presence of a British resident.

Cetshwayo attempted to re-establish himself as best he could, building a new oNdini – a shadow of its former glory – close by the ruins of the old, but the result was a catastrophe. Jubilant royalists, probably acting without the King's knowledge, promptly attacked Zibhebhu to avenge themselves for their recent wrongs. But the man who had commanded the reserve at Isandlwana, had almost trapped Buller at oNdini the day before the great battle, and had led the most determined attack on Chelmsford's square, was not to be intimidated. He ambushed the royalist forces advancing up the Msebe valley and routed them utterly, and in July 1883 made a daring attack on oNdini itself. Cetshwayo's followers were taken by surprise and utterly defeated. For the second time in its history, oNdini was put to the torch. Over fifty Zulu notables were killed by Zibhebhu's warriors, including Ntshingwayo, the victor of Isandlwana, and the heads of some of the most venerable lineages in the country. Being old and portly, they could not run fast enough.

The battle of oNdini marks the true end of the old Zulu kingdom, and it broke the threads which bound the nation together more effectively than the British had ever done. Cetshwayo escaped the slaughter with a leg wounded, and eventually took refuge in the British reserve. He died suddenly in February 1884, a broken man, worn down by disappointment and defeat. Officially, the British ascribed his death to heart failure; privately, it was widely believed that he was poisoned.

It was left to Cetshwayo's son Dinuzulu to struggle on in the royalist cause. He had successfully orchestrated the defeat of Zibhebhu in 1884 by appealing to the Transvaal Boers for help, but the possibility of Boer influence extending across Zululand provoked the British Government to take up the responsibilities of its actions upon which it had so steadfastly turned its back in 1879. In 1887 Zululand was annexed to the British Crown; in 1888 Dinuzulu led a rebellion on behalf of the Royal House. He was defeated and exiled to St Helena. Zululand was later passed over to the government of Natal, and the way was paved for a century of economic exploitation and political repression.

Lord Chelmsford never really escaped the field of Isandlwana. Always an establishment favourite, he had returned home to the blessing of Queen Victoria and the Duke of Cambridge. Honours were showered upon him – he was appointed Lieutenant of the Tower of London and later Gold Stick – but he was forced to fight a constant rearguard in the face of detractors like the journalist Archibald Forbes, or Anthony Durnford's brother, Edward.

Chelmsford never commanded troops in the field again. He collapsed and died on 9 April 1905 after a game of billiards at the United Service Club.

Index of Contributors

Contributors are listed alphabetically under ranks in which they appear in the text. Imperial officers attached to colonial units are given with their British regiments followed by local appointments. The figures in round brackets are the Accession numbers of the files from which the papers have been taken. Extracts from published works include the titles of the works in question.

Amyatt-Burney, Lieutenant H. A., 1st Dragoon Guards (6408/77–2)
Anstruther, Major Philip, 94th Regt (5705/22)
Backhouse, Lieutenant Julius, 2/3rd Regt (7602–48)
Barrow, Major Percy, 19th Hussars (6807–386–7)
Booth, Sergeant Anthony, 80th Regt (6807–386–9)
Buller, Lieutenant-Colonel Redvers, Staff, 2/60th (6807–386–9, 6807–386–14)
Chard, Lieutenant John, RE (British Parliamentary Papers (BBP) C. 2260)
Chelmsford, Lieutenant-General Lord Frederic, Commander-in-Chief, southern Africa (6807–386)
Clark, Captain Stanley, 17th Lancers (6610/540)
Clery, Major Cornelius, 32nd Regt (6807–386–8)
Cochrane, Lieutenant William, 32nd Regt (Isandlwana court of inquiry, BBP C. 2260)
Coghill, Lieutenant Nevill, 1/24th Regt (7112–38)
Coker, Midshipman Lewis, Royal Navy (6810/38)
Curling, Lieutenant Henry, Royal Artillery (Isandlwana court of inquiry, BBP C 2260)
Deacon, Private William, 80th Regt (6807–386–9)
Dennison, Captain C. G., Border Horse (6807–386–14)
Drury-Lowe, Colonel Drury, 17th Lancers (6807–386–16)
Essex, Captain Edward, 75th Regt (6807–386–8, Isandlwana court of inquiry BBP C. 2260))
Fannin, Mr James (6807–386–7)

Frere, Sir Henry, High Commissioner to the Cape (6807–386–12, BBP C. 2222)

Fynney, Mr F. B. (pamphlet on the Zulu Army; 6610/45)

Gardner, Captain Alan, 14th Hussars (6807–386–8, Isandlwana court of inquiry, BBP C. 2260)

Glyn, Colonel Richard 1/24th Regt (7112–38, 6807–386–8)

Gosset, Captain Matthew, 54th Regt (6807–386–8)

Grandier, Trooper E., Border Horse (6807–386–14)

Hamilton, Lieutenant W. des V., Royal Navy (9235/61)

Hart, Captain Alan Fitzroy, 31st Regt./2nd Natal Native Contingent, *Letters of Major-General FitzRoy Hart-Synot*, London, 1912

Harward, Lieutenant Henry, 80th Regt (6807–386–9)

Higginson, Lieutenant Walter, 2/3rd Natal Native Contingent (letters to Coghill family, quoted in *Whom the Gods Love*, edited by Patrick Coghill, 1967)

Hogan, Private Martin, 80th Regt (6807–386–9)

Leet, Major William Knox, 1/13th Regt/Wood's Irregulars (6807–386–14)

Lewis, Private Peter, 80th Regt (6807–386–9)

MacLeod, Captain Norman, Political Agent (6807–386–9)

MacSwinney, Lieutenant James, 94th Regt (6709/67, 6406/16)

Magumbi, follower of John Dunn (6807–36–7)

Malindi, 3rd Regt. Natal Native Contingent (6807–386–8)

Marshall, Major-General Sir Frederick (BBP C. 2374)

Mbamgulana, *induna* of Prince Hamu (6807–386–14)

Mehlokazulu kaSihayo, iNgobamakhosi Regt (given in Charles Norris-Newman, *In Zululand With the British Throughout the War of 1879*, London, 1880)

Moore, Captain Henry, 2/4th Regt (7411–8)

Newdigate, Major-General Edward (BBP C. 2374)

Nourse, Captain Cracroft, 1/1st Regt Natal Native Contingent (Isandlwana court of inquiry, BBP C. 2260)

Nyanda, *induna*, Mounted Native Contingent (6807–386–8)

Pearson, Colonel Charles, 3rd Regt (6807–386, 6810/38)

Raw, Lieutenant Charles, Mounted Native Contingent (6807–386–8)

Russell, Lieutenant-Colonel John, 12th Lancers (6809–386–14)

Schermbrucker, Commandant Frederick, Schermbrucker's Irregulars (6807–386–9)

Schwartzkopt, Lieutenant, Kaffrarian Rifles (6807–386–9)

Scott, Surgeon-Major F. B., Army Medical Department (6807–386–11, 6312/180)

Shepstone, Sir Theophilus, Secretary for Native Affairs (BPP C. 2222)

Sibalo kaHibana, Zulu warrior (6807–386–14)

Sihlahla, uMxhapho Regiment (British Parliamentary Papers C. 2454)

Slade, Lieutenant Frederick, Royal Artillery (6807/235)

Stanley, Col. F. A., Secretary of State for War (6807–386–19)

Strickland, Commissary-General Edward (6807–386–5)

Tuck, Bandsman M. M., 58th Regt (7005/21)

Tucker, Major Charles, 80th Regt (6807–386–9)

Wolseley, General Sir Garnet, Commander-in-Chief, southern Africa (6807–386–21)

Wood, Col. Henry Evelyn, 90th Regt (6807–386–9, 6807–386–14, also autobiography, *From Midshipman to Field Marshal*, London, 1906)

Zulu deserter from the uNokhenke regiment (reproduced in F. E. Colenso and E. Durnford, *A History of the Zulu War and its Origin*, London, 1880)

Zulu prisoner, captured at Ulundi (6807–386–17)

Zulu spy of Prince Hamu's people (6807–386–9)

Index

abaQulusi people 125–6, 127, 129, 131,
    132, 133, 136, 140, 144, 150, 152,
    154, 155, 157, 161, 171, 173, 265
Active, HMS 46, 48, 60
Afghanistan 23
Alexander, Lieutenant 268, 270
Allan, Corporal 184
amabutho 8, 15, 29, 83, 93, 140, 241, 249,
    279
amaTigulu river 52, 199–200, 206
ammunition supplies 57, 64, 99
Amyatt-Burney, Lieutenant H.A. 268–74
Anderson, Captain 137
Anstey, Lieutenant Edgar 104
Anstruther, Major Philip xviii, 230–1,
    241, 248–9, 263, 265–6, 267–8,
    275–6
    and battle of Ulundi 252, 256, 257,
    258–9
    on death of Louis Napoleon 235, 240,
    243–4
    death of 278
    travels with reinforcements 185–8,
    217–18
Ardendorff, Lieutenant 117
Attwood, Corporal 184

Babanango mountain 224, 231–2, 240,
    243, 246
Backhouse, Lieutenant Julius B. xviii, 39,
    41, 46, 47–8, 50, 51, 197, 199–200,
    201, 211, 212
    and battle of Gingindlovu 203, 208–9
    and battle of Nyezane 55–6, 59–60
    and Thukela garrison 61–2, 188–92
Baker Russell, Lieutenant-Colonel 265,
    267, 276

Barrow, Captain 200, 204, 205–6, 210
Barrow, Major Percy 48, 50, 53, 55, 64,
    190, 268
Barton, Captain 152, 157–8
BaSotho people 21, 90
Batshe river 76–7, 81, 229–30
Beach, Sir Michael Hicks 23
'beast's horns' tactic 31, 58–9
Beresford, Lord 251
Bettington's Horse 234, 235, 236
Biggarsberg heights 84
Black, Major Wilsone 112, 181–2
Blood River *see* Ncome, battle of
Boers 9, 11–12, 15, 16, 18
    boundary disputes with Zulus 18–19,
    127
    dissidents 37, 177, 193, 278, 280
    fail to support invasion 37, 127
Bonaparte, Napoleon *see* Napoleon I,
    Emperor
Booth, Sergeant Anthony 138, 139,
    140–1, 142–3
border dispute, Transvaal 18–19, 23
Border Horse 153, 157, 173
border raids 219–20
Boundary Commission 23–4, 26, 37
Bourne, Colour Sergeant Frank 113, 184
Bright, Lieutenant Arthur 167
Bromhead, Lieutenant Gonville 114,
    117–18, 177, 184
Bronkhorstspruit 278
Browne, Captain 151
Browne, Lieutenant Edward 86, 87, 92,
    110, 165
Buller, Lieutenant-Colonel Redvers 125,
    129–30, 131, 132–3, 135, 144, 145,
    146, 147, 239

Buller, Lieutenant-Colonel Redvers (*cont.*)
and battle of Hlobane 148–53, 154,
155, 156–7, 159–61
and battle of Khambula 165, 169
and battle of Ulundi 241, 243, 250,
251, 252, 254–5, 280
Bulwer, Sir Henry, Lieutenant-Governor
of Natal 23
clashes with Chelmsford 33–5, 215–17

Cambridge, Duke of 179, 185, 216, 234,
246, 280
Campbell, Captain 153–4, 156
Campbell, Captain H.J. Fletcher 48, 54,
56, 58
Canada 17
Cantwell, Wheeler 184
Cape colony 9
Cape Town 28, 275, 279
Carey, Lieutenant J. Brenton 232, 234,
235, 236, 239–40, 243–5
Carnarvon, Lord 17, 23
Carson, Private 71
cattle raids
British 146, 151
Zulu 265
cavalry
No. 1 Column 48
No. 4 Column 125
Cavalry Brigade 222, 229
Cavaye, Lieutenant 91, 94, 96
Centre Column *see* No. 3 (Centre)
Column
Cetshwayo kaMpande, King xviii, 10, 14,
16, 22, 24, 42, 135, 173, 174, 175,
223, 264
allegiance of Mbilini waMswati to 126
appoints John Dunn 43–4
coronation of 15, 27
death of 280
defeat at battle of Ulundi 257–8
defensive strategy 51–2
diplomatic initiatives 226–9, 245,
248–9, 250, 268
equips troops with guns 32
and Eshowe garrison 66–7, 197
in exile 274, 275, 279

fails to consolidate after Isandlwana
178
and Luneburg 127
and missionaries 16
orders Zulu army not to enter Natal
116, 178
plan to attack No. 4 Column 146–7,
148, 154–5, 163, 201
pursuit and capture of 265, 266,
268–74
response to 2nd British offensive 241
response to attack on Sihayo 82–3
response to ultimatum 38–9, 41
return to Zululand 279
seen as tyrannical 22, 38
to be deposed 265–6
and Transvaal boundary dispute
19–20
visits London 279
Chard, Lieutenant (later Major) John 115,
117–18, 120–1, 122, 184, 218, 243
Chelmsford, Lieutenant-General Lord
Frederic xvii–xviii, 27–9, 42, 75,
131, 142, 143, 274, 275
abandons original plan of campaign
63–4
accompanies Central Column 76
advance on oNdini 246–8, 249–50,
251–4
and battle of Gingindlovu 202–8
and battle of Isandlwana 110, 111–12,
145, 147, 179–80, 187, 257, 280
and battle of Ntombe 144
and battle of Ulundi 257, 260–1
character 28
concern for Luneburg and frontier
128
confident of victory in second
offensive 228
and Court of Inquiry 179–80, 184,
197
criticized for dividing his force 88
death of 280
and death of Prince Louis Napoleon
232, 234, 236, 239, 243
early career 27
foray into Batshe 77–8
honoured 280

Chelmsford, Lieutenant-General (*cont.*)
    invasion plan 32–7, 39, 45, 50, 128
    movement to Isandlwana 84–5
    moves to Thukela garrison 195
    plans for Centre Column 81
    plans new offensive 214–24, 226–9, 231–2
    plans relief of Eshowe 145–6, 192–9
    rebufs Zulu diplomatic initiatives 226–8, 243, 248–9
    relationship with Bulwer 33–5
    and relief of Eshowe 208–9
    reorganizes columns 221–2
    reprimands Durnford 80–1
    requests reinforcements 36, 46, 145, 177, 184–5
    returns to England 263
    returns to Pietermaritzburg 176–8
    returns to Rorke's Drift garrison 122
    states terms for peace 228, 243, 248
    superseded by Wolseley 245–6, 247–8, 260–2, 265
    troops under his command 35–6, 214–15, 245–6
Chillianwallah, battle of 82
Christianity 16
Church, Captain 110, 111
Clark, Brigadier-General 268
Clark, Captain Stanley 2–3
Clarke, Lieutenant-Colonel C.M. 265, 276
cleansing rituals 108
Clery, Major Cornelius 87, 88
Clifford, General Sir Hugh 216–17
Coates, Major 62, 189
Cochrane, Captain 91
Cochrane, Lieutenant William 180
Coghill, Lieutenant Nevill xviii, 39–40, 42, 77, 82, 84–5, 86–7, 88, 92, 102, 104, 106
    death of 107–8, 181, 183
Coker, Midshipman Lewis 60, 74
Colenso, John William, Bishop of Natal 223
Colley, General 273
Colonial Office 12, 17, 23, 246
Colours, Queen's 105–6, 181–2, 183
Confederation policy 17–18, 20–1, 22, 23, 177

Conference hill 231, 243
Court of Inquiry into Isandlwana 179–80, 184, 197
Courtney, Lieutenant 204, 206
Crealock, Major-General Henry 221, 222–3, 227, 228, 245, 260, 262
Crealock, Colonel John North 87, 204, 260, 261–2
Cunynghame, General Sir Arthur 27, 39
Curling, Lieutenant Henry 100, 102, 104, 180

Dabulamanzi, Prince 67, 70, 84, 117, 194, 201, 205, 210, 227, 263
Daily News 238
Dalton, Acting Assistant Commissary James 79–80, 118, 184
D'Arcy, Captain 170, 251
Dartnell, Major 86, 87, 88, 89, 92, 110
Deacon, Private William 140
Deleage, Paul 237, 238
Dennison, Captain C.G. 153, 157–8
Derby 33, 128, 136, 137, 138
diamonds 17
Dingane kaSenzangakhona, King 11, 22, 37, 83
Dingiswayo kaJobe 7, 8
Dinuzulu 280
disease
    Eshowe 67–8, 70, 74, 75, 189, 192, 210
    Rorke's Drift 181
    Thukela 212–13
Disraeli, Benjamin 184, 274
1st Division 221, 265
    objectives 222–3
2nd Division 221, 224, 229, 232, 240, 241, 249, 262, 265
    objectives 223, 231
Dlinza 43
1st (The King's) Dragoon Guards 1–2, 186, 214, 229, 232, 254, 267, 268, 273
Drummond, the Hon. W. 266–7
Drury-Lowe, Colonel 241, 253–4
Duncombe, Lieutenant 160–1
Dundee 224
Dunn, John 43–4, 191–2, 193–4, 201–2, 210, 211, 227, 228–9, 274, 279

Dunne, Commissary Walter 114, 121, 184
Dunn's Road 44–5
Durban 12, 46, 48, 145, 187–8, 209, 238, 239, 260, 263
Durnford, Colonel Anthony 3, 37, 45, 62–3, 113, 280
   and battle of Isandlwana 90–100, 180, 187
   death of 63, 103, 183, 230
   and Langalibalele 90–1
   orders from Chelmsford 84, 87, 90
   reprimanded by Chelmsford 80–1, 91
Durnford, Edward 280
Dutch East India Company 9
Dyson, Lieutenant 94

ebaQulusini homestead 125
eclipse, solar 103–4, 132
Ekowe *see* Eshowe
eMvutsheni 211–12
Eshowe xviii, 44, 45, 50, 52, 188, 222
   abandoned 209–10
   British garrison 61, 63, 65
   Chelmsford plans to relieve 145–6, 148, 192–9
   disease at 67–8, 70, 74, 75, 189, 192, 210
   relief of 199–209, 214
   siege at 67–75, 188–90, 191, 223
esiKlebheni homestead 246–7
eSiqwakeni homestead 70
Essex, Captain Edward 89–90, 91, 94–5, 96, 99–100, 101, 180
eZulwini homestead 210

Fannin, James (border agent) 219–20, 264
Farewell, Lieutenant Francis George 10, 12
Figaro 237, 238
Filter, Pastor 172
firearms
   plundered after Isandlwana 109, 166, 172, 208, 243, 248, 249, 271
   Zulu supply of 31–2, 44
flogging 190
Flying Column, The 221, 223, 229, 231, 240, 241, 243, 246, 249, 262, 265

Forbes, Archibald 280
Fort Chelmsford 212, 227
Fort Newdigate 242
Fort Pearson 46, 47, 48, 72, 188, 191, 260
Fort Tenedos 64, 188, 191, 193
Fowler, Private 153, 168
France
   1789 Revolution 9
   1848 Revolution 232
Frere, Sir Henry Edward Bartle 21–3, 33, 35, 63, 78, 85, 128, 176, 226, 227, 246, 259, 261
   determined to mount Zulu campaign 22, 23, 25, 27, 28
   issues ultimatum to Zulus 27, 38, 40
Frith, Lieutenant 241, 243
Frontier Light Horse 125, 129, 130, 131, 170
Fynney, F.B. 28–31, 32, 51

Gama, Vasco da 10
Gardner, Captain Alan 93–4, 99, 110, 131, 180
Gatling guns 26, 48, 60, 64, 215
German Lutheran missionaries 19–20, 127, 133–4
Gibbings, Captain 268, 270
Gifford, Captain Lord 268, 269, 273
Gingindlovu
   battle of 202–8, 211, 220, 223, 249
      casualties at 207, 210–11, 214
   camp 173, 175, 211, 212
Gladstone, William Ewart 274
Glyn, Colonel Richard xix, 37, 40, 47–8, 50, 51, 87, 229
   authority diminished by Chelmsford's presence 76, 221
   and battle of Isandlwana 105, 110, 111
   and recovery of the Queen's Colours 181–2
   at Rorke's Drift 176, 180
Godide kaNdlela, Chief 52, 53, 59, 66, 83
Godson, Captain 268, 270
Godwin-Austen, Captain Alfred 114
Gosset, Captain Matthew 110–11, 112
Grandier, Trooper E. 173–5
Graphic 238
Grey Town 40

Griqualand West 17
guerrilla campaign, prospect of 264

Hackett, Major 167, 168
Hamilton, Lieutenant W. 46–7, 57, 60, 62, 68–70, 71
Hamu, Chief 135–6, 144, 146, 147, 148, 156, 161, 163, 195, 226, 274, 279
Harford, Lieutenant 182
Harness, Colonel Arthur 110, 111, 179–80
Harrison, Lieutenant-Colonel Richard 234
Hart, Captain Fitzroy 50, 53–4, 56–7, 58, 64, 212–13, 266
    and battle of Gingindlovu 202–4, 207
    and battle of Nyezane 54, 56–7, 58, 60
Harward, Lieutenant Henry 138–44
Helpmekaar camp 41, 80, 115, 117, 118, 131, 179
Higginson, Lieutenant Walter 106, 107
Hitch, Private 184
Hlalangubo homestead 52
Hlazakazi ridge 85, 88, 89, 93
Hlobane, battle of 149–54, 155–61, 170, 173, 174–5, 197, 221, 245
    casualties at 161, 214
Hlobane range and stronghold 126, 127, 129, 130–1, 132, 135, 142, 144–5, 147–8, 265
Hlubi Molife, Chief 274
Hogan, Private Martin 140
Hook, Private 184

iklwa (short spear) 31
Illustrated London News 256
iMbube regiment 83, 164
imperialism 17
India 23
iNdlondlo regiment 25, 83, 117, 164
iNdluyengwe regiment 83, 105, 116, 164, 194, 201
iNgcugce guild 15–16
iNgobamakhosi regiment 83, 95, 98, 155, 160, 162, 164, 165, 166, 169, 194, 201, 253, 275
inkatha 247
Intumeni 46

Inyezana *see* Nyezane
iNyoni ridge 85, 90, 96, 100
iNyoni river 50–51
Isandlwana
    battle of xvii, xviii, 57, 66, 90–110, 117, 131, 143, 145, 154, 166, 171, 176, 245, 255, 259, 275, 279
    battlefield revisited 1–3, 179, 216, 229–30
    casualties at 2, 109, 214, 223–4
    Court of Inquiry into 179–80, 184, 197
    hill 81–2, 129, 130
    impact of British defeat at 145, 176–80, 182–4, 197, 207, 237
iSangqu regiment 83, 164
Ityenka Nek 129, 158, 173
izimpondo zankomo tactic 31

Johnson, Lieutenant G.C.J. 204
Jones, Private Robert 184
Jones, Private William 184

Kabul 23
Khambula
    battle of xviii, 164–75, 188, 207, 249, 255
    camp at 132, 135, 136, 137, 146, 147, 155, 156, 161, 162, 214, 224, 229
    casualties at 171, 214
Kimberley 17
Koppie Alleen 230–1
kraals, military 29
kwaGingindlovu homestead 52, 53
kwaSoxhege homestead 77

17th (The Duke of Cambridge's Own)
    Lancers 1–2, 186, 214, 229, 232, 241, 254, 265
Landman's Drift 231, 262
Langalibalele kaMthimkhulu 90, 236
Law, Colonel 192, 195
Leet, Major William Knox 148, 149, 151, 158–9, 160–1
Left Flank Column *see* No. 4 (Left Flank) Column
Lewis, Lieutenant 71
Lewis, Private Peter 140

Lloyd, Lieutenant 54, 55, 209
Lloyd, Llwellwyn 153–4, 156
Lonsdale, Captain 93, 110, 111, 117
looting 109, 257
Louis Napoleon, Prince Imperial xvii,
    232–40, 244
Lower Drift 33, 37, 43, 44, 188, 199, 214
Luneburg 19–20, 25, 127–8, 132, 275, 276
    British garrison at 127, 135, 136–7,
        138, 141, 142, 143, 172
    Zulu raid on outskirts of 133–4
Lydenburg 137
Lysons, Lieutenant 153, 156, 168

Macgregor, Captain 55, 73
MacLeod, Captain Norman 136
McMahon, Corporal 184
MacSwinney, Lieutenant James 237–8,
    239, 241–2
Magumbi, *izinduna* 194–5, 197, 201
Magwendu, Prince 84
Maiwand, battle of xvii
Majuba hill 278
Malakatha range 85, 86
Malindi 101
Manyanyoba Khubeka 126, 135, 140, 173,
    275, 276
Manzimnyama river 84, 85, 104, 105
marriage, Zulu rules on 30
Marshall, Major-General Sir Frederick
    1–2, 222, 229–30, 237
Marter, Major Richard 268–73
Matshana kaMondise 84, 85, 90
Matshana kaSitshakuza 84, 85, 90
Mavumengwana kaNdlela Ntuli 67, 84,
    100, 194, 201
Mbamgulana, *induna* 163
Mbilini waMswati, Prince 25, 26, 126–7,
    128, 131, 132, 133, 135, 137, 138,
    173, 275
    and battle of Hlobane 152, 154
    and battle of Ntombe 139–40, 142
    death of 172–3
Mbuyazi, Prince 14, 44
Mdlalose people 129
Mehlokazulu kaSihayo 24, 25, 26, 79, 98,
    102, 103, 104–5, 109, 166, 170, 256

Melvill, Lieutenant Teignmouth xix, 96,
    105–6, 107–8, 181–2, 183
Mfunzi 249
Middle Drift 33, 45, 63, 80, 219, 264
military system, Zulu 29–32
Milne, Lieutenant 110
mining 17
Misi hill 203, 204, 206
missionaries 16, 43
    German Lutheran 19–20, 127, 133–4
    Norwegian 45, 61
Mkhosana kaMvundlana, Chief 100
Mkhumbikazulu 79
Mlalazi river 70
Mnkabayi 125
Mnyamana kaNqengelele Buthelezi, Chief
    154, 162, 266, 268
Molyneux, Captain 201–2, 204
Moore, Captain Henry 274–5
Moriarty, Captain David 137–40, 142,
    143, 275
Mostyn, Captain 94, 96
Mounted Volunteers 35, 46, 76, 86
Mozambique 6, 44
Mpande, King 11–12, 13–14, 15, 16, 18,
    19, 43, 126, 127, 135
Mswagele 24
Mswati, King 126
Mthethwa people 7, 8
Mthonga kaMpande, Prince 155–6
Mthonjaneni heights 246, 248, 262
mutilation of corpses 3, 108
Mzinyathi river 1, 6, 12, 18, 33, 76, 105,
    107, 178
    crossing of 42

Napoleon I, Emperor 82, 232, 233
Napoleon III, Emperor 232–3
Natal 11, 12, 13, 14, 28, 44, 274, 279
    annexed by British 1843 12, 13
    black auxiliary forces from 34
    rift between civil and military
        authorities 216, 245
    Volunteer forces 34–5, 48
    vulnerability to counter-attack 36,
        221, 224, 264–5
    Zululand passes to government of 280
    Zulus cross into 113

Natal Mounted Police 86, 87
Natal Native Contingent (NNC) 34, 48, 50, 64, 89, 95, 115, 206, 215
  blamed for Isandlwana disaster 109, 180
Native Natal Pioneers 48, 50, 87
Naval Brigade 46, 48, 188, 193, 202, 208
  and battle of Nyezane 54, 56, 57, 58
Ncome, battle of 11
Ncome river 33, 37, 125, 127, 128, 230, 232
Ndabuko, Prince 84
Ndwandwe, Chief 227
Ndwandwe people 7
Newdigate, Major-General Edward 221, 229, 247, 266
Ngenetsheni people 135
Nkisimana 249
No. 1 (Right Flank) Column 37, 43, 46, 145
  and battle of Nyezane 54–61
  composition 48–50
  taken into 1st Division 221
  Zulu troops despatched against 52
No. 2 Column 37, 45, 62–3, 80
  and battle of Isandlwana 90–110
  to work with Centre Column 81
No. 3 (Centre) Column 37, 40, 47–8, 51–2, 70, 76, 123, 131, 145, 214, 216, 229
  at Rorke's Drift 176, 180–1, 182
  complacency of 79
No. 4 (Left Flank) Column 37, 48, 124
  composition 124–5
  objectives 128
  renamed the Flying Column 221
  see also Flying Column
No. 5 (Northern) Column 37
  objectives 128
Nondweni river 245
Norris-Newman, Charles 211
Northern Column *see* No. 5 (Northern) Column
Northey, Lieutenant-Colonel 204–5
Norwegian missionaries 45, 61
Nourse, Captain Cracroft 95
Nseka hill 129, 132, 147

Ntendeka plateau 144–5, 150, 155, 156, 160
Ntinini river 241, 243, 245, 246
Ntombe, battle of 139–44, 145, 245
  casualties at 142, 144, 214
Ntombe river 126, 127, 135, 137–8
Ntshingwayo kaMahole, Chief 83–4, 93, 100, 154, 266, 280
Numaxo, battle of 82
Nunn, Herbert 135–6
Nyanda, *induna* 96, 101, 102
Nyezane, battle of 54–61, 66, 200
  casualties at 59, 210
Nyezane river 52–3, 212
Nzibe 135

Oftebro, Ommund 61, 271
oNdini
  attacked by Zibhebhu 280
  British advance on 246, 247–8, 251–3
  burning of 257–8
  Grandier imprisoned at 174–5
  homestead xviii–xix, 24, 32, 51, 83, 116, 124, 126, 194, 201, 222, 231–2, 274
  rebuilt 279
  Wolseley marches to 265
  Zulu army assembles at 146, 154, 155, 162, 241
  see also Ulundi, battle of
O'Toole, Sergeant 251

Parnel, Colonel 58
Pearson, Colonel Charles Knight 37, 39, 41, 43, 44–5, 46, 51, 80, 83, 145
  and advance of No. 1 Column 52–3
  and battle of Nyezane 55–61, 200
  forces under 48, 50, 63–4
  occupies Eshowe 61–6
  ordered to act on own initiative 63–5
  and relief of Eshowe 209–10
  under siege at Eshowe 67–75, 188–90, 192, 195, 196
Pedis 18, 21, 276, 278
Pemberton, Colonel 195
Phongolo river 6, 19, 25, 125, 126, 136
Pietermaritzburg 12, 28, 63, 122, 176, 239, 263

polygamy 16, 44
Pope, Lieutenant 98, 99
Port Durnford 260, 275
Port Natal 12, 43
Pretoria 18, 21, 137, 278
Prior, Captain 172-3
Prior, Melton 256
provisions 35
Pulleine, Colonel 87-8, 89, 110, 111, 131
    and battle of Isandlwana 90-1,
        94-101, 105, 162, 180, 187
    death of 103, 104, 182-3

Qungebe people 77

Raw, Lieutenant Charles 92, 93, 96, 101
3rd Regiment (The Buffs) 47, 48, 50, 52,
        188, 191, 192, 193, 202
    and battle of Nyezane 54, 55, 57, 58
4th Regiment 219
21st Regiment 252, 253
24th Regiment 57n, 74, 81-2, 87-8, 89,
        208, 229, 230, 243, 252, 266, 271,
        279
    and battle of Isandlwana 91, 95,
        96-102, 104, 108, 136
    and battle of Rorke's Drift 118, 120
57th Regiment 193, 202
58th Regiment 186, 237, 242, 252, 266
60th Regiment 193, 195, 202, 204, 211
80th Regiment 136-7, 141-2, 172, 275
88th Regiment 190-1
90th (Light) Infantry 124, 131, 167
91st Regiment 193, 195, 202, 205, 208,
        211
94th Regiment 185, 217-18, 252, 263,
        275-6, 278
99th Regiment 46, 47, 48, 55, 188, 189,
        191, 193, 202, 208, 212
regiments, Zulu 29-30, 154, 164
    see also by name
reinforcements
    arrival of 184-8, 190, 209, 214-15
    requested by Chelmsford 36, 46, 145,
        177
reserves, for African population in Natal
    13
Reynolds, Surgeon James 114, 116, 184

Riebeeck, Jan van 9
Right Flank Column see No. 1 (Right
        Flank) Column
roads, condition of 79, 82, 84-5, 137-8
Roberts, Lieutenant 92, 93, 97
Rorke, Jim 76, 114
Rorke's Drift xviii, 1, 24, 33, 37, 40, 79,
        81, 84, 104, 105, 129, 223
    battle of 116-23, 155, 171, 178, 182,
        184, 243, 263
    Boundary Commision meets at 23-4
    crossing at 42, 76
    garrison at 82, 113-14, 115, 145, 214
    mission station burnt 113
Rowlands, Colonel Hugh 37, 136-7
    objectives 128
Roy, Private 184
Royal Engineers 55, 115
Royal Military Academy, Woolwich 233
Russell, Major 95, 97, 110, 111
Russell, Lieutenant-Colonel John C. 78,
        147-8
    and battle of Hlobane 150-1, 152,
        154, 155, 156, 157, 159
    and battle of Khambula 165

St Andrew's Mission Station 191, 193
San Bushmen 4
Schermbrucker, Commandant Frederick
        133-4, 150-1
Schiess, Corporal 120, 184
Schroeder, Bishop 80
Schwartzkopt, Acting Lieutenant 134-5
Scott, Surgeon-Major F.B. 236-7
Sekhukhune, King 143, 276, 278
Senzangakhona, Chief 7-8, 246
Shah, HMS 48, 193
Shaka kaSenzangakhona, King 7-11, 12,
        13, 15, 16, 22, 31, 84, 125, 246, 274,
        275
Shepstone, George 93-4, 177
Shepstone, John 25, 27
Shepstone, Theophilus 23, 25, 93, 177
    conducts coronation of Cetshwayo 15
    sees Zulu kingdom as threat to
        Confederation 20-1
    supports Boers in boundary dispute
        19

Shepstone, Theophilus (*cont.*)
    view of Zulu monarchy 20–2, 38
Shepstone's Horse 234
Shervington, Captain 72
Sibalo kaHibana 173
Sigcwelegcwele 195, 201
signalling equipment 72–3, 192, 196
Sihayo kaXongo, Chief 24, 26, 38, 77, 78,
    79, 82–3, 105, 172, 274
Sihlahla 59, 165–6, 169, 170
Sikhobobo, *induna* 129, 152
Sintwangu 228–9
Siphezi mountain 92
Sitheku, Prince 84
Sitshitshili kaMnqandi, *induna* 158
Sixth Cape Frontier War (1834–5) 11
Slade, Lieutenant Frederick 169, 239
Smith, Reverend George 116
Smith, Major Thomas 12, 102
Smith-Dorrien, Lieutenant 180
Somopho kaZikhala 195, 201
South Africa xvii
Spalding, Major 115
spies
    British 194, 201
    Zulu 74–5, 226, 238
Standard 238
Stanley, Colonel F.A., Secretary of State
    for War 177, 184–5, 192, 195, 200,
    232, 245–6, 262
Stephenson, Captain William 115, 118
Strickland, Commissary General Edward
    35, 45, 79–80, 216
Sudan xvii
Swaziland 25, 37, 128, 136
Swazis, traditional rivalry with Zulus 37,
    125, 126

Tafelberg Hill 127, 128, 137
taxation 13
Thelezeni hill 231, 232, 236
Thesiger, Frederic Augustus *see*
        Chelmsford, Lieutenant-General
        Lord Frederic
Thinta, Chief 129
Thukela garrison 73, 75, 146, 188–9, 192,
    195, 212–13

Thukela river xviii, 8, 12, 14, 25, 33, 43,
    44, 45, 178, 209, 214, 216, 219, 264
    crossing of 41, 46–8
transport 36, 216–17
    recovered from Isandlwana battlefield
        229–30
transport ships 185–7
Transvaal 278
    annexation of 18, 21, 25
    disputed territory 18–19, 23, 37
    Republican declaration in 137, 177
Trekker War (1838–40) 13
Tshotshosi river 231, 235, 240
Tuck, Bandsman M.M. 242, 251, 256,
    257, 276–8
Tucker, Major Charles 136–7, 138, 141–2
Tugela *see* Thukela river
Twentyman, Major 219, 220, 264

uDloko regiment 83, 117, 164
uDududu regiment 83, 164
uKhandempemvu regiment 83, 93, 100,
    155, 158, 162, 164, 194, 201, 250,
    268
ultimatum to Zulus 27, 37, 40, 226–7
Ulundi
    battle of 253–9, 260–1, 263
        casualties 257, 258, 267
    see also oNdini
uMbonambi regiment 83, 99, 101, 164,
    194, 201
Umhlatusi regiment 194
Umkoosana, *induna* 271, 272
Umpanda, King 24
uMxapho regiment 52, 54–5, 59, 195,
    251
uNokhenke regiment 83, 93, 108–9, 164,
    194, 201
uThulwana regiment 83, 116, 117, 164
Utrecht 19, 33, 124, 126, 127, 128, 131,
    132, 136, 164
uVe regiment 83, 98, 155, 160, 162, 164,
    169, 170, 253
Uys, Petras Lefras 37, 127, 129–30, 131,
    146, 148, 149, 159, 162

Victoria, Queen 183–4, 233–4, 279, 280
Victoria Crosses 183–4, 251

Vijn, Cornelius 249
Volunteer Cavalry *see* Mounted
    Volunteers
Volunteer forces, Natal 34–5

Wagner, Reverend 133–4
Wassall, Private Samuel 106–7, 184
Waterloo, battle of 232
weapons, Zulu 31–2
weather, impact of 79, 137–8, 178, 216
Weatherley, Colonel 152–3, 157–8
Welman, Lieutenant-Colonel 50, 51, 55
White, Commandant 151
White Mfolozi river 246, 249, 262
white settlers, Natal 13
Williams, Lieutenant 151, 152, 157
Williams, Private John 184
Witt, Reverend Otto 114, 116
Wolseley, Sir Garnet 143–4, 246, 247,
    260–1
    arrives at the front 262–3
    and peace settlement 274, 275, 278–9
    reoccupation of oNdini 265, 267
    wants unconditional surrender 268
Wombane hill 55, 56
Wood, Colonel Henry Evelyn 37, 42, 48,
    79, 80, 81, 173, 177, 178, 201, 214,
    228–9
    attacks Zungwini 130, 147
    and battle of Hlobane 144–5, 146–8,
        152–3, 154, 197
    and battle of Khambula 132, 163–72,
        188, 220–1, 255
    and battle of Ulundi 231, 246, 247,
        255
    character 124–5
    crosses Ncome 128–9
    and Flying Column 221, 223, 224
    hopes to exploit local rivalries 126,
        135–6
    impact of Isandlwana on 132
    objectives 124, 128

orders to Russell 156
and second offensive 231
troops under 137, 163
Wynne, Captain Warren 48, 55, 61, 73,
    213

Xabanga 236
Xhosa people 21, 27–8, 85

Younghusband, Captain 3, 96, 102

Zibhebhu kaMaphitha 84, 92, 117, 251,
    266, 268, 274, 279–80
Zulu army
    casualties 226
        Gingindlovu 207, 210–11, 214
        Isandlwana 109–10, 122, 230
        Khambula 171, 214
        Nyezane 66
        Ulundi 257, 258, 267
    demoralization of 215
    military capability of 28–32
    perceived threat of 220–1
    size of 32, 83, 194–5, 201
Zulu kingdom
    boundary dispute on Transvaal border
        19, 23
    break up of 264, 266, 274, 280
    history 4–14
    location 4, 6
    military system 28–31, 214
    origin of people 4, 6
    relationship with colonial Natal 13
    society 6
    succession crisis 1856 14
    topography 43
    trade with British 10, 14
Zulu War, reasons for 4, 11, 18–27, 127
Zungwini mountain stronghold 126, 129,
    130–1, 132, 147, 156, 161, 162, 171
Zwide kaLanga, Chief 7, 8

OTHER PAN BOOKS
AVAILABLE FROM PAN MACMILLAN

LORD CARVER
The National Army Museum Book of
    THE BOER WAR   0 330 36944 X   £8.99
The National Army Museum Book of
    THE TURKISH FRONT   0 330 49108 3   £7.99

JULIAN THOMPSON
The Imperial War Museum Book of
    THE WAR IN BURMA 1942–1945 0 330 48065 0   £8.99

All Pan Macmillan titles can be ordered from our website,
www.panmacmillan.com, or from your local bookshop
and are also available by post from:

Bookpost, PO Box 29, Douglas, Isle of Man IM99 1BQ
Credit cards accepted. For details:
Telephone: 01624 677237
Fax: 01624 670923
E-mail: bookshop@enterprise.net
www.bookpost.co.uk

Free postage and packing in the United Kingdom

Prices shown above were correct at the time of going to press.
Pan Macmillan reserve the right to show new retail prices on covers
which may differ from those previously advertised in the text
or elsewhere.